# Against the Death Penalty

▼   ▼   ▼

# Against the Death Penalty

*The Relentless Dissents of
Justices Brennan and Marshall*

▼  ▼  ▼

## Michael Mello

NORTHEASTERN UNIVERSITY PRESS

*Boston*

Northeastern University Press

Copyright 1996 by Michael Mello

*Library of Congress Cataloging-in-Publication Data*

Mello, Michael.
    Against the death penalty : the relentless dissents of Justices Brennan and Marshall / Michael Mello
      p.   cm.
    Includes bibliographical references and index.
    ISBN 1–55553–261–6
      1. Capital punishment—United States.
    2. Dissenting opinions—United States.
    3. Brennan, William J. (William Joseph), 1906–
    4. Marshall, Thurgood, 1908–1993.  I. Title.
    KF9227.C2M38   1996
    345.73′0773—dc20
    [347.305773]         95–45395

Designed by Joyce C. Weston

Composed in Bembo by Coghill Composition, Richmond, Virginia. Printed and bound by Thomson-Shore, Inc., in Dexter, Michigan. The paper is Supple Opaque, an acid-free sheet.

MANUFACTURED IN THE UNITED STATES OF AMERICA

00  99  98  97  96     5  4  3  2  1

*This book is for my mother, Ida Mello, and for my aunt, Harriet Anne Goldberg, for their strength, courage, unconditional love, and support; they formed the habits of my heart. And, of course, for Deanna.*

▼   ▼   ▼

# CONTENTS

▼  ▼  ▼

# ACKNOWLEDGMENTS

▼　　▼　　▼

I am deeply indebted to a sextet of extraordinarily gifted law students—Diane Bech, Nancy Gray, Deanna Lynn Peterson, Greg Beber, Ian Ridlon, and Joseph Tetrault—who put thought as well as research work into the project; but for flaws in my personality, Diane and Nancy would share authorial credit with me. Nancy Levit, Sheldon Novick, Dick Brooks, Michael Radelet, Kim Cook, and Jeffrey Robinson commented helpfully on the manuscript. I am also grateful for the help, patience, and understanding of Scott Brassart, William Frohlich, and Emily McKeigue of Northeastern University Press.

# PROLOGUE

▼   ▼   ▼

**And it seemed to me, that you lived your life**
**Like a candle in the wind;**
**Never knowing who to cling to**
**When the rains set in.**
                                                **—Elton John**

During his short life, Wilbert Evans did some hideously bad things and some courageously good things. He was convicted of murder and sentenced to die by the Commonwealth of Virginia. In 1986, while he was living on death row—waiting—there was an escape from the Mecklenberg Prison. (The several death row inmates who fled were recaptured.) During the melee, Wilbert Evans—at significant risk to himself—saved the life of a nurse who was being held hostage by the rioting prisoners. When he was later scheduled to be put to death, the nurse whose life Mr. Evans had saved pleaded with Governor Douglas Wilder to spare him. It didn't work. Nothing worked. Wilbert Evans was electrocuted on schedule.

None of this makes Mr. Evans's life or his legally sanctioned killing particularly unique; he was just another black man executed by the Commonwealth of Virginia. What is interesting, for my purposes here, is his last request. Mr. Evans asked his pro bono attorneys with the powerhouse Washington law firm of Wilmer Cutler & Pickering—Arthur Matthews and Thomas Connell among them—that he be buried along with the dissenting opinion that Justice Thurgood Marshall of the United States Supreme Court had written in his case.

Other people writing other books will tell the stories of the Wilbert Evanses of the world; those will be views from the ground. This is a book about the rarefied world inhabited by the justices of the United States Supreme Court, and about the judicial craft of a pair of jurists who bridged these two spheres. It is also a book about hope. Hope is a scarce commodity on death row. It is also a scarce commodity in the law offices of the attorneys and the investigators and the support staff who work, as often as not, for the legal system's equivalent of subminimum wage as they fight to save the condemned. As I suggest in the following chapters, the dissents of Justices Brennan and Marshall in death penalty cases were critical in providing guidance and information to death row and its lawyers about what kinds of issues the justices might be interested in considering at some future time. I call their opinions "dissents that telegraph," and they were indispensable in my own representation of condemned prisoners.

But this was not the reason I—or my clients—cherished those dissents at the time and in the years since. Even Marshall's and Brennan's boilerplate dissents from denial of plenary review communicated to us that at least *someone* was listening in the court of last resort. Brennan and Marshall might not have had the votes at the time to translate their dissenting opinions into common law, but, in a cockeyed sort of way, that wasn't what mattered. What mattered was that the dissents provided hope. The dissents were candles in the wind.

# Against the Death Penalty

▼   ▼   ▼

# The Two Justices

▼  ▼  ▼

[The dissenter is] the gladiator making a last stand against the lions.

— Benjamin Cardozo[1]

The only one that was more or less finished by the final weeks of Roger's life was *The Supreme Pork,* in part because he'd been so appalled by the Court's 5–4 majority in *Bowers v. Hardwick.* Blind by then [from AIDS], he had me read to him from the *Times* the whole of Justice Blackmun's dissent. He talked about it for days whenever one of his lawyer friends would call. Roger was the one who made me understand that a great dissent could over the course of time acquire the moral force to alter bigoted laws that seemed impregnable.

— Paul Monette[2]

Legal interpretation takes place in a field of pain and death.

— Robert Cover[3]

Cases such as these provide for me an excruciating agony of the spirit. I yield to no one in the depth of my distaste, antipathy, and, indeed, abhorrence, for the death penalty, with all its aspects of physical distress and fear and of moral judgment exercised by finite minds. That distaste is buttressed by a belief that capital punishment serves no useful purpose that can be demonstrated. For me, it violates childhood's training and life's experiences, and is not compatible with the philosophical convictions I have been able to develop. It is antagonistic to any sense of "reverence for life."

— Justice Harry Blackmun, dissenting from the majority's holding that capital punishment violates the Constitution[4]

N AN INTERVIEW held the day after Thurgood Marshall, associate justice of the Supreme Court, announced his retirement, the justice suggested that he accepted the role of a permanent opposition force. He said that in interviewing prospective law clerks, the recent law school graduates who help the justices with research and opinion writing, he always asked if they liked working on dissents. "If they said 'No,' they didn't get a job. I only pick those that liked to write dissenting opinions."[5] Throughout the interview, Marshall sat in an armchair before an array of cameras and reporters in the Court's ceremonial East Conference Room. According to one of those present, he was "by turns crotchety, cantankerous, humorous and cantankerous again. It was a pattern familiar to his friends and associates."[6] A reporter who wanted an explanation of the medical factors that Marshall (then eighty-two) cited in his letter of resignation asked him, "What's wrong with you, Sir?" The justice responded, "What's wrong with me? I'm old. I'm getting old and falling apart." Asked what his plans for retirement were, Marshall replied, "Sit on my rear end."

The retirements of William Brennan and Thurgood Marshall mark the end of an era—several eras, actually—and provide a fitting occasion to examine what made their judicial careers unique. This book explores one aspect of their uniqueness: Brennan's and Marshall's relentless dissents in capital cases.

Until 1991, capital cases in the *U.S. Reports* invariably included dissents in death cases by Justice Brennan, Justice Marshall, or both. They had doggedly voted against the death penalty—in principle and in virtually every particular case—since the Court first upheld the abstract constitutionality of capital punishment in 1976.[7] Brennan and Marshall dissented, sometimes in detail and sometimes in general terms, against the imposition of capital punishment in cases granted certiorari review by the Court. The two justices also dissented in almost every capital case where certiorari was denied, typically beginning their opinions by reiterating that they were "adhering to our views that the death penalty is in all cases cruel and unusual punishment prohibited by the Eighth and Fourteenth Amendments." Brennan and Marshall issued such dissents in more than twenty-five hundred cases between 1976 and 1991.[8] Most of these dissents simply reiterated without elaboration their conviction that capital punishment is unconstitutional. The remainder explained why, even assuming the death penalty might be constitutional, its application in the case at hand was not.

In forty-two cases decided by the Burger Court (1969–86), excluding petitions for certiorari and stays of execution decided without opinion,[9] Brennan wrote ten full opinions[10] and a brief concurring statement in fifteen others;[11] Marshall wrote fifteen full opinions[12] and added a brief statement reiterating his categorical opposition to the death penalty where the Court invalidated a sentence of death on ten occasions.[13] The Rehnquist Court (1986–), up to Brennan's retirement in 1990, decided thirty-two opinions on capital punishment; Brennan wrote ten full opinions[14] and a brief statement in five others.[15] During this period, Marshall wrote six full opinions[16] and two brief concurring statements.[17] In 1991, Marshall wrote an opinion in three[18] of seven[19] capital punishment cases decided by the Rehnquist Court. Brennan wrote but three[20] majority opinions, and Marshall spoke for the Court on four occasions.[21] Except for one case—*Strickland v. Washington* (1984)[22]—the two justices always voted identically; apart from this instance, they each wrote separate lengthy opinions in the same case on just one other occasion.[23] Thus, from 1972 to 1990 Brennan and Marshall took different perspectives in only two cases.[24]

The constant in the jurisprudence of Marshall and Brennan (and, in the end, Blackmun) on the constitutionality of the death penalty was that the result they advocated would have forestalled execution. If they joined with the majority in limiting the application of the death penalty in specific contexts, they simply concurred in the judgment.[25] If they wrote for the majority, they clarified or expanded the scope of a principle curtailing application of the penalty.[26] If they wrote dissenting opinions—as opposed to their standard dissents, which simply reiterated that executions violate the Constitution, period—the dissent incorporated two rationales. The first was a brief recapitulation of their position that the death penalty is per se unconstitutional.[27] The second was a more detailed explanation of why the state cannot execute a particular person, even if it can execute in the abstract.[28]

*Tison v. Arizona*[29] illustrates the latter approach. The majority held that the death penalty was constitutionally applied to those whose participation in the felony leading to the murder was substantial and whose mental state evidenced "reckless indifference to the value of human life," even though the condemned did not kill and did not have the actual intent to kill.[30] Brennan's ringing dissent spent little time arguing that the death penalty is unconstitutional in all cases, but instead concentrated on the attributes of the class of culpability that make it inappropriate to impose the punishment of death in a particular case.[31]

Compare Justice Harry Blackmun. A few years ago Justice Sandra Day O'Connor began a capital opinion with breezy, lawyerly detachment: "This is a case about federalism."[32] By striking rhetorical contrast, Justice Blackmun's impassioned dissent on February 22, 1994,[33] against the execution of Bruce Edwins Callins in Texas was in large part a revolt against such pronouncements; to him the delicate constitutional balance invoked by O'Connor was a jurists' self-justifying illusion. Blackmun's understanding, articulated shortly before he announced his retirement from the Court, came from two decades of grappling with capital cases as a justice following years of struggling with capital punishment as an intermediate appellate court judge.[34] "I feel morally and intellectually obliged simply to concede that the death penalty experiment has failed. . . . The death penalty remains fraught with arbitrariness, discrimination, caprice, and mistake. . . . From this date forward, I no longer shall tinker with the machinery of death."[35] Since that day Justice Blackmun has dissented from the imposition of capital punishment in every death case to reach the Court,[36] whereas in 1976 he was among the majority voting to uphold the federal constitutionality of capital punishment.[37] Once Marshall and Brennan had left the Court Blackmun had more experience with death penalty cases than any other sitting justice. His dissent came at the end of twenty years of capital punishment that his votes on the Court helped make possible. The evidence of capital punishment's intrinsic unfairness has not really changed much since 1976. Since that year 242 people, virtually all poor, have been executed in the United States. States perform executions by electric chair, gas chamber, lethal injection, firing squad, and old-fashioned noose. And yet, incremental though his journey has been, Blackmun had been moving toward his *Callins* dissent for some years, and his judicial language about capital punishment had grown progressively more urgent. "Perilously close to simple murder"[38] was how he described the death sentence of Leonel Herrera, who was executed by the State of Texas shortly after Blackmun wrote those words.[39]

This book explores the historical, jurisprudential, and strategic legitimacy of relentless dissent[40] in the context of capital punishment. Chapter 1 traces the careers of William Brennan and Thurgood Marshall. Chapter 2 seeks legitimacy for their sustained dissents in history and traces the development of dissents in general and the sustained dissent in particular. Chapter 3 seeks legitimacy for such dissent in theory and evaluates the jurisprudential function and value of the sustained dissent. Chapter 4, drawing upon the recently released papers of Justice Marshall, focuses on the strategic wisdom and tactical usefulness of this kind of dissent.

Marshall gave his papers to the Library of Congress after his retirement in 1991. The Marshall files, which were made public at the Library of Congress after his death in January 1993 at the age of eighty-four, contain private memos and drafts of decisions that circulated among all the justices and reveal new details of how the Court—one of the government's most secretive institutions—handled such issues as abortion, capital punishment, civil rights, free speech, and government power. The papers consist of some 173,700 written items from his career, mostly from his years at the Court (these files alone cover more than three thousand cases).[41] The whole collection would fill a room full of bookshelves eight feet high and nearly thirty feet long.

Typically, the public sees only portions of the Court's process: a brief announcement that a case has been accepted for plenary review; written and oral arguments; and the final ruling and written opinions. As he must have known, Thurgood Marshall's papers include no bombshells. Their value to historians and other students of the interpersonal collegiality of the Court is more subtle and more important. The Marshall papers provide a wealth of material on the steps that are rarely seen: the private debate, votes, and jockeying among the justices on which cases to take or reject; the preliminary votes at the weekly justices-only conferences; and the crucial assignments of authors for the majority and dissenting opinions. The papers also show the draft-by-draft evolution of the written opinions, as well as glimpses of the critical negotiations as one of the justices maneuvers to hold or forge a majority. "Collectively, the papers show the Court's decisionmaking process as a continuing conversation among nine distinct individuals on dozens of issues simultaneously. The exchanges are serious, sometimes scholarly, occasionally brash and personalized, but generally well-reasoned and most often cast in an understated, genteel language."[42]

In recent times, no other justice's papers have become available so soon after his departure from the Court. The papers of the late justice William O. Douglas, who retired in 1975, did not become available until a decade later. Justice Byron White, in announcing his retirement, specified that his papers would not become freely available until ten years after his death. William Brennan, who retired in 1990, strictly limited access to his papers when he gave them to the Library of Congress. He tightened the restrictions even further after several of his former colleagues said they were worried about "possible embarrassment."[43]

When the Library of Congress announced that the papers would be opened to the public, the Court threatened to bar future donations of justices' papers. As Linda Greenhouse observed at the time:

> [O]f course judges are human. Of course they change their minds, say things they later regret, enter into tactical alliances, make timely compromises. What is notable about Justice Thurgood Marshall's papers, released by the Library of Congress and spread before the public and newspaper accounts this week, is not that his Supreme Court files reveal all of this, as other justices' papers have documented before. The most striking and, at least on the surface, puzzling aspect of the affair is the evident anger and anguish of the Court itself over the disclosures. . . . The Court displayed once again its deep, almost obsessive concern for secrecy. There is a concern driven in part by the natural desire of many organizations to shield their internal workings from public view, whether the subject is the pay of top executives, the decisions of an academic tenure committee or the editing process in the newsroom. But there is something else at work here: a belief among the judges that to strip any court of its mystique is also inevitably to strip it of some of its authority and legitimacy."[44]

Juan Williams, who is writing a book about Thurgood Marshall, explained that Marshall's early release of his papers served a larger vision that was dear to his heart. "By allowing his papers to be viewed immediately after his death, he was continuing his role as the Supreme Court Justice who would not let his colleagues forget about the impact of discrimination and poverty as they deliberated on the laws of this land. The release of his papers is another reminder to the justices left behind that people are watching."[45] Chief Justice Rehnquist's "current fit of anger—he threatened to deny the Library of Congress future donations of papers and accused the institution of bad judgment—is a tactic of intimidation. After all, the work of the Court is based on the sanctity of the written word, through precedents, arguments and rulings. Unable to dictate to Marshall how his papers should be handled, he now tries to dictate to the Library of Congress. Is Rehnquist aware that, as Librarian of Congress James H. Billington notes, several other past and current justices (including Brennan, Burton, Goldberg, Douglas and White) have asked that all or part of their papers be made available immediately after, and in some cases even before, their deaths?"[46]

## The Evolving Law of Death: "The Supreme Court's Obstacle Course"[47]

In Washington, rain fell softly, steadily, on the white marble grandeur of the U.S. Supreme Court, and on a small group of protesters across the street, keeping a vigil against the death penalty. There were perhaps fifty of them, religious leaders, civil rights workers, a member of the District of Columbia City Council. They had been there since early evening. At half-past midnight, a man burst from the building, running wildly. "Marshall stayed John Spenkelink's execution!" he shouted, and a voice called back, "Amen."

Tears of relief mixed with rain on their faces as the protesters shouted and clapped their hands. A sweet, soulful voice began singing:

Paul and Silas bound in jail
Had no money for their bail.
Keep your eyes on the prize,
Hold on, hold on.[48]

The "abolitionist" position of Brennan and Marshall evolved within a context. It seems fair to say that the Court collectively has for the time being decided that the death penalty is not per se unconstitutional. The "brooding spirit of the law" and the "intelligence of a future day" are not likely to reverse their collective minds on the question of the constitutionality of the death penalty, at least not in my lifetime.

The United States Supreme Court's modern jurisprudence on the constitutionality of death as a punishment may be said to have begun with *McGautha v. California*[49] in 1971, although pressure for a ruling on the constitutionality of the penalty had been building for at least a decade.[50] In that case the defendant, Dennis McGautha, argued that the due process clause of the fourteenth amendment mandates standards to guide a capital sentencer's discretion on the penalty issue. The Court rejected his challenge, in part because development of such standards would prove impossible. Justice Harlan, writing for the majority, reasoned that to "identify before the fact those characteristics of criminal homicides and their perpetrators which call for the death penalty, and to express these characteristics in language which can be fairly understood and applied by the sentencing authority, appear to be tasks which are beyond present human ability"[51]; he concluded that the "infinite variety of cases and facets to each case would make general standards either meaningless 'boiler plate' or a statement of the obvious that no jury would need."[52]

A year later, in *Furman v. Georgia,*[53] the Court held that the eighth amendment forbade infliction of the death penalty under statutes that leave a jury with undirected discretion over the death decision. The *Furman* holding, which resulted in vacated death sentences for all 629 persons then on death row,[54] was handed down in a short per curiam opinion stating, without elaboration, that "the imposition and carrying out of the death penalty in [the cases before the Court] constitutes cruel and unusual punishment in violation of the Eighth and Fourteenth Amendments."[55] Each of the nine justices wrote separately, and no justice in the five-person majority joined any other.[56] The individual opinions suggest, however, that the central concern of the three crucial justices was that the statutes at issue in *Furman* lacked sentencing standards. Justice Douglas wrote that "[w]e deal with a system of law and justice that leaves to the uncontrolled discretion of judges or juries the determination whether defendants committing these crimes should die or be imprisoned."[57] Given this absence of guidance, it is not surprising that the penalty is applied "selectively to minorities whose numbers are few, who are outcasts of society, and who are unpopular, but whom society is willing to see suffer though it would not countenance general application of the same penalty across the board."[58] Justice Stewart also stressed the randomness of the penalty: "These death sentences are cruel and unusual in the same way that being struck by lightning is cruel and unusual. For, of all the people convicted of rapes and murders in 1967 and 1968, many of the crimes just as reprehensible as these, these petitioners are among a capriciously selected random handful upon whom the sentence of death has in fact been imposed."[59] Justice White reached the same conclusion from his experience on the Court.[60] Because Justice Brennan[61] and Justice Marshall[62] would have declared the death penalty unconstitutional as such, the "holding" of the case must be found in the opinions of Douglas, Stewart, and White. The Court has in subsequent opinions noted that "a fair statement of the consensus expressed by the Court in *Furman* is that where discretion is afforded a sentencing body on a matter so grave as the determination of whether a human life should be taken or spared, that discretion must be suitably directed and limited so as to minimize the risk of wholly arbitrary and capricious action."[63]

State legislatures, confronted with *McGautha*'s statement that the formulation of capital-sentencing standards was impossible and *Furman*'s statement that unbridled sentencing discretion violated the eighth amendment,[64] set about redrafting their death penalty statutes to conform to the Constitution. Florida, the first state to do so,[65] was followed by Georgia, and by 1976 thirty-six jurisdictions had reinstituted the death penalty.[66] The Florida and Georgia statutes, employing "guided discretion," were designed to channel the sentencer's discretion by specifying aggravating and mitigating factors that should be weighed in deciding who dies. Most of the listed aggravating circumstances referred to such objectively ascertainable facts as whether the crime was committed for pecuniary gain, whether the defendant was under sentence of imprisonment at the time of the offense, whether a defendant had a significant prior criminal history, and whether the defendant had been previously convicted of a felony.[67] But both statutes also provided for a catch-all aggravating circumstance that has proven to be of continuing concern to the Court.[68] Subsection (b)(7) of the Georgia statute authorized a death sentence if the jury found that the crime was "outrageously or wantonly vile, horrible or inhuman in that it involved torture, depravity of mind or an aggravated battery to the victim."[69] Florida's statute authorized the death penalty if the crime was "especially heinous, atrocious or cruel."[70]

The facial constitutionality of these new statutes was decided by the Supreme Court in 1976. The Court held that "on their face these [new] procedures seem to satisfy the concerns of *Furman*."[71] In *Gregg v. Georgia*, the Court stressed the "limited grant of certiorari" and emphasized it was reviewing the " 'vagueness' and 'overbreadth' of the statutory aggravating circumstances only to consider whether their imprecision renders this capital-sentencing system invalid under the Eighth and Fourteenth Amendments because it is incapable of imposing a capital punishment other than by arbitrariness or caprice."[72] The Court noted that Georgia's counterpart to Florida's (5)(b) circumstance could be construed to include "any murder involving depravity of mind or an aggravated battery." It also observed, however, that the statutory language "need not be construed this way, and there is no reason to assume that the Supreme Court of Georgia will adopt such an open-ended construction."[73] Similarly, the Court in *Proffitt v. Florida* held that the (5)(h) circumstance "must be considered as [it has] been construed by the Supreme Court of Florida.[74]

In 1978, despite Justice Rehnquist's charge that the Court was going from "pillar to post,"[75] and despite Chief Justice Burger's recognition that the Court's death penalty decisions were far from consistent,[76] the Court held that the sentencer must be permitted to consider any relevant evidence proffered in mitigation,[77] a notion reaffirmed in subsequent cases.[78] The Court has since fine-tuned the capital system it approved in 1976, sometimes ruling in favor of condemned inmates[79] but more frequently, since the 1982 Term,[80] holding against them.[81]

The "deregulation"[82] of substantive capital punishment doctrine by the Supreme Court must be understood in conjunction with the Court's increasingly restrictive view of habeas corpus. Death row inmates are unpopular, habeas petitioners only slightly less so.[83] The combination of the two can be explosive, as illustrated by the public's and politicians' reactions to the Eleventh Circuit's 1985 decisions in the Alday family cases[84] and the court's 1986 stay grants in the Theodore Bundy cases.[85]

Particularly in its procedural default cases,[86] retroactivity decisions, and rulings in cases involving successive habeas corpus petitions,[87] the Court curtailed radically the availability of the writ. Congress is poised to go even further.[88]

*Furman* and its progeny, therefore, stood during the tenures of Brennan and Marshall for the proposition that the death penalty, in the view of seven of the justices of the time, is not per se unconstitutional. The case law expounding the principles of *Furman* had reiterated, as axiomatic, that a state legislature can, consistent with the federal Constitution, enact as part of its criminal code the punishment of death for certain classes of killers and participants in crimes in which a life is taken so long as the discretion of the sentencing body is properly guided.[89] The state can, if it adheres at least in theory to the strictures of a measure of due process that is theoretically greater than that required for a deprivation of liberty or property, execute a member of the class of criminals for whom death is deemed appropriate. Although this nutshell statement does not pose as an exhaustive summary of death penalty jurisprudence, I believe it can be said to be "the law."

The question is how to deal with "the law." Brennan and Marshall dealt with it by rejecting it. My thesis is that in so doing the two justices acted legitimately. The remainder of this book traces such legitimacy in three sources: history, jurisprudence, and tactical/strategic prudence.

## William Brennan

At a press conference the day after he announced his retirement from the Supreme Court, Thurgood Marshall noted that after he concluded with his wife that he should step down, the first person he informed was Justice William Brennan.[90] After Brennan retired in 1990, Marshall became the sole force on the Court dissenting in all death penalty cases, appending a brief footnote to the published opinions. Marshall's papers in the Library of Congress "show that on occasion he tried, usually unsuccessfully, to persuade his colleagues personally, sometimes ruefully complaining when he lost that his colleagues' behavior was inexcusable."[91]

William Joseph Brennan Jr. was born April 25, 1906, in Newark, New Jersey. The second of eight children born to recent Irish immigrants William J. Brennan Sr. and Agnes McDermott,[92] young Bill Brennan, to the surprise of everyone save those who really knew him, was to become one of the most influential players in the political and social reformation of an entire country. This unimposing Irish Catholic justice who never took a law school course in constitutional law, who got his start as a union-busting corporate labor lawyer in New Jersey, indeed who got appointed to the Supreme Court almost by accident, rendered thirty-four years of devoted service as a justice. During his tenure he grew to become such a civil libertarian and so ardent a supporter of the voting, first amendment, and privacy rights that he saw as necessary to a truly free and open society that he would prompt Reagan attorney general Edwin Meese in 1985 to decry his "radical egalitarianism" as a threat to the American way of life.[93]

"Everything I am," the justice once said, "I am because of my father."[94] William Brennan Sr. was a man feared for his ferocious temper but highly respected for his incorruptible honesty. He began his life in America as a coal stoker and heaver at the Ballantine Brewery in Newark.[95] Originally a member of the International Brotherhood of Stationary Firemen, the union that represented the city's coal workers, Brennan fast became dismayed at the corruption he saw in its ranks. The dues he paid were lining the pockets of union officials rather than going toward bettering conditions for the membership. In 1908 he staged a revolt that ousted the corrupt officials; for his efforts he was elected president of his local chapter and of the Essex County Trades Council, the umbrella organization for the area's trade unions.[96] By 1913, the elder Brennan had turned his eye toward the local government, which was every bit as corrupt as the union he had helped reform. Addressing a group of city trolleymen who were striking for better wages, he called for the abolition of Newark's mayor-aldermen form of government in favor of one more representative of the people. In 1916 he was beaten severely by city police officers after one particularly intense confrontation over the demands of the trolley-car drivers.[97] The ten-year-old Bill Brennan was at home to see his bloodied father carried into the house. It was an early lesson in the potential for abuse of state power.

Within a year of that beating, the elder Brennan and his allies had gathered enough of a following to vote to change the city's charter. The city council of thirty-two members was abolished in favor of a five-member city commission.[98] William Brennan Sr. ran for a seat on that commission and finished third among eighty-six candidates,[99] securing an appointment as director of public safety, in charge of the local fire and police departments.

Though the elder Brennan was a fair and honest man, he carried out his responsibilities with an iron hand. After being splashed with slush and snow by a passing car one morning on his way to work, he stormed into the city engineer's office and demanded that every sidewalk and gutter in Newark be cleared of snow immediately. The police were to deliver the message to all homeowners, and anyone not complying would be served with formal complaints.[100] When the policemen's union approved a liberal pension plan for themselves the pro-union Brennan surprised many when he opposed it as being too generous. "The only thing I have asked from the police and firemen," he said, "is honest work for a decent wage. No man or woman in either department can say he has ever had to give a five-cent cigar for anything he or she was justly entitled to. . . . If being a friend of the police or firemen means helping them put something over on the rest of the citizens, you can put me down as no friend of theirs."[101]

When it was brought to his attention that Blacks were not being hired by the police force even though many had taken the departmental examination, Brennan saw to it that the next list of hirees contained the names of three qualified young Black men.[102] In 1925 he announced that interrogations with force would no longer be tolerated from his police. "The use of unnecessary force in making arrests, and violence in any form towards the citizens, has been done away with," he declared. "Nightsticks should last a long time. The police have been made the servants of the people and not their masters."[103] It was a theme that the younger Brennan must have noted, for it would inform his judicial decisions decades later.

As stern and demanding as William Brennan Sr. was with the police and firemen, he was no less so with his own family. From the time he was a boy the future justice's life and aspirations had been dictated to him by his father, who would accept no alternative views. As one newspaper said of the elder Brennan, "[He] doesn't give a tinker's damn what people think, when he thinks he is right."[104] Brennan Sr. chose his son's curriculum in high school, and by the time he was sixteen had informed the younger Brennan that he was to become a lawyer.[105]

Though the elder Brennan made enough money for the large family to live comfortably, young Bill held many odd-jobs to earn spending money. After high school classes he would make change for waiting passengers on the trolley platform or work in a local filling station, jockeying fifty-gallon gasoline drums to the curb to provide patrons with roadside service.[106] During the summers Brennan sold suits, served as a street repair inspector, delivered newspapers, and milked cows and delivered the milk to neighborhood homes.[107]

The imposing work ethic instilled in him by his father served Brennan well, for although he did not consider himself naturally brilliant he managed to get high marks in school, winning several academic honors largely through hard work.[108] In 1924 Brennan left home to attend the Wharton School of Finance at the University of Pennsylvania. During his senior year he fell in love with Marjorie Leonard, and the two were married in May 1928. In the fall of that year, again at his father's direction, the future justice enrolled at Harvard Law School.

When Brennan claimed that he was who he was because of his father, he did not mean merely that he had been created in the older man's image but also that his father's imposing personality played a large role in shaping his own. While he did inherit his honesty and dedication to work, thankfully the irascible temper that so seemed to characterize the elder Brennan's life was absent from his son's genuinely warm temperament. Perhaps it was from having to take his mother's side against his often overbearing father,[109] or perhaps it was the softening effect a mother's love can have on an already good-natured young man. In any event, throughout his lifetime those who have known him and worked for him have commented on his easygoing, friendly manner and on the genuine concern he showed for every individual he ever met.

Brennan's law school career at Harvard can best be described as unspectacular. Though one of the few classmates who even remembered him used the words "workaholic" and "prodigious notetaker,"[110] his grades were not good enough to get him onto Harvard's law review or to let him attain the second-tier academic honor of student adviser.[111] By his final year, however, he had managed to reach Harvard's third level of academic honors and be admitted to the Legal Aid Society, which allowed students to practice law in local Massachusetts courts on behalf of low-income or indigent clients.[112]

In May 1930 Brennan, who was still in Cambridge finishing up his second-year exams, learned that his father had died of pneumonia. Upon returning home to console his family and take care of financial matters, he discovered that his father, the honest politician who had never accepted any graft, was broke. He had spent everything he earned, leaving nothing for his wife and eight children. William J. Brennan Jr. believed that he would not be able to continue at Harvard Law School, but with the support of his family, some help from the school's administration, and another odd-job as a waiter in a Cambridge fraternity house he managed to survive his last year and to graduate with the class of 1931.[113]

Brennan's primary concern was now with his finances. In the midst of the depression he was faced with the task of supporting not only himself and his wife but also his mother and siblings. His first job offer came from the Newark firm of Pitney, Hardin, and Ward. Shelton Pitney, the senior partner, traveled to Cambridge in search of some new blood for his law firm and found William Brennan. He took an immediate liking to the New Jersey native and, after reading some of the papers he had prepared during his law school career, offered Brennan a job. Ironically, this son of a labor leader was being offered employment by a law firm that represented large corporations, one that figured out how to fire striking workers legally and prevent unions from organizing and demonstrating.[114] But the demands on Brennan's purse were paramount, and he accepted.

Diligent as always, young Brennan routinely worked up to eighteen-hour days at his new practice. His dedication and competence quickly earned him the respect of the partners in the firm, and because of his familiarity with the concerns of labor he quickly emerged as Pitney, Hardin's point man in mediating disputes between the industrial corporations that the firm represented and the unions that wanted to organize their workers.[115] Brennan's pleasant, unassuming manner endeared him to factory workers and board directors alike. And his ability to understand and communicate the needs and wishes of both often led to peaceful union organization at a time when such an occurrence was rare. In 1938 Pitney, Hardin asked Brennan to become a partner.[116]

One of the firm's better-known clients was the Johnson & Johnson Company. A progressive enterprise, it offered better than minimum wage and workers' benefits before it became fashionable. Robert Wood Johnson, the company's president, often turned to William Brennan for legal advice on how best to structure the new programs he wanted to implement.[117] Following the attack on Pearl Harbor, Johnson was one of a group of industrialists who volunteered to help in the war effort.[118] Commissioned a colonel in the army's Ordnance Division, he shortly thereafter used his influence to get Brennan recruited as well. Not wishing to offend either his best client or his country, he accepted and in July 1942 was made a major in the army.[119]

The attorney's knowledge of labor was put to use again as he greased the wheels of industry to help ensure the steady production of war materials. Within a year he was promoted to lieutenant colonel and made chief of the Labor Resources Section, Office of the Chief of Ordnance.[120] In July 1944, Brennan was named chief of the army's Industrial Personnel Division, Labor Branch; here, he found himself in the midst of a controversy concerning the order in which troops were to be scheduled to return from the European theater.[121] Some senators had requested that railroad men be given priority because their services were needed back home. Brennan flatly refused. He maintained that any such preferential treatment would have an adverse effect on the morale of the men who stayed behind in Europe. When an explanation was demanded of Brennan's actions during a Senate committee hearing his "radical egalitarianism" showed through. When such preferences were enacted after World War I, he said, "the GIs who were still fighting in the foxholes of Europe made a very real issue of the fact that some of their buddies, no better qualified than they, were permitted the soft spots in industrial employment while they had to continue fighting in Europe."[122] Reminding the committee that there was still the war in the Pacific to fight, Brennan said that a system of preferences would not be fair to those GIs who were still in the midst of battle, since the return of some of them would inevitably be postponed by any deviation from the standard system of discharge.

Shortly after he returned to private practice in September 1945, Pitney, Hardin was shaken by the deaths of its two top partners, Shelton Pitney and John Hardin.[123] Brennan had become known as the firm's top labor specialist, and in the postwar era of returning industry to commercial production his skills were much in demand. To aid the national effort during the war, unions and workers had agreed not to strike and to cap wages. But when peace came the fortunes that many large corporations had amassed through sales to the government brought immediate demands of renegotiation of workers' benefits and wages. In addition, the return of servicemen in great numbers meant there would be a glut of workers for domestic industry. To reflect Brennan's draw as a top labor lawyer, the firm changed its name to Pitney, Hardin, Ward, and Brennan.[124]

In 1946 the future justice was asked to join the editorial staff of the *New Jersey Law Journal,* the semiofficial paper of the state's bar.[125] One of its editorial causes was supporting Arthur Vanderbilt, a local lawyer who was pressing for reform of the New Jersey court system. Considered to be among the most antiquated in the country,[126] it consisted of nearly twenty different kinds of courts; these had overlapping jurisdiction and an accompanying surplus of judges. Rather than working together the courts often interfered with each other. Interminable delays were legendary.[127]

Vanderbilt's state constitutional reforms eventually became a reality, and he was appointed New Jersey's chief justice. As such, he was determined to have competent judges manning the benches in the state courts below him so his model plan would work effectively. In 1949 he offered a state superior court judgeship to William Brennan, but he was hesitant about accepting. Brennan was making close to $60,000 a year at his private practice, and a state judgeship paid only $20,000.[128] He had his wife and two sons to support, in addition to his mother and several sisters who still lived with her at home. But Vanderbilt stressed the importance of creating a model system of efficient adjudication. The new chief justice promised that if Brennan joined this effort he would use his influence to move him up to the appeals court, and then to the state supreme court, as quickly as possible.[129] With an assurance from Pitney, Hardin that his job would always be waiting for him, Brennan accepted.

During his first year as a trial court judge Brennan's typical devotion to hard work surprised many who thought he would take the opportunity to relax in a "cushy" judgeship. But within eighteen months the new judge had managed to gain control of the overwhelmingly backlogged docket for his court; he was then appointed to the New Jersey Court of Appeals.[130] During his short tenure there, presented for the first time with the power to review the decisions of lower courts and to pass upon their legality, the respect Brennan had for the principles espoused in our laws began to come through. In one case he ordered a new trial when a judge allowed a juror to use a dictionary to ascertain the meaning of a term used during the course of a trial.[131] The potential for improper influence was too great, Brennan said. "The juror's word alone that its use was limited is too weak a reed upon which to rest the difficult decision whether the verdict was subject to improper influence. . . . A new trial should be granted or refused not so much to the attainment of exact justice in the particular case; [but rather] to the ultimate effect of the decision upon the administration of justice."[132]

By March 1952, with a vacancy emerging on the New Jersey Supreme Court, Chief Justice Vanderbilt kept his promise and persuaded the governor to appoint William Brennan Jr. as its newest justice. Though his primary concern on the state's high court was at first to continue his efforts at improving courtroom efficiency, Brennan's social conscience, dampened for so many years by his family's financial circumstances, was quickly reemerging. In the 1953 case of *New Jersey v. Tune,* John Henry Tune had been convicted of murder, largely on the basis of a signed confession prepared by a police officer that presumably reflected Tune's own statements. His lawyers requested that the confession, as well as other evidence to be used by the state, be turned over to them for inspection prior to trial. The lower court agreed to let Tune see the confession, but it denied his request to view the other material. The New Jersey Supreme Court, in an opinion by Chief Justice Vanderbilt, not only upheld the lower court's refusal to let Tune's lawyers view the evidence against him but went further and reversed the part of the lower court's ruling that allowed Tune to view his own signed confession. The chief justice wrote: "Such liberal fact-finding procedures are not to be used blindly where the result would be to defeat the ends of justice. The criminal who is aware of the whole case against him will often procure perjured testimony in order to set up a false defense."[133]

Brennan was dumbfounded. Not only did this go against his notion that liberal pretrial discovery, allowing both sides to see at the outset what the other has got, was essential to the speedy adjudication of trials but it stirred something deeper within. "It shocks my sense of justice," he wrote, "that in these circumstances, counsel for an accused facing a possible death sentence should be denied inspection of his confession, which, were this a civil case, could not be denied. . . . To shackle counsel so that they cannot effectively seek out the truth and afford the accused that representation which is not his privilege but his absolute right seriously imperils our bedrock presumption of innocence."[134]

In another case Brennan delivered an opinion holding that a police officer could be held liable for damages after shooting a misdemeanor offender who was running to avoid capture.[135] Showing his abhorrence of the arbitrary imposition of state power and his reverence for the sanctity of constitutional rights, Brennan also ordered an admittedly guilty man, convicted of burning a house, freed because of errors made by the prosecution. "The plea of double jeopardy," he wrote, "must be honored though a regrettable defeat of justice may result."[136]

In April 1956 Chief Justice Vanderbilt was asked by the Eisenhower administration to come to Washington and address a symposium at the Justice Department concerning congestion in the nation's courts. The successes in New Jersey had indeed been noteworthy, and the government wanted Vanderbilt to share some of his secrets. As fate would have it, the chief justice fell ill and asked Brennan to take his place. While the two were certainly not ideological twins, they did share a passion for effective court reform, and the New Jersey chief justice knew, at least on this matter, that their views and goals were the same. Vanderbilt had long aspired to, indeed expected, a seat on the nation's highest court for himself. Ironically, by sending Brennan to Washington to speak in his place, the conservative chief justice helped make his junior colleague the next associate justice of the Supreme Court of the United States.

Brennan's speech at the symposium was not ideological; instead, he discussed such technical issues as jurisdictional controversies and the need for pretrial discovery. He impressed Attorney General Herbert Brownell, who quite mistakenly assumed that Brennan was an ideological conservative akin to Vanderbilt. In September 1956, two months before the presidential election, Justice Sherman Minton announced his retirement from the Supreme Court. Brownell informed Eisenhower that it would be the perfect time to court some of his constituencies. Cardinal Francis Spellman had met with the president only weeks before to lament the fact that there had not been a Catholic voice on the Court since the retirement of Justice Frank Murphy in 1949.[137] And the Association of State Court Judges had of late been criticizing the administration for the notable lack of sitting jurists who had been appointed to the high court.[138] Brownell's mind quickly turned to Brennan, who was a winner on both points.

After checking only to make sure that Brennan was indeed a practicing Catholic, the attorney general asked him to come to Washington immediately to meet with President Eisenhower.[139] Eisenhower was just about to leave for a tour of the midwest, as part of his reelection campaign, and his opponent, Adlai Stevenson, was getting ready for heavy canvassing in the Northeast, a trip that would take him through New Jersey. Brownell hoped the appointment of a New Jersey justice would take some of the air out of Stevenson's campaign. After a pro forma twenty-minute meeting at which no political views were discussed, Eisenhower offered the appointment. Brennan replied that he would be honored to serve. The president assumed that Brennan was "Vanderbilt's boy" and that Brownell had already asked the questions of substance.[140] In fact, not only had the attorney general failed to ask any questions of Brennan, he had not bothered to look over Brennan's decisions as a New Jersey associate justice, to consult with the state's senators or governor, or even to speak with Arthur Vanderbilt, whose "boy" Eisenhower assumed him to be.[141] The president's haste proved to be the people's good fortune.

Justice William Brennan would serve on the Court for thirty-four years. The only justice to serve longer was William O. Douglas, who sat on the high court for thirty-six. During Brennan's long tenure he helped to influence the direction of the Court in a way matched perhaps only by John Marshall, the nation's first truly great chief justice, who unified the Court and established the notion of judicial review nearly two hundred years ago. As Judge Abner J. Mikva of the Court of Appeals for the District of Columbia has noted of Brennan, "[H]is footprints are everywhere; his influence can be felt in nearly every area of the law."[142] Even Judge Robert Bork, who disagreed with Brennan's constitutional interpretation and charged that he made up law, called him "the most powerful justice of this century on the Supreme Court."[143]

Brennan's power came from an almost uncanny ability to get other justices to join in his opinions, not by cajoling or intense lobbying, as some of his colleagues were prone to do, but rather through a "special kind of perceptiveness that sees the problems of a case and can translate them in a way that appeals to the critical Justice or Justices needed for a majority."[144] Judge Mikva has said that Brennan "influences colleagues beyond measure and builds coalitions at every level—personal and intellectual, on issues and on semantics, and most of all on the strength of his own integrity."[145]

One area where Brennan's footprints are quite readily apparent is in freedom of speech and the press. As Geoffrey Stone, professor and dean of the University of Chicago Law School, notes, when Brennan joined the Court in 1956

> first amendment doctrine was still in its infancy. The Court had not
> yet addressed the issues of obscenity or libel, it had made only passing
> acquaintance with the complexities of commercial advertising and
> the concept of the public forum, . . . its protection of subversive

advocacy was more theoretical than real, and its overall free speech jurisprudence was rigid, simplistic, and incomplete. At the time of Justice Brennan's retirement some thirty-four years later, the Court's free speech doctrine was far richer, more subtle, and more speech-protective than ever before in our nation's history.[146]

In 1957, his initial term on the Court, Brennan was called upon to write the opinion in *Roth v. United States,* his first in the area of free speech and one he would come to regret. In *Roth,* Brennan declared for the Court that "obscenity is not within the area of constitutionally protected speech or press."[147] Following the jurisprudence of the day, which Judge Robert Bork would later develop into one of "original intent,"[148] Brennan referred to the status of obscenity at the time the Constitution was ratified and noted the "universal judgment that obscenity should be restrained,"[149] holding that obscenity may be banned without violating the first amendment guarantee of freedom of speech. While taking pains to articulate that sex, "one of the vital problems of human interest and public concern,"[150] is not synonymous with obscenity, and that "ceaseless vigilance" is necessary to prevent the erosion of our fundamental right to protected speech, Brennan held that obscenity is "utterly without redeeming social importance"[151] and therefore does not deserve constitutional protection.

Brennan's jurisprudence underwent profound change during his years on the Court. Immediately after *Roth,* he would begin to expand the rights of free speech, which he increasingly came to realize were essential in maintaining a free and open society and a government responsive to the concerns of its citizens. The Court would revisit the issue of obscenity many times during those years, and Brennan would come to realize the impossibility of fairly and consistently placing a judicially mandated value judgment on the societal worth of certain forms of expression. In 1973, he wrote in dissent in *Paris Adult Theatre I v. Slaton* that "the concept of 'obscenity' cannot be defined with sufficient specificity and clarity . . . to prevent substantial erosion of protected speech as a byproduct of the attempt to suppress unprotected speech"[152] and that therefore "the outright suppression of obscenity cannot be reconciled with the fundamental principles" of the first amendment.[153]

After *Roth,* Brennan wrote opinions holding unconstitutional the denial of property tax exemptions to veterans who refused to sign oaths swearing that they did not advocate the violent overthrow of the government, protecting individual citizens from retribution by Congress for not answering intrusive questions before a committee, forbidding prior restraint of printed matter, and protecting Blacks who peacefully refused to leave segregated establishments. In a controversial 1989 case, *Texas v. Johnson,* he protected the right of an American to burn the flag as an expression of political protest. "If there is a bedrock principle underlying the First Amendment," Brennan wrote, "it is that the government may not prohibit the expression of an idea simply because the society finds the idea offensive or disagreeable. . . . Government may not prohibit expression merely because it disagrees with its message."[154]

To Brennan, the public forum was a "marketplace of ideas," where all citizens had not only a right but a duty to express their views. The hallmark of a government that is the servant of the people, and not its master, is that it must listen to everyone. And even if it does not like what it hears, it does not have the right to silence the voices that criticize.

No opinion made this point more emphatically than that in *New York Times Co. v. Sullivan,* written by Brennan for a unanimous Court in 1964 and described in Anthony Lewis's compelling book *Make No Law.*[155] The *New York Times* had published a full-page advertisement critical of police actions in several southern cities, among them Montgomery, Alabama. The ad contained several small mistakes, which police commissioner L. B. Sullivan claimed constituted false criticism of him, even though he was never mentioned by name or reference. Nevertheless, Sullivan sued the New York Times Company for libel. At the time, the only defense to a libel suit by a public official was to show that the offending statements were true. Because the ad contained mistakes, Sullivan won a judgment for $500,000. Comparing the law, as it existed, to the Sedition Act of 1798 (which outlawed criticism of government), Brennan declared for the Court that "we consider this case against the background of a profound national commitment to the principle that debate on public issues should be uninhibited, robust, and wide-open, and that it may well include vehement, caustic, and sometimes unpleasantly sharp attacks on government and public officials."[156] According to Brennan, in free debate some degree of erroneous statement is inevitable and so must be protected—any other approach would lead to unacceptable "self-censorship." "[W]ould-be critics of official conduct," he said, "may be deterred from voicing their criticism, even though it is believed to be true and even though it is in fact true, because of doubt whether it can be proved in court or fear of the expense of having to do so."[157] As a result, a public official seeking damages for libel relating to official conduct cannot prevail unless the defamatory statement was made "with knowledge that it was false or with reckless disregard of whether it was false or not."[158]

*New York Times Co. v. Sullivan* shows a departure from the way in which Brennan reached his decision only seven years before in *Roth*. As the justice noted in his *Times* opinion, at the time the Constitution was adopted the law of libel was more fully developed than that of obscenity.[159] In reversing precedent Brennan was giving much less weight to popular consensus than he had in *Roth*. And while in *Roth* he declared that vagueness in the statutory definitions of obscenity did not make their usage abhorrent to the Constitution, in *Times* Brennan specifically noted that in order for our fundamental rights to have true meaning they must have "breathing space"—statutes must address a legitimate governmental concern and be precisely tailored so as not to have a "chilling effect" on protected forms of expression.[160]

Brennan did not come to the Court with his jurisprudence firmly fixed; rather, he grew into his beliefs. When he first joined the Court in 1956 it was, in the words of Harvard Law School dean Erwin Griswold, "hopelessly split into minor fragments."[161] On the one extreme was Felix Frankfurter, the former Harvard law professor. Renowned for his constitutional scholarship, his reputation was exceeded only by his own sense of self-importance. He remarked privately that he felt himself to be the only justice truly capable of writing important constitutional decisions.[162] Frankfurter was a judicial conservative, meaning that in his understanding of the Constitution, which he felt was eminently accurate, the separation of powers required that federal judges limit their own power and, with few exceptions, never involve themselves in decisions made by state legislatures. Frankfurter's imposing intellect and domineering nature often allowed him to dictate the views of four other justices and, as a result, the majority opinion.

On the other extreme sat Hugo Black and William O. Douglas, who believed that the fourteenth amendment made the entire Bill of Rights applicable to the states and who were eager to see the constitutional guarantees of freedom extended to all citizens. Earl Warren, who had been appointed chief justice by President Eisenhower in 1954, wanted to see the Court more actively involved in helping to cure the country's social ills and so eventually sided with Black and Douglas.

A large part of the controversy was over the meaning of the fourteenth amendment. Enacted in 1868 in an attempt to ensure that the states could no longer legally discriminate against Blacks, section one of the amendment reads, in part: "No State shall make or enforce any law which shall abridge the privileges or immunities of citizens of the United States; nor shall any State deprive any person of life, liberty, or property, without due process of law." While Justices Black and Douglas believed this to mean that no state could pass a law contrary to the safeguards of liberty contained in the Bill of Rights, a contrary view, espoused by Felix Frankfurter, held sway for a very long time. In *Palko v. Connecticut*,[163] decided in 1937, the Court ruled that only those liberties deemed "fundamental" were protected by the fourteenth amendment and thus not susceptible to encroachment by the states. The problem was that the Supreme Court had the prerogative of deciding what rights were "fundamental." Indeed it was not until 1925 that the Court ruled that the first amendment protections of freedom of speech and of the press were rights fundamental enough to be protected from state legislation attempting to curtail their exercise.[164] At the time of Brennan's arrival on the Court, this was the only one of the amendments in the federal Bill of Rights that applied to the states.

When Brennan came onto the Court, Frankfurter who had taught him while at Harvard, immediately began trying to bring the newest associate justice over to his conservative camp. If he could count on Brennan's vote, Frankfurter would have a solid six-member conservative majority. But the older man's condescending tone ultimately drove William Brennan away. Frankfurter was well connected both in Washington and around the world, maintaining correspondences with presidents as well as kings. Part of his strategy, Brennan remarked, was "to make you feel it was an honor to be associated with his crowd of giants."[165] On one occasion, after Frankfurter had a "discussion" with Justice Brennan that was actually more like a lecture on the virtues of judicial restraint, Brennan uncharacteristically lost his temper and told his senior colleague that he was no longer his student and expected not to be treated as one.[166] Frankfurter apologized profusely, but it was simply not in his nature to accord weight to opinions that were not his own.

During Justice Brennan's first years on the Court, he was as likely to side with Frankfurter as with Black and Douglas on issues of constitutional interpretation, but by 1960 his expansionist views of the Constitution were beginning to take hold. The case that perhaps marked the final, clear break in ideology from Frankfurter's conservative views was *Irvin v. Dowd,* decided in 1959. Irvin had been found guilty of murder and sentenced to death in an Indiana state court. He escaped custody but was later recaptured. Citing the escape, the state refused to grant him an appeal of his case, so Irvin's lawyer asked the Supreme Court to issue a writ of habeas corpus.[167] To Frankfurter and his allies, this meddling of a federal court in a state criminal prosecution was the worst transgression of the country's principles of federalism and state sovereignty. To Brennan, evidence that Irvin's jury had been tainted with prejudice (four members were seated despite their comments before the trial that they already thought he was guilty) implicated fundamental rights. His views prevailed, and a majority of the court ordered the State of Indiana to hear Irvin's appeal. Frankfurter was livid. "Something that goes to the very structure of our federal system," he wrote in dissent, "in its distribution of power between the United States and the state is not a mere bit of red tape to be cut, on the assumption that this Court has general discretion to see justice done."[168]

It was obvious that Brennan disagreed. While he came to the Court as a liberal-minded jurist who believed the extent of a judge's duty consisted of faithfully applying precedent, on the Supreme Court he became influenced by the absurd notion of Chief Justice Warren that the Court's role was in fact to see justice done, while remaining faithful to the Constitution. In fact for Brennan, perhaps an idealist, remaining faithful to the Constitution was synonymous with seeing justice done.

Increasingly, Brennan began to feel comfortable in his liberal interpretation of the Constitution; this led to expansion and protection of the liberties guaranteed the American people by that document, albeit to the dismay of Felix Frankfurter and at the expense of the states. No case better illustrates this point than *Baker v. Carr,* which came to the Court in 1962 from Tennessee.[169] There, because of how the state legislature was apportioned, a rural district comprised of a few wealthy landowners had as much political leverage as an urban community with nearly ten times the number of constituents. Voters from the less well represented urban district brought suit in federal court alleging a violation of the due process clause of the fourteenth amendment. The lower federal court dismissed the case, relying on the Supreme Court opinion in *Colegrove v. Green,* written in 1946 by Justice Frankfurter, which said the Court had no business involving itself in the "political thicket"[170] and that a federal court had no jurisdiction over the actions of a state legislature.

Brennan's contrary view was that the Constitution demanded not only that every citizen's vote count but that it count equally in relation to all others. In order to win the support of Justice Potter Stewart, Brennan agreed to limit the decision to one merely stating that federal courts did indeed have jurisdiction to correct malapportioned legislative districts, without going so far as to tell the Tennessee legislature what it must do to correct its situation. Ironically, at the last minute Justice Tom Clark changed sides and joined the Brennan majority. He had been researching his position for a dissent arguing that the Tennessee voters had not yet exhausted all avenues of relief, which he believed should have been done before bringing their case to a court of last resort. But his research revealed they had no viable alternative means; the Tennessee constitution provided no avenue for amendment by the public at large. Amendment could only be effected by the very legislature at issue.[171] With the piety of a convert, Clark now argued that Brennan's opinion did not go far enough. But Brennan had made his promise to Stewart, so, even though Stewart's vote was now unnecessary to keep a majority, the opinion came down as originally agreed upon.

A few weeks after *Baker v. Carr* was handed down Frankfurter, who was not used to having his views relegated to the minority, suffered a stroke, and in August 1962 he announced his retirement. His replacement, appointed by President Kennedy, was Arthur Goldberg, a staunch liberal activist and Kennedy's secretary of labor.[172] Along with Brennan, Black, Douglas, and Warren, Goldberg helped to create a solid liberal majority on the court. Indeed, for the next seven years, until Warren Burger replaced Earl Warren as chief justice, Brennan would find himself writing remarkably few dissents. It was during these years that the Court decided the landmark cases of *Gideon v. Wainwright* and *Miranda v. Arizona.* And Hugo Black looked on with approval as the Court ruled that the fifth amendment guarantee against self-incrimination and the eighth amendment prohibition of cruel and unusual punishment applied to the states.

By 1973, with four new Nixon appointees sitting on the Court, Brennan's skills as a builder of coalitions would again serve him, and the rights of the American people, in good stead. When the Texas case of *Roe v. Wade* came before the Court the tribunal was bitterly divided over the best approach to follow. Chief Justice Burger, originally for upholding the state's ban on abortions, tactically switched sides when it appeared that a majority of the Court was for finding the statute unconstitutional. As the senior justice in the majority, Burger was allowed to decide who would write the opinion.[173] He chose Harry Blackmun, who had seemed most unsure about the decision, in hopes of securing a narrow ruling. Blackmun, who had served as chief counsel for the Mayo Clinic, was inclined to accept the view that the Texas statute was unconstitutional only because it was too vague and because it restricted the rights of physicians to practice their trade.[174] Blackmun was at first extremely wary of the view espoused by Brennan and Douglas that the decision implicated a fundamental right to privacy. Brennan wrote in a memo to Blackmun that "liberty," as mentioned in the fourteenth amendment, encompasses "freedom of choice in the basic decisions of life, such as . . . procreation. . . . There is a sphere within which the individual may assert the supremacy of his own will and rightfully dispute the authority of any human government . . . to interfere with the exercise of that will—rather than the holding that compelling public necessity may justify intrusion into bodily freedom."[175] After many months and many drafts of his opinion, Blackmun was persuaded that his colleague's views were correct, and those views were incorporated into his now famous decision.

Justice Brennan never claimed a strict adherence to the text of the Constitution, but rather a strict adherence to its noble principles. Though the Preamble reads "We the People . . . in Order to . . . secure the Blessings of Liberty . . . ," wealthy White men wrote those words and created the laws to realize them. Blacks were not given the right to vote until 1870, and even then it was largely a right only on paper; women were likewise excluded for more than half a century after that. If "we the people" was in fact meant to apply to every member of the new nation, arguably it was a paternalistic application at the discretion of those with social, as well as political, power. "The Declaration of Independence, the Constitution, and the Bill of Rights," said Brennan,

> solemnly committed the United States to be a country where the dignity and rights of all persons were equal before all authority. In all candor we must concede that part of this egalitarianism in America has been more pretension than realized fact. But we are an aspiring people, a people with faith in progress. Our amended Constitution is the lodestar for our aspirations. Like every text worth reading, it is not crystalline. The phrasing is broad and the limitations of its provisions are not clearly marked. Its majestic generalities and ennobling pronouncements are both luminous and obscure. This ambiguity, of course, calls forth interpretation, the interaction of reader and text.[176]

This view is precisely what so frustrates those who call for a doctrine of "original intent," namely, that in order to resolve a constitutional dispute the Court must simply discern what the Framers thought of the issue and apply their intent to the case at hand. Of this, Brennan says: "It is a view that feigns self-effacing deference to the specific judgments of those who forged our original social compact. But in truth it is little more than arrogance cloaked as humility."[177] It is arrogant, the justice says, to assume that we may accurately gauge how the Framers would apply their principles to specific contemporary issues. "Those who would restrict claims of right to the values of 1789 specifically articulated in the Constitution turn a blind eye to social progress and eschew adaption of overarching principles to changes of social circumstance."[178] The proponents of original intent claim that by adhering strictly to the values of two centuries ago in interpreting the Constitution we would remove any political factor from judicial decision making. But, as Brennan observes, this is patently false. Adoption of this "facile historicism"[179] would merely result in "resolving textual ambiguities against the claim of constitutional right,"[180] favoring the wishes of the majority over the rights of the minority, a choice that would be undeniably political.

This is not to say that Brennan argues he is free to make whatever decision he chooses in interpreting the Constitution. "[T]he Constitution cannot be for me simply a contemplative haven for moral reflection."[181] Quoting Justice Benjamin Cardozo, Brennan has said: "[The judge] is not a knight-errant roaming at will in pursuit of his own ideal of beauty or of goodness. He is to draw his inspiration from consecrated principles. He is not to yield to spasmodic sentiment, to vague and unregulated benevolence."[182] Rather, what is needed is an ongoing dialogue between the heart and the head. The judicial system, in his view, has been dominated by reason for so long that it has become oblivious to the needs of men and women. Blind adherence to precedent creates an illusion that the precedent is infallible, that it is inherently objective, when in truth it stems from a very old, established, subjective norm. Justice applied mechanically is no justice at all. "Only by remaining open to the entreaties of reason and passion, of logic and of experience, can a judge come to understand the complex human meaning of a rich term such as 'liberty,' and only with such understanding can courts fulfill their constitutional responsibility to protect that value."[183]

For Brennan, the preservation of human dignity is at the very core of our constitutional protections of liberty. The first amendment's guarantee of freedom of speech ensures that individuals may express their views without fear of official retribution, for it is essential to personal dignity that people may stand up and state their conscience. The fourth amendment's guarantee against unreasonable searches and seizures protects human dignity in the sanctity of person and belongings. And the eighth amendment's guarantee against cruel and unusual punishment mandates that the state, even when it undertakes to punish an individual who has transgressed its laws, recognize the intrinsic worth of the individual as a human being. For Brennan, this is why the sentence of death is in all circumstances cruel and unusual punishment, forbidden by the Constitution. "A punishment must not be so severe," he said,

> as to be utterly and irreversibly degrading to the very essence of human dignity. Death for any crime whatsoever, and under all circumstances, is a truly awesome punishment. The calculated killing of a human being by the state involves, by its very nature, an absolute denial of the executed person's humanity. The most vile murder does not, in my view, release the state from constitutional restraints on the destruction of human dignity. Yet an executed person has lost the very right to have rights, now or ever. For me, then, the fatal constitutional infirmity of capital punishment is that it treats members of the human race as nonhumans, as objects to be toyed with and discarded.[184]

How strange that a judicial system that so prizes reason allows itself this one violent passion.

Brennan's own passion was in evidence when the Court decided a case at the intersection of capital punishment and race, *McCleskey v. Kemp,* a turning point by any measure.[185] The legal and political stakes were astronomically high. *McCleskey* was the last case, for the foreseeable future, with the potential of reaching all condemned prisoners, or at least of reaching large groups of them. Had Warren McCleskey's constitutional claim prevailed in its broadest aspects, capital punishment in Georgia (and, I believe, in most other states by implication) would have ground to a halt indefinitely. The moral stakes were higher yet. In claiming that constitutionally unacceptable racial factors permeated the system of capital sentencing that put him on death row, Mr. McCleskey demanded that the courts confront this nation's efforts to purge a racist past.[186]

Warren McCleskey, who was Black, was convicted and condemned in Georgia. He claimed, first in state court[187] and then in federal district court,[188] that Georgia's capital statute allowed factors of race to affect the administration of capital sentencing. As proof, he offered the results of the statistical study performed by Prof. David Baldus and his colleagues,[189] the most sophisticated work ever undertaken to investigate sentencing patterns.[190] The district court rejected Mr. McCleskey's claim, holding that the data base for Professor Baldus's study was flawed and that in any event the study was insufficient as a matter of law to carry McCleskey's constitutional challenges to the statute.[191] The court held that McCleskey "failed to demonstrate that racial considerations caused him to receive the death penalty."[192]

The Eleventh Circuit, using the extraordinary procedural device of taking the case en banc in the first instance, affirmed.[193] The majority opinion held that the same standards of proof govern racial discrimination challenged under the equal protection clause of the fourteenth amendment and the cruel and unusual punishment clause of the eighth amendment. Intentional discrimination must be shown under either constitutional provision.

The majority opinion recognized that "[d]ue process and cruel and unusual punishment cases do not normally focus on the intent of the governmental actor." The court ultimately concluded, however, that when "racial discrimination is claimed . . . on the basis of the decisions made within that process, then purpose, intent and motive are a natural component of the proof that discrimination actually occurred."[194] To prevail under either constitutional theory, a prisoner must offer proof of a "disparate impact [that] is so great that it compels a conclusion that the system is unprincipled, irrational, arbitrary and capricious such that purposeful discrimination . . . can be presumed to permeate the system."[195]

Applying this analytical framework to the Baldus study, the majority opinion reaffirmed previous Eleventh Circuit holdings that statistical evidence of racially disproportionate impact "may be so strong that the results permit no other inference."[196] Yet no evidentiary hearing would be required on statistical studies of capital-sentencing discrimination, regardless of their quality, unless they "reflect a disparity so great as to inevitably lead to a conclusion that the disparity results from intent or motivation."[197] The court reasoned that "it is a legal question as to how much [racial] disparity is required before a federal court will accept it as evidence of the constitutional flaws in the system."[198]

The Supreme Court granted certiorari and affirmed by a vote of 5 to 4.[199] The opinion for the majority was written by Justice Lewis Powell, the courtly Virginian whose record on matters of race as chair of the Richmond school board during the crucial period from 1952 to 1961 was mixed even according to his admirers.[200] Although I will not discuss the *McCleskey* majority and dissenting opinions in detail, in essence Justice Powell's opinion held that the touchstone of Mr. McCleskey's constitutional claims must be intentional discrimination against him personally.[201] Purporting to assume as valid the Baldus data that death sentences are four times more likely when the victim is White, the majority reasoned that discrepancies are inevitable.[202] This given, however, did "not include the assumption that the study shows that racial considerations actually enter into any sentencing decisions in Georgia."[203] Because "discretion is essential to the criminal justice process," the Court "would demand exceptionally clear proof before . . . [it] would infer that the discretion has been abused."[204] The Court found that the Baldus study did not "demonstrate a constitutionally significant risk of racial bias affecting the Georgia capital sentencing process."[205]

Justice Powell noted that statistical disparities ordinarily must be "stark" to be accepted as the sole proof of discriminatory intent.[206] Apparently the Baldus study's showing of between a 300 and 400 percent disparity based on race-of-victim effects was not sufficiently stark, even when that disparity could not credibly be explained away in a nonracist fashion.[207] That is, killers of Whites are between three and four times more likely to wind up on death row than are killers of Blacks, even when 360 variables are factored into the calculus of deciding who dies.

Justice Powell offered a rationale that had been suggested (I thought at the time tongue-in-cheek) by Justice Scalia during oral argument. Accepting McCleskey's claim of racial discrimination, Powell wrote, would mean ugly people might be the next group to whine about discrimination.[208] Criminal defendants and their crafty lawyers would not be satisfied with raising proportionality claims based on race. They would, Powell prophesied, assert claims that discrepancies in sentencing also existed based upon sex, or membership in other minority groups, or indeed "upon any arbitrary variable, such as the defendant's facial characteristics, or the physical attractiveness of the defendant or the victim."[209]

Thus did the Supreme Court equate race with any other demonstrable quality like ugliness or hair color. All were of equal insignificance to Justice Powell. Having caricatured McCleskey's claim, the Court solemnly stated the obvious: "The Constitution does not require that a State eliminate any demonstrable disparity that correlates with a potentially irrelevant factor in order to operate a criminal justice system that includes capital punishment."[210]

Justice Brennan wrote a powerful dissent,[211] one that will resonate down the years. "We cannot pretend that in three decades we have completely escaped the grip of an historical legacy spanning centuries," he observed.[212] McCleskey's evidence "confronts us with the subtle and persistent influence of the past. His message is a disturbing one to a society that has formally repudiated racism. . . . Nonetheless, we ignore him at our peril, for we remain imprisoned by the past as long as we deny its influence in the present."[213]

Perhaps most importantly, Justice Brennan's dissent refocused the case on Warren McCleskey, a Black person condemned to die in the Georgia electric chair.[214] By restoring "a face and a name"[215] to the statistical abstractions favored by the majority, Brennan reminded us that at its core the case was not about numbers, even though it was full of numbers, data, and statistical jargon. There was something numbingly banal in using all of this ciphering to resolve an ultimate question of morality. Justice Brennan captured well the human dimension lurking behind the statistics:

> At some point in this case Warren McCleskey doubtless asked his lawyer whether a jury was likely to sentence him to die. A candid reply to this question would have been disturbing. First, counsel would have to tell McCleskey that few of the details of the crime or of McCleskey's past criminal conduct were more important than the fact that his victim was white. Furthermore, counsel would feel bound to tell McCleskey that defendants charged with killing white victims in Georgia are 4.3 times as likely to be sentenced to death as defendants charged with killing blacks. In addition, frankness would compel the disclosure that it was more likely than not that the race of McCleskey's victim would determine whether he received a death sentence: 6 of every 11 defendants convicted of killing a white person would not have received the death penalty if their victims had been black, while, among defendants with aggravating and mitigating factors comparable to McCleskey's, 20 of every 34 would not have been sentenced to die if their victims had been black. Finally, the assessment would not be complete without the information that cases involving black defendants and white victims are more likely to result in a death sentence than cases featuring any other racial combination of defendant and victim. The story could be told in a variety of ways, but McCleskey could not fail to grasp its essential narrative line: there was a significant chance that race would play a prominent role in determining if he lived or died.[216]

Justice Brennan's dissent also warned that "[i]t is tempting to pretend that minorities on death row share a fate in no way connected to our own, that our treatment of them sounds no echoes beyond the chambers in which they die. Such an illusion is ultimately corrosive, for the reverberations of injustice are not so easily confined."[217] To the contrary, "the way in which we choose those who will die reveals the depth of moral commitment among the living."[218]

Justice Brennan stepped down from the Court at the end of the 1989–90 Term, at the age of eighty-four. In a tribute to him after his retirement Judge Richard Posner, who had once clerked for Brennan but who had long since left his liberal ideology behind, said of him:

Justice Brennan has not pretended that the constitutional revolution in which he has played a leading role was dictated by the text of the Constitution or by the intentions of its framers. He does not ask to be judged by his fidelity to a text and a history, or by the craft standards of the legal mandarinate. He has striven, in the American pragmatic tradition, for concrete results and will be judged in history by the results achieved, both intended and unintended. But although ultimate evaluation must be deferred, I trust that no one will question the *effectiveness* with which Justice Brennan has pursued his conception of the judicial role, or the impact of his work on contemporary legal and social thought. I have tried to suggest that the key to that effectiveness, and to that impact, lies in a personality warm and serene, and in a character that can fairly be described as noble.[219]

In a tribute of his own, Justice Thurgood Marshall concluded his praise of Justice William J. Brennan Jr. with lines from *Hamlet:* "He was a man, take him for all in all; [we] shall not look upon his like again."[220]

## Thurgood Marshall
### The Litigator

[A] few years back I researched the history of the death penalty for juveniles. In the National Archives I came across the certiorari petition filed in the United States Supreme Court on behalf of two black teenage murderers in a Mississippi case in 1947. The petition had weak legal claims—the papers seemed desperate, and succeeded only in postponing that double execution for a few months. I think I can imagine the sense of humiliation and defeat that their lawyer must have felt the night of that execution, when he watched the clock and knew he had failed so completely to stop the inexorable grinding of that racist system.

The signature at the bottom of that cert petition was Thurgood Marshall's. His work for the NAACP Legal Defense Fund may seem to have been glamorous and exciting now, when so many of the battles he fought have been at least partly won. But that night, his hopeless campaign to stop Mississippi from executing those two black teenagers must have seemed pointless, marginal, a humiliating enactment of political weakness.

Justice Marshall was the lone dissenter last week [in 1990] when Virginia electrocuted a man named Wilbert Evans. This stubborn stand again seems forlorn, and so, I suppose, it is.

But this phase in our history won't last forever. We will regain our faith in our ability to address our problems as a society, and our sense of shared responsibility and of a shared destiny as a people. And as we do, the inexorable progress of abolition will resume.

I can't say that this is the most important legal work one could be engaged in. But I do think it needs to be done. If there are some law students here tonight who think you'd like to put your shoulder to this wheel, welcome. Don't be discouraged. Push. It'll move.[221]

It seems likely that the best time life gave to Thurgood Marshall was not when he was a Supreme Court justice but when he was general counsel to the NAACP Legal Defense and Educational Fund, Inc., traveling to a South where there was no room at most inns for such as he. This experience is what made the future justice.

Anthony Lewis has reminded us that in 1908, the year Thurgood Marshall was born, eighty-nine Black men were lynched in the United States. When he went off to law school in 1930, he could not attend the University of Maryland, in his home state, because it did not admit African Americans. In the 1940s, when he traveled through the South trying cases against segregation, his life was at risk. Marshall told Lewis of a time he had to change trains in Mississippi. As he stood on the platform, a White man with a pistol sticking out of his pocket came up to him and said, "What are you doing here, boy?" "I'm waiting for the next train," Justice Marshall said he replied. "The man said, 'What did you say, boy?' Then I remembered. I said 'I'm waiting for the next train, *Sir.*' And he said 'You'd better be on it, because the sun's not going down on a live nigger in this town.' "[222]

David Margolick referred to Marshall as "the Justice with the stories that moved the world."[223] He wrote that "Justice Marshall's opinions, like those by most Supreme Court Justices these days, were assembled just as Swedish workers assemble Volvos: by team. However ringing his printed rhetoric, however stinging his dissents, Thurgood Marshall's judicial voice lacked the plain spoken, gut-wrenching eloquence of the real thing. In its power and impact, his spoken voice was separate and unequalled. That voice was something he picked up on the streets of West Baltimore, honed on the debating team at Lincoln College, polished further with Charles Hamilton Houston at Howard Law School, and sharpened, as long time counsel for the NAACP, while fighting Jim Crow justice throughout the segregated south. Fourteen times he brought it to the United States Supreme Court—a bit cleaned up, perhaps, but still passionate, dignified, to the point."[224]

Justice Marshall lived long enough to see the University of Maryland Law School, which barred him from its doors, name its library after him and to be extolled by a bar group which, well within his memory, had been as segregated as the classrooms of Little Rock or Topeka. Shortly before his death, he was extolled by a chief justice who, as a law clerk at the Supreme Court two years before the *Brown* case was decided, devised a means to uphold segregated but equal schools.[225]

Although the Supreme Court's 1954 decision in *Brown v. Board of Education* was eventually unanimous—thanks largely to the political skills of Chief Justice Earl Warren—there were deep divisions in the Court before the ruling that segregated public schools were inherently unequal and therefore unconstitutional. Nat Hentoff observed that in the course of trying to make up his mind, Justice Robert Jackson's worries included whether a ruling supporting Thurgood Marshall's arguments would appear to the country to be a "ruthless use of federal judicial power." Accordingly, Jackson asked his two clerks to send him advisory memoranda. One clerk recommended that instead of accepting Marshall's argument he should vote to retain the "separate but equal" doctrine. In the clerk's words, "I think *Plessy v. Ferguson* was right and should be reaffirmed." Keep Black students segregated. "I realize," he wrote, "that it is an unpopular and unhumanitarian position, for which I have been excoriated by 'liberal' colleagues." That clerk was William Rehnquist.

As Richard Kluger noted in his indispensable book, *Simple Justice,* when Rehnquist was nominated in 1971 to be the one hundredth justice of the United States Supreme Court, the former Jackson clerk denied that his memo to the justice represented his own views. Oh no, said Rehnquist, he was just summarizing Justice Jackson's own opinions so that Jackson could arm himself with this handy summary when arguing during the justices' conference. As Kluger says rather charitably, "There is much evidence, both internal and external, that casts doubt on the nature of Rehnquist's memorandum." Indeed, that memorandum was what Rehnquist himself believed.

There is further evidence throughout Rehnquist's subsequent record on the Supreme Court concerning his views on desegregating public schools. During the years he served with Thurgood Marshall, the two were on opposite sides of a number of crucial decisions that continued to weaken the substance and therefore the effect of *Brown*.[226]

Kathleen Sullivan has written that "great supreme court dissents lie like buried ammunition for future generations to unearth when the time comes."[227] What marked Marshall's dissents "was a candor that cut through legal abstractions to the social reality in human suffering underneath. Justice Marshall never let his colleagues forget that there is 'another world out there' and urged them not to forget on the bench all that they knew about life. When the court permitted the states greater leeway to use the death penalty, Justice Marshall, who had known first hand of lynchings during his days as a civil rights lawyer in the south, maintained that execution was cruel and unusual punishment."

Almost from the moment he graduated Howard Law School at the top of his class in 1933, until his death sixty years later, Marshall fought ardently, bravely, and endlessly to help secure equal protection under the law for all Americans. In large part because of this struggle to use the law and the courts as a means to realize the promise of equality made in the Constitution, he helped, as much as any other individual, to bring about what Justice Abe Fortas was later to describe as "the most profound and pervasive revolution ever achieved by substantially peaceful means."[228]

Thoroughgood Marshall, the younger of two sons of Norma and William Marshall, was born in Baltimore on July 2, 1908.[229] He was named after his paternal grandfather, a freeman, who took the name Thoroughgood when he was told he needed both a first and a last name in order to enlist in the Union army during the Civil War.[230] In about the second or third grade, because he got tired of spelling it out, the younger Marshall employed the courts for the first of many changes he was to work in American justice and had his name changed legally to Thurgood.[231]

There was very little indication that young Marshall would grow into a staunch legal activist in the quest for civil rights, much less go on to be the first American of African descent appointed to the nation's highest court. In his youth he was something of a hellion, causing his mother endless grief. As Marshall himself liked to recount: "We lived on a respectable street, but behind us there were back alleys where the roughnecks and the tough kids hung out. When it was time for dinner, my mother used to go to the front door and call my older brother. Then she'd go to the *back* door and call me."[232]

Throughout elementary and high school, Marshall felt there was no need for him to curtail his rambunctious nature or, in fact, even to study. His mother, Norma, was a schoolteacher and he figured, apparently correctly, that none of her peers would flunk him nor any principal expel him.[233] On one occasion an assistant principal was going to discipline Marshall and several others in a teenage gang that the future justice was running. Marshall arranged for one of the girls in the gang to meet with the assistant principal. At a predetermined, synchronized time, the girl jumped into his lap—just as Marshall and his cohorts burst into the office to catch the two "in the act." No disciplinary action was taken.[234]

What little punishment Marshall did receive actually worked to his benefit. Because the principal of his high school thought him too large for corporal punishment, he was often sent to the school's basement, given a copy of the Constitution, and told to memorize it.[235] Though "torturous" at the time, it gave him his first familiarity with the document he was to wield so mightily in a future he had not yet dreamed of.

If it seems that Marshall was rather unconcerned with his prospects in these days, perhaps it is because he realized that the futures of all Black people were necessarily limited in the climate of racial hostility and intense segregation that permeated all parts of the country. In 1906 Booker T. Washington acceded to the demands of a threatening White majority in Atlanta and agreed to restrict the aspirations of Blacks to vocational fields.[236] Bloody riots still erupted there. In 1908, the year Marshall was born, there were one hundred lynchings in America.[237] Most of the victims were Blacks accused of murder, though, for example, others were executed by mobs for "disappointment at a Colored entertainment," "offensive language," and "insulting a white woman."[238] Often these lynchings were a public spectacle, with onlookers numbering in the thousands. Even Sunday-school children attended in a picnic-like atmosphere to view with detachment the unsurprising end of a Black man who had somehow become the object of White rage.[239]

Although his parents made every effort throughout Marshall's childhood not to expose him to the truth about lynchings and the terrible plight of Black people, he could not help but hear of what went on, and be deeply affected. When he was ten years old, Marshall saw that even as African Americans returned from fighting for their country in World War I the lynchings continued, reaching in 1918 and 1919 a level of cruelty perhaps the worst in U.S. history.[240] Mary White Ovington, a founder of the NAACP, described what happened in Georgia after the lynching of what she swore was an innocent man: "His wife, Mary, after her husband's death, mourned and loudly proclaimed his innocence. For this she was slowly burned to death, watched by a crowd of men and women. She was pregnant, and as she burned, the infant fell to the ground and was trampled under a white man's heel."[241] Years later, when a fellow college student asked why Marshall had never gone to see a movie at a Whites-only theater in Baltimore, he responded: "Hell, you just didn't do it. Shit, you were told in some way every day of your life that you couldn't do it. Say we were cowed, brainwashed, but it never left your mind that you could get your ass killed just trying to go see a goddamned Tarzan movie."[242]

The North was not immune to the irrational fears and hatred that always seemed to accompany White people's reception of their darker-skinned brothers and sisters. In 1908, shortly after Thurgood was born, Norma and William Marshall joined an increasing number of Black emigrants in New York City, a place they hoped would be less susceptible to the increasingly violent racial strife so characteristic of the South.[243] Ironically, this migration incited the reactionary fears of the more "tolerant" North. Alarmed at the increasing number of Blacks who wished to make the city their home, in 1906 thousands of New Yorkers went to view *The Clansman.* This play, drawn from a novel that later became the basis of D. W. Griffith's film *The Birth of a Nation,* depicted Black men as enraged, lustful animals, whose emotions found an outlet only in violence and rape.[244] The author of the novel and the play, the Reverend Thomas Dixon Jr. warned, "The beginning of Negro equality is . . . the beginning of the end of this nation's life."[245] Signs on New York city streets bore messages like "This part of a hundred and thirty-fifth Street guaranteed against Negro invasion."[246] A mere five years after they had arrived, a disappointed Marshall family returned to Baltimore.[247]

This is not to say that all Whites everywhere treated Blacks so abominably. "There were some good white people around, even then," Marshall once recalled.[248] In fact the NAACP, through which Marshall would work for more than a quarter of a century fighting for the civil rights of all Americans, could not have been founded in 1909 had it not been for the efforts of a group of liberal Whites of conscience.[249] William English Walling was a native Southerner.[250] Mary White Ovington had done social work for Blacks in the South.[251] Dr. Henry Moskovitz worked in the office of the mayor of New York City.[252] What these three White people shared with African Americans was outrage and shame at how the promise of a free society for all was being subverted by racist laws passed under the auspices of state legislatures, was being flouted by violent mobs who seemingly could take a Black person's life and dignity with impunity, and was being ignored by a Supreme Court that refused to give substance to the words added to the Constitution in the post–Civil War amendments. Walling, Ovington, and Moskovitz enlisted the service of Oswald Garrison Villard, president of the New York Evening Post Company and grandson of the abolitionist William Lloyd Garrison, to advertise their cause.[253] He bravely laid the reputation and economic stability of his newspaper on the line to publicize the cry for action to address the issue of the unfair treatment of Blacks in the United States.[254] As he and his three colleagues saw it, this unexplained hatred of Black people threatened to turn the land of liberty and justice for all into a lawless wasteland of savage brutality. They called for a national conference to be held on May 30, 1909, and on that day the NAACP was born.[255]

These four White people and their Black colleagues managed to accomplish what, up until that time, the nation's twelve million African Americans had not been able to do—create an effective organization devoted to the pursuit of long-denied civil rights. This was not due to a lack of desire on their part; it was, rather, a consequence of the terrible oppression they faced. Though the post–Civil War amendments (the thirteenth, fourteenth, and fifteenth) were designed to ensure that Blacks would take their place in American society as full citizens, with rights identical to those of every other American, the truth was far from this ideal. Despite their significant numbers, Blacks were disenfranchised in every area necessary to ensure that this promise of equality became reality. Though the blight of slavery had been legally abolished nearly half a century before, the men, mostly White, whose duty it was to mete out justice, especially in the South, seemed bent on keeping Blacks in a position as close to slavery as possible. The economic power of African Americans was virtually nonexistent; they worked for slave wages in the cotton and peanut fields where their recent ancestors had toiled only for their lives. Their political power was likewise lacking, a cruel farce in a land where representation is the acknowledged assurance of a free republic.

Not only were Blacks woefully underrepresented in Congress, but in states throughout the Union they were systematically denied the right to vote. Whether through poll taxes, grandfather clauses (which said that if your grandfather couldn't vote neither could you), or absurd questions to determine competency such as "How many bubbles are there in a bar of soap,"[256] Blacks were relegated to a status of inferiority by a powerful White majority who took every opportunity to tell them what their place in this society was and to keep them there by hook or by crook.

Socially, too, Blacks were set apart, by design, from the "pure" White race. Segregation was everywhere—buses and trains, schools, eating and sleeping establishments, department stores. Once, when Thurgood Marshall was in downtown Baltimore, he found that he had to do something common to all human beings and go to the bathroom. But in his city there were no bathrooms that were open to Blacks.[257] Marshall boarded a trolley and headed for his home, where he might relieve himself legally. He had to go badly, and he made it only as far as his front door. It was a humiliating experience, inflicted upon him for no reason other than to appease the fears of many Whites that a race so seemingly different from their own could ever be as special, as good, as favored by God. It was an experience he would not soon forget.

The only exceptions made to the strict rules of segregation were for those Blacks in the domestic employ of Whites. And if any African American dared cross any one of these social, political, or economic lines, if he became "uppity," acting in ways that were privileged to Whites, at best a deaf ear would be turned on his entreaties for equality. At worst he would be killed, his murderers most likely convicted of disturbing the peace, if they were convicted, or even prosecuted, for anything at all. It was precisely these "lines" that the NAACP wanted to attack, to show that they were drawn by hatred and the force of a burning cross, not by some natural order in which Blacks were necessarily the social, intellectual, and biological inferiors of the White man. It was to show the arbitrary cruelty and inequality inherent in these lines that Thurgood Marshall devoted virtually every minute of his life before the bar.

Once he graduated from high school in Baltimore, Marshall applied to and was accepted at Lincoln University in Chester, Pennsylvania. The school was called "Black Princeton" because so many of the all-White faculty had studied at the Ivy League institution in New Jersey.[258] Even here it took a while for Marshall to begin to get serious about academics and his future life. He boasted that he rarely cracked a book and could be found the night before any particular exam playing pinochle or poker and drinking bourbon.[259] In fact, though he held many on- and off-campus jobs in order to pay his tuition, he boasted that his pinochle playing was good enough to keep him in spending money through most of his college career.[260] In addition Marshall was suspended briefly during his sophomore year for hazing freshmen.[261] According to the future justice, he was just getting the "horsin' around" out of his system.[262]

Though Marshall's penchant throughout his career for catching people off guard with his often irreverent humor suggests that the "horsin' around" was never really purged from his system, he finally began to get serious during his sophomore year, directing the energies of his formidable mind and oratorical skills toward the cause that was to become his passion: the freeing of a nation. Though Marshall recalled that early on in the year he stupidly stood against an uprising of students demanding that Black professors be added to the all-White faculty, he soon recanted.[263] Discussions with his sociology teacher, as well as with such classmates as Nnamdi Azikiwe (who later became president of Nigeria), Cab Calloway, and Langston Hughes,[264] made Marshall seriously consider the place of the Negro in American civilization. And concerning the matter of segregation, it made him ask the crucial question: Why?

During this critical year of transition Marshall gave up on his mother's dream for him of a stable and lucrative career as a dentist.[265] His pre-med curriculum held a hygiene course taught by Prof. H. F. Grimm.[266] Marshall disagreed with some of the things that Professor Grimm was saying. Notably, during one class on sexual intercourse, Grimm said that a man and a woman only have sex in order to conceive a child.[267] Marshall, knowing that the professor had a perfectly lovely wife and three children, raised his hand and asked if in twenty years of marriage he had only screwed his wife three times.[268] "He gave me hell," the future justice recalled, "and then he flunked me."[269]

It was also during this year that Marshall joined the school's debating team, where he began to hone the adversarial skills that his father had taught him years before.[270] William Marshall used to take Thurgood to the courthouse in Baltimore to watch trials in progress.[271] When they got home, the father would engage the son in energetic debate, making him state clearly his take on the issue and defend every aspect of it, letting him take nothing for granted. "He never told me to become a lawyer," Marshall said of his father, "but he turned me into one. He did it by teaching me to argue, by challenging my logic on every point, by making me prove every statement I made."[272] Marshall's fiery delivery and persuasive logical arguments quickly made him the star of his debating team, earning him the nickname "The Wrathful Marshall."[273] A series of impressive victories against other schools, both Black and White, among them Bates, Colby, and Bowdoin, prompted him to write to his father in 1929, "If I were taking debate for credit I would be the biggest honor student they ever had around here."[274]

One night Marshall and a group of friends went to see a movie in nearby Oxford.[275] After buying their tickets they took their seats in the comfortable orchestra section. Shortly thereafter an usher told them to move—Blacks were allowed only in the balcony, "nigger heaven," as it was called.[276] The young men pretended not to notice and stayed put. An anonymous voice called out, "Nigger, why don't you get out of here and sit where you belong?"[277] Marshall and the others said that they had paid for their tickets and intended to stay put, in the more comfortable seats. No action was taken, but Marshall recalled the incident in a letter to his parents, describing the voice from the darkness: "You can't really tell what a person like that looks like because it's just an ugly feeling that's looking at you, not a real face. . . ."[278] Marshall gave that one incident the credit for inspiring his eventual career in civil rights.[279]

Finally in this eventful year, he met Vivien Burey, an undergraduate at the University of Pennsylvania.[280] As a young man, the future justice pursued women with easily the same zeal that he showed for alcohol and cards.[281] He quipped that before "Buster," his nickname for Vivien, he was engaged at least nine times, at one point having six fraternity rings out at the same time.[282] But he saw something special in Buster, and the two soon fell in love. Norma Marshall, Thurgood's mother, liked this smart, levelheaded girl and her stabilizing influence. Indeed, Vivien would go out drinking with her beau, but at a certain point she would always tell Thurgood he'd had enough, and he would listen.[283] She told him often that he was a fine man, and that if he set his mind to it he could be someone who really made a difference in the world.[284] Again he listened. Though the two had planned on waiting until after graduation to marry, young love's sense of immediacy held sway, and they were married midway through Marshall's senior year.[285]

Despite his early antics at Lincoln University, Marshall managed to graduate with honors.[286] The impecunious couple then moved into his old room in his parents' house, which his mother had redone for them as a graduation present.[287] Vivien and Thurgood together decided that he should become a lawyer, and Marshall's parents knew that their son and daughter-in-law would have to save every penny. The logical choice for a law school was the University of Maryland; located in downtown Baltimore, it was only ten minutes away from the Marshall home by trolley,[288] and as a state school tuition would be lower than at an out-of-state institution. Unfortunately logic played little part in the admissions process. Upon receipt of his application the University of Maryland Law School promptly sent a reply stating that it simply did not admit Black students and that he would have to look elsewhere if he wanted a legal education.[289] For the first time Marshall was presented with a direct affront not only to his personal but to his intellectual freedoms and opportunities. This insult would shape his life, then and later.

As goes the law of unintended consequences, the University of Maryland actually did a great service to the cause of civil rights in this country. As a result of its actions, Marshall ended up enrolling at Howard University Law School in Washington, D.C. Here he met Charles Hamilton Houston, a man who was to have a profound effect upon the zealous young Marshall as a mentor and guide.[290] Houston, valedictorian of his undergraduate class at Amherst, had been in the top 5 percent of his law school class at Harvard.[291] Houston was recognized as a gifted student by one of his professors at Harvard, Felix Frankfurter, who took a special interest in the young African American, often inviting him to his home for meals.[292] The older man helped to instill in Houston the notion that the only way to make the country yield its constitutional promise of equality was to develop a force of competent Black lawyers to work toward that end.[293] Frankfurter also helped the young Houston win the Sheldon Traveling Fellowship in 1923, which enabled him to study abroad at the University of Madrid during the year after his graduation from Harvard.[294]

Ironically, it was in Spain that Houston met Roscoe Pound, dean of Harvard's law school.[295] Pound agreed with Frankfurter's recommendation that African Americans needed well-trained representation to fight for their rights.[296] At the time, a nation of twelve million Blacks could boast only eleven hundred lawyers, fewer than one hundred of whom had received their degrees from accredited institutions.[297] In Madrid, Pound and Houston discussed this and other issues in an environment that was foreign in a most pleasant way. They could eat together in cafés without comment or even notice—and certainly without the aura of hate that they had become used to—even though one was White and the other Black.[298] Houston found he could get a room in any hotel whose bill he could afford to pay. And he could board a bus or a train, go to see a movie or a show at the theater, and sit wherever he wanted, a luxury not afforded him in his native Washington, D.C.[299] Though he returned home to a lucrative career in his father's law firm, he discovered a hidden passion—he wanted to teach.[300] When he applied for a part-time position on Howard's law faculty in 1923, his application was accompanied by letters of recommendation from Felix Frankfurter and Roscoe Pound; he began teaching there in 1924.[301]

Howard University was chartered in 1867 as a school for freed slaves, but it admitted both Black and White students.[302] The law school opened in 1869.[303] While the student body was interracial and coeducational, Howard's law school was not widely recognized as a legal institution because it lacked accreditation from either the American Bar Association or the Association of American Law Schools.[304] Originally classes were held on an evening, part-time basis, and its facilities in such areas as classrooms, stages for moot court settings, and the resources available in its law library were less than adequate.[305] But in 1926 Dr. Mordecai Johnson was appointed Howard University's first Black president, and reform of the law school was among his top priorities.[306] Johnson was a Baptist minister who held degrees from the Atlanta Baptist College (now Morehouse College), the University of Chicago, Harvard University, and Rochester Theological Seminary.[307] He immediately set about overhauling the faculty and physical plant of the entire university, realizing its importance as one of the only institutions of graduate learning where African Americans of modest means and backgrounds could get a quality education, especially in the South.[308]

One of Johnson's closest friends was Louis Dembitz Brandeis, associate justice of the Supreme Court (and its first Jewish member).[309] The two frequently dined together at each other's homes, and the conversation often turned to the Constitution's unfulfilled promises to Black America. Brandeis took an interest in Howard's law school, and he gave Johnson advice similar to that offered to Charles Houston by Felix Frankfurter. Brandeis told his friend bluntly that he could usually tell when he was reading a brief by a Negro attorney.[310] What was needed was a solid law school to train men to go out and get the constitutional rights so long withheld from them. "Once you do this," said Brandeis, "the Supreme Court will have to hand your people their civil and constitutional rights."[311] He stressed the importance of assembling a faculty made up of qualified legal minds and of having a full-time day curriculum to prepare students for the challenges they were sure to face.[312]

In addition to recruiting distinguished educators for other departments within the university, Johnson secured first-rate academics for the law school. Among these were Leon Ransom, who graduated first in his class at Ohio State University Law School; James Madison Nabrit Jr., who was to become involved extensively with litigation for the NAACP; and William Henry Hastie, who had been editor of the law review at Harvard and who would be appointed the nation's first Black federal court judge in 1937.[313] By December 1931 Johnson and Houston had transformed Howard into a fully accredited legal institution, one staffed with a competent faculty; Houston was the law school's vice-dean.[314] Roscoe Pound, Felix Frankfurter, and even Clarence Darrow served as guest lecturers at the school on many occasions; this was a feat unmatched even by the better-funded White law schools in the area.[315]

Charles Hamilton Houston was an excellent legal strategist, with a keen mind and strong analytical skills. But Marshall remembered him just as much for the work ethic he instilled in his students. He was a perfectionist, the justice said, who would sometimes spend an entire day searching his mind for the one word that would turn a good legal brief into a great one.[316] Houston was a man driven to achieve his dream that Black lawyers be taught to wield the law effectively, so that they might secure for themselves and all Americans the promised equal protection of the laws. Houston told his students in no uncertain terms that they were to be "social engineers,"[317] that they were being given an education so that once they graduated they could give something back.[318] He was a man on a mission to gradually demolish the racist practices that operated throughout so much of the country under the aegis of government at various levels, and he would accept no lesser degree of determination or dedication from his students.

Marshall said that Houston taught him that law books were to dig in and that he should dig as deep as he could.[319] If one were assigned five cases to read, one should read eight; if assigned eight, then one should read ten.[320] But always, always go that extra step, that little bit that separates excellence from mere competency. For as Houston told Marshall, in the social climate in which these Black lawyers were to practice their trade they needed to be not only as good as their White counterparts but better.[321] Houston had a standing order to all the law school professors that they could take 5 percent off a student's grade for any reason whatsoever.[322] As a result, Marshall said, the students aimed to please. Houston's demands for excellence from his students earned him nicknames like Iron Shoes and Cement Drawers, but Marshall quickly realized what Houston was trying to do, and he began to develop a deep respect for this man whose door was always open to any student who wanted to learn.[323]

Marshall finished first in his class at the end of his first year, which enabled him to take a much-coveted job in the law school's library.[324] Thus, he no longer had to hold down the part-time jobs in Baltimore that took up so much of his time in order to help pay his tuition. It also exposed him to the late-night meetings of Houston, Nabrit, and other NAACP lawyers who gathered in Howard's library to discuss strategy for their legal attacks on segregation.[325] Walter White, NAACP executive secretary, would often attend these planning sessions. He recalls: "There was a lanky, brash young senior law student who was always present. I used to wonder at his presence and sometimes was amazed at his assertiveness in positions [taken] by Charlie [Houston] and the other lawyer. But

I soon learned of his great value to the case in doing everything he was asked, from research on obscure legal opinions to foraging for coffee and sandwiches."[326] Under the tutelage of Houston and others, Marshall was shown the tremendous talents he had and was introduced to productive and laudable goals for their expression. The irresponsible youth of only a few years before had discovered he could indeed make a difference and, more importantly, that he wanted to.

Though his law school class had originally numbered more than thirty, the rigorous curriculum and demanding atmosphere had, by graduation time, whittled that number down to six.[327] Of these, Marshall was number one.[328] In a decision he was later to recall simply as "stupid," the future justice turned down a scholarship offer from Harvard Law's dean, Roscoe Pound, that would have paid his and Buster's living expenses for a year while he earned a doctor of jurisprudence degree.[329] But having had quite enough of theory, and with Charles Houston's inspiration still fresh in his heart, Marshall wanted to enter the fray and work toward making his dreams a reality. So in 1933, after passing the bar, he opened a modest law office in downtown Baltimore—and lost between three and four thousand dollars the first year.[330] In a town dominated by White judges, many well-to-do Blacks figured they would fare better with a White lawyer to argue their case.[331] And in any event the depression years were a difficult time to find paying clients of any kind. Marshall still would not refuse his services to anyone who needed his help, however. He would take cases simply for the experience, arguing everything from traffic offenses and eviction proceedings to minor criminal matters.[332] As word spread of this passionate lawyer who would not refuse even indigent clients, Marshall's practice boomed as his finances dwindled.[333]

Luckily, neither his abilities nor his dedication went unnoticed. Carl Murphy, editor and publisher of the *Afro,* a successful weekly newspaper giving voice to the plight of the nation's African American citizens, had known the Marshall family since Thurgood was a boy.[334] An activist in his own right, he had written and published scores of stinging editorials on the evils of discrimination and segregation, at one point bringing suit against the Baltimore & Ohio Railroad for segregating him on a ferry crossing.[335] He had recently teamed up with Lillie Jackson, the young firebrand who had just become president of the Baltimore chapter of the NAACP.[336] Jackson had enlisted the financial and editorial support of

Murphy to help in her campaign to integrate the University of Maryland, desegregate Baltimore's public facilities, and equalize pay for White and Black teachers.[337] The two recognized the benefit they would derive from having the energetic Marshall involved in the legal aspects of their struggle, but they were also aware of his sketchy financial situation. Murphy employed the young attorney to handle the legal affairs of his newspaper and used his influence to help Marshall obtain a few other paying clients. He hoped that this alleviation of his financial woes would enable the lawyer to spend time working on cases of more significant social relevance for the local NAACP.[338]

No one had to ask Marshall to help alleviate legal racism, a task for which he had been trained rigorously by Houston and his other professors throughout law school. Virtually leaping at the chance to do some work for the NAACP, the first target he set his sights on (which afforded him no small measure of satisfaction) was the University of Maryland. This same institution of scholarship in law that had denied him admission four years before had just recently refused to consider another Black man who wanted apply, Donald Gaines Murray.[339] Having graduated with honors from Amherst College,[340] Murray had satisfied all of the criteria necessary for admission save one—the color of his skin. Marshall's rancor at seeing this insult heaped on yet another qualified young Black man was tempered only by knowing what he was about to do to the university and its Jim Crow policies.

Although the NAACP was always dedicated to establishing racial equality in America, during its first two decades it was hampered by a lack of funding. While it was able to become involved in select cases of national concern, or cases that received a lot of publicity, it was unable to finance the sort of large-scale strategic attack on Jim Crow that it knew was necessary to combat the institution effectively.[341] But in the late 1920s the NAACP became the beneficiary of the American Fund for Public Service, or Garland Fund.[342] A left-wing organization founded by Charles Garland, its money came from an inheritance that Garland refused to accept for himself, claiming that his father's banking and investment fortune was founded upon exploitation of the working class.[343] In 1929 the fund's grant of $100,000 allowed the NAACP to formulate a long-term strategy for overthrowing Jim Crow.[344]

The problem to overcome was the historic Supreme Court decision in *Plessy v. Ferguson* (1896), where the Court established the constitutionality of the "separate but equal" doctrine.[345] A Louisiana statute passed in 1890 mandated that all railway companies were to provide either separate cars, or separate compartments within cars, for the segregation of the White and Negro races.[346] Homer Adolph Plessy, for all intents and purposes, looked like a White man, but he was one-eighth Black. Under Louisiana law this was enough to require that he be separated from the White passengers on any train. In 1892, Plessy refused to give up his seat in the White car and was arrested. The case eventually reached the Supreme Court, and in a 7–1 opinion (one justice did not hear the case) the Court declared the separation of races constitutional as long as the facilities provided were of equal caliber. The Court reasoned that segregation did not imply inferiority of the Negro race and that any such inference was strictly of the Negro race's own making.[347] The justices "reasoned" this even though the law clearly indicated that the presence of as little as one-eighth Negro ancestry in a person's family tree was enough to taint his otherwise pure White blood and make him an unfit companion for decent White people. Notably, a Black person with one-eighth White ancestry was still considered Black.

In a vigorous lone dissent, Justice John Marshall Harlan decried the fallacy of the "separate but equal" doctrine, asserting that, arguments to the contrary notwithstanding, the obvious purpose of the Louisiana statute was "not so much to exclude whites from railroad cars occupied by blacks, as to exclude colored people from coaches occupied by or assigned to white persons. . . ."[348] He went on to say, however, that "in view of the constitution, in the eye of the law, there is in this country no dominant, ruling class of citizens. There is no caste here. Our constitution is color blind."[349] This case, prophesied Harlan, would in time prove to be as pernicious as the infamous *Dred Scott* case—where the high court decreed as the law of the land that Blacks were "considered as a subordinate and inferior class of beings, who had been subjugated by the dominant race and, whether emancipated or not, yet remained subject to their authority, and had no rights or privileges but such as those who held the power and the government might choose to grant them."[350] "The thin disguise of 'equal' accommodations," Harlan continued, "for passengers in railroad coaches will not mislead any one, nor atone for the wrong this day done."[351] Justice Harlan's views would eventually prevail, but not until over half a century had passed and hundreds of thousands of dollars, as well as many lives, had been expended in the pursuit of an unfulfilled promise of equality before the law.

As every journey begins with a single step, so every battle to bring about justice in the courtrooms of America begins with a single lawsuit. For Thurgood Marshall, this meant getting Donald Murray admitted to the University of Maryland School of Law. The legal strategy of the NAACP was to not immediately attack the constitutionality of the *Plessy* "separate but equal" doctrine.[352] It had been the law of the land for so long, was so vehemently and violently protected by its proponents in the South, and was accepted (albeit grudgingly) by so many Blacks and Whites that the NAACP knew that an immediate, direct attack was almost sure to fail. Instead, the group decided to attack "the soft underbelly" of Jim Crow.[353] The plan was to show the inequality of educational opportunity afforded Black and White students, then to get a court order forcing the state to equalize the two systems. The hope was that the process of equalization would prove prohibitively expensive, thus leaving no alternative but the admission of Black students into all-White institutions.[354] Graduate schools made attractive candidates for this first step. As Houston and others (including Marshall) at the NAACP believed, a quality professional education was essential if African Americans were ever to have the economic prosperity that must accompany their rise in social and political influence. And while most southern states did maintain Black undergraduate institutions of a sort, they had almost no Black graduate schools.[355]

The University of Maryland told Donald Murray in no uncertain terms that it would not admit African Americans under any circumstances, but if he wanted to apply for a partial state scholarship to a northern school that did admit Blacks, the university would be happy to help with the paperwork.[356] Murray had no desire to leave his native Maryland, where he wanted eventually to practice—and where he worked and paid taxes that supported the state school. So at Marshall's direction he sent in an application, along with two dollars to cover the cost of the school's reply.[357] President Raymond Pearson sent back the two dollars with a letter pointing out that Howard University was "open to [him]" and also kindly informing him that the tuition at Howard was lower than that at the University of Maryland.[358] Marshall immediately began to prepare a brief asking that the Baltimore City Court issue a writ of mandamus ordering the University of Maryland to admit Mr. Murray to classes when school opened in September.[359]

The case went to trial June 18, 1935, before Judge Eugene O'Dunne.[360] Charles Houston, who only months before had been appointed head counsel for the national office of the NAACP, recognized the suit's importance and came in by airplane to oversee.[361] He let Marshall introduce Murray to the court, establishing his qualifications for admission to the school; then, as senior attorney, he took over much of the argument.[362] Marshall recalls that seeing Houston in action in the courtroom at least matched his schooling at Howard. It set a standard that Marshall was to measure himself against during his entire career.[363]

Houston called President Pearson to the stand and got him to admit that the University of Maryland Law School was the only one in the state accredited by the American Bar Association and that it did not admit Blacks as a matter of long-standing policy.[364] Houston then called to the stand the dean of the law school, Roger Howell.[365] From Houston's questioning it became clear that the course of study was closely structured around Maryland's law and state codes. Marshall had Howell admit that twelve of the eighteen professors at the school were Maryland judges or practicing attorneys, and that any student who wished to practice in the state was being deprived of a valuable opportunity by being denied admission to the school.[366] When asked why a separate law school for African Americans had never been constructed, Howell replied that there had never been sufficient demand to warrant it.[367]

In closing arguments, Marshall told Judge O'Dunne that while the "separate" part of the "separate but equal" doctrine had been upheld by the Supreme Court, the "equal" part had never been challenged nor even come under review.[368] So while there was no precedent directly on point, Marshall assured the judge that he would be on solid constitutional ground if he ordered the university to admit Donald Murray, there being no adequate equal alternative to satisfy his constitutional right to an educational opportunity equal to that of any other Maryland citizen. The state's attorneys moved to adjourn to give the judge time to consider his ruling. Judge O'Dunne told Marshall to object, and he then ruled immediately that Murray must be admitted to the law school in September.[369]

The state immediately filed an appeal, requesting a special session of the appellate court so that review might take place before Murray was admitted.[370] The request was denied and Murray was admitted, but the state still pressed its appeal. It was heard in January 1936, and the state tried to persuade the court that by providing scholarship funds to send Black students to out-of-state schools it was satisfying its obligations under "separate but equal."[371] Marshall, again under the supervision and advice of Houston, said the state was confusing the issue of segregation and exclusion: "Donald Murray was not sent to a separate school of the University of Maryland. . . . Donald Murray was excluded from the University of Maryland entirely."[372] "What's at stake here is more than the rights of my client," Marshall proclaimed, "it's the moral commitment stated in our country's creed."[373]

The court of appeals was persuaded. Equal treatment, it reasoned, meant equality "in respect to any one facility or opportunity furnished to citizens, rather than of a balance in state bounty to be struck from the expenditures and provisions, for each race generally."[374] The state, said the court, could not export its responsibility to provide equal educational opportunities for its citizens. Judge O'Dunne's ruling was upheld.

With his first significant victory under his belt, Marshall felt the jubilation of actually achieving some of the social engineering of which he had dreamed. He knew it was only a first step, but he had made a difference, and it felt good. Marshall just could not see himself cashing in on torts cases, breach of contract, or divorce settlements when there was so much work to be done in areas he saw as infinitely more important. But his finances were abysmal. The work he had done for the Baltimore branch of the NAACP was strictly as a volunteer, and what meager remuneration they could sometimes manage for his expenses was barely enough to "keep the wolf away from my door."[375]

Nonetheless, he persevered, bringing an early action to desegregate the public high schools in Baltimore and the surrounding county, which failed,[376] and actions to equalize the pay of White and Black schoolteachers, which eventually met with success.[377] Through September 1936, Marshall had received only $200 in payment from the NAACP for his work during that year; this prompted him to propose that if he should receive a monthly retainer of $150 he might be better able to pursue his projects.[378] Charles Houston, who saw Marshall getting better exponentially with every bit of experience he gleaned, knew that his student was quickly on the way to surpassing even his own enviable abilities.[379] He convinced Walter White, executive director of the NAACP, to apply to the Garland Fund for enough money to hire Marshall for six months.[380] Houston told Marshall by letter that regular monthly payments were approved only for members of the staff, and he passed along White's offer of a six-month commitment at the national office in New York.[381] Marshall wrote back gratefully, "I have an opportunity now to do what I have always dreamed of doing. That is, to actually concentrate on the type of work the Association is doing."[382] In October 1936 Thurgood and Buster packed up their belongings from the room they still occupied in the home of William and Norma Marshall and moved to New York. The six-month commitment began a twenty-five-year career with the NAACP, during which time Marshall's skill as a litigator and his dedication to a noble cause would earn him the accolade of "Mr. Civil Rights."[383]

While his years in the NAACP would indeed be rewarding personally and socially, they were far from easy. Even as Marshall officially joined the association, it was embroiled in an ugly internal battle. W. E. B. Du Bois, who had been with the NAACP since its inception, and who is often remembered as a Black revolutionary, was preaching through the *Crisis,* the association's official magazine, that as a tactic in order to protect Black jobs during the Depression African Americans should accept some degree of segregation[384]—that in some ways Jim Crow was beneficial to both races. This infuriated the light-skinned Walter White, who, though he could easily have "passed," for a white man, was adamant in his view that equality for all people could be achieved only through desegregation.[385] White saw the accommodationist views Du Bois was spouting as nothing more than a cowardly placation of the White power structure. A separatist philosophy was, he felt, detrimental to the well-being of the nation and contrary to emerging standards of decency in the country; hence, it was utterly unacceptable. As director of the NAACP this was the only stance for the organization that he would ever accept. Their war ended with the resignation of Du Bois in 1934, an act many feared would severely damage the NAACP.[386] Instead, it created a unity of vision among the group's leaders regarding the evils of segregation.

Meanwhile, Houston and Marshall forged ahead with their attack on Jim Crow. In 1935 Lloyd Gaines was denied admission to the University of Missouri Law School.[387] Though he had graduated from Missouri's Lincoln University at the top of his class,[388] the law school said that because he was Black he should apply for a scholarship to attend a school that accepted Negroes in an adjacent state or else apply to Lincoln University.[389] Although Lincoln had no law school, the state said that if Gaines applied it would create one.[390] Though the Missouri Circuit Court and the Missouri Supreme Court held that this made adequate provision for his constitutional right to "separate but equal" schooling, the Supreme Court in 1938 disagreed.[391] Chief Justice Charles Evans Hughes said that Blacks in the state must have an opportunity equal to that of Whites. If Missouri's White citizens were given the opportunity of attending law school there, then the same opportunity must be afforded its Black citizens.[392] A promise to open a school in the future was not good enough. The decision that Marshall and Houston had won for Maryland residents in *Murray* now, because of *Gaines,* applied to every state in the Union.

The State of Missouri scrambled to open a law school at Lincoln by September 1939 so it would not have to admit Gaines to the all-White University. Lower courts held that this satisfied the mandate of the Supreme Court,[393] but the NAACP would have no opportunity to challenge the new school's equality of stature in court. Gaines, however, never enrolled. Much to Marshall's and the NAACP's dismay and disappointment (but perhaps understandably, given the pressures facing him), he simply disappeared, never to be heard from again.[394] In any event, this first Supreme Court victory in the field of "separate but equal" was a major step toward achieving the NAACP's ultimate goal.

Shortly after the conclusion of the Gaines case Charles Houston retired as lead counsel for the NAACP.[395] The strenuous schedule, involving rushing to all corners of the country to engage in litigation, was exacerbating the failure of his health. He named Thurgood Marshall, whose skills he praised as already exceeding his own, to succeed him. Marshall later recalled of the mentor whom he so revered: "This man had ignored tuberculosis to give his life to the cause of freedom for Afro-Americans. I looked at his travel schedule from one end of America to the other and saw that it was a killer."[396] When his wife, Buster, asked him how he expected to survive the grueling schedule, the thirty-year-old Marshall replied, "Shit, I'm sure I can make it till I'm forty."[397] She was not amused.

Though Buster's fears for her husband's health were certainly justified, his concern for the well-being of the underprivileged in America overrode them. In a country where the disenfranchised provided a fountain of scapegoats for the crimes of a more powerful elite, abuses of the rights of the criminally accused could not escape the swath of Marshall's legal crusade. For example, in Choctaw County, Oklahoma, early in 1940, W. D. Lyons was arrested for a gruesome triple murder.[398] Mr. and Mrs. Elmer Rogers and their four-year-old son had been killed in their home, doused with kerosene, and set on fire.[399] Marshall was convinced that Lyons had not committed the crime. Looking into the facts, he discovered that an inmate at a local prison camp had admitted to the murders shortly after they occurred.[400] The inmate, a trusty who was allowed out of the camp unattended, was at the time serving a thirty-year sentence for murdering his wife.[401] As Marshall saw it, Lyons, who had served two prison sentences—one for chicken stealing and one for burglary—presented an easy scapegoat for a local sheriff's department that did not want it known that the inmates it was letting out as trusties were committing murders.[402]

Lyons was arrested by civilians with no warrant. Though he had not been officially charged, nor brought before a magistrate, he was held for eleven days and beaten repeatedly.[403] On the evening of the eleventh day, during an interrogation that lasted nearly eight hours, he was beaten further, then taken to the Rogers' home, where a pan of charred remains was placed in his lap.[404] Lyons confessed. He was taken back to jail, then later the next day to the state penitentiary, where he signed a second, written confession.[405] It took more than a year for the state to bring his case to trial—further evidence, in Marshall's view, that the prosecutors knew Lyons was not guilty.[406] In those days a Black man accused of murder, especially the murder of a White family, did not ordinarily have to wait long to be brought before a jury.

Marshall realized that he had no chance of winning in the state court. Spectators filled the courtroom to capacity, flocking to see the "nigger lawyer," a first in Hugo, Oklahoma.[407] When Marshall used his first two peremptory challenges to exclude obviously racist jurors, the judge called him aside and informed him that after he had run through the panel of potential jurors with which he was presented the sheriff and the prosecutor would go into the street and pick whomever they saw fit.[408] During the trial Marshall cornered the police officers involved, caught them in numerous lies and inconsistencies, and elicited admissions that Lyons had indeed been beaten repeatedly—that a "special investigator" from the governor's office had used a "nigger beater" to persuade him to confess.[409] Incredibly, while the judge ruled that Lyons's first confession, after the pan-of-bones incident, was inadmissible, he ruled that the second confession was voluntary and could be admitted.[410]

The prosecution asked for the death penalty. After five hours of deliberation the all-White jury returned a verdict of guilty, but it recommended mercy and a life sentence.[411] The terrible inconsistency with normal jury findings in cases of this kind again pointed to Lyons's innocence: It is a strange society that rewards an innocent Black man with a sentence of life in prison, instead of an acquittal. An appeal was quickly filed with the Oklahoma Criminal Court of Appeals. Roscoe Dunjee, editor of the local African American paper, found hope in the fact that Bert Barefoot, a man of American Indian descent whom he regarded as a personal friend and a proponent of racial justice, would be presiding judge at the appeal.[412] In a two to one opinion, written by Barefoot, the conviction was upheld, over a bitter dissent decrying the utter unfairness of the trial Lyons had received.[413] An apologetic Barefoot supposedly remarked to Dunjee, "Don't worry. You'll win on appeal."[414]

Of the thirty-two cases that Thurgood Marshall argued before the Supreme Court during his tenure with the NAACP, he lost only four[415]— and this was one of them. Despite earlier decisions railing against the evils of coerced confessions—stating piously that "the rack and torture chamber may not be substituted for the witness stand"[416] and that the Constitution protects the right to a fair trial for every person of whatever race or creed—the Supreme Court upheld the conviction in a six to three decision. On June 5, 1944, Justice Stanley Reed wrote for the majority that the effects of the coercion used to secure the first confession had sufficiently dissipated by the time the second confession was made.[417] The effects of eleven days of physical and psychological torture had somehow ceased to exert any pressure on the accused sometime during the twelve hours when he remained in police custody, without charges having been filed against him and without the assistance of counsel. Marshall was devastated. For him this was the epitome of injustice for the underprivileged in America. It signaled to him what he already knew: that rich criminals with political connections could railroad into jail poor Blacks, or Whites, who had no powerful friends to come to their aid; that a man without money or influential friends is simply more grist for the mill; and that neither judges beholden to political allies or agendas, nor even the Supreme Court, will save him. Marshall was seeing firsthand evidence of a frightening attitude by those who made and administered the laws—that there are people in the United States who just don't matter. Lyons was pardoned by the governor of Oklahoma in 1965 after serving twenty-five years behind bars.[418]

Time and again Marshall saw the criminal laws applied with an unequal hand to persons of color. Race riots, the worst in the country in twenty-five years,[419] broke out in Detroit in June 1943. The city had long suffered from racial friction. Just a year before, Whites and Blacks had clashed when Blacks tried to move into a housing settlement after a cross had been burned there to deter them; just before that, twenty thousand White auto workers staged a walkout when three Black workers were promoted at the Packard auto plant.[420] During the 1943 riots, thirty-four persons were killed[421] and hundreds were injured. As Marshall wrote, the police "used 'persuasion' rather than firm action with white rioters while against Negroes they used the ultimate in force: night sticks, revolvers, riot guns, sub-machine guns, and deer guns. As a result 25 of the 34 persons killed were Negroes. Of the 25 Negroes killed, 17 were killed by police."[422] Not a single White was killed by law-enforcement officers. In response the police said that the Negroes they killed were in the process of committing felonies. Marshall pointed out that "[i]t is equally true that white persons were turning over and burning automobiles on Woodward Avenue. This is arson. Others were beating Negroes with iron pipes, clubs, and rocks. This is felonious assault. Several Negroes were stabbed. This is assault with intent to murder."[423] Whether the police hated Blacks, or simply anyone they could get away with hating, the end result was the same—the criminal justice system seemed free to abuse the rights of those with no adequate social or political recourse.

Even Marshall himself, this national icon of Black America who was known throughout the country as a warrior for civil rights, was not immune to the violence of racism. Perhaps one of the most astounding and harrowing experiences of his career and his life occurred in 1946 in Columbia, Tennessee. A Black woman, Gladys Stephenson, complained to a

White repairman, twenty-eight-year-old William Flemming, about a shoddy job he had done fixing her radio.[424] Flemming slapped her across the face. Stephenson's son, James, a nineteen-year-old navy veteran, quickly came to his mother's defense and knocked Flemming through a plate glass window. The Stephensons were arrested and jailed for assault, while Flemming, who sustained minor injuries, was not charged.[425] A local Black leader, fearing for the Stephensons' safety, went to the sheriff and demanded they be released on bail, which they were. Two hours later a mob of seventy-five White men, beating on the jailhouse door, demanded that the Stephensons be turned over to them. When the mob learned that the prisoners had been released on bail, all hell broke loose. Police and White citizens razed the Black community, claiming they were searching for weapons.[426] Milton Murray, an African American army veteran, had come home from duty in North Africa and Italy during World War II with a Thompson submachine gun,[427] as had another returning Black soldier. When an ambulance raced through the Black community with White men in the back firing gunshots wantonly at residents in the streets, war was declared in the small Tennessee town.[428] Murray and others set up a battle post on top of a building in the area, engaging in a firefight with the police and Klansmen who had set up a similar position on a higher building a block away. The skirmish lasted until the National Guard was called in. Murray managed to hide his weapon and only spent a night in jail on a loitering charge.[429]

When all was said and done more than a hundred Blacks as well as four Whites had been arrested, though newspaper photographs clearly showed many White civilians prowling the streets armed with sawed-off shotguns.[430] Two African Americans were killed during an interrogation when, according to police, one of them reached into a pile of guns and grabbed one that matched bullets he had allegedly smuggled in.[431] He loaded it and fired before the police realized what was happening, so they had no choice but to shoot back. Twenty-five of the arrested Blacks were eventually charged with assault with intent to commit murder. Marshall and the NAACP assisted in their defense and won acquittal for twenty-four; the convicted man received a sentence of five years, which was eventually commuted to one year.[432]

The Columbia police were very unhappy with the "tall yaller nigger"[433] who had helped secure the freedom of so many Blacks. After the trial Marshall and Z. Alexander Looby, a Nashville lawyer who had assisted in the defense, started their hundred-mile drive back to Nashville, a commute they had made every day of the trial because it was not safe for them to stay in Columbia.[434] Just outside of town Marshall's car was pulled over by a "mob . . . composed equally of state troopers and city police,"[435] and he was taken into custody for drunk driving, even though Looby was driving. The police car headed off on a side road toward the river, but because Looby remained in pursuit they headed back to town.[436] Marshall recalls that Columbia was empty because "everybody was down at the Duck River waiting for the party."[437] The local magistrate, a teetotaler, had Marshall blow in his face; unable to detect any trace of alcohol, he said that Marshall certainly was not drunk.[438] Marshall was put in a different car, with Looby and Milton Murray, and they tried to leave town again. One of the Black men displaced from that car was grabbed and beaten by policemen so severely he ended up in the hospital for a month.[439]

Outside of town, the car was pulled over yet again. This time the police told Marshall he was to accompany them down to the river. Murray and another man spotted the "party" down by the river; ostensibly, it would be the mob's task to "overpower" the police and snatch Marshall. Grabbing their impressive arsenal, the men jumped out and declared, "The party stops here!" Upon hearing "The niggers have guns!" the group by the river fled in panic.[440] Not wishing to die in a gun battle, the police told Marshall he was free to go. The next day Murray and a group of armed Blacks went to the site and cut down the rope, noose attached, still hanging from the lynching tree.[441]

Upon hearing of the incident, the NAACP wired President Truman and the attorney general demanding an investigation, but no charges were ever filed.[442] Marshall spoke often of the courage required in those days, but the bravery he praised was never his own. "I don't deserve the credit," he would say. "The people who dared to stand up, to file lawsuits, were beaten and sometimes murdered after I spoke my piece and took the fastest goddamn train I could find out of the area"—they deserve the credit.[443] Milton Murray, who had to leave Columbia after he helped avert Marshall's lynching, recalled: "Until Marshall came, the law in Columbia was whatever a white lawyer or white policeman or white judge said it was. These whites were humiliated when Marshall stood in the courthouse and told them what the Constitution said and what the statutes of Tennessee really said. . . . He just didn't give a damn how many whites he embarrassed. . . . But I was overwhelmed by the willingness of this man to come into a race-crazy community and risk his life to defend twenty-five black men he had never met."[444]

Institutionalized racism was not limited to the court proceedings of the southern states. In 1951 Marshall traveled to Korea to investigate, firsthand, disturbing stories of disproportionate Black court-martials in the army.[445] Though in 1948 President Truman had issued Executive Order 9981, mandating equality of opportunity and treatment for persons of every race, color, religion, and national origin in the armed forces, the army had been slow to comply.[446] It still maintained segregated fighting units, claiming that the mixing of the races impaired fighting morale.[447] Although African Americans were routinely given only menial duties around camp, they were sent into the most dangerous battle positions during fighting. And Black soldiers who were praised and decorated on one day for their heroism were on the next court-martialed for violating the Seventy-Fifth Article of War, misbehavior in the presence of the enemy, or cowardice.[448]

Marshall would never claim that there were no African American cowards. But although there were four times as many Whites as Blacks in the army, nearly 70 percent of all Article 75 courts-martial were directed at Blacks,[449] and the punishments they received were highly disproportionate to those given to White soldiers. In Korea, Marshall heard tales of decorated Black heroes sentenced to death for cowardice, of Black soldiers pulled from foxholes and given fifteen minutes to meet with counsel before they were sentenced to life at hard labor in a trial that lasted less than an hour.[450] One soldier, for example, though he proved he was in an army hospital during the time he was charged with leaving his post, was given ten years at hard labor. This while White soldiers were acquitted of the same charges without putting up any defense at all.[451] The sentences of the White soldiers who were found guilty typically were shorter than those of their Black counterparts by as much as a factor of ten. The dismayed and disgusted Marshall asked, "Why are so many Negroes charged with cowardice and so few white soldiers? No one has given me any answer on this yet. I have maintained that Negroes are no more or less cowards than anyone else."[452] He simply could not understand how the country's power structure could so callously and cruelly mistreat the finest young men Black America had to offer while allowing them to fight a war to protect the precious liberties they had never been allowed to know. As a result of Marshall's efforts, virtually all of the sentences in question were either reduced or withdrawn.[453]

On the civilian front, Marshall worked tirelessly to make political and educational opportunities for African Americans. With the help of his staff, in 1944 he argued and won before the Supreme Court the Texas case of *Smith v. Allwright*.[454] Nine years earlier, in *Grovey v. Townsend,* the Court had ruled that Texas could legally exclude Blacks from voting in the Democratic primary. Though earlier decisions had made clear that the state could not deny citizens the right to vote, the Texas Democratic party dissolved its association with official government entities and declared itself a private organization. As such, it then developed the Democratic primary, where the members would decide who would be the party's candidate in the upcoming election. Because this was a private body performing a private function, the Court ruled, the Democratic party could make its own rules as to who could vote.[455] Since the Democratic party dominated the South, this legal maneuver effectively denied African Americans in those states elected representation of any kind. *Smith v. Allwright,* reversing *Grovey,* declared that such exclusion was unconstitutional. Notably, the eight to one majority opinion in *Smith* was written by Justice Stanley Reed, who had voted the opposite way, with the majority, in *Grovey.*[456] During these nine years the words of the Constitution had not changed, but, at least in Reed's mind, their meaning had.

The uproar over the Court's decision was enormous. Senator John Overton of Louisiana proclaimed, "The South, at all cost, will maintain the rule of white supremacy."[457] Senator Ed Smith of South Carolina cried, "All those who love South Carolina and the white man's rule will rally in this hour of her great Gethsemane to save her from a disastrous fate."[458] And Senator Claude Pepper of Florida barked, "The South will allow nothing to impair white supremacy."[459] So much for separate but *equal.*

In 1948 Marshall argued and won *Shelley v. Kraemer,* where he convinced the Supreme Court to find that restrictive housing covenants were unconstitutional.[460] Until then, homeowners could impose upon their neighborhoods, by majority agreement, the stipulation that no home or apartment was to be rented or sold to individuals of certain minority groups.

Also in the late 1940s, Marshall was expanding on his strategy in the continuing NAACP attack on the *Plessy v. Ferguson* "separate but equal" doctrine. Ada Lois Sipuel applied for admission to the University of Oklahoma's law school. Though qualified, she was rejected on the grounds that a substantially equal law school was to be established for Negroes "at a later date."[461] Rather than rely strictly on the *Gaines* decision of a decade before, Marshall attempted a more frontal attack on *Plessy*. The use of sociological data to emphasize the impact the laws had on actual people, rather than theorizing around abstract legal principles, had grown in acceptance since Louis Brandeis originated the "Brandeis brief." When he argued *Muller v. Oregon* before the Supreme Court in 1908, he used sociological data in support of the constitutionality of federal regulations concerning working conditions for women.[462] Since then, sociological jurisprudence—whose other proponents included Oliver Wendell Holmes, Harlan Stone, Benjamin Cardozo, and Felix Frankfurter has become an accepted facet of constitutional theory.[463]

In *Sipuel v. University of Oklahoma* (1948) Marshall argued for the first time that separation in and of itself denoted inequality. His brief for petitioner read, in part: "Classifications and distinctions based on race or color have no moral or legal validity in our society. . . . [T]he 'separate but equal' doctrine is at best a bare constitutional hypothesis postulated in the absence of facts showing the circumstances and consequences of racial segregation and based upon a fallacious evaluation of the purpose and meaning inherent in any policy or theory of enforced racial segregation."[464] What Marshall was tactfully but forcefully saying was that the Supreme Court was wrong when it concluded in *Plessy* that the forced separation of the races was not intended to connote Negro inferiority. The decision cast a blind eye on the inescapable fact that the laws were intended to keep Blacks in their place, a place inferior to that of Whites. In light of this motive there could be no separate equality.

In *Sipuel,* the Court refused to address the assertion that separation was unequal, but it did rule that Ada Sipuel had to be admitted to a state law school immediately, whether it be at the University of Oklahoma or one for Negroes only.[465] Consequently, the state roped off a section in the capitol, assigned three teachers, and called it a law school.[466] Sipuel refused to enroll there. Marshall and the NAACP again drafted a brief arguing that the approach was inconsistent with the Court's ruling that Sipuel have immediate access to an education equal to that afforded applicants from other ethnic groups. The free exchange of ideas and perspectives from all members of society, argued Marshall, was an essential intangible factor that made the ad hoc law school unequal to the one at the university.[467] The Court ruled, however, that this setup did satisfy the equal protection clause of the fourteenth amendment.[468]

The negative outcome in *Sipuel* was quickly rectified by success in two cases decided in 1950. Herman Marion Sweatt applied to the University of Texas Law School and was rejected because of racial policy. A Texas district court denied a request for an order directing that he be admitted, and instead gave the state six months to come up with a substantially equal law school.[469] After an immediate appropriation of $10,000 the state rented three rooms in the basement of a building near the capitol, ordered some law books, and assigned three members of the university faculty to teach all the courses there.[470] Again, the "beneficiary" refused to enroll. The Supreme Court voted to hear his case; based on arguments essentially the same as those in *Sipuel*, it ruled that he must be admitted to the University of Texas Law School. Marshall had sociologists and anthropologists testify that a person's race had no bearing on his or her ability to learn.[471] He cited studies that showed the destructive impact on both races resulting from segregation, including mutual distrust and the "badge of inferiority" placed on Black students."[472] The Court accepted these arguments and ruled, quite apart from the tangible factors, that there were significant inequalities "incapable of objective measurement but which make for greatness in a law school."[473] Among these were reputation of the faculty, experience of the administration, standing in the community, traditions, and prestige. "The law school cannot be effective in isolation from the individuals and institutions with which the law interacts."[474]

*McLaurin v. Oklahoma State Regents* was decided just after *Sweatt*. McLaurin had applied to the University of Oklahoma to work toward a graduate degree in education. Since the state's Black college offered no such curriculum, he was admitted to the university, but on a segregated basis.[475] He was assigned a separate desk in an anteroom adjoining the classroom, he was not allowed in the library reading room (he had his own table on the mezzanine), and he was forced to eat in isolation at the school cafeteria, at special times when no White students were allowed in.[476] Again using the sociological arguments that such treatment branded McLaurin as inferior and impaired his ability to focus on his studies, Marshall and the NAACP brought his case before the Supreme Court. A unanimous Court held that the state's behavior violated the fourteenth amendment.

This set the stage for the all-out assault on the doctrine of "separate but equal" that the NAACP had long awaited. It was time to move from graduate schools to primary schools, for the arguments in *Sweatt* and *McLaurin* were no less true for six-year-olds than for twenty-six-year-olds—it was time to overrule *Plessy*. Marshall and others filed suits on behalf of grade school children from several different states. Again using the arguments that separation and equality are irreconcilable, they introduced Kenneth Clark and his dolls. Clark, a sociologist, had performed a series of studies with young Black children. He showed them two dolls, one Negro and one White, and asked them to state their preference. They invariably chose the White doll—it was "pretty" and "nice," while the Black doll was "bad."[477] This, argued Marshall, was an ingrained, learned response, reinforced and perpetuated by the stigma of being forcibly separated from the dominant race. With the exception of Delaware, all the state courts rejected this argument and dismissed the cases.[478] The Supreme Court granted review, and the cases were collectively titled *Brown v. Board of Education of Topeka*. Oral arguments were set for December 9, 1952.

Arguing for the states in favor of segregation was John W. Davis, a former solicitor general and a highly respected constitutional lawyer.[479] The thrust of his argument was that the Framers of the fourteenth amendment did not intend to eliminate segregated schools, that it was a valid exercise of the police powers of the state to separate the races if the state thought it was in the citizens' best interest, and that therefore it would be improper for the Court to step in and do what neither Congress nor the White House had been willing to do.[480]

The Court was split over how the cases should be divided. Most notably, Chief Justice Fred Vinson said he had gone as far as he wanted to go, referring to *Sweatt* and *McLaurin*.[481] Justice Vinson was not concerned with the racial discrimination that had been engendered and perpetuated by the *Plessy* "separate but equal" doctrine. Rather, he noted that there was "a whole body of law back of us on separate but equal,"[482] he wondered how, since there was segregation in the nation's capital and even immediately after the passage of the fourteenth amendment, the Framers could have intended otherwise. Justices Clark and Reed also intimated they would follow the chief justice's lead.[483] Felix Frankfurter was among those justices who thought segregation should end, but he knew that anything less than a unanimous decision in the case would be disastrous.[484] He convinced his colleagues that they should schedule the case for reargument, presenting counsel for each side with a set of five questions relating to the intent of the Framers and just how the Court should go about ordering desegregation of the schools, if that was its decision. Reargument was scheduled for December 1953.

On September 8, 1953, Fred Vinson told his wife he felt ill. A few hours later he was dead of a heart attack.[485] Said Justice Felix Frankfurter of the unfortunate incident, "This is the first indication I have ever had that there is a God."[486] Vinson's replacement was Earl Warren, who resigned his seat as California's governor when President Eisenhower asked him to lead the Court.[487] Leadership was one of Warren's specialties. He has been criticized for not being as scholarly as some of his brethren,[488] but his sense of justice and his ability to reduce complex legal issues to questions of right and wrong created a Court, eventually including Thurgood Marshall, that was proud to stand behind him. Warren was an unashamed judicial activist who believed more than anything else in egalitarianism and justice. He held these virtues to be so essential to a nation founded on justice for all that he could not conceive of a Constitution that did not embody them.

At reargument in December 1953 Marshall presented his case forcefully, stating that the plain intent of the fourteenth amendment was to raise the Negro to a level on par with other, White, Americans and that therefore state-imposed segregation was contrary to that intent. Warren, relying largely on a comprehensive study of the issue that Justice Frankfurter had one of his clerks, Alexander Bickel, prepare, came to the conclusion that the history of the fourteenth amendment was inconclusive as to the Framers' intent, and the other justices agreed.[489] So Warren posed the issue to his brethren in a simple way. He told them that as he saw it the only way segregation could be justified would be in the belief that

Blacks were inherently inferior[490]—if they followed *Plessy* it would have to be on that basis. It took four months of deliberation, campaigning, persuasion, and compromise, but Warren miraculously managed to get his desired result.

When the opinion was read on May 17, 1954, even Marshall was stunned that the decision was unanimous. Chief Justice Warren read his brief, simply stated opinion, starting with a history of the fourteenth amendment and the origins of the "separate but equal" doctrine. About halfway through he came to the central holding: "Does segregation of children in public schools solely on the basis of race, even though the physical facilities and other tangible' factors may be equal, deprive the children of the minority group of equal educational opportunities? We believe that it does."[491] To the extent that *Plessy* was in conflict with this finding *Plessy* was overruled.

This was a monumental victory for Marshall and the NAACP. By mandate of the high court, no more could any state consider the color of a person's skin in determining where he or she could get an education. While Marshall still knew that he might not live to see true equality under the laws for African Americans, after *Brown* was decided he felt closer to that goal than ever before. And though it would take many years and struggles more fierce by far to implement the Court's decision, state-enforced segregation would finally and definitely end.

Thurgood Marshall's joy in this accomplishment was soon overwhelmed by devastating news from his wife, Buster. She had recently discovered that she had advanced lung cancer.[492] Throughout Marshall's career she had been his rock in a frenetic life that led him from praise to danger all around the country. For the first time in his life he abandoned his work with the NAACP, refusing to see even his closest friends, so that he could stay home and care for his wife. On February 11, 1955, her forty-fourth birthday, Vivien Burey Marshall died.[493]

Eleven months later, Marshall married Cecilia Suyat, a Hawaiian of Filipino ancestry who was a secretary at the NAACP.[494] Though some criticized the timing, the wife of one of his friends said that in those days six months was the accepted "death etiquette" for remarriage; she also confided that Marshall was just one of those men who needed to be married.[495] He needed the stability, the love to come home to, someone to share his personal life as he had shared his public life with so many. Once people met Cecilia (or "Cissy," as she was known), the critics were usually silenced. Everyone who knew her remarked that she was a kind, caring woman, and that he was indeed a lucky man to have found her.[496] While Marshall's first marriage had been childless, Cissy bore him two boys, Thurgood Jr. and John William. Their marriage lasted twenty-seven years, until his death.

## The Judge

While Marshall continued his work with the NAACP fighting the opposition to implementing *Brown,* a young president, John F. Kennedy, looked at the federal judiciary and saw Jim Crow alive and well.[497] There were almost no minorities or women in the federal judiciary. Kennedy accordingly named ten African Americans to federal judgeships in 1961, the most controversial certainly being Thurgood Marshall.[498] The president realized the intense opposition he would face from southern Democrats, so he submitted the nomination four days before the end of the session, certain the Senate Judiciary Committee would not hold hearings until after Congress returned.[499] This allowed him to give Marshall a recess appointment, a chance to show his skill as a jurist in the hope that it would improve his chances of being confirmed for a lifetime federal judgeship. Kennedy resubmitted the nomination in January 1962, but it would be a year before the stalling tactics of Marshall's political opponents were exhausted and his nomination would be put to a vote on the Senate floor.

Senator James Eastland of Mississippi was chairman of the Senate Judiciary Committee, which he ruled dictatorially. No friend of the Black man, he once bragged that as head of its Subcommittee on Civil Rights he had bottled up 127 pieces of civil rights legislation, not allow one to go before the full committee and the Senate.[500] When Attorney General Bobby Kennedy approached Eastland about Marshall's appointment, the senator said he would be willing to send it to the floor if his old college roommate, Harold Cox, were appointed to a judgeship in the Fifth Circuit, encompassing several southern states where civil rights "agitation" was occurring. Eastland said to the attorney general, "Tell your brother that if he will give me Harold Cox, I will give him the nigger."[501] Kennedy acquiesced, much to his chagrin. Cox once told Black litigants in a voting rights case, from the bench, that they were "a bunch of niggers

. . . acting like a bunch of chimpanzees."[502] He was reversed more often on civil rights cases than any other judge in history.[503]

Despite his promise, Eastland maneuvered to delay the nomination until the uproar from Marshall's supporters proved too much for even him to combat. The committee's hearings dragged on for six session days, over the course of several months. Marshall was grilled relentlessly by the southern senators and accused of everything from being aligned with Communists to himself being a racist.[504] Despite another attempt at delay, his nomination was finally passed on to the full Senate, without recommendation, by the Judiciary Committee. On September 11, 1962, Marshall was confirmed to a seat on the Second Circuit Court of Appeals by a vote of 54 to 16,[505] with all opposed votes coming from southern Democrats. Marshall was only the second Black man to serve on any federal appellate court in the 160 years since the institution was created.[506]

During his tenure as a federal appellate judge in the Second Circuit, reviewing cases from New York, Connecticut, and Vermont, Marshall managed to silence most of the critics who doubted his abilities. Though the new judge had some embarrassing moments early on in tax law cases, where his experience was lacking, he was praised for the agility with which he quickly filled the gaps in his knowledge in all areas of law.[507] During his four years on the appellate court Marshall penned ninety-eight majority opinions (none of which was reversed), filed eight concurring opinions, and dissented twelve times.[508]

Judge Marshall also helped create important law. He ruled that the fifth amendment's guarantee against being tried twice for essentially the same crime applied not only to the federal government but also to the states by virtue of the fourteenth amendment's guarantee of due process of law.[509] The Supreme Court agreed and not only upheld his ruling for the Second Circuit, but broadened it to apply to the entire country. He also ruled a New York law requiring faculty members at state universities to sign a loyalty oath was at odds with the Constitution, and again the Supreme Court agreed.[510]

On July 12, 1965, the judge's lunch was interrupted by a phone call from the president. Lyndon Johnson said he admired Marshall's accomplishments and wanted him to become the nation's thirty-third solicitor general.[511] This is the only government official, including Supreme Court justices and attorneys general, who is required by statute to be "learned in the law."[512] The solicitor general not only serves as the government's lawyer in appeals before the Supreme Court but must decide which of the fifteen hundred or so government cases are important enough to bring under the Court's scrutiny. For Marshall to accept would mean a decrease in pay and giving up the security of a lifetime judicial appointment. But it also meant a more active role in helping to decide what cases went before the Supreme Court and how the issues in those cases would be framed for presentation.[513] The solicitor general maintained an office in the Justice Department and a chamber in the Supreme Court. He had at his disposal a staff of ten of the best lawyers in America, as well as the legal resources of all federal departments and agencies. In addition, Marshall knew that three previous solicitors general had been later named to the Supreme Court.[514] Though Johnson never intimated a Supreme Court nomination, the offer seemed too enticing to pass up.

As solicitor general Marshall found he had tremendous resources behind him to continue as a civil rights advocate. When California passed Proposition 14, making it legal for a person in the state not to sell property to someone he found objectionable, Marshall argued that this nullified the state's antidiscrimination laws. The Supreme Court agreed, holding that it was unconstitutional for a state to take actions that made private discrimination legally permissible.[515] Marshall also defended the Civil Rights Act of 1964, getting the Court to agree that Congress did have constitutional authority, through the interstate commerce clause, to prohibit discrimination at public eating and sleeping establishments.[516] He also argued several cases dealing with the Voting Rights Act of 1965, finally wiping out the last vestiges of discriminatory voting practices that denied "qualified" Black voters access to the ballot box.

Marshall also attacked a New York law that made voting eligibility dependent upon a minimum literacy in English. The statute, he argued, was a clear ploy to disenfranchise the state's growing Puerto Rican population.[517] The solicitor general also took the FBI to task when he discovered that agents were bugging the rooms of people they considered suspicious without the approval of the U.S. attorney general and without any pretext of a threat to national security.[518] One notable defeat came when Marshall argued the government's position in *Miranda v. Arizona;* here, against his conscience, he asked the Court not to uphold a decision which declared that suspects had to be apprised of their rights before being questioned by police.[519]

In June 1967 Marshall learned from Attorney General Ramsey Clark that his father, Justice Tom Clark, had resigned from the Supreme Court. While the elder Clark said it was to avoid any appearance of impropriety now that his son was attorney general, the younger Clark told Marshall it was to give President Johnson a chance to do "something he wanted to do badly."[520] Shortly thereafter he was told the president wanted to see him. He immediately called Cissy and told her of his suspicion; she was elated. Marshall knew of Johnson's penchant for grandiosity, so when the president told him of his nomination to the Supreme Court the solicitor general, not wanting to ruin the moment, feigned astonishment. "Wait until Cissy finds out," Marshall exclaimed. Johnson, very proud of himself, suggested they get her on the phone immediately. Unaware that she was on a speakerphone, she supposedly asked her husband, "So, did we get the Supreme Court appointment?" Johnson's laughter filled the room.[521]

Again before the Senate, Marshall was grilled on his views by members of a southern bloc not eager to see this civil rights activist appointed to an already liberal court. But his supporters prevailed, and by a vote of 69 to 11[522] Marshall was confirmed on August 30, 1967, as the nation's first African American Supreme Court justice. He was welcomed onto a body that shared his views on the role of the Supreme Court. Marshall had spent a lifetime in the trenches of the underrepresented in America. He had seen and experienced the devastating effects oppression by the powerful, privileged few could wreak upon the hearts, minds, and souls of a minority group with no voice in the political structure that dictate how they might live. In our government, with its intricate systems of checks and balances among the three branches, the Supreme Court opposes the majoritarian impulse, promoting justice by protecting the fundamental rights of all Americans, especially those without the ear of the dominant order. The many may dictate many things in this country, but the Supreme Court is there to ensure that they do not trample on the rights of the few. As Thomas Jefferson stated in 1798, "Free government is founded in jealousy, and not in confidence; it is jealousy, and not confidence, which prescribes limited constitutions, to bind down those whom we are obliged to trust with power."[523]

As a Supreme Court justice Marshall was a vigilant proponent of the first amendment's guarantee of freedom of speech. He argued that it should be extended to all manner of nonviolent personal expression, from sit-ins and picketing, to protests against conscription, to waving a red flag, to burning the American flag, to viewing pornography in the privacy of one's own home.[524] Marshall dissented, for example, in a case that held it was not a violation of any fundamental right for police departments to prohibit their officers from having long hair. As he saw it, "An individual's personal appearance may reflect, sustain, and nourish his personality and may well be used as a means of expressing his attitude and lifestyle."[525] The justice knew what it was like to be different in a society that resented, sometimes violently, noticeable differences. He believed passionately that the free transmission of ideas was essential to a free and equal society— that those whom we are obliged to trust with power must be bound down when they try to wield it to create a nation in their own image by criminalizing acts with which they disagree on ideological grounds. Although Marshall did not personally support all of the causes he protected, he believed fervently that even unpopular views must be acknowledged and tolerated, not suppressed by the force of majoritarian rule.

Justice Marshall also championed the constitutional right to privacy, holding that a state may not prohibit the use of contraception and that it may not reach so far into an individual's personal life as to legislate that she may not abort an unwanted pregnancy. In *Bowers v. Hardwick* (which he referred to simply as "that Georgia case") he joined in dissent against a decision that denied homosexuals constitutional protection of the right to choose, in the privacy of their own bedrooms, the sex of their desired partner. "We protect those rights," the dissent read, "not because they contribute, in some direct or material way, to the general public welfare, but because they form so central a part of an individual's life."[526]

In his concern for the underprivileged, Marshall was a constant advocate of establishing poverty as a suspect class under the Constitution. This would mean that the Court would review with particular scrutiny laws that had a disproportionate impact upon the poor. As he stated, "This is still a society in which justice is more easily available to the wealthy than to the poor."[527] In *United States v. Kras* (1973), Justice Harry Blackmun wrote for a five to four majority that even indigent debtors had to pay a $50 filing fee to get into bankruptcy court. He argued that they could easily save the money over the course of several weeks by giving up a weekly movie or a couple of packs of cigarettes. Marshall's response was venomous. "It is disgraceful for an interpretation of the Constitution to be premised upon unfounded assumptions about how people live. . . . A pack or two of cigarettes may be, for them, not a routine purchase but a luxury indulged in only rarely. The desperately poor almost never go to see a movie. . . . They have more important things to do with what little money they have."[528]

Perhaps Marshall's greatest disappointment on the Court, though, were the death penalty cases. Shortly after he was named solicitor general, President Johnson tapped him to lead a U.S. delegation to Stockholm for a United Nations congress on prevention of crime. When Marshall returned he remarked that there is "a clear tendency to favor abolition of executions, and the trend [in the United States] tells us that capital punishment is on its way out. . . ."[529] Unfortunately, he was wrong.

In Marshall's view, capital punishment in any form is unconstitutional. As cruel and unusual punishment, it is prohibited by the federal government through the eighth amendment, a prohibition applicable to the states by the fourteenth amendment's guarantee of due process of law.[530] Life in prison with no possibility of parole serves the purpose of removing killers from the population at large, where they might kill again. And the prospect of losing one's freedom for the rest of one's life is certainly enough of a deterrent (perhaps more so than death) to convince people who are capable of being deterred that murder is not a wise idea. So the only justification for the death penalty is that it is vengeance, retribution, which Marshall felt was not a proper motive for a state-sanctioned punishment.[531] As he said, "The Eighth Amendment itself was adopted to prevent punishment from becoming synonymous with vengeance."[532] The government's job is to protect its citizens. If this can be accomplished by removing a dangerous element from society through incarceration, then it is improper for the state to embrace a thinly disguised mob mentality and lash out at an individual in a crusade of an eye for an eye. In Marshall's view, the eighth amendment prohibited unnecessary cruelty in the meting out of justice.[533] Since imposing death served no purpose that lifelong incarceration would also not accomplish, he felt it an unnecessary penalty, hence one proscribed by the Constitution.

Moreover, the death penalty does not effectively deter violent crime.

Most murders are committed in the heat of passion, or on a split second's decision, in which case killers have neither the time nor the inclination to consider the ramifications of their act.[534] And those murderers who do calculatedly and purposefully plan to kill display no concern whatsoever for the punishment that awaits them if they are caught. As Marshall said, the problem with those in the latter group is that they figure they are smarter than the cops, that they won't get caught. They are incapable of being deterred by the threat of punishment. Look to seventeenth-century England, he suggested—even as a pickpocket was being hanged in public, spectators in the crowd were having their pockets picked.[535] "I don't see what's gained by it," he remarked.[536]

Further, Marshall felt, the state had shown it was not competent to mete out death in anything resembling an impartial manner. A man who committed a rape in one state would be sentenced to death, while a murderer in another would get in life in prison. Or, in a single state, the murderer of a Black man would go to prison for the rest of his life, while a similarly circumstanced murderer of a White man would be put to death. Perhaps he remembered W. D. Lyons, who, but for the grace of God and a jury with a modicum of conscience, did not get the electric chair. Or Leon Gilbert, who, but for Marshall's intervention, would have been executed by a firing squad in Korea. Even in a day when racism, ever present, is not as virulent as it was fifty years ago, it would be naïve to assert that we are not still a nation of "we's" and "them's." So long as we see our fellow human beings not only as different but as foreign from ourselves, we are susceptible to the scapegoating and related attitudes that make impartiality impossible. From the prosecutors who decide whether to seek the death penalty in a death-eligible crime, to the judges who formulate the instructions to a jury as to how it should determine whether a person lives or dies, to the twelve individuals selected from the community at large who make up a jury—throughout the process there are too many imperfect human beings involved to ensure that personal bias does not interfere with total impartiality. And while the existing system still constitutes the best method we have for dispensing criminal justice, we might at some point realize that it makes the irremediable act of taking a human life in an endeavor we should not undertake to perform.

Marshall won a significant, if brief, victory in 1972 with *Furman v. Georgia*. Until then juries had been given unfettered discretion in imposing death sentences.[537] They were simply not told that the accused's crime made him death-eligible and that they could sentence him to death if they so chose. Only Marshall and Justice William Brennan were of the opinion that the death penalty was cruel and unusual punishment in all circumstances, but they did manage to convince three other justices that the sentencing procedure as practiced was so arbitrary and capricious as to be cruel and unusual and that it therefore denied the accused due process of law.[538]

The five to four decision in *Furman* effectively made all of the death penalty statutes in the country unconstitutional, for they all followed that same procedure. Marshall hoped that this would discourage the states from attempting to execute prisoners, but in 1976 the Court heard *Gregg v. Georgia,* an aggregation of cases from five states that had revised their capital-sentencing guidelines and wished to test their constitutionality. To meet the charges that death was arbitrarily imposed, some of the new statutes provided for mandatory death sentences for certain types of murder, such as contract killing or killing a police officer.[539] Others (like Georgia's, which the Court pointed to as a model) required the jury to be informed of aggravating and mitigating circumstances surrounding the killing, after which the jury's sentence had to be reviewed by the state supreme court.[540] In a 7–2 decision the Court ruled that the new sentencing guidelines did not violate the eighth amendment. Only Justices Marshall and Brennan dissented. Unlike his colleague, who came while on the Court to the opinion that the death penalty was unconstitutional, Marshall had always held that belief. Perhaps influenced by past personal experiences, he knew the inherent arbitrariness involved in decreeing that a man was no longer fit to live, and he felt that no procedural safeguards of due process could ever produce an impartial determination of that fitness.[541]

Particularly galling to Marshall was the assertion by several in the majority that retribution was an acceptable reason for imposing the death sentence because it channeled the natural desire of man for vengeance through an appropriate avenue—the criminal justice system. Marshall wrote in his dissent, "It simply defies belief to suggest that the death penalty is necessary to prevent the American people from taking the law into their own hands."[542]

Drifting ever further away from the Court of social conscience and equality of which he dreamed, in 1987 Marshall had to endure the decision in *McCleskey v. Kemp.* Warren McCleskey, a Black man, was convicted in Georgia of killing a White police officer and was sentenced to death. Despite statistics showing clearly that a defendant convicted of killing a White man was more than four times more likely to be sentenced to death than someone who killed a Black man, a 5–4 majority held that the death penalty was not administered in a racially discriminatory manner.[543] The majority held that the statistics were constitutionally insignificant because McCleskey could not show that *he* was discriminated against. The conviction was allowed to stand.[544]

The case that finally convinced Marshall he could endure no more on a Court now dominated by ideological conservatives came on June 27, 1991, the last day of the 1990–91 Term.[545] Four years earlier Marshall had helped secure 5–4 majorities in *Booth v. Maryland* and *South Carolina v. Gathers.* These rulings had held that relatives were not allowed to deliver victim impact statements to juries before capital-sentencing deliberation.[546] *Payne v. Tennessee,* decided 6–3, reversed those decisions. Relatives could now deliver heart-wrenching renditions of how the loss of their loved one had affected them, in the hopes of inspiring the jury to return a death sentence. Aside from allowing a jury to be swayed by evidence quite apart from facts surrounding the commission of the crime, the Court seemed to be endorsing the view that taking the life of a person who was loved was more deserving of severe punishment than taking the life of one who was not. Later that day Marshall announced his retirement.[547]

Marshall's jurisprudence on the bench was marked by a compassion born of a personal understanding of how the law's promise of equal protection was either subverted or ignored by those entrusted with its administration. Though the proud claim of the United States is that we are a nation of laws, not men, the inequities that Marshall saw every day of his personal and professional life convinced him that the men who created and administered those laws had the greater power. The poor, the oppressed, the disenfranchised, the powerless—the countless minority who must rely on the goodness and objectivity of the legislatures, the police, and the judiciary—these are the people whose cause was championed by Thurgood Marshall, for he was one of them.

During the two years that George Bush had served as president at the time of Justice Marshall's retirement from the Court, 93 percent of his judicial nominees were White, 88 percent were male, and 64 percent had net worths of at least half a million dollars (more than one-third were millionaires).[548] In the twelve years of the Reagan and Bush administrations, of the 115 individuals who were appointed as appeals court judges, only 2 were Black.[549] A Pullman car porter had once said to Marshall, "I've travelled all over this country and I've never been anywhere I had to hold my hand in front of my face to know that I was black."[550] Whether by design or by habitation, racism was, and is still, an ugly reality in this country. And a Court that insisted on casting a blind eye on the fact that its decisions invariably would increase the misery of Blacks, the poor, and the uneducated was a Court on which Thurgood Marshall could no longer bear to serve.

JORDAN Steiker wrote in a perceptive essay that Thurgood Marshall always regarded the Court's 1976 cases upholding the constitutionality of capital punishment as provisional—as authorizing the death penalty only in that the new statutes and procedures actually redressed the inequalities and arbitrariness of the *ancien* capital punishment regime. Marshall was the trial lawyer as justice, who was building a record: he attempted to ground his opposition in the apparent failure of states to fulfill the particular promises upon which the modern death penalty statutes had been approved. He sought to demonstrate that, notwithstanding the seemingly scientific language of the redrafted statutes, states' administration of the death penalty remained arbitrary and discriminatory.[551]

Marshall's record-building approach reflected his role as Supreme Court Cynic—not a cynical hack like Lewis Powell, but rather a Cynic like Diogenes, the school's founder. Robert Wright has written that the roots of Cynicism lie less in suspicion of others than in suspicion of the self, and the Cynics realized that the obsession with social esteem is the enemy of principle and truth. They offered two prescriptions: eschewing all concern with public approval—the idea was to doggedly not care what anybody thinks; and walking around loudly telling the unpleasant and unpolite truths that asceticism had freed them to perceive—including, especially, the falseness of everyday life. They were the "watchdog of [human] kind" and "the surgeon whose knife sliced the cancer of cant from the minds of others." This is how Cynicism, through its self-denial akin to Buddhism, got a reputation for being cynical. It was a life of self-suspicion, yes, but the suspicion was *secondarily* trained on everyone else, too—and the results were broadcast, much to the public's discomfort. Marshall was a sort of a Buddhist with an attitude, combating brutal post-modern irony with brutal honesty. Marshall wasn't a real popular guy. Neither was Diogenes (Plato called him "Socrates gone mad"), but what can you do? Marshall didn't care; he just kept on unquietly building his record, for a future Supreme Court and for the historians and the sociologists and the anthropologists.

Nicholas Leman has written that Marshall

> didn't expend great effort in trying to influence the other justices, and so he had little effect on the overall direction of the court; his friend William Brennan would do the negotiating for liberalism, knowing that he had Marshall's vote in his pocket. Intellectually, Marshall hardened into a position of adherence to a handful of deeply held positions and did not give the impression that he was engaged in a dialectical interplay between his inclinations and the changing nature of American life.[552]

Nor did Marshall act like a Supreme Court justice.

> His un-Holmesian way of life included regular trips to racetracks and Atlantic City casinos, copious consumption (by today's standards) of Winstons and Wild Turkey and conversation filled with profanity and the 1940s boulevardier's slang. (He sometimes addressed his brethren as "baby.") All this was the style of a certain time and place—a time and place where no other justice or clerk had ever been—and also, perhaps, the style had some of the forced jauntiness of the combat soldier about it, having been adopted as a response to a life of unending fear and risk. It had often lead those who knew Marshall only towards the end of his life described him patronizingly, as a colorful character, the court's clowning token Negro.[553]

Marshall's life makes one of the great heroic stories of American history; next to it the pre-Court career of every other justice (even a former president like Taft, a leading intellectual like Frankfurter, or a great performer like Brandeis) looks like a dull bourgeois progression up the ranks of society. This is not to ascribe status to Marshall because he had "known poverty and discrimination"—the rhetoric of Clarence Thomas's handlers. What is awe inspiring about Marshall is what he *did* before he ever joined the United States Supreme Court.

"I do not believe," he told a crowd in Maui, Hawaii, on the bicentennial of the Constitution in 1987,

> that the meaning of the Constitution was forever "fixed" at the Philadelphia Convention. Nor do I find the wisdom, foresight, and sense of justice exhibited by the Framers particularly profound. To the contrary, the government they devised was defective from the start, requiring several amendments, a civil war, and momentous social transformations to attain the system of constitutional government, and its respect for the individual freedoms and human rights, we hold as fundamental today. . . .
>
> If we seek . . . a sensitive understanding of the Constitution's inherent defects, and its promising evolution through 200 years of history, the celebration of the "Miracle at Philadelphia" will, in my view, be a far more meaningful and humbling experience. We will see that the true miracle was not the birth of the Constitution, but its life.

In 1993, the Court held in a Texas case that a state death row inmate who presents belated evidence of innocence is not ordinarily entitled to a new full hearing before being executed. Its decision in *Herrera v. Collins* left open the prospect that "truly persuasive" evidence with an "extraordinarily high" chance of success might merit an exception to the general rule. But the majority found that this exception did not benefit Leonel Herrera. Convicted and sentenced to death in 1982 for the murder of two police officers, Herrera tried to reopen his case a decade later by presenting testimony that a brother who had since died had been the killer. The decision drew an angry dissent from Justice Harry Blackmun, who took the unusual step of reading his opinion from the bench. In it, he said the Court's approach sanctioned the execution of innocent people, which he called "perilously close to simple murder."

Chief Justice Rehnquist's opinion for the Court reasoned that although Herrera had presented new evidence showing he was innocent, he could not obtain a court hearing, because federal courts "sit to ensure that individuals are not imprisoned in violation of the constitution not to correct errors of fact." As Michael Meltsner wrote in the *Nation:*

> Marshall will roar over the irony of this one. "Oh, yes," the sense of his reply might go—for he would have used language more shrewdly than I can possibly imitate—"we'll save his life if the police improperly obtain a warrant, or if his lawyer was truly ineffective, or maybe even if the judge charged the jury erroneously or the prosecution withheld evidence. These are mistakes that invoke the Constitution. But that he might be innocent. That his brother may have been the murderer. Now this, you say, this doesn't violate a constitutional right. This doesn't make a lack of due process, you say. This isn't cruel and unusual punishment? Just one of those 'errors of fact,' right? So we can kill him, right?"

It wouldn't be just a matter of the death penalty, the loathsome nature of which Marshall knew firsthand, that set him against the nonsense the Court dispensed in the *Herrera* case. Nor misguided liberalism: Neither his public statements nor his private conversation betrayed the slightest sentimentality toward criminals. And certainly not naivete. There were few client dodges or lawyer tactics that Marshall couldn't spot. You simply couldn't pull the wool over eyes that had seen what his had seen. He was a lawyer who knew lynchings, race riots, kangaroo courts, perjured testimony and rigged juries as well as the subtler arts of complacent, elegant advocacy. The movement that brought him to a marble palace of justice had its origin in steamy Southern towns, where he might prepare a witness in the rowdy office above a juke joint.

The decisive factor for Marshall would be that even a Constitution born in racism was redeemable if one used the values at its core to deal humanely with the life around us. He once said that while we have a great Constitution today, "it didn't start out that way." Only the interpretations of Justices like Louis Brandeis, Earl Warren and William Brennan (and Marshall himself) replaced cramped formalism with decency. Constitutional lawyers still agonize over this sort of thing. Stray too far, they worry, and democracy will be lost. Perhaps, but trade too much fairness for efficiency or disregard the plight of the outcast or pretend that law is the same as justice and you may lose the human rights that democracy is supposed to preserve.

Thurgood Marshall was the greatest lawman of the age. He did it with a lack of pretension and a gift of humor that shaped but never detracted from the seriousness of his concerns. It might be said of him that he never forgot that in the final analysis errors of fact are the only errors that really count.[554]

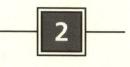

# Legitimacy in History

▼   ▼   ▼

[A]nd the first one now will later be last
— Bob Dylan[1]

## The Supreme Court: "Nine Scorpions in a Bottle"[2]

PERHAPS it all began with Job. William Safire's meditation on the Book of Job and its application to contemporary political behavior, *The First Dissident*,[3] is contrarian in a way that Brennan and Marshall might have appreciated. Safire's engagement with Job is evident and explicit: "I find the Book of Job more intellectually challenging, emotionally satisfying, spiritually uplifting, and politically instructive than any other part of the Bible." Since his undergraduate years, Safire wrote, "[t]his puzzling and infuriating biblical character has haunted my life." To be a Joban, he suggested, "is to be outraged by injustice and to be determined to right Authority's wrongs."

Job, "the first dissident," is Safire's "political metaphor for . . . principled resistance to authoritarian rule." Or, more succinctly, "[D]issent is Godly." Job becomes the precursor of Safire's modern political heroes, including Natan Sharansky, Václav Havel, Menachem Begin, Andrei Sakharov, and Mustapha al-Barzani (the Kurdish leader to whom the book is dedicated).

The Book of Job raises profoundly troubling issues about divine and human behavior. Its exploration of the correlation, if any, between sin and suffering, between human faith and divine blessing, is perennially alluring and invariably tormenting. Safire rejected any notion of a patient Job, suffering his terrible ordeal while being passively resigned to his fate. His Job, instead, symbolized "the sufferer's outrage at God's refusal to do justice."

Nor, as Jerold Auerbach observed, was Job (*pace* Mr. Safire) "the first dissident," nor even the first biblical dissenter from divine injustice. Long before Job's time, Abraham confronted God, who was prepared to destroy the righteous along with the wicked of Sodom and Gomorrah, with a stunning challenge: "Shall not the Judge of all the earth do justly?" Job may have been Abraham's worthy successor, but he was a successor nonetheless.[4]

This chapter serves two interrelated purposes. First, it provides a background discussion of judicial dissent in general. Second, it situates the idea of sustained dissent within the larger framework of judicial dissent itself.

The dissenting opinion as an institution within the United States Supreme Court has received both scorn and reverence.[5] The emergence in ever-increasing numbers of dissents and separate concurrences is a relatively recent phenomenon.[6] However, the first reported opinion of our Supreme Court contained a dissent; at a time when opinions were normally delivered orally, this probably accounted for the fact that the decision was written down at all.[7]

Chief Justice John Marshall, who broke from the English tradition of seriatim delivery of opinions to adopt the precedent of a single opinion of the Court, prized unanimity and managed to achieve consensus to a degree unparallel before or since.[8] Marshall was probably the most forceful personality ever to occupy the office of chief justice of the United States, and this gives some explanation for the seeming harmony of the Court during the period of his dominance. But his reasons for urging unanimity deserve careful consideration.

The Court as an institution had not yet established itself. Marshall undoubtedly wished to see it speak with one voice in order to minimize the cacophony of dissent and thus to send the American people a strong signal: The role of the Supreme Court is to have the last say; individual views, whether on the bench or off, must bend to the will expressed by the institutional voice.[9]

Thomas Jefferson, Marshall's political foe and a champion of the individual conscience, disagreed. He believed that there should be individual opinions in every case; each justice should "throw him self in every case on both God and his country; both will excuse him for the error and value him for his honesty."[10] It is worth remembering that Jefferson feared the growth of a strong federal judiciary.

With the passing of the John Marshall era—and perhaps because the Court was imbued with some of the institutional security that was his legacy—dissents became more frequent and more influential. Characterized by the press of his time as the "Great Dissenter," Oliver Wendell Holmes, influenced by that earlier era, was always careful to preface his magnificent dissents with an apology. In what is perhaps his most famous dissent, in *Lochner v. New York,*[11] Holmes began by stating, "I regret sincerely that I am unable to agree with the judgment in this case, and that I think it is my duty to express my dissent."[12] Although his opinion savagely mocked the majority for "attempting to read Mr. Herbert Spencer's Social Statics . . . into the Fourteenth Amendment,"[13] we have no reason to doubt the sincerity of his regret. Holmes was not the only dissenter who believed in the consensus opinion as the institutional voice of authority.[14] Having once stated their opposition to the adoption of a particular proposition as law, justices often acquiesced to the force of the precedent when it came time to apply the earlier case.

## Early History of Dissent
### Seriatim Opinions

The first published reports of the United States Supreme Court recount a history of freedom to express individual views in both concurring and dissenting opinions. Integral to the English practice of delivering opinions seriatim (separately and in sequence), this individual expression is found in the Court's handling of the first two cases reported during its 1792 Term. The case history of the early Supreme Court establishes that it consciously decided to follow the English practice of delivering opinions seriatim, particularly when encountering potentially controversial or significant decisions. In its first reported opinion, in 1792, the Court followed the English practice of delivering opinions seriatim,[15] and in the uniquely American order of inverse seniority. In *Georgia v. Brailsford*[16] each of the six justices gave an opinion either supporting or opposing Georgia's motion for an injunction in a suit in equity against two citizens of another state. The majority of the Court, Justices Iredell, Blair, Wilson, and Chief Justice Jay, gave opinions supporting the issuance of an injunction, while Justices Johnson and Cushing were opposed. Justice Thomas Johnson, sworn in just prior to the hearing of the *Brailsford* case, was the most junior member of the Court.[17] By inverse seniority, it is his dissent that is the first Supreme Court opinion reported.[18] This decision exemplifies the Court's incorporation of the seriatim practice and inverse seniority.[19]

The second decision reported during the August Term of 1792 had originated "upon the act of Congress passed the 23d of March, 1792."[20] The act stated that the circuit courts should settle the claims of widows and orphans, and establish and regulate the claims of invalided pensioners. However, the circuit courts' decisions would, under the act, be subject to the "consideration and suspension of the Secretary at War, and then to the revision of the Legislature."[21] While sitting on the circuit courts, each of the Supreme Court justices had refused to proceed in petitions of pensioners and had written letters to the president declaring the act unconstitutional: "[B]y the Constitution, neither the Secretary at War, nor any other Executive officer, nor even the Legislature, are authorized to sit as a court of errors on the judicial acts or opinions of this court."[22]

*Hayburn's Case* came before the Supreme Court in the form of a motion by the United States attorney general, Edmund Randolph, for a mandamus to the circuit court for the district of Pennsylvania commanding the court to proceed in a petition by William Hayburn. The attorney general made the motion ex officio, in the capacity of his office and not representative of any particular person.[23] Overly simplified, the question before the Court was whether the attorney general, alone, could superintend the decisions of the inferior courts.

The official report only records, "But the Court being divided in opinion on the question, the motion, made 'ex officio,' was not allowed."[24] Yet newspaper accounts of the time stated that "the debate continued from day to day until Saturday last. . . . The discussion was full and the Bench divided on the question. Judges Iredell, Johnson, and Blair declaring in favor of the attorney general and Judges Wilson, Cushing and the chief justice entertaining the contrary opinion."[25] And Attorney General Randolph wrote to James Madison that the debate "continued from day to day until yesterday, when Johnson, Iredell, and Blair were in favor of my power, and the other three against it."[26] Thus the justices of the early Court were not inhibited in the free expression of their individual opinions. Nor did division preclude each justice's views on the larger issue of the constitutionality of the act from being recorded in the official reports. Further, when confronted with the division generated by *Hayburn's Case,* the Court not only implicitly respected freedom of individual expression but went on to specifically incorporate the seriatim practice.

Under the heading of "Rule"[27] in the report of *Hayburn's Case,*[28] the attorney general "moved for information, relative to the system of practice by which the Attorneys and Counsellors of this court shall regulate themselves, and of the place in which rules in causes here depending shall be obtained." And, "THE CHIEF JUSTICE, at a subsequent day, stated, that the Court considers the practice of the courts of *Kings Bench* and *Chancery* in *England,* as affording outlines for the practice of this court; and that they will, from time to time, make such alterations therein, as circumstances may render necessary." The early Court's following of the English practice of delivering opinions seriatim was purposeful rather than accidental, and its continuation can be traced through the Court's decisions.

The English practice did not require that individual opinions be expressed in each and every case. In 1822, Jefferson observed "that from the earliest ages of the English law, from the date of the year-books, at least, to the end of the IId George, the judges of England, in all but self-evident cases, delivered their opinions seriatim, with the reasons and authorities which governed their decisions."[29] The early United States Supreme Court varied the English practice by delivering opinions seriatim in potentially controversial and significant cases.[30]

A review of the reports of these cases confirms that the issues contested represented significant legal and political controversies of the time.[31] Given the nature of the issues involved and the precarious position of the Court as an institution not yet clearly defined, the justices were individually, through seriatim opinions, assuming responsibility for the reasoning and decisions in significant cases.

The Court's determination of which cases were significant was discretionary; the exercise of this discretion turned on the potential for public and political, as well as internal, discord. In *Bas v. Tingy,*[32] Justice Chase complained that "[t]he Judges agreeing unanimously in this opinion, I presumed that the sense of the Court would have been delivered by the president, and therefore, I have not prepared a formal argument on the occasion."[33] Yet, the import of his complaint is not supported by internal disagreement in the reports of previous opinions delivered seriatim. The two dissents in the first hearing of *Georgia v. Brailsford* are the only dissenting opinions in cases in which the Court delivered opinions seriatim. Though infrequent, dissenting opinions were more common when the Court did not follow the seriatim practice: Justices Iredell and Blair dissented in the rehearing of *Georgia v. Brailsford;*[34] Justice Wilson dissented in *Wiscart v. D'Auchy,*[35] and he was joined by Justice Paterson.[36] The reports of previous opinions delivered seriatim do not support disagreement in the Court's reasoning. In *Calder v. Bull,* Justice Iredell disagreed with the reasoning of the other opinions;[37] Justice Chase, in *Calder v. Bull,* and Chief Justice Elsworth, in *Fenemore v. United States,* limited their concurrence with the Court's decisions.[38]

Public response to the justices' decision in *Bas v. Tingy* supports the ideas that the Court's discretionary following of the practice of delivering opinions seriatim was predicated upon the potential for public or political response to its decisions and that individual responsibility was intrinsic. "[F]or the first time in the history of the Government, there was uttered a suggestion that a Judge should be impeached for rendering a judicial decision, when the *Aurora* stated that the decision was 'most important and momentous to the country, and in our opinion every Judge who asserted we were in a state of war, contrary to the rights of Congress to declare it, *ought to be impeached.*' "[39] Though the justices had agreed upon interpretation of the legislation in question, the Court, in its discretion, had determined that individual expressions of reasoning, and personal responsibility for it, would clarify and strengthen the decision.

The history of the early United States Supreme Court, beginning with the first published report in 1792 and continuing through 1800, establishes that freedom of individual expression through the English practice of delivering opinions seriatim was purposely institutionalized and continued by the Court. Early case history evidences the assumption of responsibility through both concurring and dissenting opinions in potentially significant or controversial decisions. The early Court institutionalized the philosophy that its credibility as a unit would be clarified and strengthened by the individual justices' articulation of their own opinions.

## Early Opinions of "The Court"—and Early Dissents

John Marshall's appointment as chief justice signaled the Court's change from the practice of delivering opinions seriatim to the practice of delivering caucus opinions. This sudden and unexplained shift can be traced to his individual philosophy and to the strength of his personality and will. Although the Court adhered strictly to this practice for only the first four years of Marshall's tenure as chief justice, individual expression through either concurring or dissenting opinion was indelibly marked as an exception to the institution's unity. Yet, the history of unity is contemporaneous with a record of tension between the stricture of unity and individual responsibility through freedom of expression.

John Marshall was appointed Chief Justice of the United States in February 1801. In the first decision thereafter, *Talbot v. Seeman*,[40] he forever changed the practice of the Court by announcing the decision in a single opinion.[41] "The opinion of the Court" had been given in earlier, minor cases, and Chief Justice Oliver Elsworth, in *Brown v. Berry*,[42] had begun with, "In delivering the opinion of the court . . ." John Marshall went further, however, and infused the opinion with the persona of the Court by his choice of words: "But the court cannot presume"; "the court is struck with"; and "the court thinks." Marshall did not give the opinion of the majority as the chief justice of the Court, but gave the opinion of "the Court" as an entity—as a unit separate from its individual tributaries. Thus, beginning with the first decision in which he participated, Marshall changed the method of the Court from following the English practice of individual expression to one of delivering the caucus opinion of the majority, and he changed the philosophy of the Court from one that held the decision to be more than the sum of its individual parts to one that held it to be a unit independent of its individual parts.[43]

Unlike the Court's incorporation of the English practice, there is no record of announcement or institutional decision of the Court's shift to the caucus opinion. Because the change can be marked by Marshall's appointment to the bench, and because, for the next twenty-six years, the Court only reverted to the seriatim practice in his absence,[44] the change is attributed to his individual choice. In his biography of the chief justice,

Beveridge described this as "one of those acts of audacity that later marked the assumption of power which rendered his career historic."[45] This change is also traceable to Marshall's personal concept of unity and power.

In his account of the English practice, Jefferson wrote, "[w]hen Ld. Mansfield came to the bench he introduced the habit of caucus opinions. The judges met at their chambers or elsewhere, secluded from the presence of the public, and made up what was to be delivered as the opinion of the court."[46] The caucus opinion can be linked to Marshall's admiration for Mansfield, as recorded in his journal: "Mansfield's decisions had the full weight of the authority of the court of King's Bench"; "and, since his colleagues were all lawyers of great learning, the influence of his decisions was much increased."[47] In defense against an attack by Spencer Roane, Marshall's anonymous reply reflects the concept of unity behind the procedural ideal of caucus opinions: "The course of every tribunal must necessarily be, that the opinion which is to be delivered as the opinion of the court, is previously submitted to the consideration of all the judges; and, if any part of the reasoning be disproved, it must be so modified as to receive the approbation of all, before it can be delivered as the opinion of all."[48] This same concept of unity and ideal in practice was echoed in Marshall's dissent in *Bank of the United States v. Dandridge:*[49] "I should now, as is my custom, when I have the misfortune to differ from this court, acquiesce silently in its opinion. . . ." Yet, that Marshall dissented at all, and the content of his continued apology, expressed the reality of individuality that prevented complete realization of the ideal: "A full conviction that the commission of even gross error, after a deliberate exercise of judgment, is more excusable than the rash and hasty decision of an important question, without due consideration, will, I trust, constitute some apology for the time I consume in stating reasons and the imposing authorities which guided the circuit court in the judgment that has been reversed." Even the chief justice's personal ideal of the unity of the Court was subject to his individual responsibility on questions of importance.

For the first four years of Marshall's tenure, the Court did adhere to the practice of unity—it decided with opinion some twenty-six cases, and all were delivered as the unanimous opinion of the Court.[50] This unity of practice was disrupted by once, in 1804, by a one-line concurring opinion by Justice Chase.[51] That Marshall wrote for the Court in all but two opinions, those for which he had sat on the decisions below,[52] does attest to his influence: yet there were five other justices on the Court, and none of them objected to the practice. Without the support of his brethren, Marshall's concept of unity could not have become the custom of the Court, nor would it have endured through the institution's subsequent history. However, this history is also one of tension between the ideal and the reality.

After four years in which the chief justice delivered the unanimous opinion of the Court, the reality of individual responsibility began to erode the ideal of this practice.[53] Justice Chase's one-line concurring opinion of 1804 was followed by Justice Washington's dissenting opinion in 1805[54] and by Justice William Johnson's concurring opinion the same year.[55] During Marshall's absences, the Court reverted to the practice of delivering opinions seriatim, twice in 1805[56] and three times in 1806.[57] Also in 1806, Justice Paterson wrote a dissenting opinion.[58] The next year, Justice Johnson did the same.[59] In 1808 Justice Johnson wrote two concurring opinions and two dissenting opinions; Justices Washington and Livingston each wrote concurring opinions.[60] In deference to the tension between individual responsibility and the institutional unity of the Court, Marshall began to assign delivery of the majority opinion to other justices,[61] doing so three times in 1809 and once in 1810.[62] Between 1813 and 1822 Marshall averaged about fifteen opinions of the Court, and the other justices combined averaged twenty-one.[63] This action by the chief justice did not dispel the inherent tension between the freedom of individual expression and the stricture of a unified single opinion of the Court, and by the last years of his tenure individual expression had become more prevalent.

In 1827, in *Ogden v. Saunders*,[64] the Court briefly returned to its practice of delivering opinions seriatim. The majority, consisting of Justices Washington, Johnson, Thompson, and Trimble, gave opinions in this fashion; Marshall delivered a dissenting opinion for the minority, consisting of himself and Justices Duvall and Story. The practice of seriatim opinions was not reinstituted, and individual expression began to emerge by means of dissenting opinions. Of the seventy-four such opinions reported from 1805 to 1833, thirty-seven were submitted between 1827 and 1833. Conversely, of the thirty-five concurring opinions reported from 1805 to

1833, only seven were submitted between 1827 and 1833.[65] Thus, in order to reconcile the tension created by the ideal of unity promoted by the practice of caucus opinions, individual responsibility found expression primarily through dissenting opinions.

From John Marshall's first case as chief justice, he changed both the practice and the philosophy of the Court by delivering the caucus opinion of the majority as "the opinion of the Court." Because there is no record of this change being decided by the Court as a whole, and because it coincides with Marshall's appointment and his statements of conviction about strength through unity, the shift can be attributed to his individual motivation. Since the Court adhered to the practice for four years, the change was obviously embraced by the other justices. However, neither Marshall nor the Court could completely reconcile the tension between individual responsibility and the practice of caucus opinions—especially in important or potentially controversial decisions. The history of the Marshall Court is a story of tension between the ideal of unity and the reality of individual responsibility.

The early history of the United States Supreme Court records the evolution of two very diverse philosophies and practices—each representative of traditions upon which the institution rests today. The ideal of unity through a caucus-majority opinion is fundamental to the history of the Court's practice and is recognized as a source of strength and continuity. Concurrently, the reality of the expression of individual responsibility is basic to this same history. Traces of the early practice of delivering opinions seriatim have persisted through dissents and concurrences in potentially significant or controversial decisions. And, reflective of the philosophy of the early Court, individual opinions have emerged as respected assertions of individuality coterminous with individual responsibility.

The practices of the two early periods of the Court, freedom of individual expression and unanimous majority opinion, represent divergent philosophies that cannot be completely reconciled. The majority opinion has been preserved as the accepted practice of the Court.[66] However, freedom of individual expression has been, from the beginning of the practice of rendering a majority opinion during the Marshall Court, continued and accommodated by justification.

Accommodation of the dichotomy between the diverse philosophies is recorded in the opinions and writings of Supreme Court justices who supported unanimity yet practiced dissent.[67] Justice Story, who ardently supported Marshall's leadership,[68] wrote as early as 1815: "I hold it an indispensable duty not to surrender my own judgment, because a great weight of opinion is against me, a weight which no one can feel more sensibly than myself. Had this been an ordinary case I should have contented myself with silence."[69] Thus, Story justified his individual expression by citing personal responsibility, given the importance of the case. He justified a later dissent by citing the involvement of a constitutional question: "I offer no apology for this apparent exception to the course which I have generally pursued, when I have had the misfortune to differ from my brethren, in maintaining silence; for in truth it is no exception at all as upon constitutional questions I ever thought it my duty to give a public expression of my opinions, when they differed from that of the Court.[70] The justification of individual expression with responsibility in important or constitutional cases is very similar to the early Court's discretionary following of the seriatim practice, and it has persisted through the body's history.[71]

In 1847, for example, in the *License Cases,*[72] "six Judges render[ed] separate opinions upon the much vexed points as to the exclusiveness of the power of Congress to regulate commerce, and as to the definition of the word 'regulate.' "[73] In 1849, in the *Passenger Cases,* the Court virtually returned to the seriatim practice.[74] "[T]he decision holding the laws of both States [New York and Massachusetts] unconstitutional was rendered February 7, 1849, each of the Judges reading an opinion, so that seven hours were thus occupied."[75] And in 1952, in the *Steel Mill Case,* the Court emulated the seriatim practice.[76] Seven opinions were given—six concurring in denying President Truman authority to take over the steel mills and one dissenting. Finally, as discussed above, in *Furman v. Georgia* (1972) each justice wrote separately.

## Taking Dissents Seriously: Some Great Dissenters
### The Nineteenth Century

**WILLIAM JOHNSON**: Justice William Johnson was the "first dissenter" under the Marshall Court's method of caucus opinions. By writing separate concurring and dissenting opinions, he exercised individual expression akin to the seriatim practice. Focusing on individual responsibility rather than disagreement, and shaped to compromise the tension between individual and unanimous opinions, his separate holdings are often not differentiated as concurring or dissenting. However, a vindication of legislative supremacy over both executive and judicial power underlies Johnson's separate opinions.

Appointed to the Supreme Court by President Jefferson in 1804, William Johnson served through 1834, closely matching Marshall's tenure of 1801–35.[77] In 1805, in *Huidekoper's Lessee v. Douglass*,[78] he disrupted the unanimity of the Court in a concurring opinion that questioned the reasoning of the majority; two years later, he delivered a full dissent in *Ex parte Bollman*.[79] Considering the period, the persistence of Johnson's separate opinions is distinct. "Of a total of 70 dissenting opinions, 33—nearly half—were Johnson's. Similarly he submitted 24 of the 59 concurring opinions."[80] Thus, by exercising individual expression, Justice William Johnson became the "first dissenter." However, concurring opinions were integral to this individual expression.

Johnson's exercise of separate opinions was motivated more by his commitment to individual responsibility than by an inability to agree with the majority. In *Marine Insurance Co. v. Young,* it was individual responsibility that induced his rendering of a separate opinion "to avoid having an ambiguous decision hereafter imputed to me, or an opinion which I would not wish to be understood to have given."[81] In *Martin v. Hunter's Lessee,* Johnson gave two reasons for rendering a concurring opinion: "Few minds are accustomed to the same habit of thinking, and our conclusions are most satisfactory to ourselves, when arrived at in our own way"; and the question involved was one of "momentous importance."[82] Later, in his concurring opinion in *Gibbons v. Ogden,* he wrote:

> The judgment entered by the court in this cause has my entire approbation; but having adopted my conclusions on views of the subject materially different from those of my brethren, I feel it incumbent on me to exhibit those views. I have, also, another inducement; in questions of great importance and great delicacy, I feel my duty to the public best discharged by an effort to maintain my opinions in my own way.[83]

That Johnson focused on individual responsibility rather than on disagreement with the Court accounts for the fine distinction between his actual, full dissents and his dissents from the reasoning of the Court.[84]

This muted distinction is exemplified in the justice's separate opinion in (and the subsequent historical analyses of) *Fletcher v. Peck*.[85] After writing that "in this case I entertain, on two points, an opinion different from that which has been delivered by the court," Johnson's next sentences concurred with Marshall's opinion for the Court: "I do not hesitate to declare that a state does not possess the power of revoking its own grants. But I do it on a general principle, on the reason and nature of things: a principle which will impose laws even on the deity."[86] He went on to disagree with the Court's expansive construction of the contract clause because it threatened both the states' power to regulate the making and enforcing of contracts and the states' eminent domain. Historians, including Johnson's biographer, Donald Morgan, are divided as to whether he was dissenting or limiting the Court's construction of the contract clause.[87] Most analyses of the justice's opinion in *Fletcher v. Peck* ignore the second point of his dissent.[88] Yet Johnson had written that "the other point on which I dissent from the opinion of the court, is relative to the judgment which ought to be given on the first count." He went on to reason that the State of Georgia "had not a fee simple in the land," that the interest of the state in the land was "nothing more than a mere possibility," and that the land had been granted to the Native Americans. "In fact, if the Indian nation be the absolute proprietors of their soil, no other nation can be said to have the same interest in it."[89] Because Johnson's separate opinion concentrated on responsibility rather than disagreement with the opinion of the Court, it is not clear whether it is a concurrence or a dissent.[90]

A study of the consistency of Johnson's legal philosophy, his use of concurring as well as dissenting opinions, demands consideration in conjunction with his four-year "lapse into silent acquiescence" in 1819.[91] It can only be conjectured that this four-year silence grew from a compromise over delivering individual and unanimous opinions.[92]

The Court's construction of the contract clause provides a useful framework for the study of Johnson's philosophy. An advocate of legislative supremacy, he chafed at the judicial limitation of legislative action in his separate opinion in *Fletcher v. Peck*. Yet the justice acquiesced as the Court extended the clause's prohibitions on state legislation.[93] Nor did he resist the Court's expansion of the contract clause until 1823, in a concurrence that defended the power of legislatures in interstate compacts.[94] Ultimately, Johnson delivered a concurring seriatim opinion supporting the government's right "to limit and define the power of contracting, and the extent of the creditor's remedy against his debtor; to regard other rights besides his, and to modify his rights so as not to let them override entirely the general interests of society, the interests of the community itself in the talents and services of the debtor, the regard due to his happiness and to the claims of his family upon him and upon the government."[95] And "that power will be found to be measured neither by moral law alone, nor universal law alone, nor by the laws of society alone, but by a combination of the three, an operation in which the moral law is explained and applied by the law of nature, and both modified and adapted to the exigencies of society by positive law."[96] Thus, though Johnson's separate opinions were not clearly distinguished as concurring or dissenting, and though he did acquiesce in the practice of the Court for a time, there is a consistency in his individual expression. Justice William Johnson's original commitment to legislative supremacy evolved into a philosophy of positive law.[97]

By means of his separate opinions, Johnson accepted individual responsibility for his positivist philosophy. Throughout his thirty years of service, he took the position that both the executive and judicial branches must look to either the Constitution or Congress for their power. Beginning with his first dissent in *Ex parte Bollman*,[98] Johnson maintained that the Constitution granted the Court original jurisdiction but that Congress must authorize appellate jurisdiction. Thus, the Supreme Court had no general power to issue a writ of habeas corpus without express authorization when the case had been properly committed to a lower court. Johnson sustained this position in dissenting opinions throughout his years of service and expressed the same position on questions of mandamus.[99]

The same positivist philosophy animated his position that the powers of the courts were subject to the will of the legislature.[100] Thus, absent legislation, the courts lacked the power to denominate corporations as "citizens" for the purpose of a legal suit. Through dissent, Johnson refused to reconstruct article III on the premise that Congress intended that the suits should come up through the state courts.[101] He transferred this same power from federal to state legislatures, and found them to be compatible. His concurring opinion in *Ogden v. Saunders*[102] maintained that the state could regulate contracts under the contract clause. Accordingly, he reasoned that state taxation of federal securities was within the borrowing power of the state and that it was thus "no masked attack upon the powers of the general government";[103] nor was a state's issuance of a limited amount of loan office certificates, receivable in payment of debts due it, constitutionally banned as "bills of credit."[104] In attributing supreme power to the legislatures, Johnson demanded authorization for the powers of the Court. It was not authorized to dictate the bounds of state power in the right of election in a naturalization case.[105] He interpreted the implementation of the "full faith and credit" clause (article IV, section 1) to mean that one state's judgments must be carried into effect in other states, and not received merely as evidence.[106] Nor did he think that the Court was authorized to address topics that were not "essential to the case": "we are constituted to decide causes not to discuss themes or digest systems."[107]

**PETER DANIEL:** Justice Peter Daniel, the first sustained dissenter, shares little with Brennan and Marshall other than zeal. He was as relentless in his support of slavery and racism—framed in the language of federalism—as the two later justices were in their support of individual rights.

Justice Daniel served on the Taney Court for nineteen years, from 1841 to 1860, and dissented in 111 cases. Unlike the separate opinions of the first of the nineteenth-century dissenters, Justice William Johnson, Daniel's dissents were motivated by disagreement with the opinions of the Court rather than by the responsibility of individual expression. Less reflective of the seriatim practice, his dissents were not always accompanied by opinion. Even when he joined in the judgment of the Court, Daniel's concurring opinions were identifiable as vehement dissents from specific points of the majority's decision. And, unlike the opinions of the great nineteenth-century dissenter John Marshall Harlan, not one of Daniel's dissents has been remembered as "an appeal to the brooding spirit of the law, to the intelligence of a future day when a later decision may possibly correct the error into which the dissenting judge believes the court to have been betrayed."[108] His opinions simply evaporated.

Justice Peter Daniel's time on the Supreme Court does not stand out in duration when compared to Justice Johnson's thirty years and Justice Harlan's thirty-three years, eleven months. His service stands out because he delivered the opinion of the Court in 84 cases and dissented in 111.[109]

Even more significant than the sheer number of Daniel's dissents is their relentlessness.[110] His dissents, even when he concurred in the outcome of the Court's decision, left no room for compromise. Through dissent, Daniel unequivocally adhered to the sovereignty of the individual states.

In one of the first cases that Daniel reviewed, he joined in the judgment of the Court but dissented from two specific points of law. *Prigg v. Pennsylvania*[111] held that a Pennsylvania statute that made it a felony for any person by force or fraud to carry away or seduce any "colored" person from the state with intent to detain or sell him was prohibited under article IV, section 2 of the Constitution.[112] Daniel concurred that the Pennsylvania statute was unconstitutional. However, in the interest of states' rights, he could not agree that the act of Congress of 1793 prohibited any state legislation upon this subject, whether in aid of or opposition to the congressional enactment; nor could he agree that the power of legislation upon the subject was exclusive in the national government and therefore forbidden to the state legislatures.

In another infamous slavery case, fourteen years later, Daniel again concurred with the Court's decision but adamantly dissented from its reasoning. *Dred Scott v. Sandford*[113] held that a free Black was not a citizen and that a slave's residence in Minnesota, a free state, was not emancipation because "an act of Congress which deprives a citizen of the United States [the slave owner] of his liberty or property, merely because he came himself or brought his property into a particular Territory of the United States, and who had committed no offense against the laws, could hardly be dignified with the name of due process."[114] Daniel dissented from the Court's finding that slaves were the same as other property: "The only private property which the constitution has specifically recognized, and has imposed it as a direct obligation both on the States and the Federal government to protect and enforce, is the property of the master in his slave; no other property is placed by the constitution upon the same high ground, nor shielded by a similar guarantee."[115] His dissents in the slavery cases typify his dissents in other areas.

Daniel brooked no congressional infringement on the rights of the states, even for internal improvements. The Court decided two cases involving state statutes that imposed tolls on vehicles carrying the United States mail (or passengers or goods in such vehicles), traveling on a road that Congress had paid for and then ceded to the states through which it passed.[116] In both cases, he dissented from the Court's holding that the state statutes conflicted with the act ceding the road to the states: "I believe that the authority vested in Congress by the Constitution to establish roads, confers no right to open new roads, but implies nothing beyond a discretion in the government in the regulations it may make for the post-office department for the selection among various routes."[117]

Daniel's commitment to states' rights motivated his dissents from the opinions of the Court in cases interpreting the "regulation of commerce." In the *License Cases,*[118] the Court upheld a state law requiring a license for the retail sale of foreign liquors; the justices further determined that once the property passed out of the hands of the importer, or was taken from the casks in which it was imported, "it passed the line of foreign commerce, and became a part of the general mass of property in the State."[119] Although Daniel concurred in the judgment, he argued that as soon as imported goods passed from the customhouse to the importer the state had a right to tax them.[120] In the *Passenger Cases,*[121] the Court extended the term "commerce" to include all navigation and intercourse, and it held that state laws imposing taxes upon arriving aliens were unconstitutional. Daniel entered a full dissent upon the basis that persons were not "imports" within the meaning of the Constitution, and he would not extend Congress's power over "commerce" to include "intercourse" with foreign nations and among the states. In *Cooly v. Board of Port Wardens,*[122] Daniel concurred in the Court's validation of state pilotage laws but denied that the laws were regulations of commerce. He maintained that the power to enact pilotage laws was original and inherent in the states and thus not subject to the sanction of the federal government. And Daniel wrote a full dissent from the Court's extension of congressional power to rivers over which it regulated navigation.[123] Just as he dissented from any extension of the power of federal legislation, Daniel dissented from any extension of the powers of federal courts.

Although he did not object when the Court first conferred citizenship status upon corporations,[124] thereafter Daniel dissented from the Court's treatment of corporations as citizens and from the precedent of the earlier case:

> Against this position it may be urged, that this matter is no longer open for question. In answer to such an argument, I would reply,

that this is a matter involving a construction of the Constitution, and that wherever the construction or the integrity of that sacred instrument is involved, I can hold myself trammeled by no precedent or number of precedents.[125]

In ensuring years the justice "reiterated these views and emphasized his dissent, sometimes in bitter and opprobrious language, in no less than sixteen subsequent cases in which corporations were parties."[126]

Daniel also reiterated his dissent from the expansion of the admiralty jurisdiction of the district courts. When the Court extended admiralty jurisdiction beyond the earlier limits set by the law of England,[127] Daniel joined in Justice Woodbury's dissent. He dissented on the objection that the extension of admiralty jurisdiction was an encroachment upon the right to jury trial and upon state judicial power. Within the year, Daniel dissented from the Court's extension of admiralty jurisdiction to cases involving contracts beyond the limits of seamen's wages, bottomry bonds, and contracts made to be executed upon the high seas.[128] The justice never withdrew from this dissent.[129]

As in his admiralty opinions, Daniel dissented from any threat to the right to trial by jury. In *Mitchell v. Harmony*[130] he dissented because the judge had commented upon the weight and efficiency of the evidence. In *Pennsylvania v. Ravena*,[131] he wrote that "it is the peculiar province of the jury to weigh the evidence, and to draw their own independent inferences from it, and the only legitimate corrective is to be found in the award of a new trial, or by a case agreed, or a demurrer of evidence." Daniel's justified dissents do not intertwine with his commitment to states' rights, but the singularity of his commitment is no less apparent.

Even though Justice Peter Daniel "for nineteen years fought single-handedly for his convictions, and to the day of his death yielded not one jot nor one title of what he believed to be right,"[132] his dissents are rarely remembered, and not one of his sacred doctrines has been retained as law. Conversely, history recognizes Justice Benjamin Curtis as the great "dissenting justice" on the Taney Court for his lone dissent in *Dred Scott v. Sandford*.[133] In retrospect, Daniel's dissent did not weaken the authority of the Court. Rather, that authority was strengthened by the failure of his dissents to impress themselves upon the judicial consciousness. Time has solidified the approval by the people of the dominant opinion of the Court in the commerce-clause cases.[134]

JOHN MARSHALL HARLAN: Confirmed as a Supreme Court justice on November 26, 1877, John Marshall Harlan sat upon the bench until five days before his death on October 15, 1911. During these nearly thirty-four years, the justice delivered 316 dissenting opinions; he was joined by at least three colleagues in 107. Altogether, Harlan dissented 380 times.[135] He is remembered for his wonderful, lone dissent in *Plessy v. Ferguson;*[136] indeed, this dissent dramatizes the strength of commitment underlying his sustained dissents from the Court's limitation of the due process clause or legislative authority and from its extension of "judicial legislation." The dissent in *Plessy* and many of his other sustained dissents were vindicated by Court reversals or legislative action.

Harlan was committed to the legislative authority of both the state and federal legislatures. He dissented from opinions of the Court that found state laws unconstitutional in a defense of the exercise of the valid police powers of the state. For example, he defended a state statute aimed at regulating common carriers that transported liquor intrastate;[137] a state law prohibiting the sale of intoxicating liquors except for certain purposes, even when applied to "original package" sales;[138] and a state law prohibiting the introduction of oleomargarine from another state and its sale in the original package.[139] In *Lochner v. New York*[140] he defended the state's maximum hour law for bakery workers. Harlan supported the power of the states to act as guardians of the public peace and morals in the areas of child labor laws, minimum and maximum wage laws, and control of intoxicating liquors. He delineated a fine boundary between valid and unconstitutional state police power under the interstate commerce clause or the due process clause of the fourteenth amendment.

Harlan would have denied the police power of the state if it interfered with his broad interpretation of the interstate commerce clause. He dissented from upholding a West Virginia law levying wharf duties;[141] from upholding a New York law that discriminated against Pennsylvania corporations;[142] and from upholding a New York statute that allowed discriminatory taxation of foreign corporations.[143]

Harlan's belief in the paramount authority of Congress to regulate interstate commerce motivated his dissent in support of the Sherman Anti-Trust Act of 1890. In his sole dissent (of more than ten thousand words) in *United States v. E. C. Knight,*[144] he supported the right of Congress to forbid monopolies in manufacturing because manufacturing would inevitably affect commerce. Harlan continued to support the anti-trust acts in dissent in *ICC v. Alabama M. Railway.*[145] And, in his last year on the Court, in a "concurring dissent" in *Standard Oil Co. v. United States*[146] and *United States v. American Tobacco Co.,*[147] he objected to the Court's narrowing of the antitrust acts by applying a standard of reasonableness. In line with his support of congressional power over interstate commerce, Harlan dissented in the *Employer Liability Cases.*[148]

His conviction that the entire Bill of Rights was made applicable to the states through the due process clause of the fourteenth amendment motivated his dissent in due process cases. Harlan dissented from the majority's upholding of an amendment to California's constitution that permitted criminal trials, even in capital punishment cases, upon affidavit without indictment;[149] from the Court's refusal to make the "cruel and unusual punishment" clause of the eighth amendment applicable through the due process clause of the fourteenth;[150] from the Court's refusal to hold Utah to the constitutional requirement of a jury of twelve;[151] from the Court's refusal to extend the right to immunity from self-incrimination to the states;[152] and from the Court's acceptance of an accused's waiver of trial by jury.[153] Through dissent in the *Insular Cases,* Harlan advocated the application of the Bill of Rights to the territories.[154]

Originally confronted with the question of equal rights by cases that challenged the Civil Rights Act of 1875, Harlan consistently dissented from the Court's findings that the act was unconstitutional. In the first such case to be heard after his appointment,[155] Harlan dissented from the Court's finding that the Federal Anti-Klan Act of 1874 was unconstitutional. However, he dissented on jurisdictional grounds and expressed no opinion on the merits. In the next cases to come before the Court, the *Civil Rights Cases,*[156] he clarified his dissent:

> With all respect for the opinion of others, I insist that the national legislature may, without transcending the limits of the Constitution, do for human liberty and the fundamental rights of American citizenship, what it did, with the sanction of the Court, for the protection of slavery and the rights of the master of fugitive slaves.[157]

In dissent, Harlan interpreted the Peonage Abolition Act of 1867 to include the indebtedness of the peon to the master, and he reasoned that the prior debts of two African American men were enough to make out a case of returning.[158] He also argued that a private conspiracy to forcibly prevent the employment of African Americans was a reinstitution of the "badges and incidents of slavery" and a denial of rights guaranteed by the thirteenth amendment.[159] He would have issued a writ of habeas corpus in the case of an African American being held under an Alabama statute that made refusal to work prima facie evidence of a fraudulent intent to violate a contract to work.[160] Harlan also dissented from the Court's refusal to apply the fifteenth amendment's prohibition against *state* interference with voting rights to *federal* elections.[161]

In another line of cases, the justice consistently dissented against state legislation that he considered violative of the due process or equal protection clauses of the fourteenth amendment. While his most significant dissents were in opposition to the denial of equal rights to African Americans, Harlan also opposed individual states' denial of equal rights to Chinese Americans[162] and Native Americans.[163]

Four transportation cases dealing with the separation of the races came before the Court during Harlan's tenure, and he dissented in all four. In 1890, he refused to uphold the prosecution of a railroad that maintained a route through several states but failed to provide separate accommodations for the races as required by the law of one of the states.[164] In 1896, in *Plessy v. Ferguson,*[165] Harlan wrote the powerful dissent from the Court's finding that a Louisiana law requiring the separation of the races on railway cars was a reasonable regulation under the fourteenth amendment. And he dissented without opinion in two later transportation cases.[166]

In 1908, in *Berea College v. Kentucky,*[167] Harlan refused to uphold a state law forbidding any person or corporation to operate a school "where persons of the white and Negro races are both received as pupils for instruction."[168] He dissented from the Court's distinction that the law, as applied to corporations rather than to private persons or associations, reserved to the legislature the right to amend the charters of corporations. Harlan argued that the law was clearly aimed at all private institutions teaching White and African American students and that it violated the equal protection clause of the fourteenth amendment:

> Have we become so inoculated with prejudice of race that an American government, professedly based on principles of freedom, and

charged with the protection of all citizens alike, can make distinctions between citizens in the matter of their voluntary meeting for innocent purposes simply because of their respective races? . . . Many other illustrations might be given to show the mischievous, not to say cruel, character of the statute in question, and how inconsistent such legislation is with the great principle of the equality of citizens before the law.[169]

Throughout his long service, John Marshall Harlan maintained a consistent dissent in support of civil rights.[170]

## The Twentieth Century

In an era marked by two world wars, the Great Depression, the New Deal, and the social upheaval of the 1960s and 1970s, it is perhaps not surprising that the decision of the Supreme Court should reflect a lack of unanimity among the brethren. As Justice William Brennan observed:

[F]rom our beginnings, a most important consequence of the constitutional separation of powers has been the American habit . . . of casting social, economic, philosophical, and political questions in the form of actions at law and suits in equity. In this way, important aspects of the most fundamental issues confronting our democracy end up ultimately in the Supreme Court for judicial determination. They are the issues upon which our society, consciously or unconsciously, is most deeply divided.[171]

Some have criticized the "fracturing" of opinion that has been characteristic of the Court in the twentieth century; others have found it to be inevitable.[172] But if dissent on the Court reflects divisions within American society, it may be that repeated dissents illustrate the country's deepest divisions. Our legal system is, after all, based upon precedents; a justice will repeat a dissent only when she or he feels strongly enough about a particular issue to sustain the dissent against a contrary precedent. I discuss here the repeated dissents of five twentieth-century justices of the Supreme Court: Oliver Wendell Holmes, Louis Dembitz Brandeis, Hugo LaFayette Black, William Orville Douglas, and the second John Marshall Harlan. Together, these men served on the Court from 1902, when Justice Holmes took his seat, until 1975, when Justice Douglas retired. Their dissents offer a unique view of three-quarters of a century of

American law and of a society undergoing vast changes. They give special resonance to the relentless dissents of Brennan and Marshall in capital punishment cases.

**OLIVER WENDELL HOLMES AND LOUIS BRANDEIS:** Appointed by President Theodore Roosevelt in 1902, Oliver Wendell Holmes came to the United States Supreme Court from a position as chief justice of Massachusetts' highest court. During his thirty-year tenure, Holmes published 975 opinions.[173] Of these, 873 were for the full Court, 30 were concurring opinions, and 72 were in dissent.[174] Holmes also dissented without opinion in 100 cases.[175] Louis Brandeis was appointed by President Woodrow Wilson in 1916 and served until 1939. In these twenty-two years, he wrote 455 opinions for the Court, 10 concurring opinions, and 65 dissenting opinions.[176] He dissented without opinion in 150 cases.[177]

During their years together on the Court, the two associate justices found themselves "companions in dissent."[178] As a journalist of the period observed: "Oliver Wendell Holmes and Louis Dembitz Brandeis have achieved a spiritual kinship that marks them off as a separate liberal chamber of the Supreme Court. On the great issues that go down to the fundamental differences in the philosophy of government these two are nearly always together; often they are together against the rest of the court."[179] The dissents for which Holmes and Brandeis are most noted are those concerning the first amendment and those concerning the ability of the states to enact social legislation. Their views in both areas differed from those of the majority of the Court. But neither man was a "voice in the wilderness."[180] They wrote for the Court or joined in majority opinions far more frequently than they dissented. Indeed, Justice Holmes prefaced his first dissent by saying that he generally found it "useless and undesirable, as a rule, to express dissent."[181] Brandeis, too, was somewhat reticent about dissenting; he disagreed with the Court in five cases during his first term but submitted only two formal dissents. He prefaced each with an apology, saying that the importance of the particular issues had induced him to write.[182]

Although the two justices often reached the same conclusion, they arrived at it by different paths. Holmes has been characterized as a "scholar and philosopher, whose cynicism about man and society made him contemptuous of the 'upward and onward' impulse of the reformer."[183] His detachment and skepticism "at times bordered on social apathy."[184] He voted to uphold the power of state legislatures to enact social legislation, but he did not pass on the wisdom of the laws thus enacted.

On the other hand, Brandeis—the inventor of the "Brandeis Brief"—was a "social crusader"[185] who looked beyond the immediate dispute to the underlying social implications.[186] Law, for him, was essentially an instrument of social policy.[187] Brandeis often felt deeply about the necessity for the social legislation he voted to uphold. Additionally, he emphasized that "[n]o law . . . can be understood without a full knowledge of the facts out of which it arises, and to which it is to be applied."[188] Having the "temperament of a teacher,"[189] he brought the techniques he had made famous in writing briefs to his role as a judge. He often used judicial opinions to instruct his fellow justices on the factual context of a particular legal issue.

Despite their distinct approaches, Holmes and Brandeis directed dissents toward what they deemed to be an abuse of judicial discretion—the Court's propensity in the first part of this century to invalidate state social legislation as being in violation of the fourteenth amendment. Their repeated dissents document a deep division on the Court.

*Lochner v. New York,*[190] already mentioned in connection with Justice Harlan, was the first of Holmes's notable dissents in this area. The case also provides a fitting bridge between the sustained dissenters of the nineteenth century and those of the twentieth. In *Lochner,* a five-justice majority struck down a New York statute that limited bakery workers to a ten-hour day,[191] finding the law to be "meddlesome interference with the rights of the individual"[192] that was prohibited by the fourteenth amendment. In his dissent (typical in its detached view), Holmes explained the proper role of the judiciary:

This case is decided upon an economic theory which a large part of the country does not entertain. If it were a question whether I agreed with that theory, I should desire to study it further and long before making up my mind. But I do not conceive that to be my duty, because I strongly believe my agreement or disagreement has nothing to do with the right of a majority to embody their opinions in law. . . . The Fourteenth Amendment does not enact Mr. Herbert Spencer's Social Statics.[193]

Soon after *Lochner,* Holmes's view in this particular area prevailed to some degree. The Court addressed the validity of several more state laws regulating working hours and upheld them as health measures.[194] Until 1937, the Court continued to refuse to regulate wage-contract labor *as such.*

In the area of minimum wage statutes, Holmes's view was not adopted so quickly. Initially, the Court affirmed an Oregon minimum wage law in 1917 in *Stettler v. O'Hara.*[195] But in *Adkins v. Children's Hospital,*[196] the justices struck down a similar law enacted by Congress for the District of Columbia, holding it to be an infringement of liberty of contract and thus violative of the fourteenth amendment. Brandeis did not sit;[197] Holmes dissented, saying that he found the power of Congress to enact such a law to be free from doubt.[198] "[P]retty much all law consists in forbidding men to do some things they want to do, and contract is no more exempt from law than other acts."[199] When the same issue later arose in *Murphy v. Sardell*[200] and *Donaham v. West-Nelson Mfg. Co.,*[201] Holmes, believing himself bound by *stare decisis,* acquiesced in the decisions of the Court that invalidated the minimum wage statutes involved. As the *Sardell* per curiam decision makes clear, "Mr. Justice Holmes requests that it be stated that his concurrence is solely upon the ground that he regards himself bound by the decision in *Adkins v. Children's Hospital.*"[202]

Brandeis, however, differed from Holmes in the precedential value he ascribed to *Adkins.* Perhaps because Brandeis believed strongly in the value of this type of legislation, he dissented without opinion in both *Sardell* and *Donham.* After Holmes had left the bench, Brandeis again dissented from the invalidation of a minimum wage law, joining the dissenting opinions of Justices Hughes and Stone in *Morehead v. Tipaldo.*[203]

Holmes and Brandeis dissented together in cases where the Court invalidated state legislation aimed at protective rates or price fixing. In *Adams v. Tanner,*[204] the Court addressed the validity of a state law making it a crime for an employment agency to collect fees from workers seeking jobs. A majority struck down the legislation as an infringement of the fourteenth amendment. Brandeis authored a dissenting opinion, in which Holmes joined,[205] that was typical of the style of the so-called Brandeis briefs. He posited that "[w]hether a measure relating to the public welfare is arbitrary or unreasonable, whether it has no substantial relation to the end proposed is obviously not to be determined by assumptions or by *a priori* reasoning. The judgment should be based upon a consideration of relevant facts, actual or possible."[206] Then, in great detail, Brandeis marshaled those facts. He cited numerous sources and reports, and he outlined the history of abuses by employment agencies that could reasonably lead a state to enact such legislation.

In a second case, the Court again struck down state legislation licensing employment agencies and fixing the prices they could charge.[207] Holmes and Brandeis once more dissented, joining in an opinion by Justice Stone, who largely repeated Brandeis's dissent in *Adams*.[208]

In *Tyson & Brother v. Banton,*[209] the Court invalidated a New York statute regulating the prices that a theater ticket agency could charge. Holmes's dissent was typical of his attitude toward such state legislation, and it contrasted sharply with the position of Brandeis in *Adams*.

> I think the proper course is to recognize that a state legislature can do whatever it sees fit to do unless it is restrained by some express prohibition in the Constitution of the United States or of the State, and that Courts should be careful not to extend such prohibitions beyond their obvious meaning by reading into them conceptions of public policy that the particular Court may happen to entertain. . . .[210]
>
> I am far from saying that I think this particular law a wise and rational provision. That is not my affair. But if the people of the State of New York speaking by the authorized voice say that they want it, I see nothing in the Constitution of the United States to prevent their having their will.[211]

Holmes and Brandeis continued to dissent together in other cases where the Court's majority struck down state legislation as violative of the fourteenth amendment. Thus, they dissented where the Court held unconstitutional as a deprivation of due process a state law regulating the weight of bread;[212] a state prohibition against the use of shoddy in bedding;[213] a statute requiring licensing of those selling steamship tickets to foreign countries;[214] and a statute regulating chain drugstores.[215] A majority of the Court found violations of equal protection where a state, in imposing taxes on gross receipts of taxicab operators, distinguished between corporations and individuals,[216] and where a state regulated all those who transported persons or property over a regular route on public highways for compensation.[217] In dissents, Holmes and Brandeis found that the states had ample authority to legislate in these areas.

The two justices did not always see eye to eye with respect to state social legislation. In his opinion for the majority in *Pennsylvania Coal Co. v. Mahon*,[218] Holmes struck down, as a taking of property, a statute that forbade mining coal where it would cause the soil under private dwellings and streets to sink. Brandeis dissented, finding the restriction to be a valid exercise of the police power, in that it prohibited a use dangerous to the public.[219]

Holmes and Brandeis also differed in two cases addressing the validity of state statutes prohibiting the teaching of languages other than English in primary schools.[220] Brandeis joined the majority, which held the laws to be invalid. In a characteristic dissent, Holmes observed that the states might reasonably want to ensure that all their students could speak English.[221]

The Court during this period also held unconstitutional attempts by Congress to enact social legislation. In two cases, a majority of the justices held that the constitutional grant of admiralty and maritime jurisdiction to federal courts precluded states from applying workers' compensation statutes to maritime accidents. After the Court decided the first case, *Southern Pacific Co. v. Jensen*,[222] Congress attempted to overrule it by enacting legislation specifically authorizing states to apply workmen's compensation laws to accidents subject to federal admiralty and maritime jurisdiction.[223] In the second case, *Knickerbocker Ice Co. v. Stewart*,[224] the Court invalidated the legislation as an unconstitutional delegation of congressional power. Holmes dissented in both cases, joined by Brandeis.[225] In *Knickerbocker*, Holmes stated: "I thought that claimants had those rights before. I think that they do now, both for the old reasons and for the new ones."[226]

The rights of workers to organize and to strike were important social issues of the day. In a series of cases involving those rights, Holmes and Brandeis again found themselves companions in dissent. Some cases involved the power of the states to legislate, while others involved federal legislation. In addition to *Lochner*, Holmes dissented in two labor cases before Brandeis was appointed to the Court. In *Adair v. United States*,[227] the majority held unconstitutional legislation enacted by Congress under the commerce clause that made it a criminal offense for an officer or agent of an interstate carrier to discharge an employee for belonging to a labor organization. The Court found the law to be a violation of due process under the fifth amendment. In dissent, Holmes found very limited interference with freedom of contract and concluded that the Constitution did not forbid the legislation.[228] In *Coppage v. Kansas*,[229] a majority of six justices invalidated a state law providing criminal penalties for requiring an employee to agree not to join a union. The Court held the law to be an infringement of the personal liberty and property of the employer, in violation of the fourteenth amendment. Holmes's dissent called for the overruling of *Adair*. He stated that a reasonable person could well believe that he could get a fair contract only by belonging to a union.[230]

Brandeis was on the Court when it considered later union cases. In *Hitchman Coal & Coke Co. v. Mitchell*[231] and a concurrent case, *Eagle Glass & Mfg. Co. v. Rowe*,[232] the Court upheld injunctions that barred union organizers from seeking to enroll workers who had signed "yellow dog contracts." These contracts made leaving a union or agreeing not to join one a condition of employment. The majority found that the employers were entitled to an injunction to protect their constitutional right to freedom of contract. Brandeis dissented, with Holmes concurring; they would have dissolved the injunctions.[233]

Holmes and Brandeis dissented when the Court held that anti-injunction provisions of the 1914 Clayton Anti-Trust Act did not forbid enjoining pickets from conducting a secondary boycott[234] and when the Court invalidated, on fourteenth amendment grounds, an Arizona statute that prohibited state courts from issuing injunctions against peaceful picketing.[235] In the latter case, Holmes made perhaps his most emphatic statement concerning the Court's use of the fourteenth amendment to invalidate state legislation:

> There is nothing that I more deprecate than the use of the Fourteenth Amendment beyond the absolute compulsion of its words to prevent the making of social experiments than an important part of the community desires, in the insulated chambers afforded by the several states, even though the experiments may seem futile or even noxious to me and to those whose judgment I most respect.[236]

In *Bedford Cut Stone Co. v. Journeyman Stone Cutters' Association*,[237] the majority upheld an injunction to restrain a boycott on the grounds that the union was acting in restraint of trade in violation of the Sherman Anti-Trust Act. Brandeis's dissent, in which Holmes concurred, stated that the Sherman act prohibited only unreasonable restraints on trade and that, given the facts, the union's actions were not unreasonable.[238]

The two justices are equally well known for their dissents involving the first amendment. A series of freedom of speech cases arose under the Espionage Act of 1917 and state criminal anarchy and syndicalism laws. In weighing the first amendment interests of the individual against the legitimate interests of government, Holmes and Brandeis often arrived at a different balance than did the majority of the Court. They sometimes found a right to dissent where their brethren instead found criminal action.[239]

*Abrams v. United States*,[240] was Holmes's first dissent in a freedom of speech case.[241] In an opinion in which Brandeis concurred, he concluded that the defendants had been sentenced to twenty years in prison "for the publishing of two leaflets that I believe the defendants had as much right to publish as the Government has to publish the Constitution of the United States now vainly invoked by them."[242] And it was in *Abrams* that Holmes first presented his "marketplace of ideas" theory:

> [W]hen men have realized that time has upset many fighting faiths, they may come to believe even more than they believe the very foundations of their own conduct that the ultimate good desired is better reached by free trade in ideas—that the best test of truth is the power of the thought to get itself accepted in the competition of the market, and that truth is the only ground upon which their wishes safely can be carried out. That at any rate is the theory of our Constitution.[243]

After *Abrams,* Holmes joined in two Brandeis dissents reaffirming the position Holmes had staked out in that case.[244] In one of these, *Pierce v. United States,* Brandeis argued that to give a jury the power to punish statements of conclusion or opinion by declaring them to be false statements of fact was to deny small political parties the freedom to criticize and to discuss issues.[245] In a later case, *Gitlow v. New York,*[246] Holmes and Brandeis dissented when the Court upheld the conviction of a prominent socialist who had published a "Left-wing Manifesto." In his dissent,

Holmes maintained that the danger posed by such a publication was not sufficiently "clear and present."[247]

The two justices disagreed in *Gilbert v. Minnesota*,[248] where the majority sustained a conviction under a state statute that made it unlawful to interfere with or discourage enlistment in the military. Holmes concurred in the result, presumably because he felt the decisions of the Court with which he had disagreed were not binding. Brandeis dissented, advancing a new rationale (in which no other justice fully joined) for imposing greater restraints on state than federal power.[249]

Holmes and Brandeis both dissented from the majority's conclusions in two cases involving the government's control of the mails. In *Milwaukee Publishing Co. v. Burleson*,[250] the postmaster general denied second class mailing privileges, as opposed to other available rates, to a newspaper published by a prominent socialist agitator. Holmes's dissent pointed out that the Espionage Act gave the postmaster general a right to refuse only those editions of the newspaper that actually violated the act, not the entire publication.[251] Brandeis, analyzing the effect of the order, found that the postmaster general had no authority essentially to deny circulation of a newspaper because he thought it likely to violate a postal law in the future.[252] A year later, in *Leach v. Carlile*,[253] the government issued an order prohibiting the delivery of mail to Leach on the grounds that he had fraudulently advertised a patent medicine. A majority of the Court sustained the order as within the postmaster general's authority. Holmes and Brandeis dissented, on the ground that the order constituted prior restraint prohibited by the first amendment.[254]

In three naturalization cases, the two dissenters joined forces again. In *United States v. Schwimmer*,[255] *United States v. MacIntosh*,[256] and *United States v. Bland*,[257] three aliens were denied citizenship on the basis of issues related to a required oath of allegiance: Schwimmer was a pacifist who refused to bear arms; MacIntosh was a divinity professor at Yale who refused to promise in advance to bear arms unless the war was morally justified; and Bland was willing to take the oath only if it included the proviso "as far as my conscience as a Christian will allow." Holmes said in *Schwimmer* that the adequacy of the oath of allegiance was not affected by Schwimmer's statement that she would not bear arms.[258] Holmes and Brandeis concurred in the dissenting opinions of Chief Justice Hughes in

*MacIntosh*[259] and *Bland,*[260] where Hughes concluded that Congress had not made the promise to bear arms a condition of citizenship.

It is a commonplace that many of the ideas that Holmes and Brandeis expressed in dissent during their tenure on the Supreme Court have since become the law of the land. Nonetheless, the list remains impressive, standing as eloquent testimony to the value of dissenting opinions.[261] The repeated dissents of Holmes and Brandeis demonstrate a belief that "rights of property and the liberty of the individual must be remolded, from time to time, to meet the changing needs of society."[262] History has supported that belief.

**HUGO BLACK AND WILLIAM O. DOUGLAS:** After his Court-packing plan failed, President Franklin Roosevelt still found himself able to appoint two new justices relatively quickly. The first of these was Hugo Black, who was appointed in 1937.[263] He had served in the United States Senate from Alabama for ten years, where he had ardently supported New Deal legislation. During his thirty-four years on the Court, Black wrote 481 opinions for the majority, 88 concurring opinions, and 310 dissenting opinions.[264] He also concurred without opinion in 152 cases and dissented without opinion 307 times.[265]

The second justice named by Roosevelt (in 1939) was William O. Douglas, a corporate law expert who had headed the Securities and Exchange Commission.[266] At the age of forty, he was at the time the youngest justice ever appointed. When he retired thirty-six years later, in 1975, he had written 524 opinions of the Court, 154 concurring opinions, and a startling 486 dissents.[267] Douglas also concurred in 96 cases without opinion and dissented without opinion in 309 cases.[268]

Justices Black and Douglas, like Holmes and Brandeis, were very often companions in dissent.[269] However, as even a cursory inspection of voting records reveal, their dissents were very different from those of their two predecessors. Unlike Holmes and Brandeis, Black and Douglas were prolific dissenters who showed no reticence about dissenting. Black's dissents (with and without opinion) almost equaled in number the cases where he either concurred with or wrote the majority opinion of the Court. Douglas's dissents came closer to exceeding in number the concurrences and majority opinions he authored.

Both men maintained some dissents that others considered to be quixotic. For example, in *Connecticut General Life Insurance Co. v. Johnson*,[270] Black disregarded a half century of precedent[271] and found that corporations were not "persons" within the meaning of the fourteenth amendment. Douglas joined him in this "iconoclasm"[272] in *Wheeling Steel Corp. v. Glander*.[273] In dissent, he claimed that the fourteenth amendment was not meant to provide due process or equal protection rights to corporations.[274]

These two cases suggest that neither justice felt bound by the doctrine of *stare decisis* when they disagreed with the majority of the Court. One commentator said that "the effort to advance the cause of personal beliefs has been endemic with Justices Black and Douglas, and its path has been marked with monuments of disregard for precedent."[275] Indeed, Douglas plainly stated that he thought the claims of *stare decisis* to be tenuous, especially in the area of constitutional adjudication.[276] But even though Black and Douglas were alike in paying scant heed to precedent, their judicial philosophies were quite distinct. Like Holmes and Brandeis before them, they often arrived at the same conclusion by different routes.

Black was an "absolutist" or "strict constructionist" who purported to apply the words and phrases of the Constitution with "doctrinaire rigidity."[277] He found *personal* rights to be absolutely guaranteed by the Constitution; and he deplored the process of balancing those rights that was often engaged in by the rest of the Court:

> Of course the decision to provide a constitutional safeguard for a particular right, such as the fair trial requirements of the Fifth and Sixth Amendments and the right of free speech protection of the First, involves a balancing of conflicting interests. . . . I believe, however, that the Framers themselves did this balancing when they wrote the Constitution and the Bill of Rights. They appreciated the risks involved and they decided that certain rights should be guaranteed regardless of these risks. Courts have neither the right nor the power to review this original decision of the Framers and to attempt to make a different evaluation of the importance of the rights granted in the Constitution. Where conflicting values exist in the field of individual liberties protected by the Constitution, that document settles the conflict, and its policy should not be changed without constitutional amendments by the people in the manner provided by the people.[278]

At the same time, Black concluded from his reading of the words of the Constitution that the necessary and proper clause and the commerce clause left to the government the authority and the responsibility for balancing conflicts between *property* rights and the general welfare.[279] The function of the Court, then, was to separate out and distinguish those rights held absolutely from actions that could properly be regulated.[280] Thus, when Black believed a precedent "incorrectly" deprived an individual of a constitutionally guaranteed right, he consistently voted to reject precedent and uphold the right.

Where Black found guidance in the words of the Constitution, Douglas believed that document left wide gaps which could only be filled by making policy choices. "Precedents are made or unmade not on logic and history alone. The choices left by the generality of a constitution relate to policy."[281] Douglas found that such choices "must be made on the basis not of abstractions but on the realities of modern . . . life."[282] He wrote that "it is better that we make our own history than be governed by the dead."[283] Douglas believed that any search for a static security in the law was misguided.[284] Instead, security was to be attained through constant reevaluation. He quoted with full approval the words of a judge who wrote "that the duty of every judge and every court [is] to examine its own decisions . . . without fear, and to revise them without reluctance."[285]

Black and Douglas repeatedly joined in dissent in first amendment cases. Consistent with his belief concerning constitutionally guaranteed personal rights, Black found first amendment protections to be absolute;[286] in this area Douglas agreed.[287] Their belief has not been shared by other justices. Thus, they repeatedly dissented against the majority's insistence upon weighing first amendment rights of individuals against the legitimate interests of the government to determine whether speech was protected. Black and Douglas insisted in their dissents that freedom of speech could not be abridged by such balancing.[288]

In a series of cases beginning with *Roth v. United States,*[289] the two justices consistently dissented against the majority's finding that obscenity was unprotected by the first amendment.[290] In *Byrne v. Karalexis,* Douglas protested against the exception the majority made for obscenity:[291]

> If "obscenity" can be carved out of the first amendment, what other like exceptions can be created? Is "sacrilege" also beyond the pale?

Are utterances or publications made with "malice" unprotected? How about "seditious" speech or articles? . . . We forget today that under our constitutional system neither Congress nor the States have any power to pass on the value, the propriety, the Americanism,, the soundness of any idea or expression. It is that insulation from party or majoritarian control provided by the first amendment—not our gross national product or mass production or pesticides or space ships or nuclear arsenal—that distinguishes our society from the other plentary regimes.[292]

Black and Douglas also dissented when the Court upheld laws they believed imposed prior restraints on potentially "obscene" materials.[293]

The investigations of the House Un-American Activities Committee generated a series of first amendment cases that were reviewed by the Court. In *Barenblatt v. United States*,[294] a witness before the committee refused to answer questions concerning past and present affiliations with the Communist party. The witness's conviction for contempt of Congress was upheld by a majority of the Court. Black dissented, joined by Douglas and Chief Justice Warren.[295] Black argued that the conviction violated the first amendment freedoms of speech and association, as well as the fifth amendment right to due process.[296] All three justices repeated their dissent in subsequent similar cases.[297]

A decade earlier, Black and Douglas had dissented where the Court upheld loyalty programs against first amendment challenge. In *American Communications Association v. Douds*,[298] Black dissented when the Court affirmed the validity of an executive order issued by President Truman establishing a loyalty security program. Although Douglas did not sit for *Douds*, he later said of the security hearings spawned by the order: "Those hearings were primarily concerned with one's thoughts, ideas, beliefs and convictions. They were the most blatant violations of the first amendment we have ever known."[299] Black and Douglas both dissented in two later loyalty program cases, maintaining that the programs violated employees' first amendment rights.[300]

In another line of cases, Black and Douglas consistently dissented and found violations of first amendment rights when states refused to license bar applicants because of their beliefs. They dissented ni *In re Summers*,[301] where the Court upheld a state's refusal to admit an applicant to the bar because he was a conscientious objector to war. Although the applicant was willing to take the required oath to support the state constitution, the state nevertheless found that he could not meet the requirement. The Court held there was no denial of his constitutional rights under the first and fourteenth amendments. In two other cases,[302] the Court upheld the right of states to refuse bar admission to applicants who refused to answer questions about their affiliations and beliefs. The applicants argued that the questions were a violation of their first amendment rights; in dissent, Black and Douglas agreed.

In two cases, Black dissented against what he saw as another deprivation of free speech—compelled support of political causes. In *International Association of Machinists v. Street,*[303] union members sued to enjoin the use of union funds for political purposes. The Court did not reach the constitutional issue, finding that the union had no authority to spend a member's money for political purposes over the member's objection. While Douglas concurred in the majority opinion,[304] Black found that compelled contributions to promote political causes were a deprivation of free speech.[305] He repeated his dissent in *Lathrop v. Donahue,*[306] where the Court dismissed a lawyer's action to recover dues paid to an integrated state bar. The state bar admitted that the funds were used for political purposes. On this occasion, Douglas joined Black's dissent.[307]

With respect to the sixth amendment, Black and Douglas insisted in a series of dissents that defendants in criminal contempt proceedings were entitled to a jury trial.[308] After the Court adopted the view that some defendants in such cases were entitled to a jury trial, but only where the punishment for contempt exceeded six months, Black and Douglas continued to dissent.[309] Black wrote:

> I cannot say what is and what is not a "petty crime." I certainly believe, however, that where punishment of as much as six months *can* be imposed, I would not classify the offense as "petty" if that means that people tried for it are to be tried as if we had no Bill of Rights.[310]

Both Black and Douglas stubbornly asserted that the fourteenth amendment makes the protections of the Bill of Rights entirely applicable to the states. This point of view has not prevailed, although the Court has now "selectively incorporated" most of those rights into the fourteenth amendment.[311] Thus, before the fifth amendment was made applicable to the states in *Malloy v. Hogan*,[312] Black and Douglas joined in dissent where they believed that the privilege against self-incrimination should be extended to state proceedings. Similarly, they dissented when the Court determined that testimony compelled in state proceedings could be used in federal prosecutions,[313] and they claimed that the right not to be placed in double jeopardy should also be made applicable to the states.[314] In a related series of cases, the two justices dissented where the Court held that Congress could impose a gambling tax and compel disclosures that would incriminate the taxpayer under state law.[315]

Black and Douglas also steadfastly maintained that the sixth amendment should apply to the states through the fourteenth. Beginning with *Betts v. Brady*,[316] they dissented in cases where defendants in state courts were denied the right to counsel.[317] After the Court overruled *Betts* in *Gideon v. Wainwright*,[318] Black and Douglas joined Justice Stewart in two dissents from denial of certiorari, where he called for the Court to clarify whether the right to counsel was to rely merely on what label—felony or misdemeanor—a state gave a particular offense.[319]

Black and Douglas were not initially in agreement about whether the federal exclusionary rule, which barred illegally seized evidence fro federal trials, should apply to the states.[320] Douglas believed the rule to be binding upon states through the fourth and fourteenth amendments. In *Wolf v. Colorado* and later cases,[321] he dissented from the Court's holdings that the exclusionary rule was not applicable to trials in state courts. In *Wolf,* he stated that the fourth amendment had no effective sanction in the absence of such a rule.[322] Black, on the other hand, concurred in *Wolf,* saying:

> I should be for reversal of this case if I thought the Fourth Amendment not only prohibited "unreasonable searches and seizures," but also, of itself, barred the use of evidence so unlawfully obtained. But I agree with what appears to be a plain implication of the Court's opinion that the federal exclusionary rule is not a command of the Fourth Amendment but is a judicially created rule of evidence which Congress might negate.[323]

On the occasions when the Court overruled prior cases and determined that certain rights were in fact constitutionally guaranteed, or were made applicable to the states through the fourteenth amendment, Black and Douglas dissented when the Court refused to apply those rights retroactively. Thus, they dissented where the Court refused to apply *Mapp v. Ohio*[324] retroactively.[325] Black said in dissent:

> This different treatment of Miss Mapp and Linkletter points up at once the arbitrary and discriminatory nature of the judicial contrivance utilized here to break the promise of *Mapp* by keeping all people in jail who are unfortunate enough to have had their unconstitutional convictions affirmed before June 19, 1961.[326]

They dissented where the Court held the right to a jury trial in state courts to be prospective only,[327] and they dissented[328] again when the Court held that *Miranda v. Arizona*[329] applied only prospectively. Douglas, but not Black, dissented in *Desist v. United States*,[330] where the Court held that *Katz v. United States*[331] would not be applied retroactively.

Given his record as an adamant upholder of personal rights, Black's dissents in a series of civil rights cases seem surprising at first glance. Douglas did not join his colleague in these dissents, and the cases document the difference in attitude between the two toward appropriate remedies for racial discrimination. During the 1960s, the Court reviewed a series of convictions under state trespass laws where the defendants had participated in picketing or sit-ins to protest racial discrimination. Black, joined by Justices Harlan and White, dissented when the Court voted to reverse trespass convictions in *Griffin v. Maryland*[332] and to vacate and remand *Bell v. Maryland*.[333] In the latter case, Black wrote that the convictions should be confirmed because the fourteenth amendment did not prohibit privately owned restaurants from choosing their customers and because the constitutionality of the state trespass law was not at issue.[334]

In a companion case to *Bell*,[335] the same three justices dissented when the majority held that a new construction given to a state statute and applied retroactively by the state supreme court violated the defendants' due process rights under the fourteenth amendment. In yet another case, where the defendants were convicted of both criminal trespass and breach of the peace, Black wrote the majority opinion reversing the breach of peace conviction—but he dissented with White and Harlan against the Court's reversal of the trespass conviction.[336] He also dissented in two instances where the Court applied the 1964 Civil Rights Act retroactively to reverse convictions for criminal trespass.[337] The Court found that the act created federal rights that took precedence over conflicting state law. In dissent, Black stated his point of view plainly. He determined that the civil rights act could not give

> persons who are unlawfully refused service a "right" to take the law into their own hands by sitting down and occupying the premises for as long as they choose to stay. I think one of the chief purposes of the 1964 Civil Rights Act was to take such disputes out of the streets and restaurants and into the courts, which Congress has granted power to provide an adequate and orderly judicial remedy.[338]

Douglas, too, consistently dissented in a politically controversial area where Black, his usual ally, did not join him. During the Vietnam War, Douglas dissented where the Court refused to consider cases challenging the legality of both the war and the military draft. Douglas would have addressed the issues raised in the challenges—that the draft was illegal because Congress had not declared war and that the war was illegal because the United States had violated its treaty obligations.[339]

The habit of dissent apparent in the judicial records of Black and Douglas has raised the ire of some[340] and received the approbation of others.[341] It is impossible to deny, however, that in many cases they managed to garner support for their dissenting views and eventually overrule precedents with which they disagreed. In an article on the dissents of Douglas, Professor Countryman stated that it is well known that during the justice's time on the Court most of the dissents of Holmes and Brandeis became the law—but that it is "less well appreciated" that "during the same period of time even more of the dissents of Justice Douglas have become the law."[342]

Louis Brandeis once wrote in dissent in *Burnet v. Coronado Oil and Gas*[343] that "[s]tare decisis is usually a wise policy, because in most matters it is more important that the applicable rule of law be settled than that it be settled right." The repeated dissents of Hugo Black and William O. Douglas are a most emphatic rejection of that point of view. They believed that it is, in fact, of the utmost importance that the law be "settled right," particularly where constitutionally guaranteed rights of individuals are at risk.

**JOHN MARSHALL HARLAN (THE SECOND):** The second Justice Harlan was appointed to the Supreme Court by President Eisenhower in 1955.

During his sixteen-year tenure, he wrote 166 opinions of the Court, 143 concurring opinions—and 242 dissenting opinions.[344] He also concurred without opinion 67 times and dissented without opinion in 58 cases.[345]

In many ways, Harlan represents a position directly opposite that of Douglas. Where Douglas believed courts should constantly reevaluate their positions and change the law without reluctance, Harlan was a "constitutional conservative" who frequently disagreed with the "innovations" of his fellow justices on the Warren Court.[346] A large part of this attitude stemmed from his position that the Supreme Court was "not designed to be, nor should it ever be, a tool to be used to remedy the country's social and political ills."[347] In its turn this conviction grew out of his profound belief in the concept of federalism as a means of diffusing power at the national level and between the federal and state governments.[348] Harlan believed that the states should be allowed to "solve their own problems, determine their own policies, govern their own court systems, and establish their own criminal justice procedures."[349] Thus, the proper role of the Supreme Court in the arena of state law ought to be quite limited. In *Shapiro v. Thompson,* he voiced his concern with the direction he saw the Court taking:

> Today's decision, it seems to me, reflects to an unusual degree the current notion that this Court possesses a peculiar wisdom all its own whose capacity to lead this Nation out of its present troubles is contained only by the limits of judicial ingenuity in contriving new constitutional principles to meet each problem as it arises. For anyone who, like myself, believes that it is an essential function of this Court to maintain the constitutional divisions between state and federal authority and among the three branches of the Federal government, today's decision is a step in the wrong direction.[350]

As a proponent of judicial restraint, Harlan was very respectful of precedent; indeed, he has been called the "modern Court's leading accommodationist."[351] Thus, his repeated dissents have a different texture from those of Black and Douglas, or even of Holmes and Brandeis. Although Harlan often dissented from what he saw as the Court's improvidently broad interpretations of the law, most often he would afterward accord at least "interim allegiance" to the Court's position if he could not distinguish the precedent.[352] On the other hand, even though he felt bound by the principle of *stare decisis,* Harlan often spelled out the defects he saw in the Court's position in a concurring opinion, rather than joining the opinion of the majority. To the extent that he felt bound by precedent, he sometimes found himself dissenting against the majority when he believed they were not adhering to their own precedent, even though he had originally disagreed with it.[353]

As one might expect, Harlan strongly opposed the total incorporation theory of the fourteenth amendment. Not only did he reject the belief of Black and Douglas that all of the protections of the Bill of Rights were made applicable to the states by the fourteenth amendment; he also disagreed with the Court's use of selective incorporation, where a specific right or guarantee was made applicable to the states. In place of the incorporation theory, Harlan employed a test of "fundamental fairness": a state's action afforded due process to the individual if it complied with notions of "basic fairness" within the United States legal tradition.[354]

As a result of his belief that the states should be able to handle their concerns differently than the federal government, Harlan dissented in a series of cases that held specific rights in the first eight amendments to be applicable to the states through the fourteenth amendment.[355] He dissented initially when the particular right was made applicable to the states; he dissented again when he considered the Court to have been misguided in extending that right. For example, Harlan dissented in *Duncan v. Louisiana*[356] and *Bloom v. Illinois,*[357] the initial cases where the Court held that state defendants have the right to a jury trial.[358] He dissented again in *Baldwin v. New York*[359] against extending the right to trials for misdemeanors punishable by a prison term of one year. In *Baldwin,* he called upon the Court to overrule *Duncan* and to "reconsider the 'incorporation' doctrine before its leveling tendencies further retard development in the field of criminal procedure by stifling flexibility in the States and by discarding the possibility of federal leadership by example."[360]

Sometimes, however, Harlan felt bound to apply as precedent a case with which he had initially disagreed.[361] In *Griffin v. California,*[362] both the trial court and counsel had commented on a criminal defendant's failure to testify, and the Supreme Court reversed the conviction on the grounds that the fifth amendment was made applicable to the states through the fourteenth. Harlan concurred in the opinion "with great reluctance," saying that "for me the decision exemplifies the creeping paralysis with which this Court's recent adoption of the 'incorporation' doctrine is infecting the operation of the federal system."[363] In a related series of incorporation cases, Harlan wrote concurrences where he agreed with the result but argued against the policy of incorporation through the fourteenth amendment. He instead applied his test of fundamental fairness.[364]

The area of voting rights is another where Harlan's strong belief in federalism led him to oppose the position adopted by a majority of the Court. In 1946, in *Colegrove v. Green*,[365] Justice Frankfurter wrote an opinion for the Court holding that the malapportionment of congressional districts in Illinois was a non-justiciable issue that should be left to the states to correct through the political process.[366] In 1962 the Court overruled *Colegrove* in *Baker v. Carr*[367] and held that state malapportionment of voting districts is a deprivation of equal protection under the fourteenth amendment. Harlan wrote a dissenting opinion arguing that no infringement of fourteenth amendment rights had been demonstrated.[368] He reiterated his views that the states should be free to deal with their own problems and that the Court was overstepping its bounds by trying to solve social ills through judicial activism:

> [T]here is nothing in the Federal Constitution to prevent a State, acting not irrationally, from choosing any electoral legislative structure it thinks best suited to the interests, temper, and customs of its people. . . .[369]
>
> The fact that the appellants have been unable to obtain political redress of their asserted grievances appears to be regarded as a matter which should lead the Court to stretch to find some basis for judicial intervention. While the Equal Protection Clause is invoked, the opinion for the Court notably eschews explaining how, consonant with past decisions, the undisputed facts in this case can be considered to show a violation of that constitutional provision. . . . [W]hat the Court is doing reflects more an adventure in judicial experimentation than a solid piece of constitutional adjudication.[370]

Harlan repeated his dissent as the Court continued to find violations of equal protection in voting district cases; with respect to the election of trustees of a junior college district;[371] the general election of county commissioners;[372] the election of state legislators;[373] primary elections for United States senators and statewide offices;[374] and congressional districting.[375] However, the justice characteristically deferred to the majority where he believed that a prior case necessarily determined the result, however little he liked that particular outcome.[376]

One other area where Harlan repeatedly dissented has already been discussed: he joined Justices Black and White in dissenting against the Court's decisions in a series of civil rights sit-in cases where defendants were convicted under state trespass laws. Here, too, one sees Harlan's preference for federalism. For the most part, however, he did not repeatedly dissent on the same issue; instead, he tended to use concurring opinions to insist that his own point of view was the correct one. The great deference Harlan gave to the principle of *stare decisis* meant that even his dissents were often dictated by his strong belief that a judge should follow precedent. He dissented where he believed that his fellow justices were ignoring that principle.

Harlan's judicial philosophy has been compared to the point of view expressed by Herbert Wechsler in his famous "neutral principles" speech.[377] The comparison is apt. Wechsler offered a constitutional theory based not on content but on procedure. He viewed the law as a process of "reasoned explanation"[378] that could not properly be result oriented. The structure of Harlan's dissents evinces the primacy of procedure in his judicial philosophy. For the justice, the existence of a clear precedent obligated a judge to acquiesce in the Court's decisions, even where he was personally opposed to a particular outcome. Thus, Harlan's dissents epitomize Wechsler's idea that the decisions of the Court ought not to rest on immediate results; decisions are to "be framed and tested as an exercise of reason and not merely as an act of willfulness or will."[379]

## Modern Times

More recently, statistics of Supreme Court decisions show that individual expression has become more prevalent than unanimity. For the first time in the record of the Court, the justices, at the October 1943 Term, were in disagreement more than in agreement in cases with opinions.[380] And, in 1980, Archibald Cox wrote that "the most striking aspect of the work of the Burger Court has been the insistence of the Justices upon presenting individual views, and their persistence in advancing those views even after a majority has disagreed. This is not a new development, but the trend has been more pronounced."[381] Statistics for the last years of the Burger Court and the first years of the Rehnquist Court show neither a reversal of this trend nor any great disparity in the numbers. In its last two Terms, in cases decided by full opinion, the Burger Court was unanimous in 31.8 percent of the cases, while dissenting opinions were written in 59.6 percent of the cases during 1984;[382] the Court was unanimous in 18.9 percent of the cases, and dissenting opinions were written in 71 percent of the cases, during 1985.[383] In the first two Terms of the Rehnquist Court, in cases decided by full opinion, the Court was unanimous in 18.4 percent of the cases, while dissenting opinions were written in 74.3 percent of the cases during 1986;[384] the Court was unanimous in 35.9 percent of the cases, and dissenting opinions were written in 56.3 percent of the cases, during 1987.[385] These cases and statistics record a history of the tradition of individual expression and individual responsibility.

Although a unanimous opinion is the traditionally accepted ideal of practice for the United States Supreme Court, the reality of individual expression has been traditionally accommodated by justification in significant or constitutional decisions and has persisted to the point of prevalence. The accommodation of unanimity to individuality is not clearly delineated,[386] but former chief justice Charles Evans Hughes has described this tradition:

> There are some who think it desirable that dissents should not be disclosed as they detract from the force of the judgment. Undoubtedly, they do. When unanimity can be obtained without sacrifice of conviction, it strongly commends the decision to public confidence. But unanimity which is merely formal, which is recorded at the expense of strong conflicting views, is not desirable in a court of last resort, whatever may be the effect on public opinion at the time. This is so because what must ultimately sustain the court in public confidence is the character and independence of the judges. They are not simply to decide cases, but to decide them as they think they should be decided, and while it may be regrettable that they cannot always agree, it is better that their independence should be maintained and recognized than that unanimity should be secured through its sacrifice.

# Legitimacy in Theory

▼    ▼    ▼

**A** JUSTICE'S repeated dissent must be seen as a call for change in the law—the justice demonstrates her unwillingness to accommodate her view to the law as it is espoused by the majority. The more frequently the dissent is repeated, the more clearly does the justice signal her belief that the law ought to be different. Her refusal to adapt her view even temporarily to the majority position underscores the strength of her conviction.[1] As Justice Brandeis said, "[I]t is usually more important that a rule of law be settled than that it be settled right."[2] The repeat dissenter, however, believes that on this particular issue it is more important that the law be settled "right" than that it be settled.[3] This chapter will examine the jurisprudential ramifications of the relentless dissents of Justices Brennan and Marshall against the death penalty. It will also explore whether such dissents, calling as they do for a change in the law, are a legitimate use of judicial power in a democratic society.

In dissenting against the imposition of the death penalty under all circumstances, Justices Brennan and Marshall flew in the face of clear precedent.[4] In this country, the death penalty has been used to punish crimes since pre-Revolutionary times.[5] The 1972 decision in *Furman v. Georgia*[6] left the constitutionality of the death penalty temporarily in doubt, but in 1976 the Supreme Court squarely upheld the death penalty in *Gregg v. Georgia*.[7] The majority agreed that the imposition of the death penalty under a revised Georgia statute did not constitute cruel and unusual punishment under the eighth and fourteenth amendments.[8] Since *Gregg,* Justices Brennan and Marshall voted against the death penalty in virtually all cases, including every capital case where certiorari was denied. As already mentioned, their dissents often began by repeating that the justices were "adhering to [their] view that the death penalty is in all cases cruel and unusual punishment prohibited by the eighth and fourteenth amendments."[9] Thus, the two justices sought a great change in the law as it existed, by means of judicial decision.

A sustained dissent raises jurisprudential issues inseparable from those presented by the overruling of precedent. Both the repeat dissenter and the majority that overrules a precedent depart from any strict formulation of the doctrine of *stare decisis*. Yet a sustained dissent raises a distinct issue as well. There is a continuing tension between the dissenter's stance and the established precedent. A justice who repeats a dissent is necessarily aware that she is not changing the law. Indeed, it must have been apparent to Brennan and Marshall that the Court's decision on the constitutionality of the death penalty was not likely to be reversed anytime soon. Thus, it is the justice's paradoxical duty to respect the very law that she would change if only she could gather enough votes.[10] Brennan recognized the "unquestioned duty to obey and respect the law"[11] while arguing that there is no obligation to subsume one's own views under those of the majority.[12] Marshall explicitly deferred to the law in his call upon lawyers, judges, and public officials to work within the existing system to provide those facing the death penalty with the same opportunity to present their best case to the courts as noncapital defendants receive.[13]

What, then, is a sufficient reason for a judge to continue to dissent against the law she is bound to respect? When is it more important to have the law settled "right" than to have it "settled" right or wrong? Lord Denning pinpointed the reason when he wrote: "I was reluctant to dissent. But in the last resort I did so. It was for my own peace of mind. So long as I did what I thought was just, I was content. I could sleep at night. But if I did what was unjust, I stayed awake worrying."[14] The answer lies in the judge's conception of the demands of justice. But as the jurisprudence of judges varies, where justice lies in a given case inevitably will depend on the individual judge.[15] Thus, when the repeat dissenter says "Here I draw the line,"[16] she gives us an opportunity to examine her jurisprudence and to determine what, for her, constitutes ultimate justice. And, perhaps just as important, the very fact that a judge repeats a dissent on a particular issue offers insights into how she views the Court's role in achieving justice within our legal system.

The repeated dissents of Brennan and Marshall against the death penalty raise perennial questions of legal theory. One is: What is the role of morality in the law? The issue of the death penalty is of course charged with moral overtones; some commentators viewed the position of Justices Brennan and Marshall as a moralistic stance.[17] But in claiming that the death penalty is *unconstitutional,* they were making a *legal* statement. For Brennan, the Constitution itself encompassed a moral standard; the phrase "cruel and unusual" holds within it certain principles that place constraints upon the state.[18] Primary among these principles is that a punishment must not be so severe that it degrades human dignity.[19] The state fails to respect human dignity when it imposes the death penalty.[20]

It is hardly controversial to say that the law may encompass moral values.[21] But that Justice Brennan continued (despite the Court's decision in *Gregg*), to say that "cruel and unusual" means something other than what the majority of his fellow justices determined that it did said something about his view of the moral element in law. The law is not simply, as Justice Holmes put it, "[t]he prophecies of what courts will do in fact."[22] For Brennan, notwithstanding precedent to the contrary, the moral element endured.[23]

But if law is a repository of moral values, then whose moral values ought it to reflect? One theory is that because ours is a democratic society the law ought to reflect the "conventional" morality of the majority.[24] Under this view, the fact that thirty-five states reenacted death penalty statutes in the aftermath of *Furman*[25] would be a clear demonstration of the constitutionality of capital punishment.

One criticism leveled at the conventional-morality theory, as applied to constitutional adjudication, is that it would leave the protection of minorities' rights in precisely the wrong hands.[26] "[I]t makes no sense to employ the value judgments of the majority as a vehicle for protecting minorities from the value judgments of the majority."[27] In *West Virginia State Board of Education v. Barnette,* the Court itself recognized that "[t]he very purpose of a Bill of Rights was to withdraw certain subjects from the vicissitudes of political controversy, to place them beyond the reach of majorities and officials and to establish them as legal principles to be applied by the courts."[28]

Neither Brennan nor Marshall accepted the conventional-morality theory at face value. Indeed, Brennan stated repeatedly that his interpretation was one to which neither a majority of his fellow justices nor a majority of his fellow countrymen subscribed.[29] For Brennan, the intrinsic morality of the eighth amendment controlled; the Court should look to and apply the principles and values that underlay it. "It would effectively write the clause out of the Bill of Rights were we to permit legislatures to police themselves by having the last word on the scope of the protection that the clause is intended to secure against their overreaching."[30]

Both Brennan and Marshall recognized that the eighth amendment must "draw its meaning from the evolving standards of decency that mark the progress of a maturing society."[31] Each saw these evolving standards as a *limitation* on constitutionally permitted punishments, not as a means of validating otherwise unconstitutional penalties. Brennan stated that severe punishments must not be unacceptable to contemporary society.[32] He found, however, that mere legislative authorization is not sufficient to show acceptance; one must look at the actual use of the penalty by society.[33] For Justice Marshall, it was the moral values of an *informed* citizenry upon which the constitutionality of the death penalty turns;[34] he believed that if the American people were sufficiently well informed on the death penalty, they would consider it to be "shocking, unjust, and unacceptable."[35]

A second issue raised by the repeated dissent is the proper role of the doctrine of *stare decisis*. This concept—that courts should follow precedent—is based upon the idea that consistency will yield fair and predictable results. The repeat dissent is a clear demonstration of a justice's belief that there are more important values at stake in a particular case than the certainty offered by adherence to *stare decisis*. Certainly, the dissents of Justices Brennan and Marshall against the death penalty made such a statement.

Historically, there has been considerable variation in the application of the doctrine of *stare decisis*. The strictest form was adopted by the House of Lords in 1898; it was abandoned in 1966.[36] Under this interpretation, a court is absolutely bound by its prior decisions.[37] American courts have not generally adhered to this form of the doctrine,[38] following instead more relaxed[39] forms where precedents are not absolutely binding. In at least some situations, courts may depart from a previous decision.[40]

Disagreement abounds over when it is proper for a court to depart from a precedent, yet there are some recurring themes. It is often argued that *stare decisis* should have relatively greater importance in cases of statutory construction. This position rests on the perceived ability of legislatures to reverse erroneous interpretations of the legislative intent.[41] This this is a widely accepted view is supported by the fact that within the Court, "cessation of dissent occurs with some regularity . . . in cases of statutory interpretation."[42]

Many have argued that *stare decisis* is of lesser importance in constitutional adjudication.[43] The argument is often based upon the idea that in constitutional cases legislative correction is virtually impossible because as a practical matter the Court has the last word.[44] Another argument is that even where such legislative correction *is* feasible, it cannot remove "a kind of moral imprimatur" that results from the Court's upholding of a challenged activity.[45]

Thus, despite the possibility of legislative change, constitutional precedent should arguably still have diminished importance.[46] Professor Monaghan suggests, however, that "the level of indifference towards (or indeed distaste for) stare decisis has its real roots . . . [in] the substantive constitutional philosophy endorsed by the commentator."[47] Those, for example, who see constitutional clauses as open textured will consider an insistence on *stare decisis* to be self-defeating.[48]

The doctrine of *stare decisis* varies in prominence within the jurisprudence of different judges.[49] Judges simply do not agree on what values are sufficiently compelling to justify departure from precedent.[50] In constitutional cases, no Supreme Court justice sees precedent as absolutely binding.[51] Thus, for each justice there is some unacceptable balance where following precedent would threaten other values deemed more important. Repeated dissents, such as those of Justices Brennan and Marshall against the death penalty, were a clear signal that the balance reached by the majority was unacceptable. Here they drew the line.

If, in the process of judging, the benefits of *stare decisis* are indeed weighed against other values, the role of morality in the law cannot be viewed as an entirely separate issue from the role of *stare decisis*. Instead, the two concepts may be correlative within a particular legal theory. For where the moral element in law assumes great importance within the jurisprudence of a judge, the importance of precedent would seem to diminish. Reciprocally, a strong policy of *stare decisis* reflects a belief that the proper role of the judge is to rely on precedent and not on other things, such as his view of the moral element in law or even substantive justice. This in turn reflects the view that a judge is primarily a lawfinder and not a lawmaker.[52]

Of course, the proper role of the judiciary within our legal system is a third and larger issue raised by the relentless dissent. The very fact that Brennan and Marshall repeatedly dissented was a reflection of how they defined their own roles as members of our highest court. As can be seen from the preceding discussion, the question is closely related to the issues of morality and *stare decisis*.[53] And similarly, it is a question for which there seems to be no consensus on an answer.

At one end of the spectrum of possible answers is the idea that judges are lawfinders. This view is set forth in a commentary written in 1905 on the first Justice Harlan's famous dissent in *Plessy v. Ferguson*:[54]

> [T]he attitude of discussion which the Dissenting Opinion assumes, and the heat of argument which it sometimes evokes, create naturally a tendency to travel far out of the law and to extend the discussion to all manner of subjects, political, social, and economic, and cause the objecting judges to forget that it is not their province to make the law, nor even to direct its policy, but merely to interpret it. . . .[55]

Carried to its logical end, this viewpoint does not permit a judge to make or change the law or to impose his own view of justice on the law. *Stare decisis* is the principle that guides judicial decisions; morality, except as it may already be encompassed in the law, is irrelevant.

At the other end of the spectrum is the view that judges are not constrained by the rules, that they may create law. That is, judges are free to act in a legislative manner when they deem it necessary, for whatever reason.[56] Between the two ends of the spectrum lie legal theories that constrain the judge's ability to create law but do, nonetheless, view the judge as a legitimate law creator in some situations.[57]

In our democratic and representative society, there arises the question of the Court's authority to go beyond merely interpreting and applying the laws passed by Congress. Indeed, "[o]urs is not a government by the Judiciary."[58] Supreme Court justices are not elected officials. How legitimate, then, is it for the Court to create law? Just how far does a justice's discretion go?

More precisely, in the context of the repeated dissent, what is the Court's authority to change the law? Should it ever overrule clear precedents? Even if we grant such a right because of "the unique interpretive role of the Supreme Court with respect to the Constitution,"[59] should the goal of unanimity still outweigh the right of an individual justice to maintain a dissent?[60]

Any insistence that there be constraints upon a judge's law-creating or law-changing power stems from a concern for the legitimacy and authority of the judiciary within our legal system.[61] Professors Nonet and Selznick suggest that a legal theory which is concerned with establishing the legitimacy of the law will emphasize procedural fairness rather than substantive justice.[62] Under such a theory, judges are passive dispensers of impersonal justice who obey a will external to their own.[63] The rule of law is paramount. Judges are primarily lawfinders; judicial legislating is a threat to the integrity of the legal process and to the authority of the law.[64] Therefore, any opportunity for judicial legislating must be strictly limited.

Within this kind of system, the doctrine of *stare decisis* provides one form of "will" external to the judge's own—its constraints confer legitimacy on the judiciary. Adherence to the rule of law, whatever that rule may be, ought at least to result in procedural fairness.[65] Thus, procedural fairness is the concern and result of this kind of law.

At the same time, *stare decisis* is not necessarily the only kind of constraint that can confer legitimacy. What is important is that the judge even-handedly apply standards external to her own will and that her discretion be narrowly defined. Therefore, legal theories based upon natural law or natural right may also provide the necessary external constraint that limits judicial discretion.[66] The theory that conventional morality should be the standard to guide justices' decisions is another view that may fit within this type of law.

In a distinct category are legal theories that may be called result oriented or instrumentalist.[67] These theories view the law as an engine of social ordering and social change;[68] they seek to achieve substantive justice rather than procedural fairness. Proponents of such legal theories would subordinate rules to principles and policies.[69] Judges, in keeping with social purpose, can legislate for the public good.[70] Their legitimate role is that of lawmakers.

There is potential for tension between the doctrine of *stare decisis* and the ends of the legal system under either kind of legal theory. In the first, where law seeks its own legitimacy through the application of rules and procedural fairness, precedents may conflict with the "higher law" of a natural-law or natural-rights theory. Or precedents may conflict with conventional morality or other established external standards for decision making. Adhering to *stare decisis* will of course create the least tension when the system is seen to derive its legitimacy solely from such adherence. Under the second type of legal theory, which views substantive justice as the goal of adjudication, adhering to precedent in a particular case may be seen as insufficient to serve that end. When such conflicts arise between *stare decisis* and the judge's perceived end or goal of adjudication, what is her correct response? Depending upon the jurisprudence of the judge, she may see her legitimate role to be a departure from the dictates of precedent.

For Brennan and Marshall, the demands of *stare decisis* were not great enough to compel their compliance with the majority in upholding the death penalty. Certainly, the two justices believed that their repeated dissents against the imposition of the death penalty were legally legitimate. I now examine how such a viewpoint may fit within U.S. traditions of legal thought.[71]

## Natural Law[72]

Natural law has been called "the point of intersection between law and morals."[73] A characteristic shared by all natural-law theories is the idea that there are immutable principles by which enacted or positive law may be evaluated. These principles are the moral element—criteria for the goodness of positive law. A law that satisfies all of the requirements for legal validity may nonetheless by "unjust" if it does not satisfy these criteria. Thus, according to natural law, the concepts of "legality" and "justice" are distinct.[74]

According to natural-law philosophers, its principles are based on something wider and more enduring than mere convention or agreement among people. These principles are necessarily prior to any social agreement or to human institutions. It is in this sense that law is "natural"; it consists of "certain fundamental values . . . believed to be absolutely valid."[75]

Where positive law does not comport with the enduring principles of natural law, adherents of the latter have found the authority of positive law to be undermined; according to natural-law theory, positive law derives its authority only from natural law. For natural-law philosophers, "there is no such thing as 'legal obligation' apart from moral obligation. Statutory law and constitutional law do not give rise to an 'obligation' unless their dictates are congruent with moral imperatives, and then only *because of* the congruence."[76] As a result, one does "not have an 'obligation' to obey an immoral law; at best it might only be prudent . . . to do so"[77] because of the consequences of failing to obey.

Given the notion that positive law has authority only as it comports with moral principles, it would seem that the doctrine of *stare decisis* must be relegated to a lesser role in many natural-law theories. For in the context of natural law following a precedent for its own sake will not make sense, except as it may reflect a procedural aspect to the natural law.[78] Where the moral principles of natural law are substantive, a precedent that contradicts them will have no authority. Precedent may, of course, illuminate the natural-law principles to be followed in a given case.

Human reason plays a central role in natural-law philosophy—from the beginning, philosophers of this school assume the validity of logical reasoning as a means of reaching the truth.[79] They start with broad principles that are "not themselves derived from logic,"[80] but whose validity may be assessed through reason. Those principles are applied rationally to a given case or situation. "Natural law reasoning . . . is the method by which persons gifted with both clear-headed perception and logical analytic ability can reason together about the values that ought to be the basis of law. . . ."[81] For Thomas Aquinas, the law was itself brought into being through reason and consisted of "propositions or precepts articulated by reason."[82]

Despite contemporary skepticism about natural-law theories, the reasoning of this school, in a broad sense, is widespread. It has been claimed that

anyone who attempts to found concepts of justice upon reason and human nature engages in natural law philosophy. Contemporary philosophical systems based on feminism, wealth maximization, neutral conversation, liberal equality, or libertarianism are natural law philosophies. They start with assumptions about human nature and what is good for people, and they claim to employ reason to judge the relative justice or injustice of legal practices like slavery, the free market, patriarchy, and socialism. Like the man who was astonished to find that he had been speaking in prose all his life, we who make it our business to resolve differences about questions of morality and justice through the use of reason are surprised to find that we are expounding natural law. . . .

We can no more abandon natural law reasoning than we can stop speaking in prose. We are all constantly making moral judgments based on implicit views of human nature, such as whether man is naturally acquisitive or cooperative, and whether the domination of one group by another is a natural reflection of inequality or an artificial interference with natural equality.[83]

Within the context of natural-law philosophy, the repeated dissents of Brennan and Marshall can be seen as a completely legitimate exercise of judicial power. Very simply, if imposition of the death penalty does not comport with enduring moral principles, then laws permitting the death penalty are not authoritative. Thus, if "[t]he role of reason in natural law theory is to bring the moral faculty of judgment into the decision making process,"[84] a judge may reason that she has an affirmative duty to dissent from any majority decision that upholds the death penalty. The existence of precedent will be irrelevant to the judge's decision; precedent cannot affect a fundamental contradiction between imposing the death penalty and the essential moral principles that deny its validity.

In claiming that the "cruel and unusual punishment" clause prohibits punishments that do not comport with human dignity,[85] Justice Brennan spoke the language of natural law.[86] Indeed, Justice Brennan has embraced the resurgence of interest in natural law:[87]

> Perhaps some of you may detect, as I think I do, a return to the philosophy of St. Thomas Aquinas in the new jurisprudence. Call it a resurgence, if you will, of concepts of natural law—but no matter. St. Thomas, you will remember, was in complete agreement with the Greek tradition, both in its Aristotelian and Platonic modes, that

law must be concerned with seeing things whole, that it is but part of the whole human situation and draws its validity from its position in the entire scheme of things. It is folly to think that law, any more than religion and education, should serve only its own symmetry rather than ends defined by other disciplines. . . . There is pervasive recognition . . . that law, to be effective, must conform to the world in which it finds itself. That world is given; law does not make it.[88]

Brennan found defects in both positivism and sociological jurisprudence because these theories (outside natural law) are insufficiently attuned to the human situation.[89]

For Justice Brennan, a "shift from emphasis upon abstract rules to emphasis upon *justice* has profound importance for judicial decisionmaking."[90] He did not look to history and precedent to define "cruel and unusual" punishment; he looked instead to enduring principles embodied in the Constitution. The law evolves through adaptation of these broad principles to contemporary problems, without necessarily taking previous detours into account. "The genius of the Constitution resides not in any static meaning that it had in a world that is dead and gone, but in the adaptability of its great principles to cope with current problems and current needs."[91]

## Positivism

Legal positivism was first systematically formulated by John Austin, a nineteenth-century English philosopher.[92] He was concerned with distinguishing the law as it is from the law as it ought to be.[93] In his view, and in that of later positivists, law and morals were separate and distinct spheres that ought not be confused.[94] "The existence of law is one thing; its merit or demerit is another."[95] Thus, positivism concerns itself with the analysis of the law as it exists rather than with normative jurisprudence. This in not to say that moral principles cannot be written into specific laws. But for a rule to be morally desirable does not make it law, and a law is still binding even if it violates a moral standard.[96] Austin wrote that "a law, which actually exists, is a law, though we happen to dislike it."[97]

Professor Wise has suggested that the development of positivism in jurisprudence formed the essential background for the modern formulation of *stare decisis*.[98] According to Austin, law consists of the commands of the sovereign backed by threat of sanctions. Thus, the law is a set of rules that derive their obligatory status from the very fact that they have been laid down by somebody.[99] An earlier and contrasting notion of the law is evidenced in Blackstone's belief that judicial decisions are *evidence* of the common law, and not the common law itself.[100] But once the idea is established that the law is separate from its social milieu and binding in and of itself, the law takes on a life of its own. Where Austin considered the law to be the commands of the sovereign, modern positivists take a different view. According to H. L. A. Hart,[101] the leading modern positivist, the law is the intersection of what he terms "primary" and "secondary" rules.[102] Primary rules are enacted by lawmaking bodies and impose duties; they are obligatory, requiring people to act or abstain from acting.[103] Secondary rules guide the actions of the lawmakers.[104] They are rules according to which the primary rules may be introduced, extinguished, or modified.[105] Secondary rules confer power rather than impose obligations.[106]

In Hart's view, the law had an open texture.[107] The two principal devices used by the law to create standards of conduct are precedent and legislation.[108] At some point, each will prove indeterminate because of the generality and imprecision of language and because of human nature.[109] With respect to precedent, Hart concludes there is no authoritative or "correct" rule to be extracted from cases. But in applying precedent to a later case, there is often general agreement that a particular formulation is adequate.[110] Courts bound by a precedent have two choices. They may reach an opposite decision to that of the precedent by narrowing the precedent and admitting some exception. Or they may widen the rule, by rejecting some restriction because it is not required either by statute or by any precedent.[111]

Thus, in Hart's view, the role of the judge is flexible. At the margins of rules and in areas left open by precedent, she may perform a rule-producing function.[112] But the legislative activity of courts is strictly limited. As a result of our system of following precedent, there are a vast number of rules that are as determinate as any statute.[113] Where there is an established precedent that cannot be distinguished, the judge is bound to apply the precedent. It is then the role of the legislature, and not the courts, to change such an established precedent.[114]

Joseph Raz, another modern positivist, recognizes a broad law-making role for judges.[115] He distinguishes between unregulated and regulated disputes. An unregulated case is one where the applicable law has gaps and thus does not require any particular solution.[116] A regulated case is one for which the law provides a solution.[117] No judicial discretion is required.[118] The judge merely identifies the law, determines the facts, and applies the law to them.[119]

In unregulated cases, the judge can make law without changing existing law.[120] By filling in the gaps, the judge creates precedent.[121] In regulated cases, the judge may act as a lawmaker by distinguishing precedents. For, according to Raz, to distinguish a rule is to change it so that the rule which did apply to the present case no longer applies.[122]

But, beyond changing a law in a regulated case by distinguishing it, judges in some courts may also overrule a precedent.[123] Because overruling upsets established law, judges must act with restraint.[124] Raz believes that judges should resort to overruling a law only when they are certain that the new law is an improvement over the old one.[125] A judge acts improperly when he overrules a decision because he merely thinks it *likely* that the new rule will be an improvement over the old.[126]

Although he believes that a judge should act with restraint, Raz would set no standard as to how great an improvement is required.[127] He views it as a legal duty for a judge to adopt those rules that he considers to be best.[128] This legal duty arises because courts are not permitted to act in an arbitrary manner, even when making new law; in choosing the best law, the judge is not acting arbitrarily. In addition, Raz recognizes that "judges do rely and should rely on their own moral judgment."[129]

The theories of both Hart and Raz recognize a central paradox of positivism. As Raz has stated, "[T]he fact that a court may make a binding decision does not mean that it cannot err. It means that its decision is binding even if it is mistaken."[130] Similarly, Hart has written that "a supreme tribunal has the last word in saying what the law is and, when it has said it, the statement that the court was 'wrong' has no consequences within the system: no one's rights or duties are thereby altered.[131] Thus, both positivists recognize that a binding precedent is binding even if it is the result of a flawed decision-making process.[132]

From the point of view of positivist theory, the most salient problem presented by the repeated dissents of Justices Brennan and Marshall against the death penalty stems from this last observation. Even if we posit that the majority was mistaken in its interpretation of the eighth amendment and that *Gregg* was incorrectly decided, the Court in *Gregg* created a precedent that the death penalty is not per se cruel and unusual punishment. That precedent is the law, rather than any notion of how the case should have been decided. This, of course, stems from the positivist separation of law as it is and law as it ought to be. Brennan's and Marshall's broad statement that the death penalty is in all circumstances cruel and unusual is in direct opposition to the precedent. No matter how laudatory the morality implicit in their stance might be, their position is not the law.

Given the premise of a clear precedent, in Hart's view, it is now up to the legislature, and not the Court, to change the law.[133] Therefore, after *Gregg,* Brennan and Marshall may be said to have "misbehaved" when they dissented repeatedly against the imposition of the death penalty. They stepped outside their proper role as judges, as Hart posits that judges are legitimate lawmakers only within the margins of rules and where there are gaps.[134]

But the question then arises whether the problem of the legitimacy of Brennan's and Marshall's dissent stems from their breadth; the two justices find the death penalty to be unconstitutional in all circumstances, even though they often also address the majority's issues.[135] If, rather than making any blanket statement, they had distinguished each case from precedents on its particular facts, would their actions have been more legitimate? It is arguable that the justices would then be acting within Hart's quite flexible margins of rules.[136]

Measured by Raz's theory of positivism, the repeated dissents of Brennan and Marshall may have been a more legitimate exercise of judicial authority; his theory encompasses a broader lawmaking role for judges than does that of Hart. However, his standard for judicial conduct remains vague: it is unclear exactly how much discretion he would give a judge to repeat prior dissents. There can be no doubt of the certainty with which Brennan and Marshall both viewed the abolition of the death penalty to be an improvement on the law, Raz's criterion for change. Nor can there be doubt that their dissents were votes to overturn prior decisional law, not merely dissent for its own sake.[137] In keeping with Raz's belief that judges have a legal duty to adopt the best decision they can, the repeated dissents communicate their belief that opposition to the death penalty is the only possible position they can take. For them, any other stance would be arbitrary.

## Sociological Jurisprudence

The predominant viewpoint in American legal thought in the latter part of the nineteenth century was that the law was a closed, logical system.[138] Judges did not make law, but merely declared it.[139] Roscoe Pound was one of the first[140] to attack what he termed "mechanical jurisprudence,"[141] or the degeneration of a legal system into "technical rules existing for their own sake and subserving supposed ends of science, while defeating justice.[142] Pound instead called for a philosophy of law that was based on an understanding of social and political science.[143] "Sociological jurisprudence," as it was called by Pound and others, was "the movement for the adjustment of principles and doctrines to the human conditions they are to govern rather than to assumed first principles."[144]

Thus, Pound viewed the law as purposive, or instrumentalist. The end of law was the administration of justice, and the law was to be judged by the results it achieved.[145] He deplored the process of legal reasoning whereby concepts were developed logically at the expense of practical results.[146] Pound believed that judges ought to take into consideration the economic and social implications of their decisions.[147] The task of the law was to enable people "to live together in civilized society with a minimum of friction and a minimum of waste of the goods of existence."[148] The goal of judicial decisionmaking was "social engineering" to secure the maximum social benefit possible with the least sacrifice.[149] Courts were to achieve this through a process of "subsuming the claims of the parties under generalized social claims"[150] and giving effect to as many of these claims as possible.[151] Accordingly, Pound saw the contemporary values of society manifest in "generalized social claims" to be a standard for judicial decision.

Implicit in Pound's theory is the idea that as society evolves there is a need to reassess laws and the results they achieve. He argued that "what the administration of justice in America needs is . . . a redrawing of the authoritative picture of the society in which justice is administered."[152] In

Pound's view, ideals of the past are an inappropriate basis for contemporary laws because social needs change. "It is bad social engineering to administer justice to a blue print of a society of the past as a means of maintaining the jural postulates of civilization in a different society of the present."[153]

According to Phillip Selznick, a modern adherent of sociological jurisprudence,[154] it is rational public consensus concerning legitimacy that gives validity to the rule of law.[155] However, the quality of such agreement, as well as its content, is important. Selznick states that there must be broad opportunity for the emergence of public opinion through the free play of interests and ideas.[156] Public consensus is not an adequate support for the rule of law where it is not "genuine," but is instead based upon "manipulation, withholding of information, or unmitigated appeals to tradition."[157]

In Selznick's view of a developed legal system, those in authority will transcend rule by coercion. They will instead contribute to the public consensus through education and appeal to reason.[158] Accordingly, he concludes that the obligation to obey the law should ideally be closely connected to the defensibility of the rules and the official decisions that enforce them.[159]

Additionally, Selznick states that if the law is to meet the social needs and aspirations of the public there must be intrinsic within the law a capacity to sustain reasoned criticism of the rules and of official discretion.[160] Within the Anglo-American legal tradition, the freedom of the judiciary to adopt a critical stance toward received law is one source of such "institutionalized criticism."[161] This capacity for criticism is important because it creates a dialogue that may expose defective reasoning. "[W]here reasons are defective, authority is to that extent weakened and even invalidated."[162]

Within sociological jurisprudence, the application of precedent for its own sake appears to be undermined by the idea that law must be justified by its ability to achieve social goals. Of course, precedent often has a beneficial aspect; it can give stability and consistency to the law, thereby enhancing fairness. But if law is to achieve justice according to contemporary needs, the doctrine of *stare decisis* must at times give way. This balance has been expressed by Justice Cardozo, who is sometimes labeled an adherent of sociological jurisprudence.[163]

In these days, there is a good deal of discussion whether the rule of adherence to precedent ought to be abandoned altogether. I would not go so far myself. . . . But I am ready to concede that the rule of adherence to precedent, though it ought not to be abandoned, ought to be in some degree relaxed. I think that when a rule, after it has been duly tested by experience, has been found to be inconsistent with the sense of justice or with the social welfare, there should be less hesitation in frank avowal and full abandonment.[164]

Justices Brennan and Marshall believed that the law can be a vehicle for advancing the common good. For them, there was no doubt that abolishing the death penalty, rather than upholding it, best served the legitimate needs or goals of our society. Therefore, in weighing the benefits of adherence to *stare decisis* against the goal of achieving justice, they found precedent wanting.

Measured by the tenets of sociological jurisprudence, their repeated dissents against the death penalty were, at a minimum, legitimate as "institutionalized criticism." The dissents served to keep open a dialogue concerning the validity of the ultimate punishment. They may be seen as a call for a continuing rational assessment of the death penalty in light of contemporary needs, rather than mere acquiescence to practices of the past. The dissents were at once an appeal to reason and an expression of the belief that judges have an important educational role to play in the process of arriving at social consensus. Thus, the repeated dissents are consistent with principles of sociological jurisprudence.

It is Justice Marshall's point of view, found in both his concurrence in *Furman* and his dissent in *Gregg,* that most clearly comports with the attitudes of Pound, Selznick, and others of the "sociological" school: laws are to be justified by the results they achieve.[165] "The law, in Justice Marshall's eyes, is result oriented and the final cause of law is the welfare of society."[166] While Brennan's objection to the death penalty focused on upholding the broad constitutional principle of human dignity, Marshall appealed to our reason. He asked all Americans to recognize that we cannot rationally justify the death penalty as a necessary means to a legitimate social end. Therefore, we ought to do away with it altogether.[167]

Justice Marshall recognized that contemporary values are an important factor in defining the social welfare. In *Furman,* he stated that a punishment "may be invalid if popular sentiment abhors it."[168] Interestingly, Marshall's language recalled that of Professor Selznick, who insists on a "genuine" public consensus to assess the legitimacy of law.[169] The justice stated that it is the opinion of an *informed* citizenry that matter: "the American people, fully informed as to the purposes of the death penalty and its liabilities, would in my view reject it as morally unacceptable."[170]

## Legal Realism

If positivism focused on the rules of a legal system, the legal realism that arose in the 1930s out of sociological jurisprudence was characterized by a belief in the artificiality, uncertainty, and flexibility of legal rules and principles.[171] Legal realists denied that decisions were made through the purely logical application of the legal rules to the facts of a case. Instead, judicial decisions were influenced by many factors apart from the rules.[172] The legal realists were therefore concerned with understanding how decisions were actually made.[173] They focused primarily on describing how the law "really" works.

Two of the legal realism movement's most vocal proponents were Karl Llewellyn and Jerome Frank.[174] Llewellyn, taking an "institutional" approach, believed that the law could be understood only by studying how people and institutions are organized in our society.[175] He focused on the interaction between officials and those affected by their behavior.[176] According to Llewellyn, "paper" rules were the "accepted doctrine of the time and place—what the books say 'the law' is."[177] The "real" rules, however, were the actual practices of the courts.[178] He believed that study of observable behavior was necessary to deemphasize "rules and precepts and principles" and to reveal the "real" rules.[179]

Jerome Frank's theories centered on the personality of the judge.[180] He insisted that the psychology of the individual judge was of overriding importance in determining what his or her decision would be. At the trial court level, Frank asserted, judges had great discretion in determining the facts; they would assess what the facts were in different ways because of their individual biases. How a judge determined the facts would affect the outcome of the case.[181] But even at the appellate level, where judges were presented with written records rather than with live witnesses, varying individual reactions could result in judges coming to opposite conclusions.[182] Frank concluded that it was important for lawyers to learn as much as they could about the judge who would decide a case, as a means either of bringing about the decision the lawyer desired or of guessing the outcome.[183]

Both Frank and Llewellyn believed that judges rationalized their decisions in judicial opinions.[184] The published reasons were not the real reasons for deciding a case in a particular way. Instead of disclosing the decision-making process, opinions were "trained lawyers' arguments made by the judges (after the decision ha[d] been reached), intended to make the decision seem plausible, legally decent, legally right, to make it seem, indeed, legally inevitable."[185] And because opinions were written by reasoning backward from the judge's desired result, opinions citing the same "legal rule" were not necessarily decided on the same "real" basis.[186]

According to Llewellyn, investigation into the way judicial decisions are "really" made reveals that appellate courts have enormous leeway in applying precedents.[187] Given such leeway, the doctrine of *stare decisis* is not only a means of retaining the status quo but also a facile means of change within the legal system.[188] For example, wherever there are competing and equally authoritative premises leading to different conclusions, judges have a choice as to how to decide.[189] Furthermore, they always used wide discretion in dealing with precedents. Judges can limit the use of a precedent to an extremely narrow issue or give it a wide application; they may even include principles never announced in the precedent opinion at all. If there are many possible conclusions that find support in one case or a series of cases but do not follow necessarily from them, then it is clear that precedent may be interpreted in a very wide range of ways.[190] Llewellyn concluded that where the judge has so much freedom, how she chooses to apply precedent can only be justified by policy considerations.[191]

Similarly, Frank recognized the essential flexibility of the doctrine of *stare decisis,* whereby judges may easily get rid of an "obnoxious judge-made rule."[192] He directly addressed the question of whether a court should abandon or modify a rule that reflects a particular social policy when the court believes that the policy behind the rule is undesirable or unjust.[193] While Frank gave special deference to those who have relied on a particular law, his answer was clear: "[I]f the precedent system means the perpetuation of judge-made rules, shown to be unjust or undesirable

. . . then usually the courts, when they accept that system, are not performing their function—the administration of justice. They are administering injustice."[194]

Frank and Llewellyn believed that through awareness of the true nature of the legal system, it would be possible to use the system efficiently and to improve it.[195] There was, however, no agreed-upon legal realist program as to how the law ought to function ideally.[196] Where sociological jurisprudence had sought to assess laws according to whether they fulfilled the needs and aspirations of society, legal realism as a movement took no particular stance on social values, morality, or ethics.[197] There was fairly general agreement on the part of legal realists that the effects of rules should be taken into account by the courts in making or remaking rules.[198] But Llewellyn denied that there was any broad community that could be taken into account.[199] Instead, a particular part of the law was only relevant to the particular part of the community that was materially affected by it.[200] And in discussing the legal realist movement, Llewellyn acknowledged that "to get perspective on [each legal realist's] stand about ethically normative matters one must pick up the work of each man in his special field of work."

The legal realists' insight that judicial decisions are not merely the logical application of the legal rules to the facts of a case is now a widely accepted notion, at least implicitly. How else, for example, does one explain public commotion such as that raised by the nomination of Judge Robert Bork to the Supreme Court? "On a number of occasions, dramatic political debates [have been] engaged in over the question whether certain background factors would predispose a justice to decide cases in a particular way."[201]

Thus, from the legal realist point of view, it cannot be surprising that Justices Brennan and Marshall differed from other justices on the validity of the death penalty. That judges can arrive at different conclusions given the same facts is explicitly a part of the realists' descriptive scheme.

Furthermore, if judges really do have enormous leeway in using precedent either to retain the status quo or to change it, as Llewellyn and Frank claim, then it makes no sense to denigrate the dissents of Justices Brennan and Marshall as rejections of the doctrine of *stare decisis*. This is true because a majority of the Court could have arrived at the same conclusion as Brennan and Marshall, that the death penalty is unconstitutional, while claiming to rely only on precedent.

If a legal opinion is merely a postdecisional rationalization that contrives to make the decision appear logically inevitable, then we can place no faith in the reasons given by Brennan and Marshall for their repeated dissents. These reasons may or may not be the true motivation or cause for their dissents. But the corollary to this is that the reasons given by the majority for retaining the death penalty are similarly suspect. It is likely, therefore, that any objection the legal realists might have to repeated dissents by Supreme Court justices would be rooted in a sense of the importance of stability in the law.

## Wechsler, Ely, Choper

While these legal theorists can only loosely be termed a group,[202] Herbert Wechsler, John Hart Ely, and Jesse Choper have each examined the role of the Supreme Court and have each addressed what Alexander Bickel termed "the counter-majoritarian difficulty."[203] Because Supreme Court justices are appointed rather than elected, each theorist would restrict the Court's powers within certain limits in order to legitimate, justify, and protect its role within democratic government.

In a famous 1959 paper delivered at the Harvard Law School, Herbert Wechsler offered the theory of Supreme Court judicial review based on "neutral principles."[204] In defining this term, he states that a properly neutral decision is not result oriented. Instead, "[a] principled decision . . . is one that rests on . . . reasons that in their generality and their neutrality transcend any immediate result that is involved."[205] To be result oriented is to imply that "courts are free to function as a naked power organ."[206] Further, Wechsler finds that it was not the role of the Court to make choices between conflicting values.[207] In applying the Constitution, it may condemn or condone the value choices made by the legislative and executive branches.[208] But if the Court has no sufficiently generalized and neutral reasons for overturning the value choices of the democratically elected branches, it must defer to those choices.[209]

Additionally, a decision based on neutral principles must fully disclose and elaborate the grounds on which it rests.[210] Indeed, Wechsler disapproves of per curiam decisions that fail to articulate the standards on which they rely.[211] He recognizes that it may be difficult for the justices to agree on reasons for a particular result.[212] However, in such a case, disclosing variations in the positions of the different justices is essential, as the disclosure clarifies the Court's stance and delimits the principles on which the decision is based.[213]

Wechsler would have disapproved exceedingly of the repeated dissents of Justices Brennan and Marshall against the death penalty, seeing them as impermissibly value laden and result oriented. In rejecting the death penalty, Brennan would uphold human dignity as a first principle embodied in the Constitution, while Marshall would assess the "fit" between the punishment and its legitimate purposes. Analyzed according to Wechsler's standard of neutral principles (however vague it may be), each stance would be designated an impermissible attempt to impress the justices' own values on the decisions of the Supreme Court. Wechsler's position would require the justices to defer to the legislatures that have made the death penalty a legal punishment. For him, judges should not play a part in determining either the values or the social goals of the law. The majority of the Court, in upholding the value choices made by the legislatures, acts within the confines of its proper role.

John Hart Ely focuses on the role of the Court in ensuring access to the political process.[214] He contests the characterization of the Constitution itself as an evolving statement of general values,[215] asserting that "the selection and accommodation of substantive values is left almost entirely to the political process" rather than being found in the Constitution.[216] Thus, determining the meaning of open-ended clauses of the Constitution is properly left to those participating in the political process. According to Ely, the Constitution itself is concerned with procedural fairness in the resolution of individual disputes and with ensuring broad participation in the political process.[217] As a result, the Supreme Court's role is to "concern itself only with questions of participation, and not with the substantive merits of the political choice under attack."[218] For Ely, judicial review becomes an important means for "unblocking stoppages in the democratic process."[219] It does so by "clearing the channels of political change"[220] and "facilitating the representation of minorities."[221]

Thus, for Ely, the Supreme Court does have a role to play with respect to the death penalty, but it is a different one from that assumed by Justices Brennan and Marshall in *Furman* and *Gregg*. As he believes that the values embodied in the Constitution are to be left to the legislative process to define, Ely would probably reject the particular substance of Brennan's and Marshall's arguments, as he would probably reject as a misuse of judicial power their repeated broad dissents as well.

For Ely, the issue raised by the death penalty is its uneven application. "Obviously there is a very effective series of buffers at work here, protecting those who make the laws and others like them from the harshness of their application."[222] In light of his emphasis on access to the democratic process and the importance of equal protection in achieving that access, it seems possible that Ely might approve of repeated dissents that focus on and rightly point up inequities in the application of the death penalty. An example is *McCleskey v. Kemp*,[223] where, in dissent, Justice Brennan details statistical evidence of racial discrimination in the imposition of the death penalty. It seems to me that for Ely to object to this kind of repeated dissent would be fundamentally inconsistent with his belief that the Supreme Court should act to protect the access of minorities to the democratic process. The mere fact that a majority of the Court disagrees with the dissenting justices should not be enough to give a permanent imprimatur to a denial of equal protection.

For Jesse Choper, the "overriding virtue of and justification for vesting the Court with [the] awesome power [of judicial review] is to guard against governmental infringement of individual liberties secured by the Constitution."[224] His rationale for placing the guardianship of individual rights in the hands of the Court is specifically that it is the branch of government most removed from "political responsibility and unbeholden to self-absorbed and excited majoritarianism."[225] According to Choper, the smaller the aggrieved minority and the more intense the opprobrium directed toward it by the majority, the more critical is the need for protection of liberty through judicial review.[226]

According to Choper, the Supreme Court has limited "institutional capital."[227] Although judicial review is a necessary function of the Court, its exercise can result in harm to the Court itself.[228] "The Court's capacity to beget public enmity by decisions that reject political judgments believed necessary for effective governance is easily fulfilled, and its ability to obtain compliance with those mandates that thwart the popular will is greatly circumscribed."[229] To protect the Supreme Court, Choper would ration its use of judicial review. He proposes that the Court abstain from deciding constitutional questions either pertaining to national power versus states' rights or to separation of powers between Congress and the president.[230] Such a limitation would preserve the Court's prestige and allow it to act in the area where it is truly needed—protecting individual rights.

Choper explicitly rejects the idea that the Court should decline to protect individual rights until there is sufficient public consensus so that its decisions will be accepted.[231] This would be to shirk its duty and thwart its critical function as guardian of the constitutional rights of those who are without political power.[232] In his view:

> The Court's formidable and delicate task is to consult those complex sources of historic and contemporary values that are the ingredients of sound constitutional interpretation, as well as its wisdom and conscience—and then to decide. Acceptance is not the Court's responsibility, but the obligation of the people. . . . Even if the immediate decision is ignored, judicial courage is preferable to obsequious abdication. For . . . the mere articulation of cherished constitutional ideals by a Court that is "right" may carry a meaningful psychological impact that will serve the cause of liberty at a later time when popular passion has cooled.[233]

Whether or not Choper would personally agree with the stance that Justices Brennan and Marshall have taken against the death penalty, their sustained dissents are in keeping with the spirit of his argument. The two justices dissented against what they viewed as a violation of the constitutional right to be free from cruel and unusual punishment, an essential individual liberty that is the birthright of all U.S. citizens.

Just as the reintroduction of capital punishment in so many states confirms that there is a public consensus against the death penalty, the Supreme Court has repeatedly demonstrated that a majority of the justices do not agree with Brennan and Marshall that the death penalty is cruel and unusual. But Choper would not allow public sentiment to guide the choices of the Court. This, of course, means that reenactment of the death penalty by so many states should not sway the justices if constitutionally guaranteed rights are at risk. Should the majority of the Supreme Court nevertheless be able to demand compliance by the minority when that minority is convinced that individual rights are threatened? It seems to me that a logical corollary of Choper's thesis is that dissenters on the Court should not be muzzled because they differ from the majority on a question of individual rights. The position of the dissenting justices is analogous to that of the Court itself when it takes an unpopular stand. And, after all, Choper finds that "judicial courage is preferable to obsequious abdication."[234]

## Critical Theory: Critical Legal Studies and Feminist Jurisprudence

The Critical Legal Studies "movement" has been called the intellectual descendant of legal realism.[235] Feminist jurisprudence also has roots in legal realism. Like the legal realists, critical theorists have attempted to analyze and critique how our legal system really works; the CLS program has been primarily descriptive. Indeed, one of the chief complaints made by critics of CLS is that it has no constructive program.[236]

Critical theorists have adopted from the legal realists their skepticism of rules; CLS and feminist jurisprudence thus espouse the idea that legal rules are indeterminate and cannot in fact compel any particular outcome in a given case. As a result, law and politics are not distinguishable,[237] and judges can never be neutral or objective in deciding cases.[238] It is inevitable that a judge will bring to decisions her own moral values and ideological assumptions.[239] CLS critics have combined this insight with a "progressive political critique . . . [that] espouses the view that our society and its institutions fall dramatically short of our democratic and egalitarian ideas.[240]

One of the primary themes of Critical Legal Studies is that mainstream of "liberal"[241] legal thought has inherent and essential contradictions that cannot be resolved. In his book examining the movement, Mark Kelman delineates three central contradictions of liberal legal thought that have been identified by those associated with CLS.[242] First, there exists within the legal system a commitment to resolving disputes by using mechanically applicable rules in a nondiscretionary fashion.[243] At the same time, there is an equal commitment to using informal standards that allow for ad hoc decisions that are situation sensitive.[244] This rules–standards conflict results in a "logically or empirically unanswerable formal problem":[245] greater discretion can be granted, or discretion can be limited, simply through the form the legal command is made to take, and either possibility is "perfectly plausible."[246] As an example of the rules–standards conflict, Kelman points to the Supreme Court's vacillations over the death penalty.

> [I]t is hard to look at the Supreme Court's attempts over the past decade to elucidate the occasions when the death penalty may be applied constitutionally as anything more than a particularly dramatic lesson in the instability of both the rule and the standard form, with each pole rapidly and completely undercutting the other. The Court eliminates a death penalty grounded in unguided jury discretion, forcing the legislatures to write statutes establishing ostensibly rule-like aggravating circumstances that define capital murder as long as they are not applied in a rigid, rulelike, mandatory, nondiscretionary fashion, until there is a requirement, vaguely guided by statutes that now seem to have only vague exemplary power, that the jury hear of practically everything that may mitigate punishment, once they are satisfied that an aggravated form of murder has been committed.[247]

The second contradiction inherent in liberal legal thought concerns values. On the one hand, traditional liberal thought supports the idea that values or desires are arbitrary, subjective, and individual, while facts or reason are objective and universal.[248] On the other hand, it also supports the idea that social and ethical truths can be known objectively through knowledge of true human nature—that in seeking moral truth, one can transcend the distinction between subjectivity and objectivity.[249]

The third contradiction is between intentionalism and determinism.[250] In intentionalist terms, human actions are forward looking, arise from free will and are indeterminate. Intentionalism emphasizes that one has ethical responsibility for one's own actions.[251] Determinism, however, is structuralist and backward looking. It views conduct amorally, as predetermined and meriting neither respect nor condemnation.[252] According to Kelman, liberal thought "can be practically *defined* . . . by its peculiar insistence that there is some definable collective life that is coercive and determining and a definable domain of private empowerment in which free intentional action occurs."[253] He states, further, that "[i]t is . . . impossible to construct an adequate theory of individual blameworthiness that is left untouched or secure in the face of the obvious fact that circumstances clearly beyond the control of the actor have, at a minimum, a strong bearing on the possibility that he will commit wrongful acts."[254]

According to Kelman, each of the contradictions in liberal legal thought is pervasive. Even where the law appears to be clearly settled, a contradictory impulse exists, although it has been thoroughly repressed.[255] Additionally, one term in each set of contradictory impulses is privileged in mainstream legal thought; it will presumptively govern disputes in most situations, while departures from this norm are treated as exceptions that require special justification.[256] Thus, critics find that rules are privileged over standards,[257] subjective value choices of what is good will prevail over any state-defined vision of good,[258] and intentionalism is privileged over determinism.[259] Critics conclude, after examining the privileged impulses, that they mark out "a remarkably right-wing, quasilibertarian order."[260]

Mark Tushnet has found the self-contradictory nature of mainstream legal thought to run throughout American constitutional theory.[261] Mainstream theorists, in his view, seek a method of constitutional interpretation that satisfies two central criteria.[262] First, judicial invalidation of legislative action must be authorized in at least some circumstances; otherwise, the method would deny one premise of constitutionalism, the assumption that majorities sometimes overreach.[263] Thus, one goal of constitutionalists is to find a way to identify those times when majorities are behaving "tyrannically."[264] The second criterion is one of judicial restraint. Judges must not have license to overturn legislation merely because they think it is bad social policy.[265] "The method must keep judges from pretending that their policy preferences are somehow written into the Constitution."[266]

Tushnet frankly states his conviction that these two criteria are inconsistent with each other and cannot both be met at the same time.

> There is no middle ground, no method of constitutional interpretation that allows some judicial review but at the same time limits its reach. Judicial review is an "all or nothing" proposition. Either one allows judges to do whatever they want or one allows majorities to do whatever *they* want. Either choice is deeply anticonstitutional— which means, I suppose, that constitutionalism is self-contradictory.[267]

Tushnet ascribes the failure of constitutionalism to an essential contradiction between will and reason.[268] He finds that it is one of the conclusions of liberal political thought that "social decisions ought to result from the aggregation of individual choice in a world where interests, however defined, conflict.[269] This is, of course, the majoritarian idea. Tushnet argues that because it is individual wills that are aggregated, it is impossible for the outcome of aggregation to have reason as a component.[270] "The rule of law, in this context the idea of constitutionalism, attempts to transform the aggregation of individual wills into a supervening rational power."[271] Such an attempt will be "futile."[272] And in fact Tushnet finds that the "use of a collegial Court is induced by fears of judicial willfulness."[273]

As a result of the contradictions inherent in constitutionalism, only two options remain: "We can accept judicial review and live with judges doing whatever they want, or we can reject judicial review and live with the risk of majoritarian overreaching."[274]

If judges cannot be restrained in any meaningful way because of the inherent contradiction between reason and will, Tushnet suggests that they should make explicitly political judgments when deciding cases.[275] He concludes that the logical inference to be made from the legal realists' rule skepticism is that no court can create an absolutely binding precedent; therefore, "in a liberal society there simply cannot be a decision that has meaning beyond the circumstances in which it arises."[276] He asks then "that judges not delude themselves into thinking that what they do has significance different from, and broader than, what every other political actor does."[277]

Examined by the methods of Critical Legal Studies, the dissents of Justices Brennan and Marshall may perhaps be called one more example of the inherent contradictions of constitutionalism. For from the point of view of CLS these two men, like the other justices, were likely to base their legal findings not on reason but on subjective values. They cloaked the subjectivity of their decisions in supposed objectivity and enduring principles. The collegial Supreme Court, then, functions as a device for aggregating the individual wills of the individual justices.[278] Critics might find Marshall's and Brennan's repeated dissents against the death penalty merely to be a particularly clear manifestation of the fact that law does not differ in any meaningful way from politics.

For if rules are really indeterminate, there is no right answer to a particular question—even if prior cases have been decided in a certain way. If we cannot achieve any rational balance between majoritarian rule and judicial restraint, it makes no sense to say that justices cannot dissent on a repeated basis. Once we give members of the Supreme Court the power of judicial review, there is no method to prevent them from doing as they wish. Thus, the difference between Justices Brennan and Marshall and others in this regard may just come down to the idea that they place a lesser value on the doctrine of *stare decisis* as a political device.

As an additional matter, the substance of the difference between the majority of the Court and Brennan and Marshall with respect to the death penalty was a manifestation of the rules-standards conflict inherent in the cruel and unusual punishment clause—as is the Supreme Court's death penalty jurisprudence of the last decade or so. The "cruel and unusual punishment clause" is of course a standard that gives wide discretion unless it is fenced in. A decision that the death penalty is under all circumstances cruel and unusual would perhaps decrease the uncertainty and create a more rule-like standard. But it still would not answer definitively the question of what constitutes cruel and unusual punishment. That answer is fraught with conflicting impulses if, as critics claim, our society is committed both to the subjectivity of value choices and to the objectivity of moral truths. Some will find the answer in social or moral certainties; others will find those truths to be subjective. No one can have the "last word."

## A Note on Civil Disobedience

Striking French railway workers in 1910 became saboteurs when, in an attempt to slow travel and get their bosses' attention, they broke up wooden shoes (*sabots*) holding tracks together. Were the relentless dissents of Brennan and Marshall comparable to acts of civil disobedience? Is the idea of judicial civil disobedience an oxymoron?

First, civil disobedience has been defined as an *illegal* act undertaken for moral reasons.[279] Further, an act is illegal only if it may result in arrest and conviction.[280] On the other hand, a conscientious objector is one whose objection is recognized and established as a legal right.[281]

It is arguable that any claim one might make about Supreme Court justices who dissent being civil disobedients founders on the simple idea that their actions are not illegal. This, of course, is a technical point; in its favor is the idea that one should not go throwing the term "civil disobedience" about without first defining it.

It is much more appealing to think of dissenting justices as conscientious objectors. Because of their position, they have an exemption, a right to dissent that is legally protected. J. Louis Campbell uses the term "institutional disobedience" to describe dissent in the Court[282] and says that "judges . . . protesting as authorities within institutional roles [are] analogous to civilians in non-institutional roles who physically enact their protest."[283] But "disobedience" is a misnomer simply because no one can point to a binding rule that says judges cannot dissent; in fact, everyone knows that they can, and many believe that they should.

In looking at various legal philosophies, it becomes apparent that the idea of civil disobedience has more meaning in some of them than in others. For example, legal realists and their successors in Critical Legal Studies point out that rules are indeterminate and flexible, making it possible to arrive at whatever conclusion one wants. How, then, can one speak of a judge as being disobedient? Critics have essentially claimed that this is the logical conclusion of the legal realist rule skepticism.[284]

On the other hand, positivism encompasses the idea that judges can indeed misbehave. If positive law is binding, then judges who refuse to be bound could be called disobedient. There is still, however, the problem that Hart and Raz pointed out—it makes no difference to say that a judge misbehaved in coming to a particular decision.

Natural law seems a particularly appropriate way to look at civil disobedience, because then the "civil" aspect comes to the fore. A person who acts in congruence with natural-law principles but breaks a validly enacted law that conflicts with natural law may have to face the consequence of arrest. Yet it is precisely because the person believes that the particular law lacks authority that he or she is willing to break it. Natural law recognizes that even though an enacted law has no authority, there may be consequences to breaking it.

# Legitimacy in Judicial Politics

▼  ▼  ▼

In *Turning Right: The Making of the Rehnquist Supreme Court*, David Savage relates the daily encounters of Lewis Powell, recently retired from the Supreme Court, and Thurgood Marshall, doggedly serving out his final years. Powell religiously walked laps around the Supreme Court's carpeted hallway. Prodded by his doctors, the inactive Marshall began to do the same—but resolutely walked in the opposite direction. Upon their first meeting each day, Powell would say, "Good morning, Thurgood."

"What's so good about it?" Marshall would reply. The next time he passed Powell, Marshall would warn, "I'm gaining on you."

There is something irresistibly poignant in the image of these two old gentlemen, the opposite poles of segregated society, orbiting concentrically around the institution that had transformed their world.[1]

I HAVE suggested previously that the relentless dissents of Brennan and Marshall are legitimate because they have strong roots both in history and in legal philosophy. This chapter explores whether such dissents were tactically and strategically wise.

The Thurgood Marshall papers in the Manuscripts Division of the Library of Congress reveal, unsurprisingly, a justice (as well as his law clerks) actively engaged in the Court's internal political dynamics concerning capital punishment. An internal memorandum from one of Marshall's clerks to the justice, dated September 4, 1990, argued:

From a strategic standpoint, it is probably preferable to forestall for as long as possible this Court's review of the applicability of *Caldwell* to the Florida scheme. So long as the [federal court of appeals] rule remains in place, death-row inmates raising the issue presented in the [petition] can obtain vacatur of their sentences on federal habeas. Should this Court grant review, however, it is likely that a majority of Justices would side with the Florida Supreme Court, destroying [the federal court of appeals]'s better rule. In order not to draw attention to this case, I recommend that you decline from circulating a dissent from denial and that you instead merely vote your standard [federal court of appeals].[2]

In a memo sent about a week later to Justice Marshall from another of his law clerks, the clerk opined:

However, although [petitioners] have a good argument on the merits, I would recommend that, for *defensive* reasons, you not write separately. First, the Court is unlikely to take this case (the pool memo recommended a "close, but deny"), and your writing is unlikely to sway a sufficient number of votes. Second, the few state courts that have considered this issue have *upheld* joint capital sentencing, and it is dangerously possible, even likely, that if this Court did grant, it too would uphold that procedure, thereby making the law worse on a nationwide basis. For these reasons, I recommend your standard [federal court of appeals].[3]

The Supreme Court decided *Lankford v. Idaho* in the spring of 1991, shortly before Marshall's retirement The decision presents a puzzle that turns out to be a paradox. Following briefing and oral argument in *Lankford,* the justices apparently divided 5–4 in favor of affirming the conviction and death sentence—with Marshall providing the fifth vote for affirmance, and with Justice John Paul Stevens writing the opinion for the majority. On October 11, 1990, Justice Marshall wrote a one-line memo to Justice Stevens: "Dear John, I am still with you."[4] On February 21, 1991, one of Marshall's law clerks sent him a memo:

To: Justice Marshall
From: Sheryll
Re: *Lankford v. Idaho*

Over the weekend I did some research on your past record in capital cases.

With respect to cert. [petitions], you have issued approximately 2095 standard dissents from denial in which you say that you would grant the [petition] in order to vacate the death sentence. You have issued an additional 98 dissents from denial on substantive grounds that also include your standard "adhering" language.

In argued capital cases, since *Furman v. Georgia* was decided, you have joined or written majority opinions approximately 19 times. On each occasion the majority disposition was favorable to the capital [defendant]. I could not find a single case in which you joined a majority opinion that disposed of the case in a manner adverse to the capital [defendant]. In one case you even emphasized that you could not join a portion of the majority opinion that suggested that the death penalty might be imposed in other circumstances. In *Estelle v. Smith,* 451 U.S. 454, 474 (1981) you stated:

> I join in all but Part II-C of the opinion of the Court. I adhere to my consistent view that the death penalty is under all circumstances cruel and unusual punishment forbidden by the Eighth and Fourteenth Amendments. *I therefore am unable to join the suggestion in Part II-C that the penalty may ever be constitutionally imposed.* (Marshall, J., concurring in part) [emphasis added].

In *Presnell v. Georgia,* 439 U.S. 14, 17 (1978), you stated:

> While I join the opinion of the Court, I again emphasize my opinion that the death penalty in any proceeding is unconstitutional. (Marshall, J., concurring)

*Lankford* appears to be the first case in which your view of the capital [defendant's] substantive argument is at odds with your standard view that the death penalty violates the Eighth Amendment in all circumstances. The question presented in *Lankford* is "[w]hether a *death sentence* violates the Sixth, *Eighth* and Fourteenth Amendments when. . . ." [emphasis added]. I have tried to think of ways in which you could reconcile your two views—e.g., by saying there is no due process/notice violation but that there is an 8th Amend[ment] violation by virtue of the death sentence. But it seems to me that these views are inherently contradictory. By issuing some 2000 dissents from denial and countless reminders that you believe "the death penalty in *any* proceeding is unconstitutional," you have established a rather emphatic record of not adhering to the Court's precedent in this one critical area.

The Eighth Amendment is squarely raised in this case. Therefore, if you voted to reverse on your standard ground that a death sentence always violates the Eighth Amendment you would not be deciding on grounds not raised by the [petitioner].

I also think that this would be a particularly unfortunate capital case for you to vote to affirm the sentencing proceeding. Defense counsel specifically told the [trial court] in her motion for continuance that she wanted to bring to bear more mitigating evidence. She was appointed counsel only three weeks before the sentencing proceeding but was denied her request for a continuance. More importantly, she was denied her request for a copy of the trial transcript and therefore had to prepare for a capital sentencing without even knowing all of the evidence introduced at the guilt phase. Even if she had asked the [trial court] whether death was actually on the line, she could not have done much better under these circumstances. The [trial court's] rulings, I believe, make this sentencing proceeding highly questionable in terms of reliability required by the Eighth Amendment, even assuming there was adequate notice.

To be consistent with your Eighth Amendment position, I recommend that you write a short separate statement saying that you would reverse [petitioner's] death sentence on the ground that the death penalty is in all circumstances cruel and unusual punishment barred by the Eighth Amendment. If other Justices do not change their votes, you would be concurring in a judgment of reversal. You could simply note the question presented and cite your well-established Eighth Amendment views.

If you are concerned about the fact that the other four justices would only be voting for a remand for resentencing, you could also follow Justice Brennan's standard practice of saying "I would direct that the resentencing proceedings be circumscribed such that the State may not reimpose the death sentence." *Mills v. Maryland,* 486 U.S. 367, 389 (1988) (Brennan, J., concurring). Otherwise, you could just not say anything about that point, as you did in *Mills.*

The next day February 22, the same law clerk sent Marshall a follow-up memo:

> Judge, a possibility just occurred to me regarding this case which I had not thought about earlier. By your voting to affirm in this case, you are providing the fifth vote to uphold a death sentence. It seems to me, to be consistent with your established position that the death sentence is cruel and unusual in all circumstances, your posture should not be to affirm but to reverse or vacate on your standard "adhering" grounds. In this way you could remain consistent with your longstanding position on the death penalty without sanctioning the bad lawyering that so troubled you in this case. Please let me know if you would like to discuss this further.[5]

Marshall responded with a handwritten memorandum to Chief Justice Rehnquist: "I am sorry but I must ask you to re-assign *Lankford v. Idaho.* The question presented is 'whether a *death sentence* invalidates the Sixth, *Eighth* and Fourteenth amendments' [emphasis added]. I can not bring myself to endorse the death penalty under the Eighth Amendment.[6] (A typed version of Marshall's handwritten memo was dated March 5, 1991.)[7] The next day, March 6, 1991, the chief justice wrote to Justice Marshall: "At conference the vote in this case was five-to-four to affirm, with your vote being one of the five. If you have now switched to 're-verse,' that would make five votes to reverse. Since Byron and I both voted to affirm, you should then assign the case."[8] Marshall followed up with a memorandum to conference, saying in summary: "Upon reconsideration, I would now vote to reverse in *Lankford v. Idaho.* However, I would do so on grounds different from those relied upon by Harry, John, Sandra and Tony. My position is simply that the imposition of the death penalty in this case is cruel and unusual punishment under the Eighth Amendment. Because I disagree on the grounds of the disposition, I do not regard myself as the assigning Justice of the five-Justice majority to reverse."[9] On March 8, 1991, Justice Stevens wrote to Justice Blackmun: "I'll be happy to take on the opinion in this case."[10] On April 26, 1991, Justice Stevens circulated a "first draft" of the opinion for the court in *Lankford v. Idaho.*

In one 1989 capital case, the majority of justices started down one path, only to reverse direction. A majority initially voted at conference to overturn the murder conviction of Philip D. Thompkins, who was on death row in Texas. Justice Stevens circulated a twenty-eight-page draft majority opinion, saying that the systematic exclusion of Blacks from the jury may have denied Thompkins a fair trial. Then votes began to shift, and Stevens himself expressed uncertainty about some parts of the draft. Three months and thirty-one memos and draft opinions later, the justices discarded this work and upheld the conviction of Tompkins in a ten-word unsigned order. Tompkins was spared execution when the governor of Texas (citing reasons different from those in Stevens's draft opinion) commuted his sentence to life imprisonment.

The political dynamics within the Court were not limited to capital cases, of course. The *Washington Post* reported that Justice Marshall's papers reveal that he showed little interest when the Supreme Court first considered whether the Constitution should protect private homosexual acts. Only two of the nine justices voted in 1985 to hear the case of an Atlanta man arrested for having sex with another man in his own bedroom.[11] But the papers show that over the next year and a half the case known as *Bowers v. Hardwick* became a high-stakes poker game among the justices, as conservatives and liberals on the Court struggled behind the scenes to make it a definitive constitutional statement on homosexual rights.

> The twists and turns of the Georgia homosexuality case are detailed in the private papers of the late Thurgood Marshall, which were made available to the public recently, only two years after he left the court. The papers portray a group of justices concerned with such minutia as repairing the court's front steps and conducting intricate negotiations to deal with the greatest moral and legal issues of the day. . . .[12]
>
> The chronicle of the Bowers homosexuality case throughout the Marshall files described a series of shifting coalitions, with each side trying to prevent the case from even being heard when it seemed the other side might prevail. In the end, a surprise shift by Justice Lewis F. Powell gave the victory to the conservatives and the law was upheld. . . . The Marshall documents reveal a rich history as the justices imbued every move with calculations that produced a variety of shifting coalitions. In the internal debate over whether to hear the

case, the poker playing strategies became evident in the fall of 1985. Two justices initially agreed to hear the case, Byron White and Chief Justice Warren Burger, who apparently perceived an opportunity to state clearly that the constitution did not protect homosexual acts. But soon the Court's liberals tried to have the case heard because they thought they could carry the day. Suddenly, however, Justice Brennan apparently perceived that the tide had turned and he quickly withdrew his vote, hoping that there would not be the four votes needed. Justice William Rehnquist swiftly countered by adding his name. Justice Marshall apparently disagreed with Justice Brennan, and left his name on the vote to hear the case. It was a decision he came to regret.[13]

After the case was heard and debated, "Justice Powell informed his colleagues on April 8, 1986, he was anguished by the case. . . . Justice John Paul Stevens wrote a memorandum to Justice Powell wryly upbraiding him for his indecision. He told Justice Powell that his views resemble a case in which the Court, with all nine members present, said it was equally divided."[14]

The files also contain a memorandum written to Justice Marshall by Daniel B. Richman, a law clerk who is now a law professor at Fordham University. The memo noted that the

> *Bowers* case is difficult because the statute does not explicitly prohibit acts between homosexuals but specific acts usually performed by homosexuals which do not lead to procreation. [Writing in capital letters for emphasis, Mr. Richman said he feared] The justices would either forget or be ignorant of the fact That such acts including anal and oral sex are also performed by heterosexuals. "THIS IS NOT A CASE ABOUT ONLY HOMOSEXUALS. ALL SORTS OF PEOPLE DO THIS KIND OF THING."[15]

## Dissents from Cases Granted Plenary Review

One disadvantage to the abolitionist bloc for the sustained dissent is that their votes are a known factor. Whether the justices like the term or not, their votes are lobbied for. The process of collegial lobbying greatly influences the tone and substance of a finished opinion, and thus the future course of the law.[16] The judgment itself, that supposed product of the cool application of law to facts, may often depend on the results of intense lobbying by blocs or single justices in order to construct a majority.

In the typical death penalty case (if a death penalty case is ever typical), no justice need have lobbied for Brennan's or Marshall's final vote. They were givens in the calculus of the Court that determines whether a life may be taken by the state.

It is illuminating to examine the actual results engendered by the positions of Brennan and Marshall. Mark Kelman called their dissents "one-sided acceptance"[17] of the reasoning of *Furman* and its progeny. That is, when the two provided the votes needed to sustain the condemned's life in a particular situation resulting from the abstract constitutionality of the death penalty, and ad hoc alliance was formed with the three or more justices who were willing to limit the application of the death penalty in that instance or under those circumstances.[18] This is illustrated by the voting pattern in *Enmund v. Florida*, a decision holding that the death penalty was unconstitutionally severe as a punishment for an armed robber who neither took a life nor intended or contemplated that a life would be taken.[19] Marshall provided the fifth vote for the opinion by Justice White, finding Enmund's death sentence unconstitutional; he did not write separately in *Enmund*. Perhaps Marshall joined White's opinion in an attempt to strengthen the authority of the holding. Brennan wrote a one-paragraph separate concurrence, reaffirming his dissent in *Gregg*.[20]

Another example of the ad hoc alliance is the voting pattern and the rationales behind the opinions in *Coker v. Georgia*,[21] which held the death penalty unconstitutional as applied to the rapist of an adult woman. Again, Justice White announced the judgment and filed an opinion in which Justices Stewart, Blackmun, and Stevens joined. Justice Powell concurred in the judgment and dissented in part.[22] Justices Brennan and Marshall filed separate, one-paragraph statements, concurring in the judgment only.[23]

A more conspicuous example of "one-sided acceptance" can be found in *Ford v. Wainwright*,[24] which held that the Constitution forbids execution of the insane. *Ford* typifies a phenomenon discussed below: a Marshall dissent from the denial of plenary review by the Court evolving into a Marshall opinion for the majority. The resulting Marshall opinion for the Court in *Ford* reflected a curious amalgam of opinions that displayed a species of decision making seen frequently during the Burger Court.[25] Justice Marshall announced the Court's judgment and delivered an opinion that was joined by Justices Brennan, Blackmun, Powell, and Stevens (with Powell joining only as to parts of the opinion and concurring separately to say so).[26] Meanwhile, Justices O'Connor and White, while disagreeing with the majority, agreed with the result in part and dissented in part;[27] Justice Rehnquist filed a straightforward dissent, with which Chief Justice Burger joined.[28]

Of course, Marshall could not have written in *Ford* an opinion declaring that the Florida statute sought to be applied was unconstitutional on the ground that the eighth amendment forbade all executions. He would not have had the votes. The task of writing the opinion would have fallen to another Justice, who might have crafted a different rationale to support the Court's result. Marshall had to concentrate on the narrower questions of whether the eighth amendment prevented Florida from executing the insane and of what process was due the condemned who advanced the claim of insanity between the time of sentencing and the time of execution.[29] In other words, he had to assume, for the purposes of Ford's claims, that the entire body of federal death penalty law decided since *Furman* was decided correctly. It was not necessary to reiterate his views on *Furman,* as to do so would not have helped his cause. Of necessity, Marshall implicitly acknowledged that, assuming Florida can execute Ford, the question was whether Florida can do so under these circumstances.[30]

Although the votes of the abolitionist bloc were known factors (and thus these voters were not subject to lobbying by their fellow justices in the typical death penalty case), this did not diminish the fact that these seats are occupied and that these votes counted. But the lack of lobbying may have meant that the collegial argument was no longer pitched to appeal to these justices. Kelman wrote that "a justice who is willing to participate on an equal footing, doctrinally speaking, may be in a position to limit or ameliorate the [prior precedent], whereas a justice's adherence to outvoted views estranges him from the precise questions posed by succeeding cases and wastes his potential influence on the evolutionary direction of the case law."[31] What Kelman was advocating—as the most strategically sound position, as well as that which most comports with the institutional values inherent in the doctrine of *stare decisis* while maintaining some degree of intellectual self-respect—was a policy of what he termed "damage-control" or "judicial Fabianism."[32] The goal of such a policy is "the gradual reshaping of a bad decision into good, or at least less noxious, law."[33] He sees an acceptance of this policy of suspended dissent or temporary acquiescence, which limits the original, dissent-inspiring principle while furthering a consensus on the bench and thus the Court's institutional authority, in the votes of such "self-subordinators"[34] as Stewart, Blackmun, Powell and Stevens. In the minds of these justices, perhaps inspired by the example of the second Justice Harlan, there is an "institutional duty" or a "judicial responsibility"[35] to hold their personal views back and to respect precedent if they possibly can. It is perhaps coincidental that in the last fifteen years these justices have also held the balance of power on the Court, but the coincidence does give one pause.

Kelman overstated the problem, I think. Even if the views of the perennial dissenters are indeed in some sense discounted in the tactics of collegial lobbying that produce an opinion of the Court, that still left seven justices whose views *were* solicited. Assume a solid bloc of four—Rehnquist, White, Scalia, and Kennedy—who will consistently vote to uphold the death penalty in virtually every case; I shall label them the "retentionist" bloc. (This may be a misnomer, however, for the articulated concerns of this group are more directed toward considerations of federalism. That is, in their hearts they may be retentionists, but their legal position is that the state legislatures have the ultimate choice).[36] This leaves a center of three—Blackmun, Stevens, and O'Connor—who cover the spectrum from left to right. In the calculus I have posited, these three votes would have reactivated the votes and views of Brennan and Marshall. Although the pool of centrist justices shrank with the retirement of Powell (the ablest switch-hitter of the modern Court),[37] the cases decided during his tenure illustrate the tactical advantages—in orders for resentencing and in delays in execution that lead state courts to reverse or executives to commute to life—of the inflexibility of the dissenters.[38] While their impact on the course of law may have been indeterminate, the dissenters' presence caused the struggle to continue. Although there has been a large toll in executions in the past few years, all it took to stop a state-sanctioned killing, once the highest federal appellate level had been reached, was three votes. If those votes were not there, Brennan and Marshall would not have been influencing the course of the law directly, whatever their views on the law.[39]

Temporary acquiescence presents its own dilemmas and ironies. Should a justice, an original dissenter who has since acquiesced by means of a separate concurrence, adhere to her position when now, after some time, she is the key vote to overrule? Or, even more puzzling, when is the fifth, swing vote the key to unlocking the precedential value of an application of the precedent or the original precedent itself? When, as in *Furman,* two justices hold on the broad-based ground that the death penalty is unconstitutional[40] and three on the ground that the death penalty is unconstitutional as applied,[41] then the rationale of the decision is the narrowest ground.[42] But what if the three believe that the death penalty as applied is unconstitutional but take three different positions on the rationale for that view?[43] Should a swing voter acquiesce to form an artificial majority without first insisting that her reasoning become the core of the opinion? In what sense is this acquiescence?

Perhaps these dilemmas are surmountable within the secrecy of the conference room. But does not the justice who spends dissent in order to guide the lower courts and the nation as a whole and thus preserve the Court's authority, part and parcel of its "institutional capital,"[44] create a further precedent, another obstacle to eventual reversal or even reconsideration? Perhaps this is why, even when concerns for the doctrine of *stare decisis* are openly voiced, the true "self-subordinator" will always hesitate. Deep down, she will intuitively feel that the dissent was right the first time; if the principle is wrong, let us not engrave it in stone.

## Dissents from Denial of Certiorari

Although the term "dissent" most often refers to a disagreement with a majority opinion of the court, there are other types of dissents that can be equally important. One is a dissent from denial of certiorari ("cert.") Without going into great detail, a brief description of this process clarifies how important a dissent from denial of cert. can be. When a petition for writ of certiorari is filed with the Supreme Court, copies are circulated to the justices' chambers through a variety of means. From there, cases that may be considered "certworthy" are placed on what is known as the discuss list.[45] Of all types of cases, only those involving the death penalty are automatically placed on the discuss list. "Whether the rule . . . comes from general consensus, or from the knowledge that Brennan and Marshall would always put them on anyway, these cases will at least be discussed by the justices.[46]

Once on the discuss list, a case needs at least four votes to be granted plenary review. This is when a dissent from denial becomes extremely important. Such dissent is often written before a case is even denied certiorari. If a justice feels that the cases will not get the necessary votes for certiorari, she can ask to have the case "relisted," or considered later.[47] In the meantime, a dissent from denial is circulated to the other chambers. This accomplishes two purposes. First, it facilitates discussion between the chambers, which, under normal circumstances, is virtually nonexistent.[48] Second, if the dissent is strong enough, it can garner a crucial vote to grant. Through interviews with clerks and justices, Perry was able to determine that this strategy was effective in picking up ten to thirty votes per term.[49] Because these dissents are circulated before the final decision on certiorari, they are often not published, although they are generally accepted by the justices, who recognize their purpose.

An excellent example of how effective the dissent from denial of certiorari can be was contained within Justice Marshall's papers.[50] In *Parker v. Dugger*,[51] a case that applied the principles of *Lockett v. Ohio*[52] to the appellate process, the petition for writ of certiorari was slated to be denied.[53] However, Justice Brennan circulated a copy of a nine-page dissent from denial of certiorari in which he was joined by Justice Marshall.[54] It was extremely well reasoned and eventually led to garnering the votes necessary to grant certiorari. Once granted plenary review, Parker prevailed on the merits.

Although Justice Brennan's dissent from denial of certiorari in the *Parker* case was never published because the case was granted certiorari, in similar cases justices often make their dissent from denial public. Brennan and Marshall dissented from denial on all capital cases by using a "stock" statement:

> Adhering to our views that the death penalty is in all circumstances cruel and unusual punishment prohibited by the Eighth and Fourteenth Amendments, *Gregg v. Georgia,* 428 U.S. 153, 227, 231 (1976), we would grant certiorari and vacate the death sentences in these cases.[55]

The purpose of this dissent was to show their unwavering opposition to the death penalty even in cases that did not receive the notoriety of those granted certiorari. As Brennan once remarked, "Perhaps few outside the Court realize that, quite apart from his general opposition to all executions, [Marshall] has filed more than 150 dissents from 'denial of certiorari' in capital cases."[56] Sometimes, however, Brennan and Marshall would write a longer dissent from denial with a different purpose, instruction. Because death penalty cases often come up on state habeas petitions and then later on federal habeas petitions, the dissents can be instructions to the lawyer arguing the case on how the petition should be brought in order to be granted.[57] Although this is not done openly, it is a recognized occurrence.

Finally, along the same lines (and as discussed in more detail below), a dissent from denial can be used to give future litigants glimpses of what would make a case certworthy.[58] This aspect, however, is frowned upon by many members of the Court and is a good segue into the effects the dissents have on the decision-making process of certiorari.

Justice Stevens has said:

> One characteristic of all opinions dissenting from the denial of certiorari is manifest. They are totally unnecessary. They are examples of the purest form of dicta. . . . [T]hey are potentially misleading. Since the Court provides no explanation of the reasons for denying certiorari, the dissenter's arguments . . . appear to be more persuasive than most other opinions. . . .[59]

He goes on to say that because the dissents often do not mention valid reasons for denying certiorari, the practice makes the Court appear to have acted differently than it may have. Additionally, these repeated dissents can cause a "bitterness" around an issue and make a shift in doctrine that much less likely.[60]

These criticisms aside, however, that death penalty cases do automatically make at least the discuss list shows the effectiveness of the repeated dissent from denial. In fact, one justice who was not opposed to capital punishment once circulated a memo in response to these dissents saying "we just ought to summarily reverse all death cases" out of sheer frustration.[61] Thus it can be seen that the dissent from denial of certiorari can be as important a tool as a dissenting opinion in a case that has been granted certiorari.

Fortunately, the Clerk of the Court censors many of the petitions that have technical problems. If they exceed page limits for example, they are sent back to the litigants. But the ones that pass are tied up in a bundle of red tape. That is an unintended pun. There actually is a red tape that ties them up. They are put on the cart and it is walked around from chamber to chamber. You could hear it coming. You sit there and listen woefully as it rumbles down the hall. When we heard it coming, we would usually sit there and shoot rubber bands at the chandeliers. But the taxpayers didn't lose any money. From time to time we'd have to get up there and clean them out.[62]

In virtually all jurisdictions, capital trials occur in two stages. The traditional trial to determine guilt or innocence is followed by a penalty phase, essentially a separate trial on the issue of sentencing. After conviction of a capital offense and imposition of the death penalty, the condemned has a right to a plenary appeal to the state court of appeals.[63] Counsel must be provided at trial[64] and on this plenary direct appeal.[65] Beyond this point, however, the right to counsel is unclear.

After the plenary direct appeal, the death row inmate is entitled to seek certiorari in the United States Supreme Court and then to seek postconviction relief in state court. State postconviction affords a procedural mechanism for raising claims that were not or could not have been raised on the direct appeal.[66] For this reason, at least as to these issues, it is fair to characterize the state postconviction process as an extension of and a supplement to the plenary appeal. Depending on the type of claims raised and the requirements of local procedure, a state postconviction proceeding may be initiated in the state trial court; if it is denied, it may be appealed to the state appellate court; or such litigation may be initiated in the state appellate court. The prisoner may again seek certiorari review in the Supreme Court.

Following completion of state postconviction litigation, the inmate is entitled to file a petition for writ of habeas corpus in federal district court; if this is denied, he may appeal the denial to the appropriate circuit court of appeals. At least since *Brown v. Allen*,[67] the controversial[68] Great Writ of habeas corpus has permitted the relitigation of federal constitutional claims, the substance of which were presented previously to the state courts.[69] If the condemned prisoner loses in the federal circuit court of appeals, he may once again petition for certiorari in the Supreme Court.

The postconviction process in Florida is functionally typical of the collateral systems in most states. The litigation stages in Florida are as follows:

Convincing the Supreme Court to grant plenary consideration—

| STEP 1<br>Trial and sentence in state trail court | STEP 4<br>State postconviction motion in state trial court | STEP 7<br>Federal habeas corpus petition in federal district court |
| --- | --- | --- |
| STEP 2<br>Affirmance of conviction and sentence on plenary appeal to state court | STEP 5<br>Appeal to state appellate court of state postconviction motion; filing of original proceedings in state appellate court | STEP 8<br>Appeal to federal circuit court |
| STEP 3<br>Request for plenary review in U.S. Supreme Court | STEP 6<br>Request for plenary review in U.S. Supreme Court | STEP 9<br>Request for plenary review in U.S. Supreme Court |

**EXECUTIVE CLEMENCY**

"certiorari"—is *always* an uphill battle; in the 1994 Term the Rehnquist Court handed down opinions in just 93 cases out of the more than 7,000 on its docket (the lowest number since the 1955 Term, when the Warren Court decided 94 cases by written opinion, out of a far smaller docket of 1,856). Particularly in death cases, the Rehnquist/Thomas/Scalia Court is a tough room, with Clarence Thomas,[70] who recently threatened and taunted us all that "I'm going to be here on the court for 40 years. For those who don't like it, get over it" (well, it sure *sounded* like a threat, although it is nice to know that we all have something to look forward to over the next four decades), and whose dismal performance as a justice so far has already more than fulfilled my lowest and basest expectations, never asking questions at oral arguments, writing few opinions, and siding with Scalia so often that the latter is said to have two votes; Thomas does his speaking through groups of people plucked from the Rolodex of his best friend and through the brutal character of his judicial opinions, which, in addition to his strident opposition to virtually all federal rights protections, which he derides as "special treatment" (incredible as it seems, Thomas appears to believe his own press releases that Bush named him to the court regardless of his race); the gems of Thurgood Marshall's successor have included dissents in two cases where Thomas argued that the eighth amendment's prohibition against cruel and unusual punishment should not apply to the treatment of prison inmates, even when they are gratuitously and viciously beaten.

The best explanation of the Court's certiorari policy is to be found in H. W. Perry's book *Deciding to Decide*. His research and analysis documents what Court outsiders have long intuited: that death is different for the justices, and that death cases are treated differently. Perry noted: "I think it is common knowledge that all capital cases are discussed in conference. They were specially marked when we [the Supreme Court clerks] sent things in to the justice. Even if the justices thought they were frivolous, they were at least discussed in conference." This may be common knowledge, but Perry reported:

I had never heard it prior to the interviews. In the thirty–eighth interview, a clerk told me: "All of the death cases are automatically discussed, I doubt if anyone's told you that." Indeed, I had heard it several times by then. When I mentioned to a justice that I knew that all capital cases were automatically placed on the discuss list, he seemed somewhat surprised that I knew it.

PERRY: I understand that for some time, capital cases have automatically been put on the discuss list.

JUSTICE: [Pause] Yes, that is true.

PERRY: Why is that?

JUSTICE: Because of the finality of it. [Pause] That doesn't mean that they all get discussed that thoroughly though.

Regardless of the thoroughness of the discussion, the fact that all capital cases automatically make the discuss list is noteworthy. No other category of cases is guaranteed a portion of the Court's valuable conference time. Cases petitioned by the solicitor general are effectively assured a place on the list. They are different, however, because the assumption is that the SG has already screened cases. Even though most individual decisions on cert. are made prior to conference, and discussion in conference is often cursory, given the dynamics that can occur in there, chances for review are substantially increased by making the discuss list. If a case is on the list, a justice at least has the chance to demonstrate certworthiness in ways that are not particularly obvious.

> Of course, death cases got special attention. . . . On those we would often see if we could make the case on some grounds apart from the death issue. Capital cases were given a great deal of attention, although Justice _____ automatically recommended to grant vacate and remand; but still we would often look at these capital cases to see if there were other issues. We'd look for other issues that might attract other justices.

> A lot of these capital cases clearly are not certworthy and we would make distinctions. Although as a matter of principle Justice _____ did object to all the capital cases.

Justices Brennan and Marshall, of course, are on the public record opposing all capital punishment as unconstitutional.

Capital cases are advantaged not only by being automatically placed on the discuss list but also by receiving heightened scrutiny in chambers. Clerks search for any chance to review, which is quite the opposite of the normal search for any justification to deny. One would expect extra attention by Brennan and Marshall, but it was surprising to learn that every chamber treats these cases with special care. From various chambers:

> CLERK: The only particular cases that I would outline in great detail, regardless of how frivolous they were, were the death cases. . . . They all treat them seriously because of the gravity of what is involved. Everyone feels really strange about this.

> CLERK: [Capital cases] were starred for special treatment.

> CLERK: I know when I looked at the capital cases last year, I just realized how important they were, and I would go over them and look at them because you realize what it meant for the individuals.

CLERK: At some point you should remind me to tell you about death cases because they are really quite different. . . .

PERRY: . . . You suggested that I should ask you about death cases.

CLERK: Yeah, I hated death cases. But Justice A had a lot of influence on death cases. Justices B, C, and D had become very important in the death case issue, forming the plurality. And so in a sense they really determined what was to be the response. I mean you could count that Justice E and Justice F would generally uphold death penalties. Brennan and Marshall—you had their votes automatically and so in some ways the coalition that you really had to put together was Justices B, C, and D. You had to convince all three of them that under their criteria, the death penalty was not acceptable. But I hated working on these cases because I had to spend a disproportionate amount of time on them.

CLERK: Preparation of the death cases always involved a longer memo. Justice _____ took them seriously, but I don't know to what extent that they caused him a particularly big problem. It was always our fear that we'd get a stay and have to deal with the stay for the __th Circuit.

PERRY: I don't understand.

CLERK: The __th Circuit was where they kept wanting to fry people, and we had the justice who would have to make the initial response to a stay.

CLERK: Death penalty cases are treated very, very seriously.

CLERK: The only tricky ones with the i.f.p. [*in forma pauperis*] cases were the death penalty cases because . . . all death penalties are discussed at conference.

CLERK: On the memo in death cases you would always say that it was a death case, and you would state more specifically where it's at. For example, you might say that you should wait for habeas; perhaps it hadn't gone through habeas at the federal level or only at the state level. But when it came from review at the circuit court of appeals, then you began saying this was it for the poor fellow. Perry, 94–95.

Perry went on to observe that

the close attention given to all capital cases is most certainly a departure from standard operating procedures. No one would begrudge heightened scrutiny to the case of someone who is about to be killed by the state; but to place capital cases on the discuss list automatically is an interesting decision rule. The justices continually declaim that they cannot be a court to ensure justice. They often let stand what they know to be incorrectly decided cases, some of which involve lengthy periods of incarceration, but their role, so they say, is to clarify the law so that justice can be done in the courts below. It is not obvious, then, why death cases should be different. If there is any area where most lower court judges probably would be careful, for fear of reversal if nothing else, it would be in capital cases. Despite controversy in the public and among some justices who refuse to treat the issue as *stare decisis*,[71] the issue of capital punishment is *res judicata*.[72] The Court has made clear that capital punishment is allowed under certain conditions, even if it has not made clear exactly what those conditions are, or more precisely, how to determine when those conditions exist. Of course all capital cases are not directly challenging capital punishment per se. Some other procedure or happenstance may be at issue. Nevertheless, it seems that when the death penalty is involved, the justices, except perhaps Brennan and Marshall, are simply trying to ensure justice.

What is significant here is not that the justices have arbitrarily chosen to be extra careful when it comes to a capital case, a position most would applaud; rather it is that this decision rule has subtle implications. The rule suggests that there is really no such thing as a frivolous case per se, whereas the notion that there are unquestionably frivolous cases underlies much of the justification for the way the cert. decision process works. . . . We should note that justices and clerks assert that huge numbers of cases are patently and objectively frivolous because they raise no real issues of law that deserve review by the Court. That is, the petitioner simply does not like the outcome and wants one last shot at avoiding jail or paying what he owes. But it seems that even the most frivolous case, in terms of an issue of law, deserves careful consideration if the punishment is so extreme. Such a position weakens the force of the argument that cases are frivolous *prima facie*. By definition, the automatic inclusion of capital cases on the discuss list argues that the justices are saying that no case can be considered frivolous—uncertworthy perhaps but not frivolous—if the punishment involved is death. All the while, the justices are willing to accept the idea that a case can be frivolous if the punishment involves only life imprisonment. That, it seems to me, suggests the definition of "frivolous" is tautological—a frivolous case is a case the justices consider to be frivolous. Yet when I posed this definition of frivolousness to the informants (though not in the context of capital cases), virtually every one said that such a definition was preposterous. Or, as one clerk put it, the notion that "any case is potentially certworthy is a crock."

The treatment of capital cases belies the wholesale rejection of such a premise, however. Granted, reasonable people may agree most of the time that a case raises no particularly worthwhile issue for review in the Supreme Court, but that is always ultimately a subjective rather than objective evaluation. The special treatment of capital cases makes that point. It also lends some support to the view that the Supreme Court is in control of its agenda more than the textbook notion suggests. The Court has chosen to pay special attention to cases involving capital punishment, and in doing so, it gives less time to something else. Cases, on their face, do not compel acceptance or rejection. This might seem obvious, but it is not the underlying assumption of the cert. process. Perry, 95-97.

## Initial Dissents That Evolved into Opinions

> "Defend yourself," the judges said.
> "No," the accused said.
> "Why? But you must."
> "Not yet. I want you to take full responsibility."
> Albert Camus, *Notebooks,* November 1943[73]

I mentioned above that in *Ford v. Strickland* what began as a Marshall opinion dissenting from the Court's denial of plenary review ended up as an opinion on behalf of the Court. This evolution is revealed in the Thurgood Marshall papers at the Library of Congress. On November 22, 1985, Justice Marshall circulated to his colleagues a "first draft" of his dissent from denial of certiorari in *Ford*.[74] That same day, William Brennan wrote to Marshall, "please join me in your dissent."[75] On December 2, Marshall circulated a "second draft" noting that Justice Brennan had joined his dissent from denial of certiorari.[76] Over the next several months, two more justices joined Marshall and Brennan in their view that *Ford* was worth plenary consideration. The case was briefed and argued, and on June 3, 1986, Justice Marshall circulated a "first draft" of his opinion for the Court. Justice Sandra Day O'Connor wrote on the same day, "Dear Thurgood, for now I will await further writing."[77]

The next day Justice William Rehnquist wrote, "Dear Thurgood: in due course, I will circulate a dissent in this case."[78] Also on June 4, Justice Byron White wrote, "Dear Thurgood, I shall await further writing."[79] Brennan also wrote, "Dear Thurgood, I agree."[80] The following day Justice Lewis Powell—who ultimately authored an important special concurrence in *Ford v. Wainwright*—wrote to Marshall:

Dear Thurgood:

Parts I and II of your opinion are excellent, and I expect to join them. I do have some minor suggestions. On page 4, you state that we granted certiorari in order to determine the constitutionality of Florida's procedures for determining sanity. As I view this case, we granted cert to decide (i) whether the Eighth Amendment forbids execution of the insane, and (ii) if so, whether the DC [district court] should have held an evidentiary hearing on petitioner's claim. In answering these questions, we need not decide what procedures are constitutionally required, since Florida's procedures clearly do not satisfy § 2254(d), and therefore no presumption of correctness attaches to the Governor's "finding" of sanity in this case.

On page 6, you discuss the manner in which "standards of decency" have evolved. I agree that, in addition to relevant legislation, we look to state law, and to the common law that the Eighth Amendment presumably adopted. Decisions in other common law countries also are sources. I would prefer not to refer to "international opinion" or to our "own best judgment," especially when more certain sources of authority are available. Cf. *Gregg v. Georgia,* 428 U.S. 153, 173 (1976) (opinion of STEWART, J., POWELL, J., STEVENS, J.) (assessment of contemporary standards "does not call for a subjective judgment" by courts). This Court is often criticized by those who say that we base our decisions on such factors rather than on the Constitution and the law itself.

Similarly, on p. 9 your draft refers to an international study prepared at the request of the United Nations Secretary General. I would not cite this study without considering which nations have replied and what they said. Capital punishment is still extensively carried out in many sections of the world, and I doubt that the suspect's sanity receives much attention in a number of countries. I do not recall whether the Soviet Union has retained capital punishment as such, but few people doubt that in effect the sending of offenders to Siberia may result in their death.

Also on p. 9, the beautifully written paragraph that begins on that page refers to views "shared . . . around the world," and to "evidence of global restriction." I have the same negative reaction to relying on speculative "sources" such as these when we have the common law, adopted by the Eighth Amendment of the Constitution, and the numerous decisions of state courts and legislatures.

I am not comfortable with parts III and IV. Your draft apparently would require states to provide for hearings at which live testimony is taken with full cross-examination. Pp. 133, 14–15, 16. Moreover, you would require essentially "unrestricted" admission of arguably relevant evidence at such hearings, along the lines of the Court's recent decision in *Skipper v. South Carolina,* No. 84-6859. Pp. 13, 16. Finally, you specifically disapprove group psychiatric examinations on the ground that they are likely to be unreliable. P. 15, n.3. I am not prepared to agree on these points, and indeed we need not decide them in this case.

States may be able to structure fair procedures where the decision-maker determines sanity based on written reports, as long as the defendant has an opportunity to submit such a report. Also, in my view it is important as a general matter to give States a fair measure of flexibility in designing appropriate procedures for conducting psychiatric examinations as well as for making the final determination of sanity.

In sum, I expect to join parts I and II of your opinion, and I may write separately on the issues discussed in parts III and IV.[81]

On June 9, 1986, Justice Blackmun joined Marshall's opinion, writing "Dear Thurgood: Please join me."[82]

On June 16, 1986, Marshall responded to Powell's memo with one of his own:

Dear Lewis:

Thank you for your letter. After thinking about your comments, I believe we are simply not in accord on the fundamental question involved in the procedural sections of the opinion: whether the prisoner claiming insanity is entitled to only minimal due process, or whether he must be accorded an especially reliable proceeding that will protect against arbitrariness or error. Offhand, I do not know of any interest that this Court has held to be significant enough to enjoy constitutional protection, yet deserving of only a paper hearing. Indeed, in *Goldberg v. Kelly,* the Court stated that "[i]n almost every setting where important decisions turn on questions of fact, due process requires an opportunity to confront and cross-examine adverse witnesses." 297 U.S. 254, 269 (1970). In any event, I cannot agree that such a limited proceeding would adequately protect the longstanding interest of the State in avoiding execution of the insane or protect the obvious interest of the prisoner in being spared from execution while insane. Thus, on this point, I think I must stand firm.

Nevertheless, the discussion of procedures in the opinion is not necessary to the disposition of this case, and I have provided my thoughts primarily as a guide to those who must decide what will be deemed "adequate" in the future. Thus, I hope that you will be able to join the portions of the draft, circulating today, upon which we find common ground in recognizing the Eighth Amendment right and in concluding that Florida's current procedures fall short of minimal requirements.[83]

The next day, Justice Stevens wrote to Marshall, "Dear Thurgood: Please join me."[84] Also on June 17, Powell wrote to Marshall, "Dear Thurgood: Please join me in Parts I and II of your second draft. I do not agree that § 2254 or the Constitution requires a 'second trial' on insanity, I will write separately on the procedure issue. I will try to have something circulated later this week."[85] On the same day, Byron White wrote to Sandra Day O'Connor, "Dear Sandra, please join me in your separate opinion in this case."[86] Justice Rehnquist circulated a draft of his dissenting opinion on June 18, 1986, and on the following day Chief Justice Warren Burger wrote to him, "Dear Bill: I join your dissenting opinion in this case."[87]

The Marshall papers also disclose that the same evolution occurred in *Caldwell v. Mississippi,* a case I shall now examine in some detail. Bobby Caldwell was convicted in Mississippi of the shooting death of a grocery store owner during the course of a robbery. In their case for mitigation during sentencing proceedings, his lawyers asked the jury to show mercy, pointing to Caldwell's youth, character, and background. Defense counsel stressed the gravity and responsibility of sentencing a person to death.[88] In reply, the prosecutor sought to minimize the jury's responsibility for its decision, stating:

> I'm in complete disagreement with the approach the defense has taken. . . . I think it's unfair. I think the lawyers know better. Now, they would have you believe that you're going to kill this man and they know—they know that your decision is not the final decision. My God, how unfair can you be? Your job is reviewable. They know it.[89]

The trial court, over defense objections, allowed the prosecutor's statements to stand, and explained to the jury that a death penalty is automatically reviewable.[90] A closely divided Mississippi Supreme Court affirmed.

Mr. Caldwell then sought plenary review in the United States Supreme Court which the justices voted to deny.[91] On September 28, 1984, just before the Court began its 1984 Term on the first Monday in October, Marshall circulated to his fellow justices a seven-page draft opinion dissenting from the Court's decision to deny certiorari.[92] Five days later, Justice Brennan wrote his colleague a note, with copies to the other justices: "Dear Thurgood: Please join me in your dissent from denial of cert.

in [*Caldwell v. Mississippi*.]" The next day, Marshall circulated a "2nd draft" registering Brennan's joinder.

Perhaps persuaded by his draft dissent, the Justices reconsidered and agreed to receive full briefing and oral argument on Bobby Caldwell's constitutional claims. Following argument, Marshall was assigned the task of writing the opinion for the Court. He circulated a "1st draft" on April 26, 1985; its eighteen pages were an expanded version of his draft dissent from denial of certiorari.[93] That same day, Brennan signed on with a terse "I agree,"[94] while Justice Powell noted that he had taken "no part in the consideration or decision of this case."[95] Marshall circulated a "2nd Draft" on April 29,[96] the same day that Justices Stevens[97] and Blackmun[98] wrote asking to join the opinion. Marshall circulated a "3rd Draft" on May 1. On May 22, Justice White wrote Marshall that "as you may have surmised, I await the dissent in this case."[99] He did not have long to wait, since Justice Rehnquist circulated a "1st Draft" of his dissent on May 23; White joined the dissent on May 28. Near the end of the Court's Term, in June 1985, the opinions were announced.

Writing an opinion in which a plurality of four justices joined in full and Justice O'Connor joined in pertinent part, Justice Marshall held that the court-endorsed prosecutorial statements challenged by Caldwell undermined the eighth amendment's heightened "need for reliability in the determination that death is the appropriate punishment in a specific case."[100] At issue was the concern that "the sentencing process should facilitate the responsible and reliable exercise of sentencing discretion."[101] Marshall emphasized that the "qualitative difference of death from all other punishments requires a correspondingly greater degree of scrutiny of the capital sentencing determination."[102] Because the Court could not be certain that the prosecutor's statements had no effect on the sentencing decision, that decision did not meet the standard of reliability required by the eighth amendment. Although Caldwell's conviction was affirmed, his death sentence was vacated.[103]

Justice Marshall's opinion identified four reasons to fear "substantial unreliability" and a bias in favor of death sentences when there are suggestions that the jury sentencing decision is not final.[104] First, he noted the limited scope of appellate review of such decisions. Appellate courts are "wholly ill-suited to evaluate the appropriateness of death in the first instance" because of the inability of the appellate record to convey the "intangibles" that may affect a death sentence.[105] Because "most appellate courts review sentencing determinations with a presumption of correctness," a defendant's right to a fair sentencing determination would not be merely postponed, but deprived altogether.[106]

Justice Marshall observed, second, that there was an "intolerable danger" that a jury, otherwise unconvinced that death is the appropriate sentence, might wish to "send a message" of extreme disapproval of the defendant's acts. Confident that the decision could be "corrected on appeal," the jury might more freely impose a sentence of death. Justice Marshall wrote that "whatever intangibles a jury might consider in its sentencing determination, few can be gleaned from the appellate record. This inability to confront and examine the individuality of the defendant would be particularly devastating to any argument for consideration of what this Court has termed '[those] compassionate or mitigating factors stemming from the diverse frailties of mankind.' "[107]

Third, because only a death sentence is reviewable, a jury's inclination to "delegate" responsibility would necessitate imposing that sentence. This would present the "specter of the imposition of death based on a factor wholly irrelevant to legitimate sentencing concerns."[108] The death sentence resulting from the jury's desire to avoid ultimate responsibility could lead to a defendant's execution, despite a state's failure to prove that death was the appropriate punishment.

Finally, Marshall acknowledged the extremely difficult position in which the capital-sentencing juror is placed. Faced with the issue of deciding whether another should die, jurors are given "only partial guidance" and afforded "substantial discretion."[109] "Given such a situation," Marshall wrote, "the uncorrected suggestion that the responsibility for any determination of death will rest with others presents an intolerable danger that the jury will in fact choose to minimize the importance of the role."[110] This problem is compounded when the jury is made aware that the ultimate arbiters are the justices of the state's supreme court. It is possible that "many jurors will be tempted to view these respected legal authorities as having more of a 'right' to make such an important decision than has the jury."[111] The invitation to rely on judicial review "will generate a bias toward returning a death sentence that is simply too great."[112]

For these reasons, Justice Marshall's opinion observed that legal authorities have almost unanimously rejected the type of statements made by the prosecutor in *Caldwell*. Most state courts that have dealt with the question have condemned the prejudicial effect of prosecutorial conduct that minimizes any juror's sense of responsibility.[113]

Justice Marshall addressed and rejected the state's three arguments for upholding the death sentence in *Caldwell* regardless of the prosecutor's statements. First, he found no merit in the state's contention that the prosecutor's comments were "invited" as a "reasonable response" to the defense counsel's arguments.[114] Second, Marshall reasoned that the Court's decision in *Donnelly v. DeChristoforo*[115] did not preclude a finding of constitutional error in the misleading arguments of a prosecutor.[116] Third, the justice rejected the state's argument that *California v. Ramos*[117] was authority permitting states to decide freely what information about postsentencing procedure to expose to a jury. Where the prosecutor's argument about appellate review is neither accurate nor relevant, the limited, valid state interest outlined in *Ramos* is not satisfied.[118] "That appellate review is available to a capital defendant," Marshall wrote "is no valid basis for a jury to return such a sentence if otherwise it might not. It is simply a factor that in itself is wholly irrelevant to the determination of the appropriate sentence."[119] Creating an image of diminished responsibility is not a valid state interest and is not sanctioned by *Ramos*, he concluded.[120]

Justice O'Connor concurred in *Caldwell*, joining in the judgment and in Marshall's opinion for his brief treatment of *Ramos*. O'Connor, who wrote the Court's opinion in *Ramos*, agreed with Marshall's statement that the case was not controlling in *Caldwell*, reasoning that the prosecutor's comments "were impermissible because they were inaccurate and misleading in a manner that diminished the jury's sense of responsibility."[121] O'Connor disagreed with what she perceived as Marshall's implication that any information regarding appellate review would be "wholly irrelevant."[122] Jurors may not understand the limited scope of appellate review, she argued, and accurate information may be needed to educate the jury on the importance of their decision.[123] The Constitution, the justice maintained, does not preclude the giving of instructions that include such information.[124] O'Connor nonetheless agreed with Marshall's assessment that neither *Ramos* nor the Constitution permits the type of prosecutorial conduct exhibited in *Caldwell*: "I believe the prosecutor's misleading emphasis on appellate review misinformed the jury concerning the finality of its decision, thereby creating an unacceptable risk that 'the death penalty [may have been] meted out arbitrarily or capriciously.' "[125]

Justice Rehnquist wrote the dissenting opinion in *Caldwell*. He argued that the prosecutor's statements, viewed in the context of the entire closing argument, adequately stressed the importance of the jury's sentencing role.[126] Further, he disputed Marshall's assumption that a sentencing jury with a reduced sense of responsibility is more likely to vote for the death penalty.[127] Finally, Rehnquist criticized what he saw as the Court's willingness to find constitutional error in any departure from "optimum procedure" in a capital case.[128]

Cases following *Caldwell*, particularly *Romano v. Oklahoma* in 1994,[129] underscore the importance of O'Connor's concurrence.[130] During the sentencing phase of Romano's trial, the prosecutor introduced into evidence a copy of the judgment and death sentence Romano had received at another trial for another murder. The Supreme Court held that *Caldwell* was not violated because the evidence did not mislead the jury to believe that responsibility for sentencing the defendant lay elsewhere. The *Romano* Court noted that O'Connor's *Caldwell* concurrence took a narrower view of the defect in *Caldwell* than had the *Caldwell* plurality: "As Justice O'Connor supplied the fifth vote in *Caldwell*, and concurred on grounds narrower than those put forth by the plurality, her position is controlling."[131] The Court distinguished *Caldwell* from *Romano* by reasoning that "here, the jury was not affirmatively misled regarding its role in the sentencing process. The evidence at issue was neither false at the time it was admitted, nor did it even pertain to the jury's role in the sentencing process. The trial court's instruction, moreover, emphasized the importance of the jury's role."[132]

The justices in *Caldwell* identified two related constitutional evils: giving the jury misinformation about its role and giving the jury information that, even if accurate, diminished its sense of responsibility. Some courts applying *Caldwell* have focused on the case's misinformation dimension. The Supreme Court subsequently, in *Romano v. Oklahoma*[133] and other cases,[134] has emphasized the critical task of maintaining a jury's sense of responsibility. I shall focus on the diminution-of-responsibility component of *Caldwell*, as has the Court itself in its post–*Caldwell* jurisprudence.

Under the trifurcated systems of Florida, Alabama, Indiana, and Delaware, even a descriptively accurate statement of the specific roles of the judge and jury would suggest that each bears, at most, only partial responsibility for the sentence. As a result, either judge or jury could look to the other as the decision maker responsible for the hard choices—with neither ever doing so. When responsibility for a death sentence is divided, there exists the danger—identified in *Caldwell* as constitutionally intolerable—that *no one* bears ultimate responsibility for this critical decision. Juries may vote for death although not regarding a death sentence as "real" or believing it will ever be carried out, when in actuality the judge must defer to a death recommendation unless it is palpably unreasonable. Thus judge and jury may (or may not) pass the moral decision back and forth as the deadly game of blind man's bluff progresses.

This process may be conceptualized through the "Private Slovik" syndrome. The Slovik phenomenon refers to the mindset that in a multilayered system of sequential decision makers someone—someone else, somewhere else, sometime else down the line—will make a "saving" choice. In Slovik's case, however, that someone/somewhere never chose, and Slovik was executed.[135] According to William Bradford Huie's classic, *The Execution of Private Slovik:*

> I think every member of the court thought that Slovik deserved to
> be shot; and we were convinced that, for the good of the division,
> he *ought* to be shot. But in honesty—and so that people who didn't
> have to go to war can understand this thing—this must be said: I
> don't think a single member of that court actually believed that
> Slovik would ever be shot. I know I didn't believe it. . . . I had no
> reason to believe it. . . . I knew what the practice had been. I thought
> that the sentence would be cut down, probably not by General Cota,
> but certainly by Theater Command. I don't say this is what I thought
> *should* happen; I say it is what I felt *would* happen. And I thought that
> not long after the war ended—two or three years maybe—Slovik
> would be a free man.[136]

The *Caldwell* Court held that substantial unreliability and bias in favor of death sentences may result from state-induced suggestions that the capital-sentencing jury may shift its sense of responsibility to an appellate court. The type of prosecutorial misconduct and jury instructions condemned in *Caldwell*—comments about *appellate* review—had long been viewed as improper by most state courts as a matter of state law or federal due process requirements.[137] The doctrinal innovation of *Caldwell* was to elevate such impropriety to a constitutional error of eighth amendment magnitude.

Although the improper remarks in *Caldwell* referred to appellate review, state courts earlier had held that any prosecutorial or judicial comment that tended to dilute a jury's sense of responsibility in capital sentencing was erroneous. Comments that pointed to trial level judicial review, as well as to judicial review at the appellate level, were equally proscribed.[138] These cases are in accord with the broader mandate of *Caldwell* that "it is constitutionally impermissible to rest a death sentence on a determination made by a sentencer who has been led to believe that the responsibility for determining the appropriateness of the defendant's death *rests elsewhere*."[139] The danger of bias and unreliability that may stem from a diminished sense of sentencing responsibility remains just as great when a jury is told that the trial judge will review and make the ultimate sentencing determination.

The *Caldwell* Court held that, when a jury is told that the "alternative decisionmakers" are the justices of the state's highest court, "[i]t is certainly plausible to believe that many jurors will be tempted to view these respected legal authorities as having more of a 'right' to make such an important decision than has the jury."[140] Although the specter of the state's supreme court would indeed cut an impressive and formidable visage to lay jurors, the high court stands as a distant abstraction. To the capital-sentencing juror, the trial judge is posted as the immediate and tangible legal authority. She is "their" judge. As the *Caldwell* Court noted, the capital-sentencing jury is placed in a difficult and uncomfortable position, facing an awesome responsibility. Moreover, the jurors are given only partial guidance as to how their judgment should be exercised.[141]

This guidance is provided by the trial judge, along with substantial instruction and assistance through each step of the trial process. The judge becomes their ally, their guide through the legal labyrinth. In *Anatomy of a Jury,* Seymour Wishman wrote that "[m]ost jurors arrive in a courtroom with great respect for the judge, whom they see as a fair-minded father figure interested only in the implementation of justice."[142]

The respect that the jury develops for the trial judge is deliberately created, and it is reinforced by the court's control and command over the entire ritualistic proceeding. The reverence is underscored by the trappings and wardrobe of the court. According to the ABA's *Standards for Criminal Justice,* "the trial judge's appearance and demeanor should reflect the dignity of the judicial office and enhance public confidence in the administration of justice. The wearing of the judicial robe in the courtroom will contribute to these goals."[143] Cloaked in her black robe, the trial judge emerges from the recesses of her chambers. All rise as she enters the courtroom and climbs to her elevated position at the bench. These images all serve to establish and reinforce the image of the trial judge as the preeminent legal authority. It is within this context that the jury views her.

The authority and influence of the trial judge over the jury has long been recognized by the law. Because of this strong impact, the law has sought to balance promoting respect and deference with preventing undue bias and influence. As the Supreme Court noted a century ago, "it is obvious that under any system of jury trials the influence of the trial judge on the jury is necessarily and properly of great weight, and that [her] slightest word or intimation is received with deference, and may prove controlling."[144] Given the strong deference and respect accorded to the trial judge by the jury, the possibility that the jury may prefer to pass some of its frightening capital-sentencing responsibility onto the shoulders of the trial judge is very real. As the *Caldwell* Court recognized, "it is certainly plausible to believe that many jurors will be tempted to view the trial judge as having 'more of a right' to make such an important decision than has the jury."[145] The prejudicial effects identified in *Caldwell,* therefore, apply equally to suggestions that lead a jury to believe that the responsibility for its sentencing decision, whether labeled as a "recommendation" or otherwise, will rest with the trial court.

When the *Caldwell* Court laid down its general prohibition against trial comments that minimize a jury's sense of responsibility for a death sentence, it identified four ways in which bias in favor of death could result.[146] Each factor is equally salient where trial level, rather than appellate level, judicial review is posited to the penalty jury. Justice Marshall's *Caldwell* opinion first reasoned that a jury composed of lay persons might not understand the limited nature of appellate review. He wrote of the inability of the appellate court to hear evidence and to see witnesses and their demeanor; therefore, appellate courts review sentencing determinations with a presumption of correctness. Although a trial judge, in contrast, is present to weigh evidence and evaluate witnesses' credibility, in most states where the trial judge fixes the actual penalty after considering the jury's "recommendation" there is a presumption of correctness in the jury's determination. In Florida, as previously noted, where by statute the jury issues only an "advisory" sentence, the judge may disregard that sentence only where "virtually no reasonable person" could have made the recommended determination.[147] Even in the four states whose death penalty statutes authorize a trial judge to *reduce* a jury's recommendation of death,[148] this action may not be undertaken arbitrarily: the jury's sentencing determination is presumed to be correct.[149]

The second factor identified by Marshall in *Caldwell* was that a jury might reach a death verdict even when unconvinced that death was the appropriate punishment, in order to "send a message" of extreme disapproval. Given that the trial judge has the *power,* in theory if not in practice, to override the jury's death sentence, it may apply that penalty more freely, knowing that the judge has the wisdom and authority to "correct" the sentence. Whereas the prospect for appellate review raised in *Caldwell* remains a distant recourse in the mind of the hesitant or undecided juror, the trial judge is present, has heard the evidence, and, it would appear, could immediately apply the "appropriate" sentence. For this reason, the second problem posed by Justice Marshall is equally—if not more—salient where the jury is told that the trial judge is the ultimate sentencer, with mandated override authority.

Marshall's third assumption was that jurors might correctly assume that judicial review can reverse a death sentence but not a life sentence, and that they might choose to apply death in order to ensure reviewability. In the four override states (Florida, Alabama, Indiana, and Delaware), the judge has the power to override or reverse recommendations of both life and death. Technically, then, this third factor is inapplicable to those four states. Functionally, however, as documented in Chapter 3, override of death recommendations is seldom practiced. So although judicial review exists in theory, it rarely interferes with the imposition of the death sentence. In other states, where the jury's capital-sentencing role is termed a "recommendation" and the trial judge is afforded sentencing discretion, that discretion may duly be exercised to overturn a jury's recommendation of the death penalty. In those jurisdictions, therefore, the third danger addressed by Marshall is as relevant to the trial judge as it is to appellate review of a jury's sentence.

Finally, Justice Marshall wrote of the danger that jurors, otherwise reluctant to vote for a death sentence, might minimize the importance of their role where they are told that the alternative decision maker is a state supreme court justice. As previously discussed, the deference and reliance that the juror feels toward the trial judge is great, and this would create an equally unacceptable risk that the juror's sense of responsibility would be diminished.

Both the Supreme Court and lower courts have indicated that *Caldwell* applies to situations where the trial judge has been posited to the penalty jury as the final sentencing decision maker. Two months after *Caldwell* was decided, the Supreme Court summarily vacated death sentences in two cases and remanded them for reconsideration; in both, statements had been made to the capital-sentencing jury that the trial judge had the responsibility for applying the death penalty.[150] Federal circuit courts have followed this broad mandate, addressing a wide range of *Caldwell* claims. The Fifth and the Eleventh Circuits have found constitutional error in prosecutors' and judges' comments that the trial judge, not the jury, was responsible for the "final" sentencing determination.[151] The Tenth Circuit, on the other hand, has applied *Caldwell* to cases where the sentencing jury was told that its role was "part of the greater criminal justice system" and has found no constitutional error.[152]

State courts have also applied *Caldwell* to cases where the sentencing jury's sense of responsibility may have been reduced by relying upon the trial judge's power to review and "correct" a death sentence. The Supreme Court of Virginia expressly rejected the commonwealth's contention that *Caldwell* only applied to comments about appellate review.[153] Such a narrow interpretation, the court held, "ignored the sweeping language of the [*Caldwell*] Court, prohibiting any argument which leads a jury to believe that the sentencing responsibility lies 'elsewhere.' "[154] The Colorado Supreme Court similarly held that any argument leading the jury to believe that the responsibility for sentencing is "shared" with the trial court is grounds for reversal.[155]

The supreme courts and appellate courts of at least ten other states— Kentucky, Ohio, Illinois, Missouri, Georgia, California, Tennessee, Alabama, New Jersey, and Florida—have addressed *Caldwell* claims in contexts other than remarks about appellate review.[156] Of these, only Florida has found *Caldwell* inapplicable to its sentencing scheme.[157]

Given the reasoning of the Supreme Court in *Caldwell,* it is unsurprising that no court has held that the decision is applicable only to appellate judicial review. Every court that has addressed *Caldwell* claims has rejected its narrow application to appellate review alone. *Caldwell's* prohibition against comments that minimize a jury's sense of responsibility in sentencing capital defendants applies to trial judges as well as to appellate judges.

The jury override statutes of Alabama, Florida, Indiana, and Delaware divide capital-sentencing responsibility. In each state, the jury must submit a verdict on the guilt or innocence of the capital defendant. Then, this same jury must attend the sentencing phase of the bifurcated proceeding, where evidence of aggravating and mitigating circumstances is presented. The jury is asked to weigh this information carefully, to deliberate carefully, and then, finally, to set its judgment as to whether the defendant has forfeited his right to live.

At some point in the sentencing proceeding, however, the jury is provided with an additional piece of information. It is told that the ultimate sentencing responsibility rests not upon itself but with the trial judge. She or he will make the final determination; the jurors are to issue only a "recommendation" or "advisory" sentence. Whether this news is provided by the prosecution, by the defense, or by the court is of no import. The message is clear: your job is not *really* to decide whether the defendant will live or die; you are here only to provide your advice, your opinion to a court that is not bound by your recommendation. It makes no difference if the jury is informed that the trial judge must accord its recommendation "great weight"[158] or merely give it some unspecified degree of "consideration."[159] The jury is left, at best, with the sense that its sentencing decision will not necessarily be followed; at worst, it may believe that its determination is only proforma, of little relevance to the defendant's fate. Faced with its diminished sentencing role, this jury is prone toward the same death bias against which the Court warned in *Caldwell.*

Justice Marshall's *Caldwell* opinion stems from the basic intuition that jurors are naturally reluctant to impose a death sentence. This intuition is grounded in a well-established body of both legal doctrine[160] and empirical evidence.[161] Indeed, the voir dire process in a capital case is to a large extent devoted to choosing jurors who are not biased unreasonably toward the objectives of either the state or the defendant. And although the Supreme Court has approved the procedure of selecting "death-qualified" jurors,[162] a capital-sentencing scheme must meet the eighth amendment's need for heightened reliability in the determination that death is the appropriate punishment in a specific case.[163] It is the jury's natural reluctance to invoke the death penalty, the "quality of mercy" that it brings to the sentencing proceeding, that fosters the reliability required by the Constitution.[164] The bitter irony of Florida's jury override experience is that jurors in that state are among the most likely in the country to decide for death. As one trial judge in the state remarked to William Geimer and Jonathan Amsterdam, "Northern Florida is the last constitutional stronghold of people conservative about and protective of law enforcement."[165] In such an environment, where a juror may have only slight reservations about imposing a death sentence, it is difficult to ignore the bias toward death that might result from a jury's awareness that its decision is not binding.

Justice Marshall's proscription against statements that lead a capital sentencer to believe that sentencing responsibility rests elsewhere draws from a deep well of established common-law doctrine. The *Caldwell* rationale reflects a virtually unanimous response raised whenever legal authorities have confronted the question of a capital sentencer's diminished responsibility.[166] The rather sparse account of state law set forth in *Caldwell* does not fully convey the breadth and depth of the doctrinal foundation for the proposition that "it is constitutionally impermissible to rest a death sentence on a determination made by a sentencer who has been led to believe that the responsibility for determining the appropriateness of the defendant's death rests elsewhere."[167] *Caldwell* elevated these concerns from the realm of common-law notions of fairness to the level of eighth amendment constitutional imperative.

As the *Caldwell* Court noted, almost every state supreme court that had addressed the issue had condemned the specter of a diminished sense of responsibility in capital sentencing[168] prior to *Caldwell,* although never as a matter of eighth amendment law; for this reason the case's constitutional principle had not been applied retroactively to death sentences that became final prior to the *Caldwell* decision.[169] Although case law dating back to the nineteenth century may be cited,[170] the body of state law that has emerged in the last several decades establishes the near consensus. Interestingly, it is within the southern states, where the death penalty has been most enthusiastically embraced, that this doctrinal legacy has been refined. One year before the United States Supreme Court decided *Caldwell,* the Mississippi Supreme Court held that the "role of the juror in a capital murder trial brings with it an awesome responsibility."[171] Because of the "importance of the jurors' deliberations we must be cautious in avoiding any actions which tend to reduce the jurors' sense of responsibility for their decision. They must not be permitted to look down the road for someone else to pass the buck to." Jurors faced with the "portentous duty of deciding an accused's fate will take comfort in the fact of review. They may view their role as *merely advisory,* a view which can prove fatal to an accused."[172]

The Mississippi court's decision in Bobby Caldwell's case is somewhat anomalous in that state's death penalty jurisprudence. It has held consistently that comments which dilute the capital sentencer's role are impermissible.[173] In fact, the Mississippi Supreme Court's decision in Caldwell's case was four to four. Justice Lee, dissenting, reasoned that "[t]he logic of the rule [prohibiting such comments] is beyond question. Comment of this nature has the effect of lessening a juror's sense of responsibility for the fate of the accused. Those jurors who are not convinced that a defendant's life should be taken may not argue so strongly or hold their position when they are led to believe that a reviewing court will correct a mistake in their judgment."[174]

The supreme courts of Florida, Georgia, Kansas, Kentucky, Louisiana, North Carolina, and South Carolina had all joined in this view long before the United States Supreme Court addressed the issue in *Caldwell*[175]— again, never as a matter of eighth amendment doctrine. The fact that a comment or instruction was technically accurate has been equally rejected as an exception to this general prohibition against diminishing the jury's sense of sentencing responsibility.[176] As a matter of state law, any action that might diminish the jury's sense of responsibility in capital sentencing was firmly proscribed.

Nor has the common law on this issue been limited to that of the southern states composing the "death belt." The supreme courts of California, New York, and New Jersey have been among those that have addressed and set forth similar prohibitions.[177] As New York's Justice Sears reasoned in 1940: "The vice of the statements and questions of the District Attorney lies not primarily in the incorrectness of the statement that an appeal . . . is compulsory but in the suggestion that the jury's verdict, if against the defendant, cannot be seriously harmful to him because of the opportunity for review. . . . *Nothing can be permitted* to weaken the jurors' sense of obligation in the performance of their duties."[178] The fact that the remainder of jurisdictions had not addressed this issue prior to *Caldwell* indicates that such statements and instructions are viewed as fundamentally improper. It seems that few judges or prosecutors would be willing to risk reversal over so blatant an indiscretion.

It was well-established doctrine in common law prior to *Caldwell*, therefore, that capital juries must maintain a strong sense of responsibility toward their sentencing decisions. This is the case regardless of whether a jury actually fixes the sentence or makes a "mere" recommendation to the court. In *Caldwell,* the Supreme Court recognized for the first time the eighth amendment dimensions of these concerns.

The Court rested its holding squarely on the eighth amendment: "the qualitative difference of death from all other punishments requires a correspondingly greater degree of scrutiny of the capital sentencing determination."[179] Because death is different, there is a heightened need for reliability whenever a state seeks to take a defendant's life. The sentencing process, accordingly, must "facilitate the responsible and reliable exercise of sentencing discretion."[180]

The divided sentencing responsibility imposed by the override states is inimical to this requirement. Florida and Alabama have both defended their sentencing provisions against *Caldwell*-based attacks on the premise that the judge, not the jury, is the actual capital sentencer.[181] Accurate information about this fact, it is argued, neither misleads the jury nor diminishes its sense of responsibility. The judge is not bound by the jury's recommendation and carries the ultimate burden of determining the appropriate sentence. Proponents point to the language of the statutes, which requires the trial judge to undertake an independent assessment of any aggravating or mitigating factor before handing down a sentence.[182] This reasoning, appealing as it must be to pragmatists who are loath to risk reversal of the scores (if not hundreds) of death sentences so imposed, is as flawed as the statutes it defends. *Caldwell* is not retroactive. More importantly, although the trial judge is not (technically) bound by the jury's recommendation or "advisory" sentence, she is certainly (if intangibly and immeasurably) affected by it. A closer look at the policies and provisions of each of the four statutes reveals the consideration and deference that is given to the jury's advisory sentence by the trial court.

Florida's statutory language gives little clue of the true nature of its juries' sentencing role. "Notwithstanding the recommendation of the jury," it says, the judge "shall enter a sentence of life imprisonment or death."[183] Under the override standard adopted by the Florida Supreme Court in *Tedder v. State* in 1975, however, a trial judge is normally required to follow the jury's recommendation:[184] "The facts suggesting a sentence of death should be so clear and convincing that virtually no reasonable person could differ."[185] The state supreme court has scrupulously applied the standard in the last fifteen years, acknowledging that the jury's recommendation represents the judgment of the community as to whether death is the appropriate punishment in a given case. Accordingly, the jurors' decision is entitled to great weight and will not be disturbed unless it is manifestly unreasonable—which it rarely is.[186] Under the Florida Supreme Court's mandate, the recommendation of the capital-sentencing jury exercises substantial influence upon the trial judge. It is chimerical to suppose that under this regime the jury's recommendation is "merely" advisory.[187]

The United States Supreme Court, in holding the Florida statute constitutional and in discussing its application in specific cases, expressly endorsed the *Tedder* standard.[188] The United States Court of Appeals for the Eleventh Circuit has also recognized the significance of this standard and the substantive sentencing role accorded to the jury.[189] The court noted that "it would seem that the Supreme Court of Florida has recognized that a jury recommendation of death has a *sui generis* impact on the trial judge, an impact so powerful as to nullify the general presumption that a trial judge is capable of putting aside error.[190]

The force that this recommendation exerts upon the trial judge is sufficient to raise doubts about the reliability of a death sentence that is born of the divided sentencing roles imposed by the override statute. Add to this unholy alliance the fact that trial judges are elected officials, accountable to the general public, and the odds of a judge overriding a jury's recommendation of death are practically nil.[191] In reality, the number of such death overrides is negligible. For juries even partially to rely upon the prospect of a judge "correcting" a death sentence is to risk the very dangers of bias in favor of death against which *Caldwell* cautioned. There is too real a possibility that the jury might choose to "send a message" or to delegate ultimate responsibility to the judge, whom it has come to know and respect throughout the trial. In Florida, where only a majority of jurors is required for a recommendation of death, the override provision serves as an invitation to abandon the eighth amendment's requirement for heightened reliability in the capital-sentencing process. Under *Caldwell,* such a situation is constitutionally intolerable.

The override provisions of Alabama, Indiana, and Delaware were enacted after Florida's, and they were patterned after that state's law. In form, they differ little from their model, with one critical exception. The Alabama and Indiana statutes, unlike Florida's, expressly require a trial judge to give consideration to the jury's sentencing recommendation; Delaware's 1991 statute has not yet been interpreted definitively by that state's supreme court.[192] Given that Alabama and Indiana require that their statutes be interpreted based on their plain language,[193] the jury's statutory role, on its face, is far from meaningless.[194] Indiana courts recognize this; Alabama courts do not; it is too soon to tell in Delaware.

Despite the statutory provision for the jury's significant role in capital sentencing, the Alabama courts have steadfastly refused to acknowledge the effect that an advisory death sentence must have on the trial judge's ultimate sentencing decision.[195] Alabama's statute, however, contains additional, significant provisions that underscore the jury's important capital-sentencing role. Following conviction of a capital crime, the punishment phase must be held before a jury unless both parties consent and receive approval from the court for a hearing before the judge alone. All relevant factors in mitigation or aggravation are presented for the jury's consideration. A recommendation of death must be based on a vote of at least ten jurors. If the jury is unable to reach a verdict on an advisory sentence, mistrial of the sentencing hearing may result.[196] These factors all give the lie to the suggestion that the jury's sentencing role is insignificant. Although a trial judge is not statutorily bound to follow the jury's recommended sentence, it is inconceivable that she will not be influenced by the "community's voice."[197] As the United States Supreme Court noted in an Alabama case: "[I]t is manifest that the jury's verdict must have a tendency to motivate the judge to impose the same sentence that the jury did. Indeed, according to statistics submitted by the State's Attorney General, it is fair to infer that the jury verdict will ordinarily be followed by the judge even though he must hold a separate hearing . . . before he imposes sentence."[198]

The Supreme Court brief of Louise Harris, in *Harris v. Alabama*, traces the history of that state's jury override. This history, existent primarily through unreported opinions (reproduced here), has not been a happy one. The state's legislature and supreme court have evinced a commitment to maintaining the role of the jury in capital-sentencing proceedings. Drawing on the substantial part jurors have historically played in Alabama's capital-sentencing process,[199] state law requires that the jury recommendation ensue only from carefully tailored and protected procedures.

The signal importance of the jury function in capital sentencing was set out most explicitly by the Alabama Supreme Court in its seminal opinion on the death penalty, *Beck v. State*.[200] *Beck* followed the United States Supreme Court's opinion in *Beck v. Alabama*,[201] which invalidated the statute then in operation to the extent that it precluded the jury's consideration of lesser included offenses. In determining how the sentencing scheme could be restructured, the supreme court dismissed the state's contention that under Alabama constitutional and common law the judge could sentence without jury participation.[202] Invoking not only legislative intent but also the state's long history of capital jury sentencing, the court declared: "While the jury is not the final sentencing authority under the capital sentencing scheme set out in the statute, the requirement that the jury fix the punishment was deliberately included in the statute by the legislature. . . . [W]e believe that the legislature intended to have jury input in the sentencing process. Throughout Alabama's history, juries have always played a major role in capital cases."[203]

The statute presently in operation codified the jury's participation in capital sentencing.[204] The legislature fashioned Alabama's sentencing scheme around the unique importance attributed to the jury role in the state as consistently reflected in legislative and common-law traditions.[205] The jury's "key" role in sentencing is suggested in the statutory procedures outlining its participation[206] and in the case law interpreting them. It is evident that Alabama law views the jury as a vital partner in determination of punishment from its refusal to allow legal errors in the jury proceeding to go uncorrected. Although the judge is the final sentencing authority, instructional and evidentiary errors of law before the sentencing jury will require reversal even if not replicated before the sentencing judge.

For example, in *Ex parte Williams*,[207] the sentencing jury had been instructed that it could consider the aggravating circumstance that Williams was under sentence of imprisonment at the time of his crime.[208] In fact, he had not been on probation as the jury had been told, and the trial court did not find this aggravating circumstance when sentencing him to death.[209] The state argued that the error should be deemed harmless due to the proper consideration of the issue by the judge. Alabama's high court rejected this reasoning.

> The basic flaw in this rationale is that it totally discounts the significance of the jury's role in the sentencing process.
>
> The legislatively mandated role of the jury in returning an advisory verdict, based upon its consideration of aggravating and mitigating circumstances, can not be abrogated by the trial court's errorless exercise of its equally mandated role as the ultimate sentencing authority. Each part of the sentencing process is equally mandated by the statute, and the errorless application by the court of its part does not cure the erroneous application by the jury of its part. . . . To hold otherwise is to hold that the sentencing role of the jury, as required by statute, counts for nothing so long as the court's exercise of its role is without error.[210]

This has been the consistent response when the jury's role has been in some fashion undermined during the penalty phase. When juries have been improperly instructed, as in *Williams*, Alabama law has required a new jury sentencing.[211]

Despite the recognition that the jury is a significant partner in Alabama's capital-sentencing scheme, neither the statute nor the courts has provided a mechanism for governing its decision making authority relative to that of the judge. The statute's sole mention of the role of the jury in the ultimate imposition of sentence is to say that the trial court "shall consider the recommendation of the jury contained in its advisory verdict."[212] Stating simply that the jury verdict is not binding, the statute is silent as to how the trial court is to make the recommendation a part of the decision making process or what role the jury's decision should play if there is disagreement as to sentence. The appellate courts have acknowledged that no definition has been given to the relative roles of the two decision makers.[213]

The absence of guidance has led Alabama trial courts[214] to confront the advisory verdict in unpredictable ways and to accord it arbitrary degrees of deference. Treatment of the jury's role varies widely from judge to judge, and even from one defendant to another sentenced by the same judge. A central confusion among the state's sentencing judges is whether an advisory verdict of life without parole is a mitigating circumstance to be weighed (with statutory and other nonstatutory mitigation) against aggravation. A number of trial judges explicitly define the jury verdict as such and weight it directly into the balance of factors.[215] Some Alabama judges who deem the jury recommendation "mitigating" appear to do so in the belief that the statute requires as much.[216] Many courts, however, do not treat the verdict as mitigation. Several have rejected it after finding no nonstatutory mitigating circumstances.[217] Others make clear that the verdict was not one of the mitigating circumstances considered.[218] Still other courts consider the jury's recommendation according to a wholly different procedure. Their sentencing orders indicate that they do not attempt to factor the advisory verdict into the aggravation-mitigation inquiry at all, but rather take it into consideration in some separate and distinct manner. Although it is possible that the latter group of judges views the jury's advisory sentence as having an import similar to their own sentencing decisions, it is unknown what role the recommendation played in these cases.[219]

Alabama trial courts are also inconsistent in the function they assign to the jury's life-without-parole determination. Some judges assign none: they impose a sentence of death without even acknowledging in the sentencing order that the jury returned a life verdict.[220] In some cases, the jury's recommendation appears to have played no role in the judge's sentencing determination, but is simply reported in the order.[221] In others, the court states no more than that it "considered" the jury's contrary verdict without appearing to have accorded it any significance.[222] Some courts, on the other hand, read the statute to require that the jury's sentencing determination be given great deference.[223] A few Alabama judges seem to reject the jury's advisory life verdict only when a death sentence appears to them indisputable.[224]

Lacking any direction regarding the role the jury verdict should play, some judges appear to be groping for a standard. In *State v. Murry*, for example, the court rejected the advisory verdict for life in the first trial—and, following a reversal on appeal, accepted it in the second. In the first case, the court initially discussed the jury's determination as that of a separate sentencing body that was entitled to great weight; then, employing a different approach, it went on to decide that it could "only categorize the recommendation as a mitigating circumstance given the broad definition of a mitigating circumstance."[225] After the second trial, the same judge created a different role for the recommendation after stating that he was "unaware of any reported decision which suggests how much weight [should] be accorded an advisory verdict."[226]

The Alabama courts have never reversed a death sentence due to unwarranted rejection of the jury's sentencing decision.[227] They have affirmed sentences of death without even referring to the jury's life-without-parole verdict.[228] Often, no more than passing mention is given to the fact that a jury recommended life without parole: no review is undertaken to see if that recommendation was even considered.[229] The courts often observe that the trial judge considered the jury verdict and end their analysis of the case there.[230] Alabama's appellate courts have also tacitly sanctioned every conceivable approach trial courts have used to take account of the jury's role. They have implicitly approved the consideration of the jury's life verdict as a mitigating circumstance,[231] as *not* a mitigating circumstance,[232] and as something in between.[233] Overrides have been affirmed when the jury's recommendation was made part of the process of weighing aggravation against mitigation,[234] and when it was assessed in a separate analysis.[235] The appellate courts have further sanctioned whatever reasons the trial courts have given for finding the jury verdict lacking.[236]

Ironically, the Alabama Supreme Court has been quite solicitous of the integrity of jury verdicts in the *civil* context. In *Bozeman v. Busby*[237] it held that a statute authorizing trial courts to override jury verdicts awarding punitive damages in civil lawsuits and to impose additur on punitive damages awards violated the right to jury trial under the state constitution. In *Bozeman*, a trial court had granted a motion for new trial in a personal injury lawsuit after the defendant rejected the trial court's $45,000 additur to the jury's $5,000 punitive damages award.

By contrast, jury sentencing recommendations, particularly recommendations of life, matter a great deal in Indiana. There, the supreme court began its recent work in override cases by adopting a *Tedder*-like standard for life-to-death overrides in *Martinez Chavez v. State*.[238] The court pointed out that only once before[239] had it affirmed a death sentence where the jury had recommended life.[240] The standard adopted by the *Martinez Chavez* court echoed *Tedder*: "In order to sentence a defendant to death after the jury has recommended against death, the facts justifying a death sentence should be so clear and convincing that virtually no reasonable person could disagree that death was appropriate in light of the offender and his crime."[241]

The Indiana Supreme Court in 1991 articulated a standard for trial courts to use in overriding *death* recommendations given by juries.[242] It is less stringent than the *Martinez Chavez–Tedder* standard that governs life-to-death overrides. The "trial court as trier of fact must independently determine the existence of aggravators and mitigators, weigh them, consider the recommendation of the jury, and come to a separate conclusion as to whether or not to impose the death penalty. However, when the jury's recommendation is [life], it is to be given a *special—but not controlling—role* in the judge's process. . . ."[243] This indicates that the *Tedder*-type standard does not apply in Indiana cases where the jury recommends death. To override such a recommendation, the trial judge does not determine if any reasonable person could disagree; he or she simply makes a personal assessment of the aggravating and mitigating circumstances. This suggestion echoes the court's statement in 1990 that "we do not require any trial court adherence to a jury decision recommending imposition of the death penalty. When the jury recommends the death sentence, a judge is in no way bound by such recommendation."[244] Hence, at least in Indiana, it is less of a burden for the trial judge to reject a death recommendation than to reject a life recommendation. The Indiana Supreme Court, recognizing the force that a jury's recommendation exerts on a trial judge, has stated: "Notwithstanding that the sentence determination by the jury is not binding upon the judge, we do not regard it as a mere formality having no substantive value. If we did, error if any, in such regard could not be other than harmless. On the contrary, the recommendation of the jury is a very valuable contribution to the process, in that it comes from a group representative of the defendant's peers, who are likely to reflect, collectively, the standards of the community."[245]

The Eleventh Circuit's assessment of the "*sui generis* impact"[246] that a jury's advisory sentence is bound to have on a trial judge applies with equal force, then, to the jury override statutes of Alabama and Indiana (and Delaware), as well as to Florida's. Further, the specter of politics surfaces in Alabama and Indiana (and Delaware) as well as in Florida, for it cannot be said that an elected judge would lightly disregard a jury's sentence of death. Alabama Supreme Court justice Jones, dissenting, aptly described the beast when he wrote:

> The majority's judicial review "cure–all" obtains even less credence when it is understood that such guided discretion is placed upon a popularly-elected official. . . . [T]o leave sentence reduction in the prerogative of the trial court is to place undue pressures upon this office. Again, admittedly, a trial judge must often be the bulwark of the legal system when presented with unpopular causes and adverse public opinion. This State's recent history, however, reflects the outcry of unjustified criticism attendant with a trial judge's reduction of a sentence to life imprisonment without possibility of parole, after a jury has returned a sentence of death. Clearly, this pressure constituted an undue compulsion on the trial judge to conform the sentence which he imposes with that previously returned by the jury.[247]

Finally, that judges generally follow a jury's recommendation of death is borne out by the override's history: death-to-life overrides in Alabama and Indiana remain relatively rare occurrences.[248]

Thus, in Florida and Indiana (and perhaps eventually in Delaware), the jury's sentencing role is far greater than its statutory description would suggest. Even a technically accurate description of its sentence as a "recommendation" or "advisory sentence" does not convey the true import of the jury's determination. It is impractical simply to not inform the jury of the true nature of its sentencing role. It is not difficult to imagine the confusion and outrage that might result when a jury deliberates upon the fate of the defendant, only to learn that the judge may—and has—completely disregarded its sentencing determination. It is most likely, in any case, that the average venireperson would be aware of the potential for override, and treat this divided responsibility as requiring that he or she issue only an advisory decision.

The other alternative, of attempting to inform the jury fully and accurately of the importance of its recommendation, is bound for failure. Any qualification of the jury's role as being "advisory" or a "recommendation" will still engender the possibility of a juror attaching diminished consequences to his or her sentencing decision. As one Kentucky Supreme Court justice argued, any use of the word "recommendation" to describe the jury's sentencing role, although accurate, sends the message that its "awesome responsibility" is lessened because its decision is not the final one:

> Continuously we are confronted by the fact that these words are used before the jury to minimize its responsibility in deciding on the death penalty. Sometimes we sidestep the problem by saying that the word was not overused, and sometimes, as in the present case . . . we recognize that the prejudice is too serious to ignore. . . . While it is true that [the Kentucky statute] provides that the jury "shall recommend a sentence for the defendant," the fact is that when the jury votes for the death penalty, it is much more than merely a recommendation. . . . If the jury so recommends, almost without exception the trial judge has followed the jury's recommendation by imposing the death penalty. . . . [O]nce and for all, we should get rid of the unfair prejudice inhering in use of the word "recommend" to describe the jury's function in setting a penalty.[249]

The problem lies, therefore, not with the administration of the override provisions but with their fundamental unfairness. The exact quality of consideration that a trial judge accords this determination may vary, but it is certainly a significant factor that cannot wholly be ignored by the judicial "ultimate sentencer." The jury, on the other hand, instructed or reminded that its role is advisory, may at best treat its decision as not bearing the weight of deciding upon another person's death. Although the degree to which a juror's sense of responsibility is lessened may likewise vary, one cannot say that it will have "no effect" on the outcome of the sentencing proceeding.[250] Under such a capital-sentencing scheme, both judge and jury may take comfort in the knowledge that neither is ultimately, fully responsible for the fate of a defendant. The concerns of *Caldwell*—the danger of a bias toward a death sentence—are implicated here.

The Court in *Caldwell* reasoned that information diminishing a capital sentencer's sense of responsibility created dangers that the Court found constitutionally intolerable. The constitutional logic of *Caldwell* suggests the invalidity of sentencing schemes that divide sentencing responsibility at the trial level. The Court's *Caldwell* reasoning, and its extension to the jury override statutes, finds validation in the empirical literature.

Although the precise degree of consideration that a trial judge gives to the jury's advisory sentence in the override states remains indeterminate, there is little doubt that sentencing responsibility is, to some extent, divided and shared. The trial judge, though not "bound" by the advisory sentence in any one of the four override states, is certainly subject to its influence. Under these singular sentencing provisions, the judge is by no means the sole sentencer.

Most critical, however, is the possibility that the capital juror, informed that his or her sentencing role is advisory, will succumb to the dangers of bias toward a death sentence that *Caldwell* and its precursors exposed. Before invalidating these statutes or voiding death sentences imposed under them, courts ought not require proof that jurors actually were adversely influenced by the divided sentencing roles. It is sufficiently intolerable that even the risk of such a phenomenon exists.

The *Caldwell* legal doctrine is important enough, but the decision's principle may also contain a larger message about the death penalty itself at this moment in American history. As David Bruck perceptively and eloquently argued:

> In their astute analysis of *Furman*'s aftermath, Frank Zimring and Gordon Hawkins conclude that the derailment of abolition in the United States after *Furman* was a product of the peculiarly American system of divided government, which by diffusing responsibility for such profound moral decisions permitted the country's political leadership to avoid the courageous actions of their Western European and Canadian counterparts. Zimring and Hawkins point out the remarkable fact that in no country did public opinion favor abolition before the fact. Everywhere but here, elected leadership actually took

the lead, abolishing capital punishment while the public opinion polls still favored it. Only in the United States could the political branches pander to retentionist public sentiment in the knowledge that the courts would step in and sort out who, if anyone, would actually get killed.

When *Gregg v. Georgia* ratified the derailment of abolition in the United States in 1976, the handful of lawyers engaged in the struggle against the death penalty expected that executions would begin relatively soon, and in large numbers. But fourteen years later, the average annual rate of executions still stands at only ten, and the backlog of prisoners on death row has exploded to four times the total who waited at the time of *Furman*.

Why has it taken so long?

Obviously, the pace of executions will quicken, as the Rehnquist Court steadily removes legal obstacles, and slashes away at the federal habeas system. But I don't think that executions will even remotely approach the 250 or 300 death sentences imposed each year around the country. Americans' enthusiasm for executions is inversely proportionate to the responsibility they bear for carrying them out. Wherever responsibility comes to rest, there you will find a bottleneck. Lift the responsibility from the federal courts, and the cases will pile up in the state courts. If the state courts start letting more cases through, you'll begin to see increased jury reluctance to impose death sentences—as appears to have happened in Louisiana, where new death sentences have dwindled to almost zero in the years after the execution binge of the mid-1980s.

This reluctance to assume personal responsibility for large numbers of executions should not be surprising. It tells us that the United States has not veered so far after all from the abolitionist path of the other democratic countries of the West. The practice of killing unarmed prisoners has run its course here too. It's just that we lack the political means to say so.[251]

As the importance of the *Caldwell* decision increases ever time, the importance of Marshall's initial dissent from the majority's decision to deny plenary review also increases. Had he not written his original dissent, it is likely that the Court never would have given Bobby Caldwell's case the attention we now know that it warranted.

## Dissents That Telegraph

Justice Marshall and Justice Brennan opposed capital punishment as a matter of principle, and they felt so strongly about it that they always dissented. Sometimes, however, they may have been doing more. The two justices used dissents from denial of certiorari in capital cases, Perry wrote, "to send advice to counsel below."[252] I don't know if you understand how death cases work, but eventually what happens is that it goes back down and can come up on state habeas, and then if not there it can go back and come up on federal habeas. Brennan and Marshall's dissents from denial [were] not necessarily arguments to persuade the Supreme Court to take it, but they [became] briefs for the lawyers when the lawyer [was] arguing in a state court or federal court on why habeas should be granted.

Several of Perry's informants at the Court noted the signaling aspects of dissents.

> When an issue came up again they could point to what was said in the dissent from denial.
>
> [I]n some ways it serves as an early warning system to litigants. It says these are the issues that we are interested in. It gets the message both to the litigants to go and find cases, and to the other members on the Court—effectively saying, "[W]hen you publish these dissents from denials we're going to keep bitching until you take one of these cases."
>
> Of course there is an increase in dissent from denials. Some justices abuse this, I think. Denials are often attempts to persuade other justices—at least threats of denials are. Sometimes they are published as a way of communicating to future litigants.

Dissents from denial of certiorari may also send a signal to lower court judges: "We are watching you." Many observers have viewed summary decisions as sending such a signal, but some of Perry's informants thought that dissents from denial also perform this function. One clerk stated:

> So though sometimes a case isn't important, they will take the case and say, "look, you can't ignore us." Sometimes do that by dissents [from denial of cert.]. A justice will write to point out that the Supreme Court has taken note of this and that you can't fool anyone, and don't think you are getting away with this unnoticed.

The same clerk agreed this means that sometimes a dissent is published with the goodwill of the rest of the Court. Another clerk observed that dissent from denial is "often used to express revulsion to a decision below even though they don't expect the court to take it."

When Perry asked about the idea that dissents might be used to let lower courts know that they were being watched, most other clerks said that they did not know; some thought the idea sounded plausible, and others said no. Thus, responses were mixed on the use of dissents as signals to lower court judges to "behave." Many clerks, however, did see dissents as a form of communication to actors below, be they judges, attorneys, or litigants.

In some cases, what may have begun as a dissent from denial, perhaps intended as a message to those below, has become a per curiam opinion.

> Sometimes if the justice was worked up we would help write a dissent from denial of cert. And sometimes those dissents from denial became per curiam opinions.

Perry asked the justices about dissents becoming per curiam opinions, and they agreed that it happened, but they differed somewhat on the frequency. One justice stated, for example, "Yes that does happen, and I think they are some of our worst per curiam opinions."

Another said:

> I think that is very rare. If you have fewer than four voting for cert., the chances of picking up three votes to reverse are very unusual.[253] What is more likely is to have three who would say the case is so wrong that they would grant and reverse but not hear. Three others might say that "it seems to me that it ought to be reversed, but I am not willing to vote without hearing arguments," and the discussion would take that tone.

Whether it happens rarely or frequently, the potential for such an occurrence means that a justice must take a threat to dissent seriously. From his perspective, it may be a strategic error to let a case get decided this way. While he may well prefer to vote to deny, he may also figure that if the case is going to be decided plenary consideration is preferable to a summary disposition.

## Defensive Denials

Acting truly strategically, Brennan and Marshall might have preferred to pass over some capital cases in order to get a better case for their desired doctrinal outcome. There are areas of law generally, and cases specifically, where a justice believes that if a case is reviewed he will not like the outcome on the merits. Therefore, even if he believes the case is certworthy, and perhaps even believes that the ruling below is a horrible injustice, he still will vote to deny the case. This is a "defensive denial." The reasoning is, why make a bad situation worse? A denial of cert. has no precedential value, and refusal to take a case in no way signifies that the Supreme Court agrees with the ruling below. Difficult as it may be for a justice to let a ruling stand, by doing so he has let the precedent remain only for its immediate jurisdiction—for example, only the Second Circuit—rather than for the entire country.

All of the justices Perry interviewed acknowledged the existence of defensive denials. This strategy antedates the current Court. One justice told Perry:

> When I was in law school, Felix Frankfurter once came out to lecture and he said that he knew of cases where four wanted cert., but when the vote was taken, cert. was denied because only three would be in dissent. The reason for this was practicality. The four were convinced that if they went to full argument they would lose, so they would not take this case and would try for another day. He made this as a flat statement in the classroom.[254]

Capital cases seem to be the only category that are off-limits to defensive denials as such, at least in terms of attempts to avoid discussion. Remember that all capital cases are put on the discuss list, and Brennan and Marshall dissented every time. However, several informants said that there were distinctions among capital cases, and that Brennan and Marshall pushed harder on some than on others.

# Epilogue

▼ ▼ ▼

The retirement of William Brennan and Thurgood Marshall provides a fitting moment to reexamine what made their judicial careers unique. This book has explored one aspect of their singularity: Brennan's and Marshall's relentless dissents in capital cases. Except for one case— *Strickland v. Washington* (1984)[1]—the two justices always voted identically; apart from this instance, they each wrote separate lengthy opinions in the same case on just one other occasion.[2] Thus, from 1972 to 1990 (the year of Brennan's retirement), they took different perspectives in just two cases.[3]

This book has explored the historical, jurisprudential, and strategic legitimacy of relentless dissent[4] in the context of capital punishment. After examining the careers of William Brennan and Thurgood Marshall, I traced the history of dissents in general and the sustained dissent in particular. I then sought legitimacy in theory and evaluated the jurisprudential function and value of the sustained dissent. Finally, I focused on the strategic wisdom and tactical usefulness of such dissents.

It is fitting to close with a reminder about the public release of Marshall's papers and the horror of at least some of the justices at making the papers available to the public. Like Marshall's dissents, his papers were intended to fill in gaps between the aspirations of the Court's opinions and the reality of the people whose lives were touched—oftentimes fatally—by those decisions. In his papers and dissents, the justice was building a record for historians, anthropologists, and some future majority of the Supreme Court.

On January 25, 1993, the Supreme Court issued its decision in *Graham v. Collins*. The case presented the question of whether the Texas death penalty statute could constitutionally be applied in instances where capital juries might not have known that they could properly consider the fact that the defendant committed murder before the age of eighteen. The majority did not actually reach that question because the decision, written by Justice Byron White, concluded that the challenge could not be brought through a petition for a writ of habeas corpus in federal court. *Graham v. Collins* was a five to four decision. Had Justice Marshall, who retired in 1991, still been on the Court, the issue would have been reached, the evidence considered, and the statute declared unconstitutional as applied.

The *Graham* decision was announced on a day when flags flew at half staff to mark the death of Thurgood Marshall. Chief Justice Rehnquist called him an "extraordinary man" and a "champion of equal justice."[5]

# NOTES

▼ ▼ ▼

## Chapter 1

1. B. Cardozo, Law & Literature 34 (1931). I am grateful to Henry Schwartzschild for bringing this reference to my attention.

2. Paul Monette, West of Yesterday, East of Summer: Collected Poems xvii (1994).

3. Cover, *Violence and the Word*, 95 Yale L.J. 1601, 1601 (1986).

4. Furman v. Georgia, 408 U.S. 238, 405–06 (1972) (Blackmun, J., dissenting).

5. Neil A. Lewis, *Marshall Urges Bush to Pick "the Best,"* N.Y. Times, June 29, 1991, at 8.

6. *Id.*

7. Gregg v. Georgia, 428 U.S. 193 (1976).

8. WESTLAW search; *see also* Burt, *Disorder in the Court,* 85 Mich. L. Rev. 1741 (1987) (quoting Villereal, Dissents to the Denial of Certiorari in Death Penalty Cases of Justices Brennan and Marshall) (July 11, 1985) (unpublished Yale Law School paper, listing result of LEXIS search) (noting that Brennan and Marshall had dissented from the denial of certiorari in more than four hundred cases between 1976 and 1985).

9. Furman v. Georgia, 408 U.S. 238 (1972); Jackson v. Georgia, 408 U.S. 238, *reh'g denied,* 409 U.S. 902 (1972); Branch v. Texas, 408 U.S. 238, *reh'g denied,* 409 U.S. 902 (1972); McGautha v. California, 402 U.S. 183 (1971), *reh'g denied,* 406 U.S. 978 (1972); Crampton v. Ohio, 402 U.S. 183 (1971), *vacated,* 408 U.S. 941 (1972).

10. Glass v. Louisiana, 471 U.S. 1080 (1985) (Brennan, J., dissenting); Wainwright v. Witt, 469 U.S. 412 (1985) (Brennan, J., dissenting); Francis v. Franklin, 471 U.S. 307 (1985) (Brennan, J., for the majority); Strickland v. Washington, 466 U.S. 668 (1984) (Brennan, J., concurring in part and dissenting in part); Pully v. Harris, 465 U.S. 37 (1984) (Brennan, J., dissenting); Maggio v. Williams, 464 U.S. 46 (1983) (Brennan, J., dissenting); Sandstrom v. Montana, 442 U.S. 510 (1979) (Brennan, J., for the majority); Gregg v. Georgia, 428 U.S. 153 (1976) (Brennan, J., dissenting); Furman v. Georgia, 408 U.S. 238 (1972) (Brennan, J., concurring); McGautha v. California, 402 U.S. 183 (1971), (1972) (Brennan, J., dissenting).

11. Turner v. Murray, 476 U.S. 28 (1986) (Brennan, J., concurring in part and dissenting in part); Cabana v. Bullock, 474 U.S. 376 (1986) (Brennan, J., dissenting); Campbell v. Washington, 103 Wash. 2d 1, 691 P.2d 929, *cert. denied,* 471 U.S. 1094 (1985) (Brennan, J., concurring); Baldwin v. Alabama, 472 U.S. 372 (1985) (Brennan, J., dissenting); Smith v. Kemp, 717 F.2d 1401 (11th Cir.), *cert. denied,* 464 U.S. 1032 (Brennan, J., concurring); Enmund v. Florda, 458 U.S. 782 (1982) (Brennan,

J., concurring); Eddings v. Oklahoma, 455 U.S. 104 (1982) (Brennan, J., concurring); Estelle v. Smith, 451 U.S. 454 (1981) (Brennan, J., concurring); Adams v. Texas, 448 U.S. 38 (1980) (Brennan, J., concurring); Beck v. Alabama, 447 U.S. 625 (1980) (Brennan, J., concurring); Green v. Georgia, 442 U.S. 95 (1979) (Brennan, J., concurring); Coker v. Georgia, 433 U.S. 584 (1977) (Brennan, J., concurring); Dobbert v. Florida, 432 U.S. 282 (1977) (Brennan, J., concurring); Roberts v. Louisiana, 428 U.S. 325, *reh'g denied,* 429 U.S. 890 (1976) (Brennan, J., concurring); Woodson v. North Carolina, 428 U.S. 280 (1976) (Brennan, J., concurring).

12. Ford v. Wainwright, 477 U.S. 399 (1986) (Marshall, J., for the majority); Caldwell v. Mississippi, 472 U.S. 320 (1985) (Marshall, J., for the majority); Ake v. Oklahoma, 470 U.S. 68 (1985) (Marshall, J., for the majority); Strickland v. Washington, 466 U.S. 668 (1984) (Marshall, J., dissenting); Gray v. Lucas, 677 F.2d 1086 (5th Cir.), *cert. denied,* 463 U.S. 1237 (1983) (Marshall, J., dissenting); Barefoot v. Estelle, 463 U.S. 880 (1983) (Marshall, J., dissenting); Zant v. Stephens, 462 U.S. 862 (1983) (Marshall, J., dissenting); California v. Ramos, 463 U.S. 992 (1983) (Marshall, J., dissenting); Barclay v. Florida, 463 U.S. 939 (1983) (Marshall, J., dissenting); Coleman v. Balkcom, 451 U.S. 949 (1981) (Marshall, J., concurring); Lockett v. Ohio, 438 U.S. 586 (1978) (Marshall, J., concurring); Coker v. Georgia, 433 U.S. 584 (1977) (Marshall, J., concurring); Gardner v. Florida, 430 U.S. 349 (1977) (Marshall, J., concurring); Gregg v. Georgia, 428 U.S. 153 (1976) (Marshall, J., dissenting); Furman v. Georgia, 408 U.S. 238 (1972) (Marshall, J., concurring).

13. Turner v. Murray, 476 U.S. 28 (1986) (Marshall, J., concurring in part and dissenting in part); Estelle v. Smith, 451 U.S. 454 (1981) (Marshall, J., concurring); Adams v. Texas, 448 U.S. 38 (1980) (Marshall, J., concurring); Beck v. Alabama, 477 U.S. 625 (1980) (Marshall, J., concurring); Green v. Georgia, 442 U.S. 95 (1979) (Marshall, J., concurring); Bell v. Ohio, 438 U.S. 637 (1978) (Marshall, J., concurring); Dobbert v. Florida, 432 U.S. 282, *reh'g denied,* 434 U.S. 882 (1977) (Marshall, J., concurring); Jurek v. Texas, 428 U.S. 262 (1976) (Marshall, J., dissenting); Woodson v. North Carolina, 428 U.S. 280 (1976) (Marshall, J., concurring); Roberts v. Louisiana, 428 U.S. 325 (1976) (Marshall, J., concurring).

14. Demosthenes v. Baal, 110 S. Ct. 2223 (1990) (Brennan, J., dissenting); Walton v. Arizona, 110 S. Ct. 3047 (1990) (Brennan, J., dissenting; also applied to Lewis v. Jeffers, 110 S. Ct. 3092 (1990)); Blystone v. Pennsylvania, 110 S. Ct. 1078 (1990) (Brennan, J., dissenting); Saffle v. Parks, 110 S. Ct. 1257 (1990) (Brennan, J., dissenting); Stanford v. Kentucky, 492 U.S. 361 (1989) (Brennan, J. dissenting); Penry v. Lynaugh, 492 U.S. 302 (1989) (Brennan, J., concurring in part and dissenting in part); South Carolina v. Gathers, 490 U.S. 805 (1989) (Brennan, J., for the majority); McCleskey v. Kemp, 481 U.S. 279 (1987) (Brennan, J., dissenting); Tison v. Arizona, 481 U.S. 137 (1987) (Brennan, J., dissenting).

15. Clemons v. Mississippi, 494 U.S. 738 (1990) (Brennan, J., concurring in part and dissenting in part); Hildwin v. Florida, 490 U.S. 638 (1989) (Brennan, J., dissenting); Mills v. Maryland, 486 U.S. 367 (1988) (Brennan, J., concurring); Johnson v.

Mississippi, 486 U.S. 578 (1988) (Brennan, J., concurring); Maynard v. Cartwright, 486 U.S. 356 (1988) (Brennan, J., concurring).

16. McKoy v. North Carolina, 494 U.S. 433 (1990) (Marshall, J., for the majority); Whitmore v. Arkansas, 110 S. Ct. 1717 (1990) (Marshall, J., dissenting); Sawyer v. Smith, 110 S. Ct. 2822 (1990) (Marshall, J., dissenting); Shell v. Mississippi, 111 S. Ct. 313 (1990) (Marshall, J., concurring); Lowenfield v. Phelps, 484 U.S. 231 (1988) (Marshall, J., dissenting); Satterwhite v. Texas, 486 U.S. 249 (1988) (Marshall, J., concurring).

17. Boyde v. California, 494 U.S. 370 (1990) (Marshall, J., dissenting); Hildwin v. Florida, 490 U.S. 638 (1989) (Marshall, J., dissenting).

18. Mu'Min v. Virginia, 111 S. Ct. 1899 (1991) (Marshall, J., dissenting); McCleskey v. Zant, 111 S. Ct. 1454 (1991) (Marshall, J., dissenting); Payne v. Tennessee, 111 S. Ct. 2597 (1991) (Marshall, J., dissenting).

19. Parker v. Dugger, 111 S. Ct. 731 (1991); McCleskey v. Zant, 111 S. Ct. 1454 (1991); Lankford v. Idaho, 111 S. Ct. 1723 (1991); Yates v. Evatt, 111 S. Ct. 1884 (1991); Mu'Min v. Virginia, 111 S. Ct. 1899 (1991); Schad v. Arizona, 111 S. Ct. 2491 (1991); Payne v. Tennessee, 111 S. Ct. 2597 (1991).

20. South Carolina v. Gathers, 490 U.S. 805 (1989); Francis v. Franklin, 471 U.S. 307 (1985); Sandstrom v. Montana, 442 U.S. 510 (1979).

21. McKoy v. North Carolina, 494 U.S. 433 (1990); Ford v. Wainwright, 477 U.S. 399 (1986); Caldwell v. Mississippi, 472 U.S. 320 (1985); Ake v. Oklahoma, 470 U.S. 68 (1985).

22. 466 U.S. 668 (1984) (Brennan, J., concurring in part and dissenting in part) (Marshall, J., dissenting).

23. *Furman,* 408 U.S. 238 (1972) (Brennan, J., concurring) (Marshall, J., concurring).

24. *Strickland,* 466 U.S. 668 (1990); *Furman,* 408 U.S. 238 (1972).

25. *E.g.,* Enmund v. Florida, 458 U.S. 782 (1982); Coker v. Georgia, 433 U.S. 584 (1977); Lockett v. Ohio, 438 U.S. 586 (1978).

26. *E.g.,* Ford v. Wainwright, 106 S. Ct. 2595 (1986); Caldwell v. Mississippi, 105 S. Ct. 2633 (1985).

27. *E.g.,* Barefoot v. Estelle, 463 U.S. 880, 916 (1983) (dissenting opinion of Marshall, J., joined by Brennan, J., in which Marshall reiterates his adherence to his dissents in *Gregg* and *Furman*).

28. *E.g., id.*

29. 107 S. Ct. 1676 (1987).

30. *Id.* at 1688.

31. *Id.* at 1693.

32. Coleman v. Thompson, 111 S. Ct. 2546, 2548. Roger Coleman claimed he was innocent. Jill Smolowe, "Must This Man Die?" TIME, May 18, 1991, at 40. He was executed on January 23, 1992.

33. Callins v. Collins, 114 S. Ct. 1127 (1994).

34. *E.g.,* Feguer v. United States, 302 F.2d 214 (8th Cir. 1962); Pope v. United States, 372 F.2d 710 (8th Cir. 1967).

35. 114 S. Ct. at 1130. After the United States Supreme Court denied him a stay, Callins received one from a lower court.

David von Drehle wickedly described Blackmun's *Callins* opinion as revealing "the secret":

> For years, the American government—lawmakers, executives and courts—has been keeping a secret from the public. Supreme Court Justice Harry Blackmun recently raised the veil. "I feel morally and intellectually obliged simply to concede that the death penalty experiment has failed," he announced.
>
> Predictably, Blackmun got some stern scoldings. These came from insiders—like Blackmun's colleague, Justice Antonin Scalia. Also from outsiders, still beguiled, like columnist George Will. This is the familiar fate of government whistleblowers, now visited on Harry Blackmun.
>
> More than 20 years ago, the U.S. Supreme Court swept away existing death penalty laws and invited the states to begin anew. They were instructed to draft new laws that would consistently and reliably identify only the very worst arch-demons among America's vast criminal population, cull them and kill them. The effort has turned out to be as taxing and fruitless as the medieval exercise of counting angels on the head of a pin. The soul of a villain is very hard to plumb, we have discovered, and the nature of evil impossible to corral.
>
> Hundreds of millions of dollars have been spent. The death penalty, affecting a minuscule slice of the criminal population, has come to consume time and energy beyond belief: Nearly half the working hours of the Florida Supreme Court, for example; a third or more of the resources of the Eleventh Circuit Court of Appeals. The results? Last year, the number of executions climbed steeply, reaching the highest level in 30 years. Yet for every execution, there were roughly six new death sentences. Death rows continue to expand rapidly—the main force containing them is the number of death sentences reversed on appeal. These far outnumber the executions, owing to a permanent confusion as to the standards governing capital punishment. The population of America's condemned is approaching 3,000.
>
> Here is the truth: If the United States suddenly outlawed all death row appeals, and began executing prisoners at the swiftest rate in history—200 per year—death row would keep growing. What should a man on death row fear most: electrocution, gassing or lethal injection?
>
> Try: Old age.
>
> Anyone who wants to take the time to dig can unearth the secret. This isn't some gentle whim of Blackmun's; it has been bubbling through the legal community for more than a decade.

---

One of the first to break ranks was a former chief justice of the Florida Supreme Court, Arthur England. During his tenure, in the late 1970s and early '80s, the state of Florida was in the vanguard: It has the nation's largest death row and was the only state to execute a man who had not voluntarily abandoned his appeals. England voted to send that man to the electric chair, just as he voted to affirm some 40 other death sentences. When he was finished, England concluded that the rationality and consistency demanded of capital punishment was, in fact, a chimera. "I thought the Supreme Court of Florida would be able to set standards that made sense that we could enforce," he told me. "My experience . . . was that it's impossible to set standards and adhere to them." In 1987, Maryland's chief judge, Robert Murphy, expressed a similar conclusion to the state legislature. He explained that the U.S. Supreme Court had set a very high standard for the death penalty, installing safeguards that are "extremely difficult and complicated . . . difficult and expensive." People may wonder, Murphy continued, "whether the time is close at hand when most of the legal problems have been ironed out. . . . I doubt seriously that that day, if it ever comes, is close at hand."

Philosophy is not the problem. The problem resides in the essential enterprise—trying to define shades of evil on a consistent basis. Chief Justice William Rehnquist, one of the great conservative jurists of the century, has conceded that the death penalty requires "especially careful review of the fairness of the trial, the accuracy of the fact-finding process and the fairness of the sentencing." When you look at death row in America—nearly 3,000 strong, including men who have been there nearly 20 years—you discover the real reason applying the death penalty has been so problematic. "Especially careful review" has crushed the system.

Justice Scalia, echoed by George Will, scolded Harry Blackmun for ignorance. The death penalty is mentioned in the Constitution and is, ergo, constitutional, they intoned. Furthermore, a murderous terror is loose in America.

Blackmun deserved more credit. He made the Scalia-Will argument himself, in his dissent from the Supreme Court's 1972 decision to abolish the death penalty as it then existed. Blackmun wrote: "Our task here, as must so frequently be emphasized and reemphasized, is to pass upon the constitutionality of legislation. . . . That is the sole task for judges. We should not allow our personal preferences as to the wisdom of legislative and congressional action, or our distaste for such action, to guide our judicial decisions in cases such as these. . . ."

"These cases are here because offenses to innocent victims were perpetrated," Blackmun continued. "This fact, and the terror that occasioned it, and the fear that stalks the streets of many of our cities today. . . ."

Of the current members of the Supreme Court, only Blackmun and Rehnquist have been with capital punishment through thick and then— resisting the decision to outlaw it, supporting the decision to restore it. Now Blackmun has given up. He has let the secret out of the bag.— David von Drehle, *When Harry Met Scalia: Why the Death Penalty Is Dying*, WASH. POST, March 6, 1994, at C3.

36. See, for example, Davis v. Florida, 114 S. Ct. 1205 (1994) (Blackmun, J., dissenting from denial of certiorari); Osborne v. Georgia, 114 S. Ct. 1205 (1994) (Blackmun, J., dissenting from denial of certiorari); Robinson v. California, 114 S. Ct. 1205 (1994) (Blackmun, J., dissenting from denial of certiorari); Moody v. Texas, 114 S. Ct. 1205 (1994) (Blackmun, J., dissenting from denial of certiorari); Lambright v. Arizona, 114 S. Ct. 1237 (1994) (Blackmun, J., dissenting from denial of certiorari); Collins v. Byrd, 114 S. Ct. 1288 (1994) (Blackmun, J., dissenting from denial of certiorari); Campbell v. Wood, 114 S. Ct. 1337 (1994) (Blackmun, J., dissenting from denial of certiorari); San Miguel v. Texas, 114 S. Ct. 1339 (1994) (Blackmun, J., dissenting from denial of certiorari); Camacho v. Texas, 114 S. Ct. 1339 (1994) (Blackmun, J., dissenting from denial of certiorari); Aldridge v. Texas, 114 S. Ct. 1339 (1994) (Blackmun, J., dissenting from denial of certiorari); Howell v. Tennessee, 114 S. Ct. 1339 (1994) (Blackmun, J., dissenting from denial of certiorari); Callins v. Texas, 114 S. Ct. 1339 (1994) (Blackmun, J., dissenting from denial of certiorari); Willis v. Texas, 114 S. Ct. 1867 (1994) (Blackmun, J., dissenting from denial of certiorari); Mann v. Oklahoma, 114 S. Ct. 1869 (1994) (Blackmun, J., dissenting from denial of certiorari); Alexander v. Texas, 114 S. Ct. 1869 (1994) (Blackmun, J., dissenting from denial of certiorari); Marek v. Singletary, 114 S. Ct. 1869 (1994) (Blackmun, J., dissenting from denial of certiorari); Chambers v. Texas, 114 S. Ct. 1871 (1994) (Blackmun, J., dissenting from denial of certiorari); Buell v. Ohio, 114 S. Ct. 1871 (1994) (Blackmun, J., dissenting from denial of certiorari); Conklin v. Zant, 114 S. Ct. 1871 (1994) (Blackmun, J., dissenting from denial of certiorari); Gay v. California, 114 S. Ct. 1576 (1994) (Blackmun, J., dissenting from denial of certiorari); Gosch v. Texas, 114 S. Ct. 1576 (1994) (Blackmun, J., dissenting from denial of certiorari); Cummings v. California, 114 S. Ct. 1576 (1994) (Blackmun, J., dissenting from denial of certiorari); Jefferson v. Zant, 114 S. Ct. 1577 (1994) (Blackmun, J., dissenting from denial of certiorari); Johnson v. Texas, 114 S. Ct. 1577 (1994) (Blackmun, J., dissenting from denial of certiorari); Van Tran v. Tennessee, 114 S. Ct. 1577 (1994) (Blackmun, J., dissenting from denial of certiorari); Van McHone v. North Carolina, 114 S. Ct. 1577 (1994) (Blackmun, J., dissenting from denial of certiorari); Schackart v. Arizona, 114 S. Ct. 1578 (1994) (Blackmun, J., dissenting from denial of certiorari); Bible v. Arizona, 114 S. Ct. 1578 (1994) (Blackmun, J., dissenting from denial of certiorari); Lopez v. Arizona, 114 S. Ct. 1578 (1994) (Blackmun, J., dissenting from denial of certiorari); Cade v. Alabama, 114 S. Ct. 1579 (1994) (Blackmun, J., dissenting from denial of certiorari); Johnson v. Texas,

114 S. Ct. 1579 (1994) (Blackmun, J., dissenting from denial of certiorari); Stewart v. Chiles, 114 S. Ct. 1586 (1994) (Blackmun, J., dissenting from denial of certiorari); Stewart v. Singletary, 114 S. Ct. 1586 (1994) (Blackmun, J., dissenting from denial of certiorari); Stewart v. Florida, 114 S. Ct. 1586 (1994) (Blackmun, J., dissenting from denial of certiorari); Richley v. Norris, 114 S. Ct. 1633 (1994) (Blackmun, J., dissenting from denial of certiorari); Holmes v. Norris, 114 S. Ct. 1634 (1994) (Blackmun, J., dissenting from denial of certiorari); Smith v. Indiana, 114 S. Ct. 1634 (1994) (Blackmun, J., dissenting from denial of certiorari); Madison v. Texas, 114 S. Ct. 1634 (1994) (Blackmun, J., dissenting from denial of certiorari); Elkins v. South Carolina, 114 S. Ct. 1634 (1994) (Blackmun, J., dissenting from denial of certiorari); Barnes v. Texas, 114 S. Ct. 1635 (1994) (Blackmun, J., dissenting from denial of certiorari); West v. Arizona, 114 S. Ct. 1635 (1994) (Blackmun, J., dissenting from denial of certiorari); Anderson v. Collins, 114 S. Ct. 1637 (1994) (Blackmun, J., dissenting from denial of certiorari); Spencer v. Wright, 114 S. Ct. 1638 (1994) (Blackmun, J., dissenting from denial of certiorari); Baker v. Maryland, 114 S. Ct. 1664 (1994) (Blackmun, J., dissenting from denial of certiorari); Ramsey v. Missouri, 114 S. Ct. 1664 (1994) (Blackmun, J., dissenting from denial of certiorari); Ford v. Alabama, 114 S. Ct. 1664 (1994) (Blackmun, J., dissenting from denial of certiorari); Tarver v. Alabama 114 S. Ct. 1664 (1994) (Blackmun, J., dissenting from denial of certiorari); Montgomery v. Ohio & Greer v. Ohio, 114 S. Ct. 1665 (1994) (Blackmun, J., dissenting from denial of certiorari); Rogeau v. Texas, 114 S. Ct. 1667 (1994) (Blackmun, J., dissenting from denial of certiorari); Gacy v. Page, 114 S. Ct. 1667 (1994) (Blackmun, J., dissenting from denial of certiorari); Whitmore v. Gaines, 114 S. Ct. 1667 (1994) (Blackmun, J., dissenting from denial of certiorari); Pickens v. Tucker, 114 S. Ct. 1668 (1994) (Blackmun, J., dissenting from denial of certiorari); Hoffman v. Idaho, 114 S. Ct. 1387 (1994) (Blackmun, J., dissenting from denial of certiorari); Williams v. Alabama, 114 S. Ct. 1387 (1994) (Blackmun, J., dissenting from denial of certiorari); Coral v. Alabama 114 S. Ct. 1387 (1994) (Blackmun, J., dissenting from denial of certiorari); Ogan v. Texas, 114 S. Ct. 1388 (1994) (Blackmun, J., dissenting from denial of certiorari); Tucker v. Texas, 114 S. Ct. 1388 (1994) (Blackmun, J., dissenting from denial of certiorari); Jones v. Illinois, 114 S. Ct. 1388 (1994) (Blackmun, J., dissenting from denial of certiorari); Behringer v. Texas, 114 S. Ct. 1388 (1994) (Blackmun, J., dissenting from denial of certiorari); Jenkins v. Alabama, 114 S. Ct. 1388 (1994) (Blackmun, J., dissenting from denial of certiorari); Moreno v. Texas, 114 S. Ct. 1389 (1994) (Blackmun, J., dissenting from denial of certiorari); Dubois v. Virginia, 114 S. Ct. 1389 (1994) (Blackmun, J., dissenting from denial of certiorari); Young v. Pennsylvania, 114 S. Ct. 1389 (1994) (Blackmun, J., dissenting from denial of certiorari); Johnson v. California, 114 S. Ct. 1391 (1994) (Blackmun, J., dissenting from denial of certiorari); Webb v. Collins, 114 S. Ct. 1392 (1994) (Blackmun, J., dissenting from denial of certiorari); Hance v. Zant, 114 S. Ct. 1392 (1994) (Blackmun, J., dissenting from denial of certiorari); Lamberty v. Texas, 114 S. Ct. 1393 (1994) (Blackmun, J., dissenting from denial of certiorari); Beavers v. Collins, 114 S. Ct. 1393 (1994) (Blackmun, J., dissenting from denial of certiorari);

Mu'Min v. Murray, 114 S. Ct. 1416 (1994) (Blackmun, J., dissenting from denial of certiorari); Nethery v. Collins, 114 S. Ct. 1416 (1994) (Blackmun, J., dissenting from denial of certiorari); Comer v. Arizona, 114 S. Ct. 1417 (1994) (Blackmun, J., dissenting from denial of certiorari); Davis v. Arkansas, 114 S. Ct. 1417 (1994) (Blackmun, J., dissenting from denial of certiorari); Davis v. Florida, 114 S. Ct. 1205 (1994) (Blackmun, J., dissenting from denial of certiorari); Osborne v. Georgia, 114 S. Ct. (1994) (Blackmun, J., dissenting from denial of certiorari); Robinson v. Florida, 114 S. Ct. 1205 (1994) (Blackmun, J., dissenting from denial of certiorari); Moody v. Texas, 114 S. Ct. 1205 (1994) (Blackmun, J., dissenting from denial of certiorari); Pickens v. Norris, 114 S. Ct. 1206 (1994) (Blackmun, J., dissenting from denial of certiorari); Sweet v. Florida, 114 S. Ct. 1206 (1994) (Blackmun, J., dissenting from denial of certiorari); Hunt v. Maryland, 114 S. Ct. 1206 (1994) (Blackmun, J., dissenting from denial of certiorari); Collins v. Maryland, 114 S. Ct. 1206 (1994) (Blackmun, J., dissenting from denial of certiorari); Carroll v. Alabama, 114 S. Ct. 1207 (1994) (Blackmun, J., dissenting from denial of certiorari); Dunlap v. Idaho, 114 S. Ct. 1207 (1994) (Blackmun, J., dissenting from denial of certiorari); Workman v. Tennessee, 114 S. Ct. 1207 (1994) (Blackmun, J., dissenting from denial of certiorari); Drew v. Collins, 114 S. Ct. 1207 (1994) (Blackmun, J., dissenting from denial of certiorari); Spencer v. Murray, 114 S. Ct. 1208 (1994) (Blackmun, J., dissenting from denial of certiorari); Holladay v. Alabama, 114 S. Ct. 1208 (1994) (Blackmun, J., dissenting from denial of certiorari); Lawson v. Dixon, 114 S. Ct. 1208 (1994) (Blackmun, J., dissenting from denial of certiorari); Russell v. Collins, 114 S. Ct. 1236 (1994) (Blackmun, J., dissenting from denial of certiorari); Trevino v. Texas, 114 S. Ct. 1237 (1994) (Blackmun, J., dissenting from denial of certiorari); Lewis v. Ohio, 114 S. Ct. 1237 (1994) (Blackmun, J., dissenting from denial of certiorari); Smith v. Arizona, 114 S. Ct. 1237 (1994) (Blackmun, J., dissenting from denial of certiorari); Lambright v. Arizona, 114 S. Ct. 1237 (1994) (Blackmun, J., dissenting from denial of certiorari).

37. Gregg v. Georgia, 428 U.S. 153 (1976); Proffitt v. Florida, 428 U.S. 242 (1976); Jurek v. Texas, 428 U.S. 262 (1976).

38. Herrera v. Collins, 113 s. Ct. 853 (1993).

39. Lewis Powell's post-judicial conversion to the abolitionist position is worth a footnote. As described by his biographer, Justice Powell in retirement came to believe capital punishment unconstitutional. J. JEFFRIES, JUSTICE LEWIS F. POWELL, JR. 451–52 (1994). I prefer the view of Powell held by Scharlette Holdman and Gail Rowland of the Florida Clearinghouse on Criminal Justice, an operation existing to find and help lawyers willing to represent that state's death row inmates pro bono.

> By Spring of 1984, Holdman was spending an hour a day just keeping her ledger [of condemned Florida inmates] up to date. And the work kept expanding. Every few weeks another family would arrive in North Florida to face the possible extinction of a son, a brother, a father. Scharlette Holdman raised their bus fares, found them someplace to stay. Some of those sons and brothers and fathers did die; Holdman arranged the

funerals. Gail Rowland became an overnight expert in the laws governing interstate transportation of corpses. Holdman, as always, worked the phone: "I need $300 for a funeral; can your church group handle it?" Or, "You've got six acres out there; can we bury somebody on your land?" Holdman's son Tad came home one day to find a station wagon in the carport with a big box in the back. "Is that what I think it is?" he asked. It was—the dead followed her home.

She worked constantly—her first day off that year came in November—but she confided that she cried as much as she worked. She cried though she hated to be seen crying. (When a photographer got a picture of her sobbing at a vigil for Anthony Antone, Holdman announced that she would no longer attend such protests.) Death became her life, and it subsumed the lives of those around her. "I got to the point where all I did was buy black clothes," said Gail Rowland. "I learned so many damn funeral songs. I hope I never sing 'Amazing Grace' or 'Will the Circle Be Unbroken' again."

There were moments when the tension broke, moments of bitter laughter. Gail Rowland's puppet, for example. At the U.S. Supreme Court, one justice was assigned to each region of the country to handle emergency appeals. Florida's justice was Lewis Powell; naturally be became a particular target of Holdman's scorn. So Rowland made a hand-puppet that she called "Mr. Justice Powell," and the puppet offered running commentary on the events in the office. Say Holdman and Craig Barnard were talking about filing an appeal based on an inmate's deprived background. Mr. Justice Powell would pop up and shout, "Oh, shut up!" Not another bed-wetting darkie!" Or Jimmy Lohman would strum a folk tune on his guitar, and Mr. Justice Powell would chime in with some grossly racist, sexist lyrics. Holdman either laughed or cried; it was a time of emotional extremes; her nerves glowed like incandescent filaments.—D. Von Drehle, Among The Lowest of the Dead (1995)

40. Professor Kelman refers to repeated dissent on the same issue as "sustained dissent." Kelman, *The Forked Path of Dissent,* 1985 Sup. Ct. Rev. 227, at 248–58.

41. Benjamin W. Eiser & Joan Biskupic, *Rare Look Behind Bench: Late Justice's Papers Offer Glimpse of Sitting Court,* Wash. Post, May 23, 1993, at A1.

42. *Id.*

43. *Id.*

44. Linda Greenhouse, *Protecting Its Mystique: High Court's Anger over Marshall Papers Is Fueled by More than Pomp and Privacy,* N.Y. Times, May 27, 1993, at 1.

45. Juan Williams, *Thurgood Marshall's Continuing Impact,* Valley News (Vt.), June 1, 1993.

46. *Id.*

47. The phrase is the subtitle to Raoul Berger, Death Penalties (1982).

48. Von Drehle, *supra* note 39, at 77–78. The stay proved merely temporary.

49. 402 U.S. 183 (1971).

50. *See generally* MICHAEL MELTSNER, CRUEL AND UNUSUAL (1974) (tracing pre-*Furman* litigation strategy of death penalty abolitionists).

51. 402 U.S. at 204.

52. *Id.* at 206.

53. 408 U.S. 233 (1972).

54. Greenberg, *Capital Punishment as a System,* 91 YALE L.J. 908, 915 (1982).

55. 408 U.S. at 239–40.

56. *See* Daniel Polsby, *The Death of Capital Punishment? Furman v. Georgia,* 1972 SUP. CT. REV. 1 (analyzing separate opinions).

57. 408 U.S. at 253 (Douglas, J., concurring).

58. *Id.* at 345.

59. *Id.* at 309–10 (Stewart, J., concurring).

60. *Id.* at 313–14 (White, J., concurring).

61. *Id.* at 257–306.

62. *Id.* at 314–71.

63. Zant v. Stephens, 103 S. Ct. 2733, 2741 (1983) (quoting Gregg v. Georgia, 428 U.S. 153, 189 (1976)).

64. The tension between *McGautha* and *Furman* was noted by the dissenters in *Furman, see* 408 U.S. at 399 (Burger, C.J., dissenting); *id.* at 427 n.11 (Powell, J., dissenting) and by several commentators. *See, e.g.,* Polsby, *supra* note 56, at 1–4; Margaret Radin, *Cruel Punishment and Respect for Persons: Super Due Process for Death,* 53 S. CAL. L. REV. 1143, 1148–49 (1980); Note, *The Bitter Fruit of McGautha: Eddings v. Oklahoma and the Need for Weighing Method Articulation in Capital Sentencing,* 20 AM. CRIM. L. REV. 63, 63–64 (1982). *See generally* Weisberg, *Deregulating Death,* 1983 SUP. CT. REV. 305.

65. *See generally* Ehrhardt & Levinson, *Florida's Legislative Response to Furman: An Exercise in Futility?* 64 J. CRIM. L. & CRIMINOLOGY 10 (1973); Note, *Florida's Legislative and Judicial Response to Furman v. Georgia: An Analysis and Criticism,* 2 FLA. ST. U. L. REV. 108 (1974).

66. Gregg v. Georgia, 426 U.S. at 179–80 n.23.

67. *Compare* Gregg v. Georgia, 428 U.S. at 106 n.9, *with* Proffitt v. Florida, 428 U.S. 242–49 n.66 (1976).

68. *E.g.,* Espinosa v. Florida; Sochor v. Florida; Stringer v. Black; Maynard v. Cartwright; Lewis v. Jeffers.

69. GA. CODE ANN. § 17-10-30(b)(7) (1973). This provision has received much attention in the legal literature. *See, e.g.,* C. BLACK, CAPITAL PUNISHMENT 74–78 (2d ed. 1982); J. ELY, DEMOCRACY AND DISTRUST 175 (180); Dix, *Appellate Review of the Decision to Impose Death,* 68 GEO. L.J. 97, 112–17 (1979); Donohue, *Godfrey v. Georgia: Creative Federalism, the Eighth Amendment and the Evolving Law of Death,* 30 CATH. U. L. REV. 13 (1981); Richards & Hoffman, *Death Among the Shifting Standards: Capital Punishment After Furman,* 28 S.D. L. REV. 243 (1981); Note, *The Death Penalty in Georgia: An Aggravating Circumstance,* 30 AM. U. L. REV. 335 (1981); Note, *Consti-*

*tutional Procedure for the Imposition of the Death Penalty—Godfrey v. Georgia,* 30 DePaul L. Rev. 721 (1981).

70. Fla. Stat. § 921.141(5)(b) (1983).

71. Gregg v. Georgia, 428 U.S. 153, 196 (1976).

72. *Id.* at 301 n.51.

73. *Id.* at 201.

74. 426 U.S. 242, 25 (1976).

75. Lockett v. Ohio, 438 U.S. 586, 629 (1978) (Rehnquist, J., concurring in part and dissenting in part).

76. *Id.* at 597–602 (opinion of Burger, C.J., joined by Stewart, Powell, and Stevens, JJ.).

77. *Id.* at 604–05 (opinion of Burger, C.J.) (holding that although individualized sentencing was matter of public policy in noncapital cases, individualized decision including consideration of all relevant mitigating factors is constitutionally required for "profoundly different" sentence of death).

78. For examples of Supreme Court decisions vacating death sentences because the sentencer was precluded from considering mitigating factors, see Penry v. Lynaugh, 492 U.S. 302 (1989), Sumner v. Shumann, 483 U.S. 67 (1987); Hitchcock v. Dugger, 481 U.S. 393 (1987); Skipper v. South Carolina, 476 U.S. 1 (1986).

Justice Scalia recently rejected this line of cases as fundamentally inconsistent with *Furman. See* Walton v. Arizona, 110 S. Ct. 3047, 3058–68 (1990) (Scalia, J., concurring in part). For a discussion of the tension between *Furman* and *Lockett,* see Sundby, *The* Lockett *Paradox: Reconciling Guided Discretion and Unguided Mitigation in Capital Sentencing,* 38 UCLA L. Rev. 1147 (1991).

79. *E.g.,* McFarland v. Collins, __ S. Ct. __ (1994); Espinosa v. Florida, 112 S. Ct. 2926 (1993); Lankford v. Idaho, 111 S. Ct. 1723 (1991); McKoy v. North Carolina, 110 S. Ct. 1227 (1990) (jury cannot be required to agree unanimously on the existence of mitigating circumstances); Johnson v. Mississippi, 486 U.S. 578 (1988) (sentencer's consideration of invalid prior conviction tainted resulting death sentence); Booth v. Maryland, 482 U.S. 496 (1987) (use of victim impact statement, including family's emotional reaction to and characterization of murderer and his crime, held to violate Constitution), *overruled,* Payne v. Tennessee, 111 S. Ct. 2597 (1991); Ford v. Wainwright, 477 U.S. 399 (1986) (mere cursory review used to determine inmate's sanity prior to execution held insufficient); Caldwell v. Mississippi, 472 U.S. 320 (1985) (prosecutor's and judge's comments to jury indicating that appeals court would correct any mistakes by jury held to be error of constitutional magnitude); Enmund v. Florida, 458 U.S. 782 (1982) (death sentence for felony murder when defendant did not himself kill, attempt to kill, or intend that killing take place or lethal force be used); Bullington v. Missouri, 451 U.S. 430 (1981) (state's request for death penalty on retrial violated double jeopardy clause when jury had previously imposed lesser sentence); Godfrey v. Georgia, 446 U.S. 420 (1980) (no showing of "consciousness materially more 'depraved' than that of any person guilty of murder" when victims were killed immediately, defendant suffered extreme

emotional distress as a result of their deaths, and defendant admitted responsibility shortly after crimes); Lockett v. Ohio, 438 U.S. 586 (1978) (limitation on sentencer's consideration of mitigating factors held unconstitutional); Coker v. Georgia, 433 U.S. 584 (1977) (death penalty unconstitutionally disproportionate sentence for crime of rape of an adult woman).

80. In all but one of the fifteen fully argued capital cases decided between 1976 and the end of the 1981 Term, the Court reversed or vacated the death sentence. Weisberg, *supra* note 64, at 305 n.1. The Court rendered four capital cases at the end of the 1982 Term, all of which found against the condemned inmate. *See* California v. Ramos, 463 U.S. 992 (1983) (rejecting challenge that jury instruction that governor may commune life sentence without parole was speculative or impermissibly shifts focus from defendant); Barclay v. Florida, 463 U.S. 939 (1983) (finding no constitutional violation in sentencer's consideration of nonstatutory aggravating circumstances); Barefoot v. Estelle, 463 U.S. 880 (1983) (upholding procedures for expedited consideration of capital habeas cases and allowing use of psychiatric testimony on future dangerousness at capital-sentencing proceeding even when based on hypothetical questions concerning particular defendant); Zant v. Stephens, 462 U.S. 862 (1983) (holding that invalidity of one aggravating circumstance did not render death sentence unconstitutional when other valid aggravating factors were present).

81. *E.g.,* Graham v. Collins, 113 S. Ct. 1406 (1993); Herrera v. Collins, 113 S. Ct. 853 (1993); Sawyer v. Whitley, 112 S. Ct. 2514 (1992); Mu'min v. Virginia, 111 S. Ct. 1899 (1991); Coleman v. Thompson, 111 S. Ct. 2546 (1991); Payne v. Tennessee, 111 S. Ct. 2597 (1991); McCleskey v. Zant, 111 S. Ct. 1454 (1991); Lewis v. Jeffers, 110 S. Ct. 3092 (1990); Boyde v. California, 494 U.S. 370 (1990); Walton v. Arizona, 110 S. Ct. 3047 (1990); Butler v. McKellar, 494 U.S. 407 (1990); Stanford v. Kentucky, 109 S. Ct. 2969 (1990); Murray v. Giarratano, 109 S. Ct. 2765 (1989); Franklin v. Lynaugh, 487 U.S. 164 (1988); Ricketts v. Adamson, 483 U.S. 1 (1987) (no double jeopardy bar to reprosecution for first-degree murder when defendant breached plea bargain to second-degree murder); McCleskey v. Kemp, 481 U.S. 279 (1987) (no constitutional violation on showing of statistical disparity between imposition of death penalty in cases of Black defendants with White victims and cases of White defendants with Black victims); Tison v. Arizona, 481 U.S. 137, 158 (1987) (upholding death sentence resting on felony-murder conviction on showing of "major participation" in felony and "reckless indifference to human life"); California v. Brown, 479 U.S. 538, 542 (1987) (affirming death sentence following instruction that jury should not be swayed by "mere sentiment, conjecture, sympathy, passion, prejudice, public opinion or public feeling," because jury would not single out "sympathy" and would likely consider instruction admonishment not to consider sympathy arising from other than aggravating and mitigating circumstances presented); Smith v. Murray, 477 U.S. 527 (1987) (procedural default); Darden v. Wainwright, 477 U.S. 168 (1986) (finding no constitutional violation in exclusion of juror who would refuse to impose death penalty or in prosecutor's improper closing arguments); Lockhart v. McCree, 476 U.S. 162 (1986) (no constitutional error in

removal of jurors who would not impose death sentence under any circumstances); Poland v. Arizona, 476 U.S. 147 (1986) (finding no double jeopardy bar to further capital-sentencing proceedings when appeals court finds evidence insufficient to support sole aggravating factor on which sentencing judge relied but not insufficient to support death sentence because judge misconstrued availability of another aggravating factor); Heath v. Alabama, 474 U.S. 82 (1985) (finding no double jeopardy bar to prosecution present when defendant is tried for murder by one sovereign (Alabama) after having pled guilty to offense arising from same occurrence in prosecution by another sovereign (Georgia)); Baldwin v. Alabama, 472 U.S. 372 (1985) (statute requiring jury to impose death sentence if it convicted defendant of aggravated crime did not violate Constitution because jury's sentence is only a recommendation and the judge must weigh mitigating and aggravating circumstances at a separate sentencing hearing); Wainwright v. Witt, 469 U.S. 412 (1985) (no constitutional violation in exclusion of juror who would not vote for death penalty regardless of circumstances of crime); Spaziano v. Florida, 468 U.S. 447 (1984) (no eighth amendment violation when judge sentences defendant to death despite jury's recommendation of life sentence); Pulley v. Harris, 465 U.S. 37 (1984) (no eighth amendment requirement that states conduct proportionality review in capital cases).

82. Use of the term in this this sense is taken from Weisberg, *supra* note 64. Some states have responded to this "deregulation" by interpreting their won constitutions more broadly than the federal constitutional minima. *See generally* Acker & Walsh, *Challenging the Death Penalty Under State Constitutions,* 42 VAND. L. REV. 1299 (1989); *cf.* Mello, *The Jurisdiction to Do Justice: Florida's Jury Override and the State Constitution,* 18 FLA. ST. U. L. REV. 923 (1991).

83. For a sampling of the academic debate surrounding the federal courts' redetermination of federal questions decided in state criminal proceedings, see Bator, *Finality in Criminal Law and Federal Habeas Corpus for State Prisoners,* 76 HARV. L. REV. 441 (1963); Brennan, *Federal Habeas Corpus and State Prisoners: An Exercise in Federalism,* 7 UTAH L. REV. 423 (1961); Friendly, *Is Innocence Irrelevant? Collateral Attack on Criminal Judgments,* 38 U. CHI. L. REV. 142 (1970); Neuborne, *The Myth of Parity,* 90 HARV. L. REV. 1105 (1977); Peller, *In Defense of Federal Habeas Corpus Relitigation,* 16 HARV. C.R.-C.L. L. REV. 579 (1982); Robbins, *The Habeas Corpus Certificate of Probable Cause,* 44 OHIO ST. L.J. 307 (1983); TAGUE, *Federal Habeas Corpus and Ineffective Representation of Counsel: The Supreme Court Has Work to Do,* 31 STAN. L. REV. 1 (1978).

84. In 1985 the Eleventh Circuit unleashed a firestorm of criticism, much of it directed specifically at the court, when a panel ordered new trials because of pervasive pretrial publicity for three Georgia inmates, Wayne Carl Coleman, George Elder Dungee, and Carl J. Isaacs, who had been condemned to death for murdering several members of the Alday family. The Eleventh Circuit's opinions are reported as Coleman v. Kemp, 788 F.2d 1487 (11th Cir. 1985), *cert. denied,* 476 U.S. 1164 (1986). Three days after the rulings, one newspaper reported that with one notable exception editorial pages across Georgia "blasted the 11th U.S. Circuit Court of Appeals deci-

sion." *Most State Editorial Pages Decry Alday Ruling,* MACON TELEGRAPH & NEWS (Ga.), Dec. 12, 1985, at B1. *E.g.,* Resch, *Midstate Judge Has Tried His Share of 'Glamour Cases,'* MACON TELEGRAPH & NEWS (Ga.), July 21, 1986, at B2 (quoting state superior court judge Walter C. McMillan, who was assigned to retry the Alday case: "I'm completely put out by the federal government on the death system. . . . The general public equates the inability of federal courts to establish finality on death verdicts with the entire court system"); Grimm, *"We'll Never Be the Same": Court's Decision Granting New Trial to Defendants in Alday Rulings Case Has Opened Old Wounds,* MACON TELEGRAPH & NEWS (Ga.), June 10, 1986, at B1 ("[T]hose rulings are regarded as the inexplicable acts of madmen. They solidified all the local mistrust of everything urban and Washington, of slick lawyers and their technical maneuvering, of ivory tower judges and their niggling fascination with the seemingly irrelevant. 'Ought to hang them judges.' "); *Measure Hits Court Ruling in Alday Case,* ATLANTA J.–ATLANTA CONST., Jan. 18, 1986, at B3 (40 members of the Georgia House of Representatives cosponsored resolution condemning Alday rulings); McLeon, *Newspaper Would Do Nothing Different in Covering Alday Murders,* ATLANTA J.–ATLANTA CONST., Dec. 22, 1985, at D6 ("We have saddled ourselves with people ruling who are far removed from real life, who are trying to reach forth and grab powers they don't have and use them for purposes only they can explain."); *Justice Left on Legal Scrap Heap,* MACON TELEGRAPH & NEWS (Ga.), December 20, 1985, at A11 (letter to the editor) ("[I]t is just such stupid decisions by men such as [the Eleventh Circuit panel of judges] that one day will force the very best of en to begin to take revenge, for most good men in America have about come to feel that there is no justice at all left in America."); Woolner, *The "Faceless" Men of the 11th Circuit Court,* ATLANTA CONST., Dec. 18, 1985, at 9A (in week following rulings, the court "was beseiged with phone calls—more calls than the 4-year-old court had ever received on a case. According to court personnel many callers simply wanted to know the names of the faceless men who set aside the convictions. . . ."); Corson, *Alday Retrial Decision Vehemently Opposed,* MACON TELEGRAPH & NEWS (Ga.), Dec. 13, 1985, at A14 ("As might be expected, the readers' hot line Wednesday was dominated by the subject of the federal appeals court's decision," some callers stating that the judges "should be disqualified and disbarred."); Allen, *Alday Jury, Not Appeals Judges, Upheld the Law,* ATLANTA CONST., Dec. 12, 1985, at A2 (decisions were a product of "the rarefied atmosphere of a life appointment to the federal bench" and of federal judges who are "actively hostile to capital punishment"); Hansen, *Harris Vents "Shock" over Alday Case,* ATLANTA CONST., Dec. 12, 1985, at 38A (Georgia governor quoted aas calling decisions a "flaw in our system"); McKerley, *Anger, Disbelief Greet Alday Ruling,* MACON TELEGRAPH & NEWS (Ga.), Dec. 11, 1985, at A1 (describing "anger and frustration" of local residents concerning the rulings); Thompson, *Bowers: Alday Ruling Marks Demand for Perfection,* ATLANTA CONST., Dec. 11, 1985, at A6 (quoting Georgia attorney general as saying "appeals courts are holding trial court judges to impossibly high standards"); Thompson, *Bowers: Alday Ruling Shows Legal Delimma,* ATLANTA J., Dec. 11, 1985, at C9; Montgomery, *Ruling in*

*Alday Case Reopens Old Wounds: Anger of Seminole Community Mirrors "Outrage" of Governor*, ATLANTA CONST., Dec. 11, 1985, at A1 (quoting governor of Georgia as being "outraged" by court's decisions: "It indicates that something is terribly wrong with our judicial system. How can the system be defended?"); Boyd, *Time to Pull the Switch*, MACON TELEGRAPH & NEWS (Ga.), Dec. 11, 1985, at B1 (condemning multiple levels of review of capital cases and "high-and-mighty judges"); Montgomery & Woolner, *Seminole Outraged at Alday Ruling*, ATLANTA J., Dec. 10, 1985, at A1 (quoting local citizen as saying, "[M]aybe they ought to turn [the killers] loose and hang same judges."); Woolner, *Alday Murder Convictions Overturned*, ATLANTA CONST., Dec. 10, 1985, at A1 (quoting Georgia lieutenant governor as calling the rulings the "outrage of the century" and saying that "[t]he judges ought to be required to go down to Seminole County, lay down on the Alday family graves and apologize."). *But cf.* Editorials, *Decision Shocking but Also Necessary*, MACON TELEGRAPH & NEWS (Ga.), Dec. 12, 1985, at A14 (state courts "dropped the ball. Finally, after all these years, the federal appeals court had to pick it up and do what the state courts apparently lacked the courage to do—something unpopular, yet important to our freedoms."); Teepen, *Buck Stopped at 11th Circuit*, ATLANTA CONST., Dec. 12, 1985, at A22; *Tough, but Correct, Alday Ruling*, ATLANTA CONST., Nov. 11, 1985, at A12.

A Georgia grand jury reportedly accused the Eleventh Circuit judges of "callous disregard for the rights of crime victims and their families." *Lowndes Grand Jury Faults Judges' Lifetime Appointment*, ATLANTA J.–ATLANTA CONST., Feb. 15, 1986, at C7. The press reported that in a voluminous petition, one hundred thousand citizens asked Congress to impeach the three Eleventh Circuit judges who took part in the Alday decisions. *See A Stand on Judicial Principal*, ATLANTA CONST., Oct. 29, 1986, at A14; Thompson, *Contractor Behind Alday Petition Moves into Politics*, ATLANTA CONST., Oct. 29, 1986, at A10; McDonald, *Judges in Alday Case Can't Be Impeached, Panel Rules*, ATLANTA CONST., Oct. 17, 1986, at A26; King, *Petitioner Vows He Will Continue Fight*, MACON TELEGRAPH & NEWS (Ga.), June 3, 1986, at A1; Dart, *Congress Asked to Impeach Judges in Alday Appeal*, ATLANTA CONST., Mar. 20, 1986, at A28; Beasley, *Petitions to Impeach Judges in Alday Ruling Spreading Across State*, ATLANTA CONST., Jan. 29, 1986, at A20.

At the retrials mandated by the Eleventh Circuit, juries resentenced Coleman, Dungee, and Isaacs to life imprisonment.

85. Eleventh Circuit panels twice stayed Bundy's execution and twice remanded his cases for evidentiary hearings. The public was not pleased. *E.g.*, Leguire, *Grant Blasts Bundy Delays*, LAKE CITY REPORTER (Fla.), Feb. 22, 1988, at A1 ("Saying that convicted murderer Ted Bundy has made a mockery of the law, Congressman Bill Grant, D-Madison, is calling for an overhaul of the judicial system which would hasten executions. . . ."). The federal district judge in Bundy's case disingenuously cited it as an example of lawyers manipulating the legal system; the judge did so at a time when he must have known that Bundy's case was likely to come before him again, as it in fact did. Cotterell, *Death-Appeals Process Examined*, TALLAHASSEE DEMOCRAT, Feb. 27, 1988, at C3.

The Alday rulings, discussed above, also prompted Georgia officials and legislators to call for "reforms" in the federal judiciary and in habeas corpus. *E.g.,* McDonald, *Judges in Alday Case Can't Be Impeached, Panel Rules,* ATLANTA CONST., Oct. 17, 1986, at A26 (Congressman Charles Hatcher of Georgia quoted as saying he planned to "co-sponsor legislation when Congress reconvenes next year that would limit the powers of federal courts in deciding whether to overturn or grant new trials for convicted murderers"); *Death Appeals Resolution Approved,* ATLANTA CONST., Feb. 7, 1986, at A8 (describing Georgia state senate resolution urging Congress to require all appeals in death cases to be filed within twelve months); McAlister, *Alday Case Calls for New Legislation, Not Outrage,* ATLANTA J., June 4, 1986, at A14 ("At the federal level, Rep. Newt Gingrich has called on Congress to enact a law to speed action in death-penalty cases. He would eliminate the U.S. District Court from the appeals process, limit the federal portion of the appeal [sic] to two years and require that all grounds be included in one appeal [sic]."); Cowles, *Court Won't Reconsider Alday Ruling,* ATLANTA CONST., Feb. 1, 1986, at B1 (Georgia lieutenant governor quoted as saying that he "will lead an effort to have federal judges face election every eight years"). The outpouring of rage led former U.S. attorney general Griffin Bell to suggest that issuance of habeas corpus writs be limited to three years after exclusion of state court remedies or after the appearance of new evidence. Brady, *Right of Habeas Corpus Endangered, Griffin Bell Says,* ATLANTA CONST., Jan. 9, 1986, at A24.

86. *E.g.,* Coleman v. Thompson, 111 S. Ct. 2546 (1991); Lewis v. Jeffers, 110 S. Ct. 3092 (1990); Dugger v. Adams, 489 U.S. 401 (1989); Murray v. Carrier, 477 U.S. 478 (1986); Wainwright v. Sykes, 433 U.S. 72 (1977).

87. McClesky v. Zant, 111 S. Ct. 1454 (1991); Butler v. McKellar, 494 U.S. 407 (1990); Saffle v. Parks, 494 U.S. 484 (1990); Sawyer v. Smith, 110 S. Ct. 2822 (1990); Teague v. Lane, 489 U.S. 288 (1989); Penry v. Lynaugh, 492 U.S. 302 (1989). On retroactivity generally, see Blume & Pratt, *Understanding* Teague v. Lane, 18 N.Y.U. REV. L. & SOC. CHANGE 325 (1990–91); Ledewitz, *Habeas Corpus as a Safety Valve for Innocence,* 18 N.Y.U. REV. L. & SOC. CHANGE, 415 (1990–91); Liebman, *More than "Slightly Retro": The Rehnquist Court's Rout of Habeas Corpus,* 18 N.Y.U. REV. L. & SOC. CHANGE (1991); Weisburg, *A Great Writ While It Lasted,* 81 J. CRIM. L. & CRIMINOLOGY 9 (1990); Arkin, *The Prisoner's Dilemma: Life in the Lower Federal Courts After* Teague v. Lane, N.C. L. REV. (1991).

88. *E.g.,* S. 635, 102d Cong., 1st Sess. (1991); H.R. REP. No. 1400, 102d Cong., 1st Sess. (1991); S. REP. No. 1760, CONG. REC., Oct. 16, 1989; *Report on Habeas Corpus in Capital Cases,* 45 CRIM. L. REP. 3239 (1989). For outstanding critiques of these proposals to "reform" capital habeas, see ABA, *Toward a More Just and Effective System of Review in State Death Penalty Cases: A Report Containing the American Bar Association's Recommendations Concerning Death Penalty Habeas Corpus and Related Materials from the American Bar Association Criminal Justice Section's Project on Death Penalty Habeas Corpus,* 40 AM. U. L. REV. 53 (1990); Berger, *Justice Delayed or Justice Denied—A Comment on Recent Proposals to Reform Death Penalty Habeas Corpus,* 90 COLUM. L. REV. 1665 (1990).

89. Gregg v. Georgia, 428 U.S. 153 (1976); Jurek v. Texas, 428 U.S. 262 (1976); Proffitt v. Florida, 428 U.S. 242 (1976).

90. Lewis, *supra* note 5, at 8.

91. Neil A. Lewis, *In Marshall Papers, Rare Glimpse at Court,* N.Y. TIMES, May 23, 1993, at A1, A16.

92. EISLER, A JUSTICE FOR ALL: WILLIAM J. BRENNAN, JR., AND THE DECISIONS THAT TRANSFORMED AMERICA 17–18 (1993).

93. Meese, *The Supreme Court of the United States: Bulwark of a Limited Constitution, 27* S. TEX. L.J. 455, 464 (1985).

94. Hopkins, *Mr. Justice Brennan and Freedom of Expression 4 (1991).*

95. EISLER, *supra* note 92, at 18.

96. *Id.* at 19.

97. *Id.*

98. *Id.* at 20.

99. Hopkins, *supra* note 94, at 4.

100. EISLER, *supra* note 92, at 20.

101. *Id.* at 23, 24.

102. *Id.* at 26.

103. *Id.* at 25.

104. *Id.* at 21.

105. *Id.* at 21, 22.

106. *Id.* at 22.

107. *Id.*

108. *Id.* at 23.

109. *Id.* at 22.

110. *Id.* at 28.

111. *Id.*

112. *Id.*

113. *Id.* at 31.

114. *Id.* at 33, 34.

115. *Id.* at 38.

116. *Id.*

117. *Id.* at 43.

118. *Id.*

119. *Id.*

120. *Id.* at 44.

121. *Id.* at 45.

122. *Id.* at 46.

123. *Id.* at 51, 52.

124. *Id.* at 53.

125. *Id.* at 63.

126. *Id.*

127. *Id.* at 64.

128. *Id.*

129. *Id.* at 65.

130. *Id.* at 69.

131. *Id.* at 70.

132. *Id.*

133. *Id.* at 78.

134. *Id.* at 80.

135. *Id.*

136. *Id.* at 81.

137. *Id.* at 89.

138. *Id.*

139. *Id.*

140. *Id.* at 90.

141. *Id.*

142. Hopkins, *supra* note 94, at 3.

143. *Id.*

144. Totenberg, A Tribute to William J. Brennan, Jr., 104 HARV. L. REV. 33, 38 (1990).

145. Mikva, A Tribute to William J. Brennan, Jr., 104 HARV. L. REV. 9, 10, (1990).

146. Stone, *Justice Brennan and the Freedom of Speech: A First Amendment Odyssey,* 139 U. PA. L. REV. 1333, 1333 (1991).

147. *Id.* at 1335, citing *Roth v. United States,* 354 U.S. 476, 485 (1957).

148. *Id.*

149. *Id.*

150. Hopkins, *supra* note 94, at 22.

151. *Id.*

152. *Id.* at 34.

153. Stone, *supra* note 146, at 1345.

154. EISLER, *supra* note 92, at 276.

155. A. LEWIS, MAKE NO LAW (1991).

156. WILLIAM J. BRENNAN, JR., AN AFFAIR WITH FREEDOM 71 (Friedman ed., 1967).

157. Stone, *supra* note 146, at 1342–1343.

158. *Id.*

159. *Id.* at 1343.

160. *Id.* at 1344.

161. Hopkins, *supra* note 94, at 4.

162. EISLER, *supra* note 92, at 140.

163. Palko v. Connecticut, 302 U.S. 319 (1937).

164. Gitlow v. New York, 268 U.S. 652 (1925).

165. EISLER, *supra* note 92, at 102.

166. *Id.* at 104.

167. Irvin v. Dowd, 359 U.S. 394 (1959); *Eisler, supra* note 92, at 160.

168. *Eisler, supra* note 92, at 161, 162.

169. Baker v. Carr, 369 U.S. 186 (1962); *Eisler, supra* note 92, at 161, 162.

170. *Id.*

171. *Id.* at 174.

172. *Id.* at 177.

173. *Id.* at 223.

174. *Id.* at 228.

175. *Id.* at 224.

176. Brennan, *The Constitution of the United States: Contemporary Ratification,* 27 S. Tex. L. J. 433, 433 (1986).

177. *Id.* at 435.

178. *Id.* at 436.

179. *Id.*

180. *Id.*

181. *Id.* at 433.

182. Warren, *Reason, Passion, and "The Progress of the Law,"* 10 Cardozo L. Rev. 3, 11 (1988).

183. *Id.*

184. Brennan, *supra* note 176, at 444.

185. Johnson, *Unconscious Racism and the Criminal Law,* Cornell L. Rev. 1016, 1017 (1988).

186. McCleskey v. Kemp, 481 U.S. 279, 328–45 (1988) (Brennan, J., dissenting).

187. McCleskey v. State, 245 Ga. 108, 263 S.E.2d 146, *cert. denied,* 449 U.S. 891 (1980).

188. McCleskey v. Zant, 580 F. Supp. 338 (N.D. Ga. 1984), *aff'd in relevant part,* 753 F.2d 877 (11th Cir. 1985) (en banc), *aff'd in relevant part,* 481 U.S. 279 (1987).

189. *McCleskey,* 580 F. Supp. at 352.

190. The study by Baldus, George G. Woodworth, and Charles A. Pulaski, Jr., has been published in D. Baldus et al., Equal Justice and the Death Penalty: A Legal and Empirical Analysis (1990). Earlier portions of the study were published in Baldus et al., *Comparative Review of Death Sentences: An Empirical Study of the Georgia Experience,* 74 J. Crim. L. & Criminology 661 (1983); Baldus et al., *Arbitrariness and Discrimination in the Administration of the Death Penalty: A Challenge to State Supreme Courts,* 15 Stetson L. Rev. 133 (1986); Baldus et al., *Monitoring and Evaluating Contemporary Death Sentencing Systems: Lessons from Georgia,* 18 U.C. Davis L. Rev. 1375 (1985).

Georgia has been the most heavily studied jurisdiction in the United States. An accessible yet sophisticated treatment of the Georgia data is Gross, *Race and Death: The Judicial Evaluation of Evidence of Discrimination in Capital Sentencing,* 18 U.C. Davis L. Rev. 1275 (1985). For studies of Georgia and other jurisdictions, see W. Bowers, Legal Homicide: Death as Punishment in America, 1864–1982 (1984); S. Gross & A. Mauro, Death and Discrimination: Racial Disparities in Capital

SENTENCING (1989); Bowers, *The Pervasiveness of Arbitrariness and Discrimination Under Post-Furman Capital Statutes,* 74 J. CRIM. L. & CRIMINOLOGY 1067 (1983); Gross & Mauro, *Patterns of Death: An Analysis of Racial Disparities in Capital Sentencing and Homocide Victimization,* 37 STAN. L. REV. 27 (1984); Jacoby & Paternoster, *Sentencing Disparity and Jury Packing: Further Challenges to the Death Penalty,* 73 J. CRIM. L. & CRIMINOLOGY 379 (1982); Johnson, *Selective Factors in Capital Punishment,* 36 SOCIAL FORCES 165 (1957); Koeninger, *Capital Punishment in Texas, 1924–1968,* 15 CRIME & DELINQ. 132 (1969); Paternoster, *Prosecutorial Discretion in Requesting the Death Penalty; A Case of Victim-Based Racial Discrimination,* 18 LAW & SOC'Y REV. 437 (1984); Paternoster, *Race of Victim and Location of Crime: The Decision to Seek the Death Penalty in South Carolina,* 74 CRIM. L. & CRIMINOLOGY 754 (1983); Paternoster & Kazyaka, *Racial Considerations in Capital Punishment: The Failure of Evenhanded Justice,* in CHALLENGING CAPITAL PUNISHMENT (K. Haas & J. Inciardi eds., 1988); Radelet, *Racial Characteristics and the Imposition of the Death Penalty,* 946 AM. SOC. REV. 918 (1981); Radelet & Pierce, *Race and Prosecutorial Discretion in Homicide Cases,* 19 LAW & SOC'Y REV. 587 (1985); Smith, *Patterns of Discrimination in Assessments of the Death Penalty: The Case of Louisiana,* 15 J. CRIM. JUST. 279 (1987); Wolfgang & Riedel, *Race, Judicial Discretion, and the Death Penalty,* 407 ANNALS 119 (1973); Zeisel, *Race Bias in the Administration of the Death Penalty: The Florida Experience,* 95 HARV. L. REV. 456 (1981).

191. *McClesky,* 580 F. Supp. at 379–80.

192. *Id.* at 380. The district court granted habeas relief based on a prosecutorial misconduct issue, a claim specific to Mr. McCleskey's case. The Eleventh Circuit reversed this holding of the district court. The Supreme Court did not address the issue in its opinion affirming the Eleventh Circuit. McCleskey v. Kemp, 753 F.2d 877 (11th Cir. 1985), *aff'd.,* 481 U.S. 279 (1987). The *New York Times* recently reported that for the first time in almost fifty years a White person was executed for killing a Black: Not since 1944, "when a Kansas man was executed for killing a black in an attempted robbery, has a white person in the United States received the death penalty for killing a black. No white man has been executed in South Carolina for such a killing since 1880." N.Y. TIMES, September 7, 1991, at A1.

193. McCleskey v. Kemp, 753 F.2d 877 (11th Cir. 1985) (en banc), *aff'd,* 481 U.S. 279 (1987).

194. *Id.* at 892.

195. *Id.*

196. *Id.* (quoting Smith v. Balkcom, 671 F.2d 858, 859 (5th Cir. Unit B), *cert. denied,* 459 U.S. 882 (1982)).

197. *Id.* at 894.

198. *Id.* at 893.

199. The Court commented recently in a capital case that 5–4 decisions containing spirited dissents are especially strong candidates for overruling. Payne v. Tennessee, 111 S. Ct. 2597 (1991) (overruling Booth v. Maryland, 482 U.S. 496 (1988)). Perhaps there is still hope for Mr. McCleskey's claim, although he would not benefit

from its ultimate vindication. But probably not. *McCleskey* was most likely not the case the Court had in mind when it wrote *Payne*.

200. Then-professor (now Fourth Circuit judge) J. Harvie Wilkison III, an admirer and former clerk of Justice Powell, provided a balanced view of his activities:

> As chairman of the Richmond school board from 1952 to 1961, Powell wrestled with the agonies of transition *Brown* had brought to the South. At the Senate hearings on his confirmation [to the Court], two quite opposite views emerged on his tenure. The first was that of a man "in a position of complex responsibility during some very turbulent and confused times" whose "primary concern was to keep the schools of Virginia open and to preserve the public education system for all pupils." Possibly "Mr. Powell's outstanding contribution to Virginia," noted the Norfolk *Virginian-Pilot*, "was his leadership in the quiet sabotage by a business-industrial-professional group of Senator [Harry F.] Byrd's Massive Resistance." In later articles Powell blamed much of the lawlessness of the 1960s on southern defiance of the *Brown* decision. He was not unsympathetic to the Negro's plight: "It is true," he noted in 1966, "that the Negro has had, until recent years, little reason to respect the law. The entire legal process, from the police and sheriff to the citizens who serve on juries, has too often applied a double standard of justice. Even some of the courts at lower levels have failed to administer equal justice. . . . There were also the discriminatory state and local laws, the denial of voting rights, and the absence of economic and educational opportunity for the Negro. Finally, there was the small and depraved minority which resorted to physical violence and intimidation. These conditions, which have sullied our proud boast of equal justice under law, set the stage for the civil rights movement."
>
> By most measures of opinion in the aftermath of *Brown*, Powell was very much a moderate. That meant that he was also a gradualist, a symbol to Negroes of the frustrating pace of process in the South. By 1961, when Powell left the school board, only 37 Richmond Negroes out of more than 23,000 had enrolled in white schools. Shortly afterward [in 1963, in *Bradley v. Richmond School Bd.*, 317 F.2d 429 (4th Cir. 1963)], the Fourth Circuit found in Richmond a system of dual attendance zones and feeder schools designed to keep racial integration to a minimum. "Notwithstanding the fact that the [state] Pupil Placement Board assigns pupils to the various Richmond schools without recommendation of the local officials," observed the Fourth Circuit, "we do not believe that the City School Board can disavow all responsibility for the maintenance of the discriminatory system which has apparently undergone no basic change since its adoption." Simply because Powell "had sense enough to recognize the futility of the massive resistance program and to go for a more sophisticated scheme of evading the *Brown* decision

[should] not affect your decision," argued the prominent Richmond black attorney Henry Marsh to the Senate Judiciary Committee. "The Constitution outlaws the ingenious as well as the obvious scheme, and the fact that Mr. Powell had the knowledge to . . . evade the Constitution more effectively, as he did in the City of Richmond during the massive resistance era, without having integration, does not commend him to the Supreme Court." John Conyers of Michigan, representing the Congressional Black Caucus, was more explicit: "We would conclude . . . Mr. Powell's own activities on the boards of education, his close association with a variety of corporate giants, . . . his membership in the largest all-white law firm in Richmond, his support of segregated social clubs, and his defense of the status quo, are inconsistent with the kind of jurist that . . . is desperately needed for the court in the 1970's and the 1980's."—J. WILKINSON, FROM BROWN TO BAKKE 163–64 (1979) (citations omitted).

201. McCleskey v. Kemp, 481 U.S. 279, 292 (1987).

202. *Id.* at 291 n.7.

203. *Id.*

204. *Id.* at 297.

205. *Id.* at 313.

206. *Id.* at 293 (quoting Arlington Heights v. Metropolitan Hous. Dev. Corp., 429 U.S. 252, 266 (1977)).

207. *Id.* at 286–87.

208. *Id.* at 317–18.

209. *Id.* at 317 (citation omitted).

210. *Id.* at 319.

211. Justice Powell graciously acknowledged the dissent's eloquence. *See id.* at 313 n.37.

For a fascinating discussion in another context of Justice Brennan's use of rhetorical and literary techniques, *see* Phinney, *Feminism, Epistemology, and the Rhetoric of Law: Reading Bowen v. Gilliard,* 12 HARV. WOMEN'S L.J. 151 (1989). Bowen v. Gilliard, 483 U.S. 587 (1987) was decided during the same Term as *McCleskey,* and Justice Brennan's dissents in the two cases share striking rhetorical similarities. *Compare id.* at 609 (Brennan, J., dissenting). For an accessible survey of the recent body of writings on the uses of literary theory in aid of legal interpretation, *see* R. POSNER, LAW AND LITERATURE 269–316 (1988); *see also* B. THOMAS, CROSS-EXAMINATIONS OF LAW AND LITERATURE (1987); INTERPRETING LAW AND LITERATURE: A HERMENEUTIC READER (S. Levinson & S. Meilloux eds., 1988); R. WEISBURG, THE FAILURE OF THE WORD (1984); J. WHITE, THE LEGAL IMAGINATION (1985); J. WHITE, HERACLES' BOW: ESSAYS ON THE RHETORIC AND POETICS OF THE LAW (1985); J. WHITE, WHEN WORDS LOSE THEIR MEANING (1984); Cover, *supra* note 3; Gibson, *Literary Minds and Judicial Style,* 36 N.Y.U. L. REV. 915 (1961); Heilbrun & Resnik, *Convergences: Law, Literature and Feminism,* 99 YALE L.J. 1913 (1990); Weisberg, *Law, Literature, and Cardozo's Judicial Poetics,* 1 CARDOZO L. REV. 283 (1979); Weisberg, *How Judges Speak: Some Lessons on Adjudication in* Billy Budd, Sailor, *with an Application to Justice Rehnquist,* 57 N.Y.U. L. REV. 1, 49–52 (1982); West, *Jurisprudence as Narrative: An Aesthetic Analysis of Modern Legal Theory,* 60 N.Y.U. L. REV. 145 (1985).

The writings on law and literature tend to place textual interpretation at the center of the project of law. For a haunting discussion of death sentences as interpretive acts of violence, see Cover, *supra* note 3, at 1622–28.

212. *McCleskey,* 418 U.S. at 344 (Brennan, J., dissenting).

213. *Id.*

214. *Cf.* Phinney, *supra* note 211, at 158–61 (similar technique used in Brennan's dissent in *Bowen v. Gilliard).*

215. *Id.* at 161.

216. *McCleskey,* 481 U.S. at 321 (Brennan, J., dissenting) (citations omitted).

217. *Id.* at 344.

218. *Id.*

219. Posner, *A Tribute to William J. Brennan, Jr.,* 104 HARV. L. REV. 13, 14 (1990) (emphasis in original).

220. Marshall, *A Tribute to William J. Brennan, Jr.,* 104 HARV. L. REV. 1, 8 (1990).

221. David Bruck, Does the Death Penalty Matter?, Address Given at Austin Hall, Harvard Law School (Oct. 22, 1990).

222. Anthony Lewis, Abroad at Home, *Mr. Justice Marshall,* N.Y. TIMES, July 1, 1991, at A13.

223. David Margolick, *The Justice with the Stories That Moved the World,* N.Y. TIMES, Jan. 31, 1993, at E4.

224. *Id.*

225. *Id.*

226. Nat Hentoff, *Thurgood Marshall and The Chief,* VILLAGE VOICE, March 8, 1993, at 22.

227. Kathleen M. Sullivan, *Marshall, the Great Dissenter,* N.Y. TIMES, June 29, 1991, at 23.

228. B. SCHWARTZ, A HISTORY OF THE SUPREME COURT 334 (1993).

229. C. ROWAN, DREAM MAKERS, DREAM BREAKERS: THE WORLD OF JUSTICE THURGOOD MARSHALL 23 (1993).

230. M. DAVIS & H. CLARK, THURGOOD MARSHALL: WARRIOR AT THE BAR, REBEL ON THE BENCH 31 (1992).

231. *Id.*

232. R. GOLDMAN & D. GALLEN, THURGOOD MARSHALL: JUSTICE FOR ALL 24 (1992).

233. ROWAN, *supra* note 229, at 35.

234. *Id.*

235. *Id.*

236. *Id.* at 23.

237. *Id.* at 28.

238. *Id.*

239. *Id.*

240. *Id.* at 30.

241. *Id.*

242. *Id.* at 66.

243. *Id.* at 27.

244. *Id.* at 23.

245. *Id.*

246. *Id.* at 37.

247. *Id.* at 28.

248. *Id.* at 36.

249. DAVIS & CLARK, *supra* note 230, at 96.

250. ROWAN, *supra* note 229, at 24.

252. *Id.* at 25.

252. *Id.*

253. *Id.*

254. *Id.* at 25, 26.

255. *Id.* at 27.

256. *Id.* at 291.

257. DAVIS & CLARK, *supra* note 230, at 41.

258. GOLDMAN & GALLEN, *supra* note 232, at 24.

259. ROWAN, *supra* note 229, at 43.

260. GOLDMAN & GALLEN, *supra* note 232, at 43.

261. *Id.* at 44.

262. *Id.*

263. *Id.* at 144.

264. *Id.* at 144, 145.

265. ROWAN, *supra* note 229, at 44.

266. *Id.* at 43.

267. *Id.*

268. *Id.* at 43, 44.

269. *Id.* at 44.

270. DAVIS & CLARK, *supra* note 230, at 46.

271. *Id.* at 37.

272. *Id.*

273. GOLDMAN & GALLEN, *supra* note 232, at 46.

274. *Id.*

275. *Id.* at 45.

276. *Id.*

277. *Id.*

278. *Id.*

279. *Id.*

280. *Id.*

281. ROWAN, *supra* note 229, at 43.
282. *Id.*
283. *Id.* at 45.
284. *Id.*
285. *Id.*
286. DAVIS & CLARK, *supra* note 230, at 46.
287. *Id.*
288. *Id.* at 47.
289. ROWAN, *supra* note 229, at 45, 46.
290. *Id.* at 46.
291. DAVIS & CLARK, *supra* note 230, at 52.
292. *Id.* at 53.
293. *Id.*
294. *Id.* at 54.
295. *Id.*
296. *Id.* at 53.
297. *Id.* at 52.
298. *Id.* at 53.
299. *Id.*
300. *Id.*
301. *Id.* at 54.
302. *Id.* at 48.
303. *Id.* at 49.
304. *Id.*
305. *Id.*
306. *Id.* at 50.
307. *Id.*
308. *Id.*
309. *Id.* at 51, 52.
310. *Id.*
311. *Id.*
312. *Id.*
313. *Id.* at 51.
314. *Id.* at 57.
315. *Id.* at 55.
316. ROWAN, *supra* note 229, at 46.
317. DAVIS & CLARK, *supra* note 230, at 56.
318. ROWAN, *supra* note 229, at 47.
319. DAVIS & CLARK, *supra* note 230, at 48.
320. *Id.* at 55.
321. GOLDMAN & GALLEN, *supra* note 232, at 145.
322. ROWAN, *supra* note 229, at 46.
323. DAVIS & CLARK, *supra* note 230, at 55.

324. *Id.* at 57.

325. *Id.*

326. *Id.* at 58.

327. Goldman & Gallen, *supra* note 232, at 145.

328. *Id.*

329. Rowan, *supra* note 229, at 47.

330. *Id.*

331. Davis & Clark, *supra* note 230, at 70.

332. *Id.*

333. *Id.*

334. *Id.* at 72.

335. *Id.* at 71.

336. *Id.* at 73.

337. *Id.* at 72.

338. *Id.*

339. M. Tushnet, Making Civil Rights Law: Thurgood Marshall and the Supreme Court, 1936–1961, at 11 (1994).

340. Davis & Clark, *supra* note 230, at 78.

341. Tushnet, *supra* note 339, at 11.

342. *Id.*

343. *Id.*

344. *Id.* at 12.

345. Plessy v. Ferguson, 163 U.S. 537 (1896).

346. Davis & Clark, *supra* note 230, at 65.

347. *Plessy,* 163 U.S. at 551.

348. *Id.* at 557.

349. *Id.* at 559.

350. *Id.* at 559, 560.

351. *Id.* at 562.

352. Davis & Clark, *supra* note 230, at 66, 67.

353. Goldman & Gallen, *supra* note 232, at 30.

354. *Id.*

355. Tushnet, *supra* note 339, at 13.

356. Davis & Clark, *supra* note 230, at 82.

357. Rowan, *supra* note 229, at 51.

358. *Id.*

359. *Id.*

360. *Id.*

361. *Id.*

362. *Id.*

363. Tushnet, *supra* note 339, at 15.

364. Rowan, *supra* note 229, at 52.

365. Davis & Clark, *supra* note 230, at 85.

366. *Id.*

367. *Id.*

368. *Id.* at 87.

369. TUSHNET, *supra* note 339, at 14.

370. *Id.*

371. *Id.*

372. *Id.* at 14, 15.

373. *Id.* at 14.

374. *Id.* at 15.

375. *Id.* at 17.

376. DAVIS & CLARK, *supra* note 230, at 91, 92.

377. *Id.* at 76.

378. TUSHNET, *supra* note 339, at 18, 19.

379. *Id.* at 17.

380. *Id.* at 19.

381. *Id.* at 18.

382. *Id.* at 19.

383. GOLDMAN & GALLEN, *supra* note 232, at 27.

384. ROWAN, *supra* note 229, at 59.

385. *Id.* at 58.

386. *Id.* at 65.

387. *Id.* at 71.

388. *Id.*

389. TUSHNET, *supra* note 339, at 70.

390. *Id.*

391. DAVIS & CLARK, *supra* note 230, at 94.

392. *Id.* at 94, 95.

393. TUSHNET, *supra* note 339, at 70.

394. *Id.*

395. ROWAN, *supra* note 229, at 75.

396. *Id.* at 76.

397. *Id.*

398. *Id.* at 86, 87.

399. *Id.*

400. TUSHNET, *supra* note 339, at 62.

401. ROWAN, *supra* note 229, at 86.

402. TUSHNET, *supra* note 339, at 62.

403. *Id.* at 61.

404. *Id.*

405. *Id.*

406. *Id.* at 62.

407. *Id.*

408. ROWAN, *supra* note 229, at 91.

409. *Id.*

410. Tushnet, *supra* note 339, at 63.

411. *Id.*

412. Rowan, *supra* note 229, at 93.

413. *Id.* at 95.

414. *Id.*

415. Goldman & Gallen, *supra* note 232, at 44, 45.

416. Rowan, *supra* note 229, at 94.

417. *Id.* at 96.

418. *Id.* at 97.

419. *Id.* at 100.

420. *Id.*

421. *Id.* at 101.

422. *Id.*

423. *Id.* at 101, 102.

424. *Id.* at 107.

425. *Id.*

426. *Id.* at 108.

427. *Id.* at 110.

428. *Id.*

429. *Id.*

430. *Id.* at 108.

431. *Id.*

432. Tushnet, *supra* note 339, at 54.

433. Rowan, *supra* note 229, at 109.

434. *Id.* at 111.

435. *Id.* at 108.

436. Tushnet, *supra* note 339, at 55.

437. *Id.*

438. *Id.*

439. Rowan, *supra* note 229, at 109.

440. *Id.* at 111.

441. *Id.*

442. *Id.* at 112.

443. *Id.* at 112, 113.

444. *Id.* at 111.

445. Goldman & Gallen, *supra* note 232, at 114.

446. Rowan, *supra* note 229, at 161.

447. *Id.*

448. *Id.* at 160.

449. *Id.* at 166.

450. *Id.*

451. *Id.* at 167.

452. *Id.*

453. GOLDMAN & GALLEN, *supra* note 232, at 115.

454. ROWAN, *supra* note 229, at 126.

455. *Id.* at 125.

456. *Id.* at 126.

457. *Id.*

458. *Id.* at 127.

459. *Id.*

460. DAVIS & CLARK, *supra* note 230, at 145.

461. GOLDMAN & GALLEN, *supra* note 232, at 82.

462. *Id.* at 71.

463. *Id.*

464. *Id.* at 84.

465. *Id.* at 86.

466. *Id.*

467. *Id.* at 86, 87.

468. *Id.*

469. TUSHNET, *supra* note 339, at 131.

470. *Id.*

471. *Id.* at 132.

472. GOLDMAN & GALLEN, *supra* note 232, at 88.

473. *Id.* at 90.

474. Sweatt v. Painter, 339 U.S. 629 (1950).

475. GOLDMAN & GALLEN, *supra* note 232, at 90, 91.

476. *Id.*

477. *Id.* at 94.

478. *Id.*

479. *Id.* at 99.

480. *Id.*

481. SCHWARTZ, *supra* note 228, at 287.

482. *Id.*

483. *Id.*

484. *Id.* at 288.

485. ROWAN, *supra* note 229, at 208.

486. SCHWARTZ, *supra* note 228, at 286.

487. *Id.* at 291.

488. *Id.* at 265, 266.

489. *Id.* at 291.

490. *Id.* at 293.

491. *Id.* at 306.

492. ROWAN, *supra* note 229, at 224.

493. *Id.* at 225.

494. DAVIS & CLARK, *supra* note 230, at 181.

495. *Id.*

496. Rowan, *supra* note 229, at 234.

497. *Id.* at 272.

498. *Id.* at 273.

499. *Id.*

500. Davis & Clark, *supra* note 230, at 235, 236.

501. *Id.* at 236.

502. *Id.* at 240.

503. *Id.*

504. *Id.* at 238, 239.

505. *Id.* at 240.

506. Rowan, *supra* note 229, at 283.

507. Davis & Clark, *supra* note 230, at 243.

508. *Id.* at 240.

509. *Id.*

510. *Id.* at 241.

511. *Id.* at 244, 245.

512. *Id.* at 245.

513. Rowan, *supra* note 229, at 289.

514. *Id.*

515. *Id.* at 293.

516. Davis & Clark, *supra* note 230, at 247.

517. Rowan, *supra* note 229, at 292.

518. *Id.* at 291.

519. *Id.* at 295.

520. *Id.* at 296.

521. *Id.* at 296, 297.

522. Davis & Clark, *supra* note 230, at 275.

523. Rowan, *supra* note 229, at 341.

524. *Id.* at 339.

525. Kelley v. Johnson, 425 U.S. 238, 250–51 (1975).

526. Rowan, *supra* note 229, at 443.

527. *Id.* at 345.

528. *Id.*

529. *Id.* at 290.

530. *Id.* at 447.

531. *Id.* at 381.

532. *Id.*

533. Bigel, *Justices William J. Brennan, Jr., and Thurgood Marshall on Capital Punishment: Its Constitutionality, Morality, Deterrent Effect, and Interpretation by the Court*, 8 Notre Dame J.L. Ethics & Pub. Pol'y. 121 (1994).

534. *Id.* at 318.

535. *Id.*

536. Davis & Clark, *supra* note 230, at 374.

537. *Id.* at 320, 21.

538. *Id.* at 323.

539. *Id.* at 348.

540. *Id.*

541. Bigel, *supra* note 533, at 128.

542. *Id.* at 349.

543. Goldman & Gallen, *supra* note 232, at 201.

544. Schwartz, *supra* note 228, at 373.

545. Rowan, *supra* note 229, at 402.

546. *Id.* at 396.

547. *Id.* at 403.

548. *Id.* at 309.

549. *Id.*

550. *Id.*

551. Jordan Steiker, *The Long Road Up from Barbarism,* 71 Tex. L. Rev. 1131 (1993).

552. Nicholas Leman, *The Lawyer as Hero,* New Republic, Sept. 13, 1993, at 32.

553. *Id.*

554. Michael Meltsner, *The Late Justice,* Nation, Feb. 15, 1993, at 184.

## Chapter 2

1. Bob Dylan, *The Times They Are a-Changin',* on The Times They Are A-Changin' (Columbia Records 1964).

2. Max Lerner, Nine Scorpions in a Bottle: Great Judges and Cases in the Supreme Court (Richard Cummings ed., 1994).

3. William Safire, The First Dissident: The Book of Job in Today's Politics (1993).

4. Jerold S. Auerbach, *Into the Whirlwind,* National Review, Mar. 29, 1993, at 66.

5. *See generally* Brennan, *In Defence of Dissents,* 37 Hastings L.J. 427 (1986); Kelman, *The Forked Path of Dissent,* 1985 Sup. Ct. Rev. 227; Campbell, *The Spirit of Dissent,* 66 Judicature 304 (1983); R. Barth, Prophets with Honor: Great Dissents and Great Dissenters in the Supreme Court (1974); Zobell, *Division of Opinion in the Supreme Court: A History of Judicial Disintegration,* 44 Cornell L.Q. 186 (1959); McWhinney, *Judicial Concurrences and Dissents: A Comparative View of Opinion-Writing in Final Appellate Tribunals,* 6 Cal. Bar Rev. 595 (1953).

6. For a thoughtful analysis, *see* P. Freund, The Supreme Court of the United States 51 (1967). "It is not remarkable that the process of constitutional decision has become more self-conscious, more avowedly an expression of political philosophy, than ever before. Our present judges have gone to school, so to speak, to Holmes and Cardozo." *Id.* Professor Freund, in recounting the history of the incorporation debate, noted: "Cleavages in the Court . . . significant as they are,

hardly constitute a Great Divide. Intensity of feeling, however, generally varies inversely with the distance separating the disputants, and, more obloquy, has usually been heaped more on heretics than on infidels." *Id*. A separate concurrence may therefore inspire more judicial wrath than a dissenting opinion.

7. Georgia v. Brailsford, 2 U.S. (2 Dall.) 402 (1792) (Iredell, J., dissenting) ("It is my misfortune to dissent from the opinion entertained by the Court upon the present occasion; but I am bound to decide according to the dictates of my own judgment.").

8. For a thorough analysis of both the English practice and that of the Marshall era, *see* Zobell, *supra* note 5, at 187–98.

9. HAND, THE BILL OF RIGHTS 72–73 (1958) ("[D]isunity cancels the impact of monolithic solidarity on which the authority of a bench of judges so largely depends. People become aware that the answer to the controversy is uncertain, even to the best qualified, and they feel free, unless especially docile, to ignore it if they are reasonably sure they will not be caught. The reasoning of both sides is usually beyond their comprehension, and is apt to appear as verbiage assigned to sustain one side of a dispute that in the end might be decided either way, which is generally the truth").

10. 7 T. JEFFERSON, WORKS 276 (letter to William Johnson, March 4, 1823).

11. 198 U.S. 45 (1905).

12. *Id*. at 74.

13. *Id*. at 75.

14. *E.g.,* West Virginia Board of Education v. Barnette, 319 U.S. 624, 646 (1943) (Frankfurter, J., dissenting).

15. "During most of its first decade, the Supreme Court followed the custom of The King's Bench—its decisions were announced through the seriatim opinions of its members. (Unlike King's Bench practice, however, the opinions were delivered in inverse order of seniority.)" Zobell, *supra* note 5, at 192; *see* Evans, *Dissenting Opinion: Its Use and Abuse,* 3 MISSOURI L. REV. 120 (1938); Levin, *Mr. Justice William Johnson, Creative Dissenter,* 43 MICH. L. REV. 497, 512 (1944); Charles Warren, *The First Decade of the Supreme Court of the United States,* 7 U. CHI. L. REV. 631, 637–38 (1940).

16. 2 U.S. (2 Dall.) 402 (1792).

17. August Term, 1792, 2 U.S. (2 Dall.) 402.

18. 2 U.S. (2 Dall.) 402, 405.

19. This neat formulation perhaps came about because the decision was to be fully reported, not because of the presence of a dissent.

Neither Justice Johnson, as the junior member of the Court, nor Justice Cushing apologized for his dissent: Justice Johnson simply stated, "[I]t is my opinion that there is not a proper foundation for issuing an injunction."; Justice Cushing said, "I think that an injuction ought not to be awarded." 2 U.S. (2 Dall.) at 405 and 408.

20. Hayburn's Case, 2 U.S. (2 Dall.) 409 (1792).

21. Letter of the circuit court for the district of New York to the president—reported in a note to Hayburn's Case, 2 U.S. (2 Dall.) at 410.

22. Each of these letters was reported in Hayburn's Case, 2 U.S. (2 Dall.) at 410–14.

23. *See id.* at 409.

24. *Id.*

25. GENERAL ADVERTISER (Phil.), Aug. 16, 1792; GAZETTE OF THE UNITED STATES, Aug. 25, 1792; UNITED STATES CHRONICLE (Prov.), Aug. 30, 1792; MASSACHUSETTS SPY, Aug. 30, 1792; *in* 1 WARREN, THE SUPREME COURT IN UNITED STATES HISTORY I, at 77–78.

26. M. CONWAY, OMITTED CHAPTERS OF HISTORY DISCLOSED IN THE LIFE AND PAPERS OF EDMUND RANDOLPH 145 (1888); Letter of Aug. 12, 1792, *cited in* 1 WARREN, *supra* note 25, at 79.

27. "During the August, 1792, term' in considering the adoption of rules, the Court considered 'the practice of the courts of King's Bench and Chancery in England, as affording outlines for the practice of this court'; and added 'that they will, from time to time, make such alterations therein, as circumstances may render necessary.' " P. JACKSON, DISSENT IN THE SUPREME COURT 21–22 (1969).

Jackson is the only writer that I have read who points out this "rule." Zobell, *supra* note 5, and Levin, *supra* note 15, state the use of the seriatim practice but do not mention this rule. Morgan wrote that "[b]efore Marshall, the justices employed no standardized mode of opinion-giving; their frequent resort to seriatim opinions, some of them in leading decisions, bears witness to the freedom of expression which had prevailed." Morgan, *Mr. Justice William Johnson and the Constitution,* 57 HARV. L. REV. 328, 331 (1944).

28. 2 U.S. (2 Dall.) 409, 411–13 (1792).

29. 29 T. JEFFERSON, THE WRITINGS OF THOMAS JEFFERSON 223–25 (P. Ford ed., 1899), *cited in* Levin, *supra* note 15; D. MORGAN, JUSTICE WILLIAM JOHNSON: THE FIRST DISSENTER 168 (1954).

30. "Out of sixty-three cases reported for the period [before 1801] twelve [actually thirteen] appeared as seriatim opinions; thus nearly one-fifth of the adjudications found all the justices expressing their individual convictions, and among the number were such pivotal cases as *Chisholm v. Georgia, Hylton v. United States, Ware v. Hylton,* and *Calder v. Bull.*" MORGAN, *supra* note 29, at 45–46; *see* Morgan, *supra* note 27, at 331 n.13 (leading decisions); Levin, *supra* note 15, at 512 n.42.

31. The Court granted an injunction to Georgia, in a suit in equity by that state against two citizens of South Carolina, even though the state was not a party to the original action at common law (Justices Johnson and Cushing dissenting), Georgia v. Brailsford, 2 Dall. 402 (1792); the Court held that a state could be sued by a citizen of another sovereign state (the holding was overruled by passage of the eleventh amendment), *Chisholm v. Georgia,* 2 Dall. 419 (1793); the Court upheld removal of an action for prize money from the Circuit Court to the Court of Admiralty (the court was divided on, and therefore could not award, a writ of *Venise Facias de novo),*

*Bingham v. Cabot*, 3 Dall. 19 (1795); the Court held that the Federal Circuit Court could effectuate the decrees of the Old Prize Court of Appeals that existed under the Articles of Confederation, *Penhallow v. Doane's Administrators*, 3 Dall. 54 (1795); the Court issued a decree of restitution for a captured Dutch vessel, holding that capture without commission was a violation of the laws of nations, and that the captor could not renounce U.S. citizenship by renouncing allegiance to the State of Virginia while continuing to be domiciled within the United States, *Talbot v. Janson*, 3 Dall. 133 (1795); the Court upheld the constitutional validity of an act of Congress, the federal tax on carriages, *Hylton v. United States*, 3 Dall. 171 (1796); the Court held that the provisions of a British treaty prevailed over state laws (fundamental doctrine of American law), Ware v. Hylton, 3 Dall. 199 (1796); the Court held that the United States Treasury had the right to affirm a certificate ("a public paper medium"), even though it had been acquired by fraud, and to recover the value of the certificate and the interest, Fenemore v. United States, 3 Dall. 357 (1797); the Court found that the legislature of the State of Connecticut did not violate the federal Constitution by exercising a general superintending power over its courts of law in granting new trials: the act could not be regarded as an ex post facto law because that prohibition extended only to criminal, not civil, cases, and the state had the right to empower the legislature to superintend the Courts of Justice, Calder v. Bull, 3 Dall. 386 (1798); the Court held that a case only belonged to the jurisdiction of the United States Supreme Court, on account of the interest that a state has in the controversy, when the state is either nominally or substantially a party, Fowler v. Lindsey, 3 Dall. 411 (1799); the Court held that in the case of an "offending citizen," a traitor who had served His Britannic Majesty, the right to confiscate [money that Cooper had bonded to Telfair] and banish must belong to every government (the right was not within the judicial power but was a power that grew out of the nature of the social compact and was inherent to the legislature), *Cooper v. Telfair*, 4 Dall. 14 (1800); the Court construed the act for licensing and regulating ships and vessels by "conforming to the letter of the statute" (although the letter of § 19, which they found controlling, was contradicted by the "ambiguous" wording in § 33 of the same statute), Priestman v. United States, 4 Dall. 28 (1800); and the Court held that "limited, partial"—though undeclared—war existed with France, and construed the act of 1799, providing salvage for ships "retaken from the enemy," to include ships retaken from France, Bas v. Tingy, 4 Dall. 37 (1800).

MORGAN, *supra* note 29, at 46 n.15, gave a "full" list of the twelve cases in which the Court followed the seriatim practice: [Georgia v. Braisford], 2 Dall. 402 (1792); Chisholm v. Georgia, 2 Dall. 419 (1793); Bingham v. Cabot, 3 Dall. 19 (1795); Penhallow v. Doane's Administrators, 3 Dall. 54 (1795); Talbot v. Janson, 3 Dall. 133 (1795); Hylton v. United States, 3 Dall. 171 (1796); Ware v. Hylton, 3 Dall. 199 (1796); Fenemore v. United States, 3 Dall. 357 (1797); Calder v. Bull, 3 Dall. 386 (1798); Cooper v. Telfiar, 4 Dall. 14 (1800); Priestman v. United States, 4 Dall. 28 (1800); and Bas v. Tingy, 4 Dall. 37 (1800).

This list, however, is not complete. Morgan omitted Fowler v. Lindsey, 3 U.S.

(3 Dall.) 411 (1799), which was included in a partial list by Zobell, *supra* note 5, at 192 n.38. However, Zobell included Wiscart v. D'Auchy, 3 U.S. (3 Dall.) 321 (1796), which was not delivered seriatim.

32. 4 Dall. 37, 43 (1800).

33. 1 WARREN, *supra* note 25, at 654 n.1, uses Chase's opinion to establish that the practice of having the opinion of the Court delivered by the chief justice did not originate with Marshall.

Warren also pointed out that Chase's absence from the August 1800 Term had drawn "savage attack from the Anti-Federalist newspapers . . . for he was speaking in Maryland in behalf of Adams' candidacy for Presidency." *Id.* at 156 n.1. Thus, Chase may have been complaining about the criticism more than the Court's following of the seriatim practice.

34. 2 U.S. (2 Dall.) 415 (1792).

35. 3 U.S. (3 Dall.) 321 (1796).

36. *See* Jennings v. Perseverance, 3 U.S. (3 Dall.) 336, 337 (1797): "Though I was silent on the occasion, I concurred in opinion with Judge Wilson upon the second rule laid down in *Wiscart v. D'Auchy*."

37. "Though I concur in the general result of the opinions, which have been delivered, I cannot entirely adopt the reasons that are assigned upon the occasion." 3 U.S. (3 Dall.) 386, 398 (1798).

38. Justice Chase: "But I will go no farther than I feel myself bound to do, and if I ever exercise the jurisdiction I will not decide *any law to be void* but *in a very clear case.*" 3 U.S. (3 Dall.) 386, 395 (1798) (emphasis in the original).

Chief Justice Elsworth: "With respect, however, to the right of disaffirmance, I wish to be understood, as limiting it to the continuance of the certificate in the hands of the original party for, if the certificate had passed into the hands of a bona fide purchaser, even a court of equity would, I think, refuse to invalidate it. . . ." 3 U.S. (3 Dall.) 357, 364 (1797).

39. *Aurora*, Aug. 22, 23, 25, 1800 (emphasis in the original); cited by WARREN, *supra* note 25.

40. 5 U.S. (1 Cranch) 1 (1801).

41. P. Jackson, *supra,*: "It is undeniable that in the first case in which he participated and which he decided, following his accession to the bench, Marshall undertook to put the English seriatim practice, which had theretofore been followed by the Court, at rest, by writing for the Court."

Zobell, *supra* note 5, at : "Only after consideration of the early English practice and of the embryonic custom of the Supreme Court does one become aware of the striking nature of the innovation which was introduced when, in the first case decided after he became Chief Justice, 'Marshall, C.J., delivered the opinion of the Court.' "

42. 5 U.S. (1 Cranch) 1 (1801).

43. Zobell, *supra* note 5: "When 'the Chief Justice delivered the opinion of the Court,' he intended that the words he wrote should bear the imprimatur of the

Supreme Court of the United States. For the first time, the Court as a judicial unit had been committed to an opinion—a ratio decidendi—in support of its judgment."

44. In Ogden v. Saunders, 25 U.S. (12 Wheat.) 213, 358 (1827), Marshall delivered a dissenting opinion seriatim.

45. 3 A. BEVERIDGE, THE LIFE OF JOHN MARSHALL 16 (1919). Beveridge continued: "For the first time the chief Justice disregarded the custom of the delivery of opinions by the Justices seriatim, and, instead, calmly assumed the function of announcing, himself, the views of that tribunal. Thus Marshall took the first steps in impressing the country with the unity of the highest court of the Nation."

46. T. JEFFERSON, *supra* note 29.

47. The speculation and notes come from Marshall's Paris Journal 52–67 (Library of Congress), *cited in* L. Baker, *John Marshall: A Life in Law* 414–15 (1974).

48. 4 A. BEVERIDGE, THE LIFE OF JOHN MARSHALL 320 (1919).

49. 25 U.S. (12 Wheat.) 64, 90 (1827).

50. Morgan, *supra* note 29. *See* Jackson, *supra* note 27: "Of forty-seven cases found in the first two volumes of Cranch's reports (1801–1805), following Marshall's appointment, the Chief Justice wrote for the Court in twenty-eight cases; he did not participate in two, the Court acted or spoke per curiam in sixteen, and one was left for future reargument." *See also* Machen, *Dissent and Stare Decisis in the Supreme Court,* 45 MD. ST. B. ASS'N 79, 81 (1940): "In 1st Cranch every opinion of the Court was delivered by Marshall save one, in which Marshall had sat below and graciously permitted Mr. Justice Paterson to affirm him."

51. Head & Amory v. Providence Ins. Co., 2 Cranch 127, 169 (1804).

52. Stuart v. Laird, 1 Cranch 299 (1803); Ogden v. Blackledge, 2 Cranch 272 (1804).

53. A legal realist would advance an alternative rationale for Justice Johnson's break from Chief Justice Marshall's delivery of a single opinion of the Court. Justice Johnson had been nominated by President Thomas Jefferson, a staunch proponent of state's rights. Since Chief Justice Marshall supported a strong central government, the conflicting political ideologies manifested themselves in Justice Johnson's dissents.

54. United States v. Fisher, 2 Cranch 358, 397 (1805).

55. Huidekoper's Lessee v. Douglas, 3 Cranch 1, 72 (1805).

56. Lambert's Lessee v. Paine, 3 Cranch 97 (1805); Marine Insurance Company of Alexandria v. Wilson, 3 Cranch 187 (1805). Many of these figures were compiled by MORGAN, *supra* note 29, at 179 n.52: he observes that, "[i]n contrast to later practice, the judges gave their opinions according to the order which was followed before Marshall's term; thus, Johnson, as junior justice, gave the first opinion at the *Lambert* ruling. . . ." *Id.*

57. Marine Insurance Company of Alexandria v. Tucker, 3 Cranch 357 (1806); United States v. Heth, 3 Cranch 399 (1806); Randolph v. Ware, 3 Cranch 503 (1806).

58. Simms and Wise v. Slacum, 3 Cranch 300 (1806).

59. *Ex parte* Bollman and Startwout, 4 Cranch 75 (1807).

60. MORGAN, *supra* note 29, at app. II 306–307.

61. *Id.* at 180: "And by 1809 Marshall had surrendered his supreme preroga-tive—delivering the opinion of the Court." *See also* Machen, *supra* note 50, at 81: "Even in 7 Cranch, where the rudiments of the present system of assigning different justices to write the opinion of the Court are observable, Marshall delivered 38 opin-ions, Washington and Story 8 each, Johnson 7, Livingston 6, Duvall 2, and Todd 1, so that Marshall's opinions (38) outnumbered those of all the other justices combined (32)."

There are indications that this change was not so much motivated by external political factors as by internal pressure. Although Marshall altered his practice be-tween 1809 and 1813, attack by Roane and Jefferson did not become acute until the early 1820s. But Justice Johnson referred back to this change in a letter to Jefferson, and ascribed it to internal pressure:

> Some case soon occurred in which I differed from my brethren, and I thought it a thing of course to deliver my opinion. But, during the rest of the session I heard nothing but lectures on the indecency of judges cutting at each other, and the loss of reputation which the Virginia appel-late court has sustained by pursuing such a course. At length I found that I must either submit to circumstances or become such a cipher in our consultations as to effect no good at all. I therefore bent to the current, and persevered until I got them to adopt the course they now pursue, which is to appoint someone to deliver the opinion of the majority, but leave it to the discretion of the rest of the judges to record their opinions or not ad libitum. —Letter from William Johnson, associate justice of the Supreme Court, to T. Jefferson (Dec. 10, 1822) (Jefferson Papers; MSS; Library of Congress).

62. MORGAN, *supra* note 30, at n.56: Washington spoke for the Court in Pierce v. Turner, 5 Cranch 154 (1809); Cushing, in Marine Insurance Company of Alexan-dria v. Young, 5 Cranch 187 (1809); and Livingston, in Keene v. United States, 5 Cranch 304 (1809); and in Hudson v. Guestier, 6 Cranch 281 (1810). The reports give no indication that Marshall was absent from any of these decisions.

63. MORGAN, *supra* note 29, at 180 n. 57.

64. 12 Wheat. 213 (1827).

65. These numbers are deduced from figures compiled by MORGAN, *supra* note 29, at app. II 306–07, and tbl. 2, 189. *See also* Evans, *supra* note 15, at 138 tbl I. Although this table was compiled by volumes rather than by years, one can use it to estimate roughly that the rates of dissents from vols. 5–10 through vols. 21–30 rose from 4 percent to 8 percent and that the rates of concurring opinions decreased from 3 percent to less than 2 percent.

66. Preservation of the majority opinion was codified from 1924 to 1972 in Canon 19 of the American Bar Association's Canons of Judicial Ethics:

> It is of high importance that judges constituting a court of last resort should use effort and self-restraint to promote solidarity of conclusions

and the consequent influence of judicial decisions. A judge should not yield to pride of opinion or value more highly his individual reputation than that of the court to which he should be loyal. Except in case of conscientious difference of opinion on fundamental principle, dissenting opinions should be discouraged in courts of last resort.

Yet even this prescript accommodated individual responsibility "on fundamental principle."

67. John Marshall himself wrote nine dissenting opinions. *See* Machen, *supra* note 50, at 99.

68. For example, Story once wrote to the chief justice: "I trust in God . . . that the Supreme Court will continue fearlessly to do its duty; & I pray that your invaluable life may be long preserved to guide us in our defence of the Constitution. Will you excuse me for saying that your appointment to the Bench has in my judgment more contributed under Providence to the preservation of the true principles of the Constitution than any other circumstance in our domestic history." Letter from Joseph Story, associate justice of the Supreme Court, to John Marshall, chief justice of the Supreme Court, June 27, 1821, *quoted in* WARREN, THE STORY-MARSHALL CORRESPONDENCE, 1819-1831, at 7 n.2.

69. The Nereide, 9 Cranch 388 (1815).

70. Briscoe v. Bank of Kentucky, 36 U.S. 257, 329 (1837).

71. West River Bridge v. Dix, 6 How. 507, 536, 539 (1848). Justice Woodbury wrote:

> In the decisions of this Court on constitutional questions it has happened frequently, that, though its members were united in judgment, great differences existed among them in the reasons for it, or in the limitations on some of the principles involved. Hence it has been customary in such cases to express their views separately. I conform to that usage in this case the more readily, as it is one of first impression before the tribunal, very important in its consequences, as a great landmark of the States as well as the general government, and, from shades of difference and even conflicts in opinion, will be open to misconstruction.

Justice McLean wrote, "[A]s this is a constitutional question of considerable practical importance, I will state, succinctly, my general views on the subject."

*See also* Justice Frankfurter's concurring opinion in Graves v. New York, 306 U.S. 466, 487 (1939):

> I join in the Court's opinion but deem it appropriate to add a few remarks. The volume of the Court's business has long since made impossible the early healthy practice whereby the Justices gave expression to individual opinions. But the old tradition still has relevance when an important shift in constitutional doctrine is announced after a reconstruction in the membership of the Court. Such shifts of opinion should not be derived from mere private judgment. They must be duly mindful of the necessary demands of continuity in civilized society. A reversal of

a long current of decisions can be justified only if rooted in the Constitution itself as an historic document designed for a developing nation.

72. Thurlow v. Massachusetts; Fletcher v. Rhode Island; Pierce v. New Hampshire, 5 How. 504, 573 (1847).

73. 2 WARREN, THE SUPREME COURT IN UNITED STATES HISTORY 154.

74. Smith v. Turner; Norris v. Boston, 7 How. 283 (1849).

75. 2 WARREN, *supra* note 73, at 178.

76. Youngstown Sheet and Tube Co. v. Sawyer, 343 U.S. 579 (1952).

77. *Id.*

78. 7 U.S. (3 Cranch) 1, 72 (1805).

79. 8 U.S. (4 Cranch) 75 (1807).

80. Morgan, *supra* note 27, at 332.

81. 5 Cranch 187, 191 (1809) (added by erratum).

82. 1 Wheat. 304, 362 (1816).

83. 22 U.S. (9 Wheat.) 1, 222-23 (1824).

84. "In this group of concurring opinions will be found some of his best opinions, wherein, although he followed the majority of the Court, his reasoning was so different as to possess the quality of real dissent so much so as to perplex some scholars." Levin, *supra* note 15, 522-23.

85. 10 U.S. (6 Cranch) 87 (1810).

86. *Id.* at 143.

87. Authorities identifying it as a concurring opinion include MORGAN, *supra* note 29, at 210-16; Morgan, *supra* note 27, at 352-53; Levin, *Mr. Justice William Johnson and the Common Incidents of Life,* 44 MICH. L. REV. 59, 90-91 (1945); C. PETER MAGRATH, YAZOO: LAW AND POLITICS IN THE NEW REPUBLIC 70 (1966).

Authorities identifying it as a dissenting opinion include DILLON, JOHN MARSHALL, COMPLETE CONSTITUTIONAL DECISIONS 216 (1903); J. COTTON, CONSTITUTIONAL DECISIONS OF JOHN MARSHALL 231 (1905); Hale, *The Supreme Court and the Contract Clause,* 57 HARV. L. REV. 852, 873 (1944); A. SIEGEL, THE MARSHALL COURT, 1805-1835, at 116-17 (1987); JACKSON, *supra* note 27.

88. Johnson's biographer, Donald Morgan, *supra* note 29, completely avoided his reference to the "sovereignty" of the Native American nations. MAGRATH, *supra* note 87, at 5, in a book devoted to analyzing *Fletcher,* refers only to President Washington's warning in 1790 not to interfere with the treaty rights of the Indians, and determines that "there was an appropriate conclusion to the unusual Yazoo fraud: it produced no losers." Magrath lists the fraudulent-speculators' gain, various political gains, and the state and federal governments' gains, with no reference to the Native Americans. *Id.* at 116-17. Only JACKSON, *supra* note 27, at 31 remarked upon Johnson's "sovereignty" reference.

89. 10 U.S. (6 Cranch) 87, 143-48 (1810).

90. Cotton mistakes Johnson's concurring opinion in Gibbons v. Ogden, 22 U.S. (9 Wheat.) 1 (1824), for a dissenting opinion. 2 J. COTTON, CONSTITUTIONAL DECISIONS OF JOHN MARSHALL 37 (1905).

91. MORGAN, *supra* note 29, at 290.

92. *See* Letter from Johnson to Jefferson, *supra* note 61. In Ogden v. Saunders, 12 Wheat. 213, 272–73 (1827), Johnson revealed that the unanimous decision in Sturges v. Crowninshield, 4 Wheat. 122 (1819), had been the result of a "compromise" with the minority.

92. New Jersey v. Wilson, 7 Cranch. 164 (1812); Trustees of Dartmouth College v. Woodward, 4 Wheat. 518 (1819); Sturges v. Crowninshield, 4 Wheat. 122 (1819).

94. Green v. Biddle, 8 Wheat. 1 (1823).

95. Ogden v. Saunders, 12 Wheat. at 291–92.

96. *Id.* at 282.

97. *See* Morgan, *supra* note 27, at 360; *see also* Levin, *Mr. Justice William Johnson and the Unenviable Dilemma,* 42 MICH. L. REV. 803 (1944) (equates Johnson's "functional interpretation of judicial power" to Holmes's philosophy of judicial restraint); Levin, *supra* note 15, at 500 ("Holmes began a judicial re-examination which harkened back to the earlier dissents of Johnson."). But Oliver Wendell Holmes's reasons were quite different. *See* S. NOVICK, HONORABLE JUSTICE 444 n.24 (1989).

98. 4 Cranch 75, 106–07 (1807) (Johnson, J., dissenting); *see also Ex parte* Crane, 5 Pet. 190 (1831) (Baldwin, J., joined by Johnson, J., concurring); *Ex parte* Watkins, 7 Pet. 568 (1833) (Johnson, J., dissenting).

99. Johnson's majority opinions in mandamus cases include M'Intire v. Wood, 7 Cranch 504 (1813), and M'Clung v. Silliman, 6 Wheat. 598 (1821).

100. Yeaton v. Bank of Alexandria, 5 Cranch 49, 54 (1809) (Johnson, J., dissenting).

101. United States v. Planter's Bank of Georgia, 9 Wheat. 904 (1824) (Johnson, J., dissenting); Osborn v. Bank of Georgia, 9 Wheat. 738, 871 (1824) (bank was a federal entity, but there was no federal question.)

102. 12 Wheat. 213 (1827).

103. Weston v. City Council of Charleston, 2 Pet. 449, 472 (1829) (Johnson, J., dissenting).

104. Craig v. Missouri, 4 Pet. 410, 444 (1830) (Johnson, J., dissenting).

105. Shanks v. Dupont, 3 Pet. 242, 250 (1830) (Johnson, J., dissenting).

106. Mills v. Duryee, 7 Cranch 481 (1813) (Johnson, J., dissenting).

107. United States v. Palmer, 3 Wheat. 610, 641 (1818) (Johnson, J., dissenting); *Atlanta,* 3 Wheat. 409, 419 (1818).

108. C. HUGHES, THE SUPREME COURT OF THE UNITED STATES 68 (1928).

109. Brown, *The Dissenting Opinions of Mr. Justice Daniel,* 21 AM. L. REV. 869, 870 (1887).

110. "One of the most pertinacious dissentients was Peter Daniel. . . . A protomodern dissenter in frequency and tenacity was Justice Peter Daniel (1841–60)." HENDRICK, BULWARK OF THE REPUBLIC 417 (1937).

111. 16 Pet. 539 (1842).

112. U.S. CONST., art. IV, § 2, cl. 3 (repealed 1865): "No Person held to Service or Labor in one State, under the Laws thereof, escaping into another, shall, on Con-

sequence of any Law of Regulation therein, be discharged from such Service or Labor, but shall be delivered up on Claim of the Party to whom such Service or Labor may be due."

113. 60 U.S. (19 How.) 393 (1856).

114. *Id.* at 450.

115. *Id.* at 473.

116. Searight v. Stokes, 3 How. 151 (1845); McNeil v. State of Ohio, 3 How. 720 (1845).

117. *Searight,* 3 How. at 180.

118. 46 U.S. (5 How.) 504 (1847).

119. *Id.* at 575.

120. *Id.* at 611.

121. 7 How. 283 (1849).

122. 12 How. 299 (1851).

123. Pennsylvania v. Wheeling Bridge Co., 13 How. 518 (1851).

124. Louisville & Cincinnati R.R. Co. v. Letson, 2 How. 497 (1844).

125. Rundle v. The Delaware & Raritan Canal Co., 14 How. 80, 95 (1852).

126. Brown, *supra* note 109, at 869. *See also* Northern Indiana R.R. v. Mich. Cent. R.R., 15 How. 233, 251 (1854).

127. Waring v. Clark, 5 How. 441 (1847).

128. New Jersey Steam Navigation Co. v. The Merchant's Bank, 6 How. 344 (1848).

129. *E.g.,* St. Johnson v. Paine, 10 How. 557 (1850) (Daniel, J., dissenting); Newton v. Stebbins, 10 How. 596 (1850) (Daniel, J., dissenting); Rich v. Lambert, 12 How. 347 (1851) (Daniel, J., dissenting); The Howard, 18 How. 231, 234 (1855) (Daniel, J., dissenting); The Genessee Chief, 12 How. 449 (1851) (Daniel, J., dissenting); Fretz v. Bull, 12 How. 466 (1851) (Daniel, J., dissenting); The New World, 16 How. 469, 478 (1853) (Daniel, J., dissenting); The Monticello, 17 How. 152 (1854) (Daniel, J., dissenting); The New York, 18 How. 223, 226 (1855) (Daniel, J., dissenting); Ward v. Peck, 18 How. 296 (1855) (Daniel, J., dissenting); The Magnolia, 20 How. 296 (1857) (Daniel, J., dissenting); "In other cases too numerous to mention, he simply announced his dissent." Brown, *supra* note 109, at 894.

130. 13 How. 138 (1851).

131. 21 How. 803, 818 (1858).

132. Brown, *supra* note 109, at 900.

133. Curtis filed 7 dissenting opinions and cast 12 dissenting votes during his tenure (when the Court decided 467 cases). Zobell, *supra* note 5, at 198, n.69.

134. Brown, *The Dissenting Opinions of Mr. Justice Harlan,* 46 Am. L. Rev. 321, 351 (1912).

135. Abraham, *John Marshall Harlan: A Justice Neglected,* 41 Va. L. Rev. 871, 872, 874 (1955).

136. 163 U.S. 537 (1896).

137. Bowman v. Chicago & Nw. Ry., 125 U.S. 465 (1888).

138. Leisy v. Hardin, 135 U.S. 100 (1890).

139. Schollenberger v. Pennsylvania, 171 U.S. 1 (1898).

140. 198 U.S. 45 (1905).

141. Transportation Co. v. Parkersburg, 107 U.S. 691 (1882).

142. Philadelphia Fire Ass'n v. New York, 119 U.S. 110 (1886).

143. New York v. Roberts, 171 U.S. 658 (1898). Harlan's sustained dissent continued to make this distinction in Geer v. Connecticut, 161 U.S. 519 (1895); Fidelity Mutual Life Insurance Assoc. v. Metler, 185 U.S. 308 (1901); Atchison T. & S. F. R. Co. v. Mathews, 174 U.S. 96 (1898); Hooper v. California, 155 U.S. 648 (1893), Doyle v. Continental Insurance Co., 94 U.S. 535 (1876); Barron v. Burnside, 163 U.S. 299 (1895); and Security Insurance Co. v. Prewitt, 202 U.S. 246 (1905).

144. 156 U.S. 1 (1895).

145. 168 U.S. 144 (1897).

146. 221 U.S. 1 (1911).

147. Id. at 106.

148. 207 U.S. 463 (1908). These dissents are also in line with his repeated dissents restricting the "fellow servant" rule: Central R.R. Co. v. Reegan, 160 U.S. 259; North Pacific R.R. v. Peterson, 162 U.S. 346; North Pacific v. Charless, 162 U.S. 359; Alaska Mining Co. v. Whelan, 168 U.S. 86; Martin v. Atchison [& R.R.], 166 U.S. 399.

149. Hurtado v. California, 110 U.S. 516 (1884).

150. O'Neil v. Vermont, 144 U.S. (1892).

151. Maxwell v. Dow, 176 U.S. 581 (1900).

152. Twining v. New Jersey, 211 U.S. 78 (1908).

153. Schick v. United States, 195 U.S. 65 (1904).

154. Downes v. Bidwell, 182 U.S. 244 (1901) (Harlan, J., dissenting); Hawaii v. Mankichi, 190 U.S. 197 (1903) (Harlan, J., dissenting); Dorr v. United States, 195 U.S. 138 (1904) (Harlan, J., dissenting).

155. United States v. Harris, 106 U.S. 629 (1883).

156. *United States v. Stanley, United States v. Ryan, United States v. Nichols, United States v. Singleton,* and *Robinson v. Memphis & Charleston R.R.* were later consolidated in 109 U.S. 3 (1883).

157. Id. at 25 (Harlan, J., dissenting).

158. Clyde v. United States, 197 U.S. 207 (1905).

159. Hodges v. United States, 203 U.S. 1 (1906).

160. Bailey v. Alabama, 211 U.S. 452 (1908).

161. James v. Bowman, 190 U.S. 127 (1903).

162. United States v. Wong Kinm Ark, 169 U.S. 649 (1898) (Fuller, J., dissenting; joined by Harlan, J.); Baldwin v. Franks, 120 U.S. 678 (1887) (Harlan, J., dissenting).

163. Elk v. Wilkins, 112 U.S. 94 (1884) (Harlan, J., dissenting).

164. Louisville, New Orleans & Texas Ry. v. Mississippi, 133 U.S. 587 (1890) (Harlan, J., dissenting).

165. 163 U.S. 537 (1896) (Harlan, J., dissenting).

166. Chesapeake & Ohio Ry. v. Kentucky, 179 U.S. 388 (1900) (Harlan, J., dissenting); Chiles v. Chesapeake & Ohio Ry., 218 U.S. 71 (1910) (Harlan, J., dissenting).

167. 211 U.S. 45 (1908).

168. *Id.* at 69.

169. *Id.*

170. His opinion for the Court in Cumming v. Board of Education, 175 U.S. 528 (1899), has been read to contradict his stance for equal protection, but in *Cumming* there was no proof of unequal treatment due to race. The board was charged with not establishing a high school for African-American children, yet it had never established a high school for White boys. Since the board did appropriate taxes to subsidize a White girls high school, the distinction turned on sex rather than race. Also, one must remember that the right to education is not a fundamental one, that the Georgia constitution provided for an "elementary" school education (a provision that was being met), and that the plaintiffs had no contention with the separation of the races. *Id.* at 543–544.

The vindications of Harlan's dissents affirm their appeal to "the brooding spirit of the law" and "the intelligence of a future day":

> Plessy v. Ferguson (1896), overruled by Brown v. Board of Education, 347 U.S. 483 (1954); Bolling v. Sharp, 347 U.S. 497 (1954)
>
> Louisville, New Orleans & Texas Ry. v. Mississippi (1890) and Chesapeake & Ohio Ry. v. Kentucky (1900), involving segregated railroad accommodations, overruled by Morgan v. Virginia, 328 U.S. 373 (1946)
>
> United States v. E.C. Knight (1899), overruled by NLRB v. Jones & Laughlin Steel Corp., 301 U.S. 1 (1937)
>
> Leisy v. Hardin (1889), nullified by twenty-first amendment, which accomplished absolute state regulation of liquor sales and traffic
>
> Lochner v. New York (1905), overruled by Bunting v. Oregon, 243 U.S. 426 (1917)
>
> Robertson v. Baldwin (1897), rectified by passage of the Federal Seaman's Act of 1915
>
> Pollack v. Farmers Loan and Trust Co. (1895), inapplicable after ratification of the sixteenth amendment (1913)
>
> Employer's Liability Cases (1908), overruled by Second Employer's Liability Cases, 223 U.S. 1 (1912)

Abraham, *supra* note 135, at 890–91. In contrast, *see* Brown, *supra* note 134, at 321, 336; from the perspective of 1912, before *Brown v. Board of Education*, Brown wrote about the Civil Rights Cases: "Twenty-eight years have elapsed since this decision was rendered, and while it has met with the general approval of the country, there is still a lingering doubt whether the spirit of the amendments was not intended to secure the equality of the races in all places affected with a public interest."

171. Brennan, *How Goes the Supreme Court?*, 36 Mercer L. Rev. 781, 785 (1985).

172. *E.g.,* Easterbrook, *Agreement Among the Justices: An Empirical Note,* 1984 Sup. Ct. Rev. 389, 389–90 ("No doubt the number and length of separate and dissenting opinions continue to increase. This is not necessarily bad. Fracturing is inevitable. The Court selects hard cases for decision, and cases are hard because existing precedents and the temper of the times allow more than one outcome."); Hughes, *Address,* 13 Am. L. Inst. Proc. 61, 64 (1936) (*quoted in* F. Frankfurter, Of Law and Men 42 (1956)) (Chief Justice Hughes expressed surprise "that in the midst of controversies on every conceivable subject, one should expect unanimity upon difficult legal questions.").

173. P. Blaustein & R. Mersky, The First One Hundred Justices 144 (1978). For a list of Holmes's constitutional opinions through February 24, 1931, arranged topically, *see* Frankfurter, 44 Harv. L. Rev. 820 (1931).

174. Blaustein & Mersky, *supra* note 173, at 144.

175. *Id.* Holmes has sometimes been called the "Great Dissenter," but justification for the title does not stem from the number of his dissents; at least ten other justices have published more. *See* Blaustein & Mersky, *supra* note 173, at 102. Instead, many of the points of view he expressed in dissent have been vindicated by time. "If any Supreme Court dissenter can be said to have influenced the thinking of his successors, it was Justice Holmes." Kelman, *supra* note 5, at 225–26 (1985).

176. Blaustein & Mersky, *supra* note 173, at 145.

177. *Id.*

178. Konefsky, *Holmes and Brandeis: Companions in Dissent,* 10 Vand. L. Rev. 269 (1957).

179. C.G. Ross, St. Louis Post-Dispatch, June 19, 1927 (*quoted in* H. Dillard, Mr. Justice Brandeis, Great American 14 (1941)).

180. Kirchwey, *Foreword to* Lief, The Dissenting Opinions of Mr. Justice Holmes (1929).

181. Northern Securities Co. v. United States, 193 U.S. 197, 400 (1904).

182. Konefsky, *supra* note 178, at 271. *See also* Freund, The Unpublished Opinions of Mr. Justice Brandeis (1957).

183. Konefsky, *supra* note 178, at 281.

184. *Id.*

185. *Id.*

186. A. Mason, *Mr. Justice Brandeis and the Constitution,* 80 U. Pa. L. Rev. 799, 812 (1932).

187. *Id.* at 837.

188. Brandeis, *The Living Law,* 10 Ill. L. Rev. 461, 467, (1916).

189. Freund, *supra* note 182, at xx.

190. 198 U.S. 45 (1905).

191. In Holden v. Hardy, 169 U.S. 366 (1898), the Court had previously upheld a Utah statute limiting miners to an eight-hour workday as a proper exercise of the police power.

192. *Lochner,* 198 U.S. at 61.

193. *Id.* at 25–26.

194. *E.g.,* Muller v. Oregon, 231 U.S. 412 (1908) (Oregon statute limiting women to a ten-hour workday); Sturges v. Beauchamp, 231 U.S. 320 (1913) (Illinois child labor law); Riley v. Massachusetts, 232 U.S. 671 (1914) (Massachusetts statute limiting women to a fifty-five-hour workweek); Miller v. Wilson, 236 U.S. 373 (1915); Bosley v. McLaughlin, 236 U.S. 385 (1915); Bunting v. Oregon, 243 U.S. 426 (Oregon statute limiting work hours of men in certain industries).

195. 243 U.S. 629 (1917) (per curiam). Brandeis, who had defended the Oregon law in 1914, did not sit. JACKSON, *supra* note 27, at 106–07. The Court split evenly on the issue.

196. 261 U.S. 525 (1923).

197. *Id.*

198. *Id.* at 567.

199. *Id.* at 568.

200. 269 U.S. 530 (1925).

201. 273 U.S. 657 (1926).

202. 269 U.S. at 530. In United States v. Lehigh Valley R.R., 254 U.S. 255 (1920), Holmes (along with Chief Justice White) also stated that he was acquiescing in the majority's opinion because he felt constrained by the precedents.

203. 298 U.S. 587 (1936).

204. 244 U.S. 590 (1917).

205. *Id.* at 597 (Brandeis, J., dissenting).

206. *Id.* at 600.

207. Ribnik v. McBride, 277 U.S. 350 (1928).

208. *Id.* at 359 (Stone, J., dissenting). The employment agency cases were eventually overruled in Olsen v. Nebraska, 313 U.S. 236 (1941).

209. 273 U.S. 418 (1926).

210. *Id.* at 446 (Holmes, J., dissenting).

211. *Id.* at 447 (Holmes, J., dissenting).

212. Burns Baking Co. v. Bryan, 264 U.S. 504 (1924).

213. Weaver v. Palmer Bros. Co., 270 U.S. 402 (1926).

214. DiSanto v. Pennsylvania, 273 U.S. 34 (1927).

215. Liggett Co. v. Baldridge, 278 U.S. 105 (1928).

216. Quaker City Cab Co. v. Pennsylvania, 277 U.S. 398 (1928).

217. Frost & Frost Trucking Co. v. California, 271 U.S. 583 (1926).

218. 260 U.S. 393 (1922).

219. *Id.* at 417 (Brandeis, J., dissenting).

220. Meyer v. Nebraska, 262 U.S. 390 (1923); Bartels v. Iowa, 262 U.S. 404 (1923).

221. Bartels v. Iowa, 262 U.S. at 412 (Holmes, J., dissenting).

222. 244 U.S. 204 (1917).

223. Act of October 6, 1917, ch. 97, §§ 1, 2, 40 Stat. 395 (Repealed by act of June 25, 1948, ch. 646, 62 Stat. 869, 931).

224. 253 U.S. 149 (1920).

225. Holmes had famously dissented in Massachusetts labor cases, *e.g.,* Vegelahn v. Guntner, 167 Mass. 92, 44 N.E. 1007 (1896) (Sup. J. Ct. of Mass.), vindicated by Plant v. Woods, 176 Mass 492, 47 N.E. 1011 (Mass. 1900) in Massachusetts, and then *Coronado Coal.*

226. *Id.* at 167 (Holmes, J., dissenting). As Justice Stevens pointed out, Holmes considered it "entirely proper to continue to rely on the reasons that had been rejected by the majority in *Jensen;* the repetition of his dissenting views was not foreclosed by the doctrine of *stare decisis.*" Stevens, *The Life Span of a Judge-Made Rule,* 58 N.Y.U. L. REV. 1, 7 (1983).

227. 208 U.S. 161 (1908).

228. *Id.* at 190–92 (Holmes, J., dissenting).

229. 236 U.S. 1 (1915).

230. *Id.* at 26–27 (Holmes, J., dissenting).

231. 245 U.S. 229 (1917).

232. 245 U.S. 275 (1917).

233. Brandeis's argument is an interesting one; after looking at the facts, he found no evidence that any employee had joined the union in violation of the contract. Furthermore, the organizer was asking employees only to agree to join at some later date, when there were enough employees willing to join so that the union would have some clout. Brandeis did not deny that for an employee to join the union and remain employed would be a violation of the contract. *Id.* at 263–74 (Brandeis, J., dissenting).

234. Duplex Print Co. v. Deering, 254 U.S. 443 (1921).

235. Truax v. Corrigan, 257 U.S. 312 (1921).

236. *Id.* at 344 (Holmes, J., dissenting). This was the issue in *Vegelahn* on which Holmes had dissented in Massachusetts almost thirty years earlier.

237. 274 U.S. 37 (1927).

238. *Id.* at 58.

239. I have classified the first amendment dissents of Holmes and Brandeis as "repeated dissents." I realize that this may be a tenuous characterization; these dissents are not like the repeated dissents of Black and Douglas or of Brennan and Marshall, where it is clear that the justices are dissenting for the same reason again and again. Nevertheless, Holmes's and Brandeis's first amendment dissents are an important part of their record, and this is an area where they differed from a majority of the Court on a fairly regular basis.

240. 250 U.S. 616, 624 (1919).

241. Before parting ways with the majority, Holmes worked out a standard that, in conjunction with the work of Brandeis, was to form the basis for twentieth-century freedom of speech jurisprudence. *See* A. MASON, BRANDEIS: A FREE MAN'S LIFE 562 (1946). In Schenck v. United States, 249 U.S. 47 (1919), Holmes wrote for a unanimous Court that the first amendment would not protect speech which created "a clear and present danger" of evils that Congress had a right to prevent. The

application of that test to the particular situation in *Schenck* seems less than clear; the defendants in *Schenck* were convicted under the Espionage Act of 1917 for conspiracy to obstruct enlistment during wartime by publishing a leaflet. There is, however, evidence that Holmes wrote the opinion reluctantly. In writing to a friend later, he commented that "it is one of the ironies, that I, who probably take the extremist view in favor of free speech (in which, in the abstract, I have no very enthusiastic belief, though I hope I would die for it), that I should have been selected for blowing up." 2 DEWOLFE, HOLMES-POLLOCK LETTERS 29 (1941).

Holmes also wrote the opinion of the Court in two concurrent cases, Frohwerk v. United States, 249 U.S. 204 (1919) and Debs v. United States, 249 U.S. 211 (1919).

In another letter, Holmes wrote: "I sent you yesterday some opinions in the *Debs* and other similar cases. . . . I greatly regretted having to write them—and *(between ourselves)* that the Government pressed them to a hearing. . . . But on the only questions before us I could not doubt about the law. 1 DEWOLFE, HOLMES-LASKI LETTERS 142 (1963).

242. *Abrams,* 250 U.S. at 629 (Holmes, J., dissenting).

243. *Id.* at 630 (Holmes, J., dissenting).

244. Schaefer v. United States, 251 U.S. 466, 482 (1920); Pierce v. United States, 252 U.S. 239 (1920).

245. *Pierce,* 252 U.S. at 269 (Brandeis, J., dissenting).

246. 268 U.S. 652 (1925).

247. In a letter to his friend, Holmes wrote: "My last performance . . . was a dissent . . . in favor of the rights of an anarchist (so-called) to talk drool in favor of the proletarian dictatorship. But the prevailing notion of free speech seems to be that you may say what you choose if you don't shock me." 2 DEWOLFE, *supra* note 241, at 163.

248. 254 U.S. 325 (1921). *Gitlow* presented a new issue of state power. Holmes was no longer willing to dissent in cases of federal law, and therefore there was no dissent from him in *Gilbert.*

249. *Id.* at 335–36 (Brandeis, J., dissenting). Brandeis eventually gained Holmes's concurrence for a greatly modified statement of his new view in Whitney v. California.

250. 255 U.S. 407 (1921).

251. Holmes also wrote: "The United States may give up the Post Office when it sees fit, but while it carries it on, the use of the mails is almost as much a part of free speech as the right to use our tongues; and it would take very strong language to convince me that Congress ever intended to give such a practically despotic power to any one man." *Id.* at 437.

252. *Id.* at 436 (Brandeis, J., dissenting).

253. 258 U.S. 138 (1922).

254. *Id.* at 140–41 (Holmes, J., dissenting).

255. 279 U.S. 644 (1929).

256. 283 U.S. 605 (1931).

257. 283 U.S. 636 (1931).

258. *Schwimmer,* 279 U.S. at 653–55 (Holmes, J., dissenting).

259. *MacIntosh,* 283 U.S. at 627 (Hughes, C.J., dissenting).

260. *Bland,* 283 U.S. at 637 (Hughes, C.J., dissenting).

261. After *Lochner,* for example, and after Roosevelt's Court-packing plan failed, the Court proceeded to uphold a variety of state laws regulating the working hours of employees. A year after the Court had struck down a minimum wage statute in Morehead v. Tipaldo, 298 U.S. 587 (1936), a majority held a Washington State minimum wage statute to be constitutional in West Coast Hotel Co. v. Parrish, 300 U.S. 379 (1937). (Justice Roberts was the "swing-justice" whose vote changed in *West Coast Hotel.*) The employment agency case was eventually overruled in Olsen v. Nebraska, 313 U.S. 236 (1941).

Adair v. United States, 208 U.S. 161 (1908), and Coppage v. Kansas, 236 U.S. 1 (1915), which had held that neither the states nor Congress could prohibit an employer from discharging or refusing to hire workers because they were union members, were expressly overruled in Phelps Dodge Corp. v. NLRB, 313 U.S. 177 (1941). Congress agreed with Brandeis's dissent in Duplex Print Co. v. Deering, 254 U.S. 443 (1921), and in 1932 extended anti-injunction provisions to secondary boycotts through the Norris–La Guardia Anti-Injunction Act.

In matters involving the first amendment, the "clear and present danger" standard set forth in *Schenck* and refined in the dissents of Holmes and Brandeis provided guidance for the Court in post–World War II political subversion cases. The naturalization cases were expressly overruled in Girouard v. United States, 328 U.S. 61 (1946), where, in an opinion by Justice Douglas, the majority held that one unwilling to take up arms in the country's defense could not on that basis be deprived of citizenship.

262. Truax v. Corrigan, 257 U.S. 312, 376 (1921) (Brandeis, J., dissenting).

263. Black's appointment met with strong public disapprobation because of his erstwhile membership in the Ku Klux Klan. His background notwithstanding, Black became "a staunch defender of dissident voices during the McCarthy era, a protector of the constitutional rights of the accused . . . [and] a proponent for rights of racial equality" and for the one-man, one-vote doctrine. Decker, *Justice Hugo L. Black: The Balancer of Absolutes,* 59 Cal. L. Rev. 1335 (1971).

264. Blaustein & Mersky, *supra* note 174 at 145.

265. *Id.*

266. "It is interesting to note that the appointment was viewed somewhat askance by the left wing. *The Nation,* for example, commented, 'We wonder how hardy Mr. Douglas's liberalism would prove to be in the cold isolation of the Supreme Court.' " Irish, *Mr. Justice Douglas and Judicial Restraint,* 6 Univ. of Fla. L. Rev. 537, 538 (1953) (citation omitted).

267. Blaustein & Mersky, *supra* note 173, at 145.

268. *Id.*

269. "From the outset Black and Douglas have been in almost complete agreement, whether in the heyday of the Roosevelt Court, when they were with the majority on social legislation, or more recently, when they are likely to be determined dissenters on civil rights." Irish, *supra* note 266, at 549.

270. 303 U.S. 77, 87 (1938) (Black, J., dissenting).

271. Santa Clara Co. v. Southern Pacific R.R., 118 U.S. 394, 396 (1886); Minneapolis R.R. v. Beckwith, 129 U.S. 26, 28 (1889).

272. JACKSON, *supra* note 27, at 12.

273. 337 U.S. 562, 576 (1949) (Douglas, J., dissenting).

274. Douglas mentioned elsewhere the great possibilities for development and exploitation afforded by arming corporations with constitutional prerogatives. Douglas, *Stare Decisis,* 49 COLUM. L. REV. 735, 738 (1949).

275. JACKSON, *supra* note 27, at 13.

276. *See* Douglas, *supra* 274, at 737: "So far as constitutional law is concerned *stare decisis* must give way before the dynamic component of history."

277. Decker, *supra* 263, at 1354.

278. Black, *The Bill of Rights,* 35 N.Y.U. L. REV. 865, 879 (1960).

279. Decker, *supra* note 263, at 1345.

280. *Id.* at 1353.

281. Douglas, *supra* note 274, at 739.

282. Standard Oil Co. of Cal. v. United States, 337 U.S. 293, 320 (1949).

283. Douglas, *supra* note 274, at 739.

284. *Id.* at 735.

285. *Id.* at 747 (quoting Baker v. Lorillard, 4 N.Y. 257, 261 (1850)).

286. The first amendment formed a vital part of Black's jurisprudence. "[T]he guaranties of the first amendment [are] the foundation upon which our government structure rests and without which it could not continue to endure as conceived and planned. Freedom to speak and write about public questions is as important to the life of our government as is the heart to the human body. If that heart be weakened, the result is debilitation; if it be stilled, the result is death." Milk Wagon Drivers Local 753 v. Meadowmoor Dairies, Inc., 312 U.S. 287, 301–02 (1951) (Black, J., dissenting).

287. As he observed in one case:

The first amendment says that freedom of speech, freedom of press, and the free exercise of religion shall not be abridged. That is a negation of power on the part of each and every department of government. Free speech, free press, free exercise of religion are placed separate and apart; they are above and beyond the police power; they are not subject to regulation in the manner of factories, slums, apartment houses, production of oil, and the like.—Beauharnais v. Illinois, 343 U.S. 250, 286 (1952) (Douglas, J., dissenting).

288. *E.g.,* Feiner v. New York, 340 U.S. 315 (1951) (upholding conviction for disorderly conduct of a student addressing a crowd and making derogatory remarks

about public officials); Breard v. Alexandria, 341 U.S. 622 (1951) (upholding ordinance prohibiting door-to-door solicitation for magazine subscriptions); Beauharnais v. Illinois, 343 U.S. 250 (1952) (affirming conviction under state statute prohibiting group defamation); Poulos v. New Hampshire, 345 U.S. 395 (1953) (statute requiring license for open-air meeting valid on its face where speaker who was refused license failed to seek judicial relief and proceeded without license.)

289. 354 U.S. 476 (1957).

290. Black and Douglas both dissented in Ginsburg v. United States, 383 U.S. 433 (1966) (upholding conviction of publisher for "pandering" in advertising and methods of distribution where the literature itself was not obscene); Mishkin v. New York, 383 U.S. 502 (1966) (upholding conviction of publisher of literature designed to appeal to the prurient interest of a "clearly defined deviant sexual group," though not to the prurient interest of the "average" person); Ginsberg v. New York, 390 U.S. 629 (1968) (upholding state statute forbidding sale to minors under 177 of magazines depicting nudity, sexual excitement, sexual conduct and sadomasochistic abuse where such magazines were not obscene for adults); Byrne v. Karalexis, 396 U.S. 976 (1969); United States v. Thirty-Seven (37) Photographs, 402 U.S. 363 (1971) (first amendment does not protect against seizure of obscene photographs by Customs agents); United States v. Reidel, 402 U.S. 351 (1971) (first amendment does not protect booksellers who mail obscene materials to adults for their private use).

291. 396 U.S. 976, 977 (1969).

292. *Id.*

293. *E.g.,* Kingsley Books v. Brown, 354 U.S. 436 (1957) (New York statute permitting a municipality to sue to enjoin the sale or distribution of obscene written or printed matter); Times Film Corp. v. Chicago, 365 U.S. 43 (1961) (municipal ordinance requiring movies to be submitted for examination by a censor as a prerequisite to public exhibition). Black and Douglas both concurred in the majority opinion in Freedman v. Maryland, 380 U.S. 51 (1965), which held that a statute requiring submission of a film to a censor must provide procedural safeguards to eliminate the dangers of censorship.

294. 360 U.S. 109 (1959).

295. *Id.* at 134 (Black, J., dissenting).

296. Additionally, Black determined that Congress was impermissibly seeking to impose punishment, a role it was denied by the separation of powers.

297. *E.g.,* Wilkinson v. United States, 365 U.S. 399, 415, 423 (1961); Braden v. United States, 365 U.S. 431, 438, 446 (1961).

In Uphaus v. Wyman, 360 U.S. 72 (1959), the Court sustained the conviction of the operator of a summer camp who refused to produce for a *state* committee the names of attendees at purportedly Communist activities at the camp. Again, Black, Douglas, and Warren dissented, joining the opinion of Justice Brennan. Brennan wrote that the camp activities were protected by the first and fourteenth amendments. *Id.* at 86–87 (Brennan, J., dissenting).

298. 339 U.S. 382 (1950).

299. Brandenburg v. Ohio, 395 U.S. 444, 456 (1968) (Douglas, J., concurring).

300. Garner v. Board of Public Works, 341 U.S. 716 (1951) (upholding city ordinance requiring public employees to take oath and sign affidavit that they had never been affiliated with any group advocating overthrow of the government); Adler v. Board of Education, 342 U.S. 485 (1952) (no violation of first amendment where membership in a "listed" organization was prima facie evidence of disqualification for employment).

301. 325 U.S. 561, 573 (1945) (Black, J., dissenting).

302. Konigsberg v. State Bar, 366 U.S. 36 (1961); In re Anastaplo, 336 U.S. 82 (1961). See also Law Students Civil Rights Research Council, Inc. v. Wadmond, 401 U.S. 154 (1971).

303. 367 U.S. 740 (1961).

304. In his concurrence, Douglas said that "there is a practical problem of mustering five Justices for a judgment in this case. . . . So I have concluded dubitante to agree to the one suggested by Mr. Justice Brennan. . . ." Id. at 778–79.

305. Id. at 780.

306. 367 U.S. 820 (1961).

307. In at least one area of first amendment law, Black and Douglas did not agree. Douglas dissented in a line of cases upholding Sunday closing laws, while Black joined the majority. Douglas believed that state laws which required businesses to close on Sundays violated both the free exercise and establishment clauses of the first amendment. Braunfeld v. Brown, 366 U.S. 599 (1961); Gallagher v. Crown Kosher Super Market, 366 U.S. 617 (1961); McGowen v. Maryland, 366 U.S. 420, 561 (1961); Arlan's Department Store v. Kentucky, 371 U.S. 218 (1962).

308. Sacher v. United States, 343 U.S. 1 (1952); Isserman v. Ethics Committee, 345 U.S. 927 (1953); Green v. United States, 356 U.S. 165 (1958); Piemonte v. United States, 367 U.S. 556 (1961); United States v. Barnett, 376 U.S. 681 (1964).

309. Frank v. United States, 395 U.S. 147 (1969); Dyke v. Taylor Implement Mfg. Co., 391 U.S. 216 (1968); Cheff v. Schnackenberg, 384 U.S. 373 (1966). See also Muniz v. Hoffman, 422 U.S. 454 (1975); Johnson v. Nebraska, 419 U.S. 949 (1974).

310. Frank v. United States, 395 U.S. at 159–60 (Black, J., dissenting).

311. See generally L. TRIBE, American Constitutional Law 772 (2d ed. 1988). In his separate opinion in Gideon v. Wainwright, 372 U.S. 335 (1963), Douglas stated that ten justices have thought that the Bill of Rights applied to the states. They were Justices Field; Harlan (I); himself; Black; Murphy; Rutledge in Adamson v. California, 332 U.S. 46 (1947); Bradley and Swayne in the Slaughter House Cases, 16 Wall. 36 (1873); "probably" Brewer, in O'Neil v. Vermont, 144 U.S. 323 (1892); and "seemingly" Clifford in his dissent in Walker v. Sauvinet, 92 U.S. 90 (1876).

312. 378 U.S. 1 (1964).

313. Feldman v. United States, 322 U.S. 487 (1944); Knapp v. Schweitzer, 357 U.S. 371 (1958).

314. 336 U.S. 684 (1949); Bartkus v. Illinois, 359 U.S. 121 (1959); Abbate v. United States, 359 U.S. 187 (1959).

315. United States v. Kahriger, 345 U.S. 22 (1953); Irvine v. California, 347 U.S. 128 (1954); Lewis v. United States, 348 U.S. 419 (1955).

Black called this a "squeezing device contrived to put a man in federal prison if he refuses to confess himself into a state prison as a violator of state gambling laws." *Kahriger,* 345 U.S. at 36–37 (Black, J., dissenting).

316. 316 U.S. 455 (1942). In his dissent in *Betts* (where he was joined by Douglas), Black stated: "I believe that the Fourteenth Amendment made the Sixth applicable to the states. But this view, although often used in dissents, has never been accepted by a majority of this Court and is not accepted today." *Id.* at 474–75. "A practice cannot be reconciled with 'common and fundamental ideas of fairness and right' which subjects innocent men to increased dangers of conviction merely because of their poverty." *Id.* at 476.

317. Foster v. Illinois, 332 U.S. 134 (1947); Bute v. Illinois, 333 U.S. 640 (1948); Gayes v. New York, 332 U.S. 145 (1947); Gryger v. Burke, 334 U.S. 728 (1948).

Professor Kelman noted in *The Forked Path of Dissent, supra* note 5, that Black oscillated between his own "anti-*Betts*" view and a generous application of the *Betts* exception. Professor Kelman calls this a "one-sided" dissent. The constant in Black's actions was "that he never failed to support the claim for appointment of counsel."

318. 372 U.S. 335 (1963). Black wrote the majority opinion in *Gideon,* where he "proceeded, in a dignified way, to crow." JACKSON, *supra* note 27, at 233.

319. Winters v. Beck, 385 U.S. 907 (1966); DeJoseph v. Connecticut, 385 U.S. 982 (1966).

320. The federal exclusionary rule was established in Weeks v. United States, 232 U.S. 383 (1914).

321. Wolf v. Colorado, 338 U.S. 25 (1949); Stefanelli v. Minard, 342 U.S. 117 (1951); Salsburg v. Maryland, 356 U.S. 545 (1954); Irvine v. California, 347 U.S. 128 (1954).

322. 338 U.S. at 40 (Douglas, J., dissenting).

323. 338 U.S. at 39–40 (Black, J., concurring). When the fourth amendment (including the exclusionary rule) was made applicable to the states in Mapp v. Ohio, 367 U.S. 643 (1961), Black concurred. He said that upon reflection he had determined that although the fourth amendment standing alone was not sufficient to bar illegally seized evidence, the fourth in conjunction with the fifth amendment's ban against compelled self-incrimination did establish a basis for requiring the exclusionary rule. *Mapp,* 367 U.S. at 661–62.

324. 367 U.S. 643 (1961).

325. Linkletter v. Walker, 381 U.S. 618 (1965); Angelet v. Fay, 381 U.S. 654 (1965).

326. *Linkletter,* 381 U.S. at 641 (Black, J., dissenting).

327. DeStefano v. Woods, 392 U.S. 631 (1968). The right to jury trial in state

courts was established in Duncan v. Louisiana, 341 U.S. 145 (1968) and Bloom v. Illinois, 391 U.S. 194 (1968).

328. Johnson v. New Jersey, 384 U.S. 719 (1966).

329. 384 U.S. 436 (1966).

330. 394 U.S. 244 (1969).

331. 389 U.S. 347 (1967).

332. 378 U.S. 130 (1964).

333. 378 U.S. 226 (1964).

334. Bell, 378 U.S. at 318 (Black, J., dissenting). In contrast, Douglas wrote in a concurring opinion in Bell:

> Segregation of Negroes in the restaurants and lunch counters of parts of America is a relic of slavery. It is a badge of second-class citizenship. It is a denial of a privilege and immunity of national citizenship and of the equal protection guaranteed by the Fourteenth Amendment against abridgement by the States. When the state police, the state prosecutor, and the state courts unite to convict Negroes for renouncing that relic of slavery, the "State" violates the Fourteenth Amendment.—Id. at 260.

335. Bouie v. Columbia, 378 U.S. 347 (1964).

336. Barr v. Columbia, 378 U.S. 146 (1964).

337. Hamm v. Rock Hill, 379 U.S. 312 (1964); Lupper v. Arkansas, 379 U.S. 306 (1964); Blow v. North Carolina, 379 U.S. 684 (1965).

338. Hamm, 379 U.S. at 318–19 (Black, J., dissenting).

339. Massachusetts v. Laird, 400 U.S. 886 (1970) (Douglas, J., dissenting from denial of motion to file complaint); McArthur v. Clifford, 393 U.S. 1002 (1968) (Douglas, J., dissenting from denial of cert.); United States v. O'Brien, 391 U.S. 367 (1968) (Douglas, J., dissenting from denial of cert.); Hart v. United States, 391 U.S. 956 (1968) (Douglas, J., dissenting from denial of cert.); Mora v. McNamara, 389 U.S. 934 (1967) (Stewart, J., dissenting from denial of cert. and joined in dissent by Douglas, J.); Mitchell v. United States, 386 U.S. 972 (1967) (Douglas, J., dissenting from denial of cert.); Holmes v. United States, 391 U.S. 936 (1968) (Douglas, J., dissenting from denial of cert.). See also Morse v. Boswell, 393 U.S. 1052 (1969) (Douglas, J., dissenting from denial of cert.); Johnson v. Powell, 393 U.S. 920 (1968) (Douglas, J., dissenting from denial of application for stay of deployment); Hawthorne v. Hardaway, 393 U.S. 802 (1968) (Douglas, J., dissenting from denial of application for stay).

340. E.g., JACKSON, supra note 27, at 11–13.

341. E.g., Countryman, The Contribution of the Douglas Dissents, 10 GA. L. REV. 331 (1976); Decker, supra note 263.

342. Countryman, supra note 341, at 331. A majority of the Court has never accepted the view of Black and Douglas that the first amendment's guarantees are absolute. Nevertheless, the two justices had some success in this area. In particular, their point of view in the loyalty program cases was eventually upheld in Keyishian v. Board of Regents, 385 U.S. 589 (1967), where Adler v. Board of Education, 342

U.S. 485 (1952), was reconsidered and rejected. Additionally, one commentator has seen the influence of Black's absolutist view in the Court's current position on libel and slander. Decker, *supra* note 263, at 1354.

With respect to the insistence by Black and Douglas that the Bill of Rights was made applicable to the states through the fourteenth amendment, "While they never won that war, they won most of the battles." Countryman, *supra* note 341, at 344. Jackson called this a "war of attrition." JACKSON, *supra* note 27, at 12. Through selective incorporation, the Court made many of the rights guaranteed by the first eight amendments binding upon the states. Among these are the fourth amendment, Wolf v. Colorado, 338 U.S. 25 (1949); the fifth amendment privilege against self-incrimination, Malloy v. Hogan, 378 U.S. 1 (1964); the fifth amendment guarantee against double jeopardy, Benton v. Maryland, 395 U.S. 784 (1969); the sixth amendment right to jury trial, Duncan v. Louisiana, 391 U.S. 145 (1968); and the sixth amendment right to the assistance of counsel, Gideon v. Wainwright, 372 U.S. 335 (1963). These are all areas where Black and Douglas sustained dissents against the majority of the Court.

343. 285 U.S. 393, 406 (1932) (Brandeis, J., dissenting).

344. BLAUSTEIN & MERSKY, *supra* note 173, at 146.

345. *Id.*

346. *See generally* Dorsen, *The Second Mr. Justice Harlan: A Constitutional Conservative,* 44 N.Y.U. L. REV. 249 (1969).

347. Dane, *The Second Justice Harlan,* 51 U. CIN. L. REV. 545, 569 (1982).

348. Days, *Justice John M. Harlan,* 12 N.C. CENT. L. REV. 250, 251 (1981).

349. Bourguignon, *The Second Mr. Justice Harlan: His Principles of Judicial Decision Making,* 1979 SUP. CT. REV. 251, 252.

350. 394 U.S. 618, 677 (1969) (Harlan, J., dissenting) (majority holding that state residency requirement for welfare recipients violates equal protection).

351. Kelman, *supra* note 5, at 274.

352. *Id.* Harlan would, however, vote according to his own view for the remainder of a Term in which he disagreed with the majority and only acquiesce in the Court's position the following Term. *See, e.g.,* North Carolina v. Pearce, 345 U.S. 711, 744 (1968), where he explained that he was not following his usual practice.

353. An example is Harlan's dissent in Miranda v. Arizona, 384 U.S. 436, 506 (1966). He later dissented in Jenkins v. Delaware, 395 U.S. 213, 222 (1968), where he wrote: "As one who has never agreed with the *Miranda* case but nonetheless felt bound by it, I now find myself in the uncomfortable position of having to dissent from a holding which actually serves to curtail the impact of that direction."

354. Dane, *supra* note 347, at 553, 557.

355. Baldwin v. New York, 399 U.S. 66, 117 (1970) (right to jury trial by those accused of a misdemeanor punishable by a maximum of one year in prison); Benton v. Maryland, 395 U.S. 784, 801 (1969) (double jeopardy clause of the fifth amendment applicable to the states); Bloom v. Illinois, 391 U.S. 194, 215 (1968) (jury trial for criminal contempt punishable by two years in prison); Duncan v. Louisiana, 391

U.S. 145, 171 (1968) (right to impartial jury); Miranda v. Arizona, 384 U.S. 436, 504 (1966); Malloy v. Hogan, 378 U.S. 1 (1964) (privilege against self-incrimination); Mapp v. Ohio, 367 U.S. 643 (1961) (exclusion of illegally obtained evidence). *See also* Smith v. Illinois, 390 U.S. 129 (1968) (right to cross-examine witness).

356. 391 U.S. 145, 171 (1968).

357. 391 U.S. 194, 215 (1968).

358. He was following his usual practice of maintaining a dissent throughout the same Term in similar cases.

359. 399 U.S. 66, 117 (1970).

360. *Baldwin,* 399 U.S. at 138.

361. *E.g.,* Griffin v. California, 380 U.S. 609 (1965) (Harlan, J., concurring); Ashe v. Swenson, 397 U.S. 436 (1970) (Harlan, J., concurring); North Carolina v. Pearce, 345 U.S. 711, 744 (1968) (Harlan, J., concurring in part and dissenting in part).

362. 380 U.S. 609 (1965). In *Griffin,* Harlan wrote: "I would not, but for *Malloy,* apply the no-comment rule to the states." *Id.* at 612.

363. *Id.* at 615–16.

364. Klopfer v. North Carolina, 386 U.S. 213 (1967) (Harlan, J., concurring); Douglas v. Alabama, 380 U.S. 415 (1965) (Harlan, J., concurring); Pointer v. Texas, 380 U.S. 400 (1965) (Harlan, J., concurring); Ker v. California, 374 U.S. 23 (1963) (Harlan, J., concurring); Gideon v. Wainwright, 372 U.S. 335 (1963) (Harlan, J., concurring); Lanza v. New York, 370 U.S. 139 (1962) (Harlan, J., concurring).

365. 388 U.S. 549 (1946).

366. Black, Douglas, and Murphy dissented from the Court's opinion and strongly supported the proposition of one person, one vote. In his dissent, Black stated that as the districts were currently drawn some citizens had a vote only one-ninth as effective as the vote of other citizens of the state. *Id.* at 569 (Black, J., dissenting).

367. 369 U.S. 186 (1962).

368. *Id.* at 300 (Harlan, J., dissenting).

369. *Id.* at 334 (Harlan, J., dissenting).

370. *Id.* at 339 (Harlan, J., dissenting).

371. Hadley v. Junior College District, 347 U.S. 50, 69 (1970).

372. Avery v. Midland County, 390 U.S. 479, 486 (1968).

373. Swann v. Adams, 385 U.S. 440, 447 (1967); Reynolds v. Sims, 377 U.S. 533, 589 (1964). *See also* WMCA v. Lomenzo, 377 U.S. 633 (1964) (companion case to *Reynolds v. Sims*); Maryland Committee v. Tawes, 377 U.S. 656 (1964) (same); Davis v. Mann, 377 U.S. 678 (1964) (same); Roman v. Sincock, 377 U.S. 695 (1964) (same); Lucas v. Forty-Fourth General Assembly, 377 U.S. 713 (1964) (same).

374. Gray v. Sanders, 377 U.S. 368, 390 (1963).

375. Wells v. Rockefeller, 394 U.S. 542, 549 (1969); Kirkpatrick v. Preisler, 394 U.S. 526 (1969); Rockefeller v. Wells, 389 U.S. 421 (1967); Lucas v. Rhodes, 389 U.S. 212 (1964); Wesberry v. Sanders, 376 U.S. 1, 20 (1964).

376. For example, Harlan concurred in Jordan v. Silver, 381 U.S. 415, 419 (1965), where the Court held the senatorial apportionment of California to be invalid. "Finding . . . that the judgment of the District Court is squarely required by Lucas v. Forty Fourth General Assembly . . . I reluctantly acquiesce in the Court's summary affirmance."

377. Bourguignon, *supra* note 349, at 288–89 (citing Wechsler, *Toward Neutral Principles of Constitutional Law,* 73 HARV. L. REV. 1 (1959)).

378. Wechsler, *supra* note 377, at 15.

379. *Id.* at 11.

380. C. Pritchett, *Dissent on the Supreme Court, 1943–44,* 39 AM. POL. SCI. REV. 43 (1945). *See also* PRITCHETT, THE ROOSEVELT COURT: A STUDY IN JUDICIAL POLITICS AND VALUES, 1937–47, at 25–26.

381. Cox, *Freedom of Expression in the Burger Court,* 94 HARV. L. REV. 1, 72 (1980).

382. *The Supreme Court, 1984 Term,* 99 HARV. L. REV. 324 (Table I[C]) (1985).

383. *The Supreme Court, 1985 Term,* 100 HARV. L. REV. 306 (Table I[C]) (1986).

384. *The Supreme Court, 1986 Term,* 101 HARV. L. REV. 364 (Table I[C]) (1987).

385. *The Supreme Court, 1987 Term,* 102 HARV. L. REV. 352 (Table I[C]) (1988).

386. *See* Kelman, *supra* note 5, at 228–29.

## Chapter 3

1. Kelman, *The Forked Path of Dissent,* 1985 SUP. CT. REV. 227, 254. According to Professor Kelman: "In favor of the course of unremitting dissent as against the alternative of temporary subordination of minority views is its quality of directness. The dissenter speaks in his own unmistakable voice, says what he thinks the law ought to be, and wields his vote in conformity to that vision."

2. Di Santo v. Pennsylvania, 273 U.S. 34, 42 (1927) (Brandeis, J., dissenting).

3. As discussed in Mello, *supra* note 5, the sustained dissent has a tactical dimension. Continuing to exhibit opposition shows the world that the issue is still in dispute, thus inviting fresh assaults on the official position. *See* Kelman, *supra* note 1, at 254.

4. As the stance of Justices Brennan and Marshall that the death penalty constitutes cruel and unusual punishment is squarely in opposition to the Court's ruling in *Gregg v. Georgia,* I will not directly address the jurisprudential issues related to judicial discretion in cases where there is no clear precedent.

5. Furman v. Georgia, 408 U.S. 238, 335 (Marshall, J., concurring) (*citing* Filler, *Movements to Abolish the Death Penalty in the United States,* 284 ANNALS AM. ACAD. POL. & SOC. SCI. 124 (1952)). In his *Furman* opinion, Marshall traced the history of the death penalty as well as the movement in the United States for its abolition. He concluded that the use of the death penalty was tempered considerably in its move from Europe to America. But although strong abolitionist movements have existed, they have never been completely successful; no more than one-fourth of the states have at any one time abolished the death penalty. *Id.* at 341.

Justice Black used the fact that the death penalty existed in the United States when the Bill of Rights was enacted as the basis of his concurring opinion in McGautha v. California, 402 U.S. 183, 226 (1971), where he stated: "The Eighth Amendment forbids 'cruel and unusual punishments.' In my view, these words cannot be read to outlaw capital punishment because that penalty was in common use and authorized by law here and in the countries from which our ancestors came at the time the Amendment was adopted."

6. 408 U.S. 238 (1972).

7. 428 U.S. 193 (1976).

8. *Id.*

9. *E.g.,* McCleskey v. Kemp, 107 S. Ct. 1756, 1781 (1987) (Brennan, J., dissenting).

10. This paradoxical position may explain to some extent what Professor Kelman terms the "one-sided acceptance." Kelman, *supra* note 1, at 263. A justice who believes both in her duty to respect the law and in her right to repeat a dissent may find that in some cases she need not dissent. Instead, she may join the majority opinion because its result coincides with her view of how justice is best served in the case. This is perhaps analogous to the doctrine that the Court is conservative and will only reach constitutional issues where the case cannot be resolved on another, lesser basis.

11. Brennan, *In Defense of Dissents,* 37 HASTINGS L.J. 427 (1986).

12. *Id.* Brennan also says, however, that a dissent for its own sake is not justifiable. *Id.* at 435.

13. Marshall, *Remarks on the Death Penalty Made at the Judicial Conference of the Second Circuit,* 86 COLUM. L. REV. 1, 8 (1986).

14. P. DENNING, THE FAMILY STORY 183 (1981).

15. Justice Jackson wrote that "the Court functions less as one deliberative body than as nine." R. JACKSON, THE SUPREME COURT IN THE AMERICAN SYSTEM OF GOVERNMENT 16 (1955). Justice Powell characterized the Court as "nine small, independent law firms." Justice Lewis F. Powell Jr., address at the American Bar Association Annual Meeting (1976), *excerpted in What the Justices are Saying . . . ,"* 62 A.B.A.J. 1454 (1976). Additionally, Professor Tribe argued that the appointment of just one justice to the Court can have a great impact on the direction of its decisions. L. TRIBE, GOD SAVE THIS HONORABLE COURT (1985).

For an article that takes the idea a step further, *see* Maltz, *The Concept of the Doctrine of the Court in Constitutional Law,* 16 GA. L. REV. 357 (1982). Professor Maltz offers what he calls the "atomistic approach" to constitutional analysis; it is based on viewing a decision of the Supreme Court as an aggregate of individual approaches rather than as the product of a single unified theory.

16. Brennan, *supra* note 11, at 437.

17. *E.g.,* W. BERNS, FOR CAPITAL PUNISHMENT: CRIME AND THE MORALITY OF THE DEATH PENALTY (1979).

18. In his concurring opinion in *Furman,* Brennan set out the standards of a cumulative test for whether a punishment is cruel and unusual within the meaning

of the eighth amendment. Primary among the amendment's implicit principles is that a punishment must not be so severe as to be degrading to human dignity. Mental as well as physical pain can cause a punishment to be severe. Extreme severity is degrading to human dignity because it treats humans as objects to be discarded. The second related principle is that the state must not inflict a severe punishment in an arbitrary manner. Brennan argues that where a punishment is inflicted as rarely as the death penalty it is likely to be administered arbitrarily. The third principle is that a severe punishment must not be unacceptable to contemporary society. In order to determine what is unacceptable, it is necessary to look at objective factors. We must look not to whether a punishment is authorized by legislatures, but instead to the actual use of an authorized punishment. The final factor is that a punishment must not be excessive. A punishment is excessive if, in view of its purposes, a significantly less severe punishment is adequate. *Furman,* 408 U.S. at 269–82.

19. In *Gregg v. Georgia,* Brennan stated that he would hold on this ground alone that the death penalty is a cruel and unusual punishment. 428 U.S. at 227–31 (Brennan, J., dissenting).

20. *Id.* at 230–31; Brennan, *Constitutional Adjudication and the Death Penalty: A View from the Court,* 100 HARV. L. REV. 313 (1986).

21. *E.g.,* HOLMES, *The Path of the Law, in* COLLECTED LEGAL PAPERS 167, 170 (1920) ("The law is the witness and external deposit of our moral life. Its history is the history of the moral development of the race."); H.L.A. HART, THE CONCEPT OF LAW 7 (1979) ("Not only do law and morals share a vocabulary so that there are both legal and moral obligations, duties, and rights; but all municipal legal systems reproduce the substance of certain fundamental moral requirements.").

22. HOLMES, *supra* note 21, at 173.

23. Enduring elements of law are not, however, limited to the moral. *See* Brennan, *supra* note 11, at 437. ("[I]n my judgment, when a justice perceives an interpretation of the text to have departed so far from its essential meaning, that justice is bound, by a larger constitutional duty to the community, to expose the departure and point toward a different path.").

24. Wellington, *Common Law Rules and Constitutional Double Standards: Some Notes on Adjudication,* 83 YALE L.J. 221, 246–47 (1973) ("The Court's task is to ascertain the weight of the principle in conventional morality and to convert the moral principle into a legal one by connecting it with the body of constitutional law.").

For an article that evaluates the conventional-morality theory of judicial review, see Sadurski, *Conventional Morality and Judicial Standards,* 73 VA. L. REV. 339 (1987).

25. Gregg v. Georgia, 428 U.S. 228, 232 (1976) (Marshall, J., dissenting).

26. ELY, DEMOCRACY AND DISTRUST 69 (1980).

27. *Id.* (citation omitted).

28. 319 U.S. 624, 638 (1934).

29. *E.g.,* Brennan, *supra* note 11, at 437; Brennan, *The Constitution of the United States: Contemporary Ratification,* 27 S. TEX. L.J. 433, 444 (1986).

30. Brennan, *supra* note 11.

31. Trop v. Dulles, 356 U.S. 86, 101 (1958).

32. *Furman,* 408 U.S. at 277.

33. Brennan concluded in *Furman* that society has essentially rejected the death penalty because we have developed supposedly more humane methods of inflicting death, we no longer permit public executions because they are debasing and brutalizing, the number of crimes for which death is imposed have been drastically reduced, mandatory death sentences are no longer in common use and the death sentence is rarely imposed. *Furman,* 408 U.S. at 296–300.

Despite the reenactment of the death penalty in so many states, Brennan's empirical observations remain accurate. In 1976, the Court held mandatory capital punishment statutes unconstitutional. The Court curtailed the use of the death penalty in Coker v. Georgia, 433 U.S. 584 (1977), where it held that punishment to be unconstitutional as applied to the rapist of an adult woman. And from 1980 through May 24, 1991, there were only 146 executions in the United States; death is still a relatively rarely inflicted punishment, given that there are more than 2,000 people on death row. NAACP Legal Defense and Educational Fund, Inc., Death Row U.S.A. 1 (May 24, 1991) (unpublished compilation).

34. Furman v. Georgia, 408 U.S. at 360–69. In *Furman,* Marshall delineated four reasons that a punishment may be deemed cruel and unusual. First, there are certain punishments, such as use of the rack or the thumbscrew, that inherently involve so much physical pain and suffering that civilized people cannot tolerate them. These have been barred since the adoption of the Bill of Rights. Second, there are punishments that are unusual in that they were previously unknown as penalties for a given offense. If an innovative punishment is no more cruel than the punishment it supersedes, it is probably constitutional. It may also be constitutional if it is intended to serve a humane purpose. The third reason for holding a punishment to be cruel and unusual is because it is excessive and serves no valid legislative purpose. Marshall finds this kind of punishment to be unconstitutional even though popular sentiment may favor it. Fourth, where a punishment is not excessive and serves a valid legislative purpose, it still may be invalid if popular sentiment abhors it. *Id.* at 330–32.

35. *Id.* at 361.

36. Wise, *The Doctrine of Stare Decisis,* 21 WAYNE L. REV. 1043, 1045–46 (1975) (citing *London Street Tramways Co. v. London County Council,* [1898] A.C. 375 and Practice Statement [1966] W.L.R. 1234 [H.L.(E.)]).

37. *Id.* at 1045.

38. *Id.* at 1046.

39. Professor Wise called the more easygoing forms "latitudinarian." *Id.* at 1045.

40. *Cf.* Easterbrook, *Ways of Criticizing the Court,* 95 HARV. L. REV. 802, 818 n.39 (1982) ("*Stare decisis* is applied so loosely that it seems fair to say that it does not exist as a doctrine. The Court frequently changes rules it views as mistaken, invoking stare decisis only when the first decision induced substantial detrimental reliance.").

41. *E.g.,* Illinois Brick Co. v. Illinois, 431 U.S. 720, 736 (1977).

42. Kelman, *supra* note 1, at 237. As a confirming illustration of the sway of *stare decisis* in statutory construction, Professor Kelman cites a case where Brennan and Marshall, "evidently still in disagreement with the decision" in Buffalo Forge Co. v. Steelworkers, 428 U.S. 397 (1976), abandoned their dissent in Jacksonville Bulk Terminals v. International Longshoremen's Ass'n. 457 U.S. 702 (1982). In Professor Kelman's view, evidently, the example has special force because Brennan and Marshall are "two justices who are not usually identified with stare decisis self-denial." *Id.*

43. *E.g.,* Wengler v. Druggists Mut. Ins. Co., 446 U.S. 142, 153–54 (1980) (Rehnquist, J., dissenting) (adhering to his previous dissent in Califano v. Goldfarb, 430 U.S. 199 (1977) and stating his belief that *stare decisis* should be relaxed in constitutional cases); Brennan, *supra* note 29 ("In my judgment . . . the unique interpretive role of the Supreme Court with respect to the Constitution demands some flexibility with respect to the call of *stare decisis.* Because we are the last word on the meaning of the Constitution, our views must be subject to revision over time, or the Constitution falls captive . . . to the anachronistic views of long-gone generations.").

44. Burnet v. Coronado Oil and Gas, 285 U.S. 393, 406 (1932) (Brandeis, J., dissenting).

45. Maltz, *The Nature of Precedent,* 66 N.C. L. Rev. 367, 392–93 (1988).

46. *Id.*

47. Monaghan, *Taking Supreme Court Opinions Seriously,* 39 Md. L. Rev. 1, 4 (1979).

48. *Id.* Professor Monaghan says that the minimal role of *stare decisis* in constitutional adjudication reflects the weakness of the doctrine in common-law cases. He ascribes this weakness to an influx of judges who are "quite comfortable simply overruling precedents which they are unable to rerationalize." *Id.* at 5.

49. Maltz, *supra* note 15, at 370–74.

50. *Id.* at 386.

51. *See generally* Monaghan, *Our Perfect Constitution,* 56 N.Y.U. L. Rev. 353, 387 (1981).

52. Maltz, *supra* note 15, at 371.

53. I have discussed the issues of *stare decisis* and morality in the law first because they seem to be the initial and most immediately apparent questions pertaining to Brennan's and Marshall's repeated dissents. However, I view them as part of the larger issue of the proper role of the judge, a very large issue that has engendered endless debate. All I attempt to do here is to outline general arguments.

54. 163 U.S. 537 (1896).

55. Bowen, *Dissenting Opinions,* 17 Green Bag 690, 697 (1905).

56. A permutation of this idea appears in Easterbrook, *supra* note 40, at 828–29. Judge Easterbrook does not argue that there are no out-of-bounds choices for justices. He "would argue vigorously that the Court must discover and carry out the design of any given provision; that cost-benefit and moral concerns play no legitimate role in the process . . . [and] that the 'evolution' of society after a provision has

been drafted should be ignored by the Court." *Id.* at 828 (citations omitted). He does, however, argue that there is no way of ruling any set of choices that Supreme Court justices might make to be out of bounds. This is so because there is no one authorized to refuse to count the votes of a justice who selects an inadmissible option. "To decide what is out of bounds is effectively to decide the case before the Court; the body that made the out-of-bounds decision for the Justices would acquire its problems as well." *Id.*

Similarly, H.L.A. Hart has written that "a supreme tribunal has the last word in saying what the law is and, when it has said it, the statement that the court was 'wrong' has no consequences within the system; no one's rights or duties are thereby altered." HART, *supra* note 21. However, he also says that "at any given moment judges, even those of a supreme court, are parts of a system the rules of which are determinate enough at the centre to supply standards of correct judicial decision. These are regarded by the courts as something which they are not free to disregard. . . ." *Id.* at 141–42.

57. *E.g.,* HART, *supra* note 21, at 121–50; RAZ, THE AUTHORITY OF LAW 180–209 (1979); B. CARDOZO, THE NATURE OF THE JUDICIAL PROCESS 112–14 (1921).

58. Sierra Club v. Morton, 405 U.S. 727 (1972) (appendix to opinion of Douglas, J., dissenting) (extract from oral argument of the solicitor general).

59. Brennan, *supra* note 29, at 437.

60. Chief Justice Taney once stated to a colleague, "I don't approve of dissents generally, for I think in many cases where I differ from the majority, it is more important to stand by the Court and give its judgment weight than merely to record my individual dissent." MASON, WILLIAM HOWARD TAFT: CHIEF JUSTICE 223–24 (1965).

For citations to the related issue of criticism of plurality decisions, *see* Easterbrook, *supra* note 40, at 804 n.3.

61. *See generally* NONET & SELZNICK, LAW AND SOCIETY IN TRANSITION: TOWARD RESPONSIVE LAW (1978).

62. *Id.* Professors Nonet and Selznick call this kind of law "autonomous law." They include within autonomous law the legal theories of positivists Hans Kelsen and H.L.A. Hart and natural-law theorist Lon Fuller. *Id.* at 18.

Among other theories that seem to fit is that of John Hart. Dean Ely has suggested that the legitimate role of the Court in constitutional adjudication ought to be to ensure that all individuals have procedural access to the system. "[T]he general theory is one that bounds judicial review under the Constitution's open-ended provisions by insisting that it can appropriately concern itself with questions of participation, and not with the substantive merits of the political choice under attack." *Ely, supra* note 26, at 181.

I have used the model set forth by Professors Nonet and Selznick because it seems to help in understanding the motivation of both those who favor the use of the repeated dissent and those who find its use to be undesirable. I do not adopt their particular point of view, which is within sociological jurisprudence.

I also do not suggest that those who adhere to what Professors Nonet and Selznick call "autonomous law" are somehow uninterested in achieving substantive justice. First, it is difficult to draw an absolute line between procedure and substance, no matter how helpful it may be to try; they inform each other. Second, the judiciary is just one part of our legal system. While a legal theory may view the role of the judiciary as restricted to obtaining procedural fairness, it nevertheless sees the overall goal of a legal system as substantive justice.

63. NONET & SELZNICK, *supra* note 61, at 57.

64. *Id.* at 60.

65. The danger of this kind of legal system is that it is "vulnerable to formalism and legalism." *Id.* at 16.

66. *Id.* at 18. Professors Nonet and Selznick cast Lon Fuller's natural-law theory within "autonomous law." Fuller's theory is a kind of minimalist natural-law theory that is concerned with the legitimacy of the legal system as a whole, and not necessarily with individual laws. Thus it is more concerned with procedural aspects of the law than with its substance, and fits within "autonomous law."

67. Professors Nonet and Selznick term these "responsive law" and include among them legal realism and sociological jurisprudence. *Id.* at 73.

Although I discuss these two kinds of legal theories as distinct categories, they are not mutually exclusive. "[A]ny given legal order or legal institution is likely to have a 'mixed' character, incorporating aspects of all . . . types of law." *Id.* at 17.

68. *Id.* at 74.

69. *Id.* at 73–113.

70. Professor Monaghan, who takes a "relatively narrow view of judicial authority under the Constitution," casts aspersions on "the new breed of social engineers who are assuming judicial office in increasing numbers." Monaghan, *supra* note 47, at 1, 7, 5.

The problem accompanying a result-oriented legal system is, of course, the risk of unchecked judicial discretion. Professors Nonet and Selznick recognize this problem and attempt to solve it by saying that the integrity of an institution is protected when the institution is strongly committed to a distinctive mission. "Purposes set standards for criticizing established practice . . . [and] can control administrative discretion." *See* NONET & SELZNICK, *supra* note 61, at 76–77.

71. Because of the complexity and great variety of the topic, this examination can only be preliminary. Since I cannot explore all of American legal thought within this subsection I have rather arbitrarily limited its scope. I examine positivism, sociological jurisprudence, legal realism, the legal theories of a loosely defined group that includes H. Wechsler, J.H. Ely, and J. Choper (each of whom has examined the role of the Supreme Court), natural-law theory, and the Critical Legal Studies movement. Even with such limitation, it is impossible to explore more than a few facets in each area or to characterize accurately the beliefs of all of the proponents of a particular school of thought.

72. Natural-law views were widely held in the United States during the Revolu-

tionary period and have had a lasting impact on our law through the form given to the Constitution.

> For the generation that framed the Constitution, the concept of a "higher law," protecting "natural rights," and taking precedence over ordinary positive law as a matter of political obligation, was widely shared and deeply felt. An essential element of American constitutionalism was the reduction to written form—and hence to positive law—of some of the principles of natural rights. But at the same time, it was generally recognized that written constitutions could not completely codify the higher law. Thus in the framing of the original American constitutions it was widely accepted that there remained unwritten but still binding principles of higher law.—Grey, *Do We Have an Unwritten Constitution?*, 27 STAN. L. REV. 703, 715–16 (1975).

73. PASSERIN D'ENTREVES, NATURAL LAW: A HISTORICAL SURVEY 116 (1965).

74. For an overview and comparison of natural-law, legal positivist, and social good (utilitarian) philosophies and philosophers, *see* BIRD, THE IDEA OF JUSTICE (1967).

75. PASSERIN D'ENTREVES, *supra* note 73, at 117. Many natural-law philosophers have found such fundamental values in innate characteristics of human nature or in essential human rights. Modern representatives of natural-law theories grounded in rights are R. DWORKIN, TAKING RIGHTS SERIOUSLY 1978); R. DWORKIN, LAW'S EMPIRE (1986); FINNIS, NATURAL LAW AND NATURAL RIGHTS (1981); and J. RAWLS, A THEORY OF JUSTICE (1971).

76. D'Amato, *Lon Fuller and Substantive Natural Law*, 26 AM. J. JURIS. 202, 215 (1981).

77. *Id.* at 215.

78. For example, Lon Fuller espoused a natural-law theory that may be termed procedural. According to Fuller, a legal system will fail where: issues are decided on an ad hoc basis rather than by rules; there is a failure to publicize or make available to the affected party the rules he or she is expected to observe; legislation is applied retroactively; the rules are not made understandable; contradictory rules are enacted; rules require conduct beyond the powers of the affected party; the rules are frequently changed so that the subject cannot orient his or her action by them; or there is a failure of congruence between the rules as announced and their actual administration. L. FULLER, THE MORALITY OF LAW 33 (1964).

79. Johnson, *Some Thoughts About Natural Law*, 75 CAL. L. REV. 217, 218 (1987).

80. *Id.*

81. *Id.*

82. May, *The Meaning and Nature of the Natural Law in Thomas Aquinas*, 22 AM. J. JURIS. 168, 170–71 (1977).

83. Johnson, *supra* note 79, at 218–19. Professor Johnson adds: "The embarrassment of asserting supposedly self-evident principles in an intellectual atmosphere in which everything is automatically called into question makes us try to get by on as

few such principles as possible—hence the prevalence in our day of natural law systems that are based on a single governing concept: economic efficiency, equality, neutrality, autonomy (neutral conversation), or utility." *Id.* at 219.

84. McCauliff, *Constitutional Jurisprudence of History and Natural Law: Complementary or Rival Modes of Discourse?*, 24 CAL. W.L. REV. 287, 321 (1988) (citing Gewirth, *The Ontological Basis of Natural Law: A Critique and an Alternative*, 29 AM. J. JURIS. 95, 96 (1984)).

85. *E.g., Furman v. Georgia*, 408 U.S. 238, 257–306 (1972) (Brennan, J., concurring).

86. Justice Brennan ascribed a similar philosophy to his colleague in dissent, Justice Marshall. Compare the language of Brennan, *How Goes the Supreme Court?*, 36 MERCER L. REV. 781, 787–88 (1985) [hereinafter Brennan, *How Goes the Supreme Court?*], to that in Brennan, *Justice Thurgood Marshall: Advocate for Human Need in American Jurisprudence*, 40 MD. L. REV. 390 (1981) [hereinafter Brennan, *Justice Thurgood Marshall*]. However, where Brennan's death penalty jurisprudence was openly aspirational, Justice Marshall's had an instrumentalist cast. Marshall's dissent in *Gregg v. Georgia*, 428 U.S. 153, 231–41 (1976), turned on the idea that the death penalty is cruel and unusual because it is excessive and serves no valid legislative purpose where life imprisonment would do as well. I discuss Marshall's jurisprudence in more detail below in connection with sociological jurisprudence.

87. Brennan, *How Goes the Supreme Court?, supra* note 86, at 786–88.

88. *Id.* at 787–88 (citation omitted).

89. *Id.* Brennan calls positivism "a notion of law wholly unconcerned with the broader extralegal values pursued by society at large or by the individual. It lived in a heaven of abstract technicalities and legal forms, and found its answers to human problems in an aggregation of already existing rules, or found to answers at all." *Id.* at 787.

"[S]ociological jurisprudence too had a defect: 'While it shifted the emphasis away from positivism . . . it did so at the expense of reality by substituting the abstract idea of society for the actuality of the individual human beings who constitute society in fact.'" *Id.* (quoting Rooney, *Report of Committee on New Trends in Comparative Jurisprudence and Legal Philosophy*, 1964 A.B.A. SEC. OF INT'L & COMP. L. 195).

90. *Id.* at 788 (emphasis added). Brennan's natural-law philosophy was explored in McCauliff, *supra* note 84, at 287. Professor McCauliff contrasts the historical approach of Justice Burger to a natural-law approach of Justice Brennan with respect to their first amendment jurisprudence. Although fairly hostile to the use of natural law in constitutional adjudication, Professor McCauliff makes some observations that seem to apply equally well to Brennan's death penalty dissents. For example, he stated that "Jutice Brennan is less patient with indirect, experiential extraction of jurisprudential values from history. He presents his own public distillation of constitutional values, and directly applies them as absolute principles in the context of case-by-case claims of constitutional guarantees." *Id.* at 287. Brennan, of course, insisted that the meaning of the "cruel and unusual" punishments clause is that punishments

must comport with the overriding principle of human dignity. *Furman v. Georgia,* 408 U.S. 238, 257–306 (1972) (Brennan, J., concurring). "The constant for Americans, for our ancestors, for ourselves, and we hope for future generations, is our commitment to the constitutional ideal of libertarian dignity protected through the law." Brennan, *Justice Thurgood Marshall, supra* note 86, at 394.

Professor McCauliff also noted that "[a]dherence to natural law frees Justice Brennan from the constraints of history"; he compares his jurisprudence to that of Justice Stephen Field, who "often urged a move away from immediate precedent by couching his opinions in terms of natural law." McCauliff, *supra* note 84, at 290, 291. "[T]he use of natural law in opinion writing is ideal for setting forth a new departure from the precedential *status quo.* It simply does not matter if the view set forth is currently out of fashion[,] because a natural law position claims for itself, not historical development, but unchanging validity. According to natural law theory, although society may have in error departed from that view sanctioned by natural law, the erroneous departure does not, to the natural law jurist, signify challenge to the validity of its principles but merely underscores the human error of that departure. Thus the validity of the principle remains untouched." *Id.* at 333.

"While Justice Brennan's jurisprudence is not derived from history but from abstract principles of natural law, the historical survival of exceptional practices which deviate from those principles does not carry weight with Justice Brennan. The practices are simply long-standing wrongs which can now be righted by the application of the proper principles." *Id.* at 328. Finally, "Justice Brennan always puts forth his own consistent position, even if he must assert his views in lone dissent." *Id.* at 331.

91. Brennan, *Justice Thurgood Marshall, supra* note 86, at 394.

92. Austin's works include J. Austin, The Province of Jurisprudence Determined (1832); J. Austin, Lectures on Jurisprudence, or the Philosophy of Positive Law (1863); J. Austin, Essay on the Uses of the Study of Jurisprudence (1863).

93. Hart, *Positivism and the Separation of Law and Morals,* 71 Harv. L. Rev. 593, 594 (1958).

94. *E.g.,* Holmes, *supra* note 21, at 167.

95. J. Austin, The Province of Jurisprudence Determined 184–85 (Library of Ideas 1954) (1832).

96. Hart, *supra* note 93, at 599.

97. Austin, *supra* note 95, at 184–85.

98. Wise, *supra* note 36, at 1049.

99. *Id.* at 1048.

100. 1 W. Blackstone, Commentaries 70–71. *See also* Brennan, *How Goes the Supreme Court?, supra* note 86, at 786 ("When the common law flourished greatly, law was merged . . . with the other disciplines and sources of human value. Custom, for example, was the cherished source of the common law of that time. What was declared custom but the accumulated wisdom of social problems of society itself?

The function of law was to formalize and preserve this wisdom, but it certainly did not purport to originate it.").

101. H.L.A. Hart held the Chair in Jurisprudence at Oxford University until 1969.

102. HART, *supra* note 21, at 78–79.

103. *Id.*

104. *Id.* at 79.

105. *Id.*

106. *Id.* Hart distinguishes among three kinds of secondary rules. *Id.* at 92–94. The first is the "rule of recognition." This is a rule for conclusive identification of the primary rules of obligation. *Id.* at 92. In a developed legal system, the rule of recognition will be complex; it may identify primary rules by reference to some characteristic they possess, such as having been enacted by a specific body, long customary practice, or their relation to judicial decision. *Id.*

The next kind of secondary rules in Hart's scheme are the "rules of change." *Id.* at 93. These provide for the introduction of new rules and for the elimination of old ones. *Id.* Such rules may specify who may legislate and what procedures are to be followed. *Id.* There is a close connection between the rules of change and the rule of recognition; where rules of change exist, the rule of recognition will include legislation as a means of identifying primary rules. *Id.*

"Rules of adjudication" are the last kind of secondary rule. *Id.* at 94. These confer authority on individuals to make authoritative determinations of whether a particular primary rule has been broken. *Id.* These rules identify those who are to adjudicate and the procedures to be followed. Hart points out that a system which has rules of adjudication is committed to a rule of recognition. *Id.* This is so because, where courts can make authoritative determinations that a rule has been broken, they also necessarily make authoritative determinations of what the rules are. *Id.* at 94–95.

107. *Id.* at 124.

108. *Id.* at 121.

109. *Id.* at 124–25.

110. *Id.* at 131.

111. *Id.*

112. *Id.* at 132. Hart compares that function to the exercise of delegated rule-making powers by an administrative body. *Id.*

Although later criticism of Austinian positivism was based on the idea that it took a "mechanical" view of the judicial process, even Austin realized that at times judges must legislate. "I cannot understand how any person who has considered the subject can suppose that society could possibly have gone on if judges had not legislated." AUSTIN, *supra* note 95, at 191.

113. *Id.* at 132.

114. *Id.*

115. Raz distinguishes between judicial lawmaking and legislation, stating that there are no pure judicial law-creating cases. Judges' law-creating powers are limited.

Additionally, judge-made law is constantly subject to revision, and in this sense can be said to be less binding than enacted law. J. RAZ, THE AUTHORITY OF LAW 195 (1979). Finally, judicial lawmaking tends to be piecemeal; judges avoid making broad statements of principles. *Id.* at 198.

116. *Id.* at 181. In unregulated cases, the law may, however, rule out some solutions as inappropriate and offer some guidance as to the choice among some or all of the remaining possible solutions. *Id.* "Unregulated cases are partly, not wholly, unregulated." *Id.* at 195.

117. *Id.* at 182.

118. *Id.* at 181.

119. *Id.* at 182.

120. *Id.*

121. *Id.* at 195.

122. *Id.* at 185.

123. Raz states that there are two kinds of cases of overruling. A superior court may overrule the rule of an inferior court, or a court may overrule its own previous decision. He finds that the power to overrule is necessarily limited to certain courts; otherwise the legal system would not recognize the binding power of precedents. *Id.* at 189–90.

124. *Id.* at 191.

125. *Id.* at 190. Raz states that when courts exercise their lawmaking power, they should "act as one expects Parliament to act, i.e., by adopting the best rules they can find." *Id.* at 197. In response to the criticism that courts do not have lawmaking power because they are not democratically elected, Raz says that, given the supremacy of Parliament in Great Britain, judge-made law is no more undemocratic that much delegated legislation. *Id.* at 197–98. In the United States, of course, some constitutional cases cannot be reversed by the legislative branch. Raz notes that the justification for such powers resting in the Supreme Court is then bound up with the justification for having a Constitution that limits the power of the majority. *Id.* at 198 n. 17.

126. *Id.* at 190.

127. *Id.* at 191.

128. *Id.* at 197. Raz recognizes, but does not directly address, the fact that there may be other legal duties which courts are bound to observe that "may prevent them from adopting the best rule and may force them on occasion to settle for second best." *Id.*

129. *Id.* at 199. Raz recognizes moral restrictions on judges that do not apply to legislators. These stem from the piecemeal manner in which judge-made law changes existing law. Thus, the judge has to weigh any changes in the law against the possibility that they will result in pragmatically inconsistent law. This leads to courts being generally, although not always, conservative in their attempts at law reform. Raz finds this conservatism to be justified only at some times. *Id.* at 200–01.

130. *Id.* at 108.

131. HART, *supra* note 21, at 138.

132. According to Hart, a legal system gives up infallibility for the advantages of being able to reach final decisions. HART, *Id.* at 139.

This is apart from any consideration of the potential threat to a legal system when judges fail to abide by the correct standards of judicial decision on more than an incidental or exceptional basis. Hart analogizes the court to the scorer of a game, where his rulings are authoritative and final. However, Hart points out, the scoring rule for the particular game remains what it was before there was a scorer, and it is the scorer's duty to apply the rule as best he can. If he repudiates the scoring rule and makes repeated aberrant findings at his own discretion, there will come a point when the players will no longer accept the scorer's rulings or, if they do accept them, when the game has changed. Hart calls the new game "scorer's discretion." Similarly, judges are parts of a system of rules that is determinate enough to supply standards of correct judicial decision. They must adhere to the standards in order to maintain them, but the judges do not make the rules. *Id.* at 138–44.

133. *Id.* at 132.

134. *Id.*

135. Kelman, *supra* note 1, at 265.

136. This is a very unsatisfactory conclusion. One cannot help but feel that Hart's scheme does not sufficiently address overruling of precedent—it would allow a court to distinguish a law to the point where it is no longer a law, but prohibit a direct overruling.

Furthermore, Hart recognizes that the secondary rules of a legal system include rules of change. HART, *supra* note 21, at 93. In our legal system, it is not only legislatures that change the law—we must also take account of a majority of five justices of the Supreme Court. Where, then, does one draw the theoretical line between two justices and five justices voting to change the law?

137. "Deep conviction" may be, as Professor Kelman has stated, "the fuel that drives dissent past the limits of hope, beyond appeal to the intelligence of a future day, and into the realm of the quixotic. . . . *But the other factor behind continued dissent is distinctly the child of hope.*" Kelman, *supra* note 1, at 257 (emphasis added).

138. G. GILMORE, THE AGES OF AMERICAN LAW 62 (1977).

139. *Id.*

140. *Id.* at 69 n.4.

141. Pound, *Mechanical Jurisprudence,* 8 COLUM. L. REV. 605 (1908).

142. *Id.* For Pound, judicial discretion was a part of any legal system.

> Probably it is true that even in the earliest and rudest justice the will of the judge is not exercised entirely as such, wholly free from the constraint of acknowledged rules of action or principles of decision. On the other hand it is equally true that in no legal system, however minute and detailed its body of rules, is justice administered wholly by rule, without any recourse to the will of the judge and his personal sense of what should be done to achieve justice in the cause before him. Both elements

are to be found in all administration of justice. But sometimes, as in oriental justice, the one element preponderates; at other times, as in Europe and America of the nineteenth century, the other element all but holds the whole field.—Pound, *Justice According to Law,* 13 COLUM. L. REV. 696, 713 (1913) [hereinafter Pound, *Justice According to Law*].

Pound later qualified his attack on mechanical jurisprudence. He found that such an application of the law is appropriate in both property law and commercial transactions. His rationale was that there was no need in these areas for judicial discretion, as "the social interests in security of acquisitions and security of transactions—the economic side of human activity in civilized society—call for rule or conception authoritatively prescribed in advance and mechanically applied." Pound, *The Theory of Judicial Decision,* 36 HARV. L. REV. 940, 957 (1923) [hereinafter Pount, *Theory of Judicial Decision*]. "In matters of property and commercial law . . . mechanical application of fixed, detailed rules or of rigid deductions from fixed conceptions is a wise social engineering." R. POUND, INTERPRETATION OF LEGAL HISTORY 154 (1923).

For an article connecting the development of sociological jurisprudence and legal realism to the American Progressive movement and the New Deal respectively, *see* T. WHITE, FROM SOCIOLOGICAL JURISPRUDENCE TO REALISM; JURISPRUDENCE AND SOCIAL CHANGE IN EARLY TWENTIETH-CENTURY AMERICA, *reprinted in* PATTERNS OF AMERICAN LEGAL THOUGHT 99 (1978).

143. Pound, *Do We Need a Philosophy of Law?,* 5 COLUM, L. REV. 339, 344, 351 (1905).

144. Pound, *Liberty of Contract,* 18 YALE L.J. 454, 464 (1909).

145. Pound, *supra* note 141, at 605.

146. Pound, *supra* note 144, at 457.

147. Pound, *Law in Books and Law in Action,* 44 AM. L. REV. 12 (1910). Holmes expressed a similar point of view: "I think that the judges themselves have failed adequately to recognize their duty of weighing considerations of social advantage. The duty is inevitable, and the result of the often proclaimed judicial aversion to deal with such considerations is simply to leave the very ground and foundation of judgments inarticulate, and often unconscious." HOLMES, *supra* note 21, at 184.

148. R. POUND, CONTEMPORARY JURISTIC THEORY 82 (1940). According to Pound, the legal order must take account of individual, public, and social interests. *Id.* at 61. Of course, not every claim can be recognized, so the law must classify claims, select those which are to be recognized, and fix the limits within which they will be given effect, as none can be recognized fully, in view of other recognized claims. *Id.* at 59.

149. Pound, *Theory of Judicial Decision, supra* note 142, at 941, 955.

150. *Id.* at 958.

151. *Id.*

152. POUND, *supra* note 148, at 83.

153. *Id.*

154. Contemporary sociological jurisprudence can be divided into two camps.

One includes those who believe that how the law *ought* to behave is beyond the jurisdiction of sociology. Donald Black is a leading proponent of this theory. *See* DONALD BLACK, Sociological Justice (1989). Under this view, the proper sociological perspective is that of an observer of the social characteristics or "social structure" of a case. *Id.* at 7, 20. Sociological principles can predict and explain the outcome of a particular case. *Id.* at 20. But "a purely sociological approach to law should involve not an assessment of legal policy, but rather, a scientific analysis of legal life as a system of behavior." Black, *The Boundaries of Legal Sociology,* 81 YALE L.J. 1086, 1087 (1972). It is thus not surprising that Black describes himself as "an uncompromising adherent of the positivist approach." Black, Book Review, 78 AM. J. SOC. 709 (1972). It might be said that Black's view of legal sociology is not in fact a jurisprudential view at all. This is the thrust of an article by Philippe Nonet in which he faults Black for his insistence on separating sociology from normative philosophy. Nonet, *For Jurispruden-tial Sociology,* 1976 LAW & SOC'Y 525.

Pound's "jurisprudence of ends" characterizes the sociological jurisprudence of the other camp. Phillip Selznick and Philippe Nonet are two proponents of this position. For adherents of this point of view, empirical study of legal institutions is but a means to an end. A legal system should be more than procedurally fair; "it should help define the public interest and be committed to the achievement of substantive justice." NONET & SELZNICK, *supra* note 61, at 74. Under this view, sociological jurisprudence is legitimately evaluative. It sets normative standards and uses impirical data to assess the competency and limitations of different kinds of legal institutions. Nonet, *supra* at 544: "[S]ociology must have redeeming value for policy" rather than "stand[ing] on its theoretical merits along." *Id.* at 529 (emphasis omitted).

155. Selznick, *The Sociology of Law,* 9 INTERNATIONAL ENCYCLOPEDIA OF THE SO-CIAL SCIENCES 50, 53, (1972).

156. *Id.* at 53.

157. *Id.*

158. *Id.* at 52.

159. *Id.* at 54.

160. *Id.*

161. *Id.* Other sources of institutionalized criticism within the Anglo-American legal tradition are the availability of counsel and the adversary concept of the legal process. *Id.*

162. *Id.* at 53.

163. Justice Cardozo has also been labeled a legal realist.

164. CARDOZO, *supra* note 57, at 149–50 (citations omitted). Justice Cardozo added that "we have had to do this sometimes in the field of constitutional law." *Id.* at 150.

165. Pound, *supra* note 141, at 605. *See* Daniels, *Non Occides: Thurgood Marshall and the Death Penalty,* S. TEX. L.J. 243, 260, for a discussion that compares Justice Marshall's death penalty jurisprudence to the jurisprudence of Justice Cardozo. The latter wrote: "Few rules in our time are so well established that they may not be

called upon any day to justify their existence as means adapted to an end. If they do not function, they are diseased. If they are diseased, they must not propagate their kind." CARDOZO, *supra* note 57, at 98 (quoted by Daniels, *supra* at 252).

166. Daniels, *supra* note 165, at 260.

167. Justice Marshall considers six conceivable purposes for imposing the death penalty: retribution, deterrence, preventing repetitive criminal acts, encouraging guilty pleas and confessions, eugenics, and economy. *Furman v. Georgia,* 408 U.S. at 343 (Marshall, J., concurring). He eliminates each. In particular, he finds that retribution by itself is not a legitimate goal of punishment, because "the Eighth Amendment itself was adopted to prevent punishment from becoming synonymous with vengeance." *Id.; see also Gregg v. Georgia,* 428 U.S. at 236–42 (Marshall, J., dissenting). Additionally, he rejects arguments that the death penalty is a necessary deterrent to crime in our society. In *Furman,* Justice Marshall cites research that appears to support the idea that the death penalty is no more effective a deterrent than life imprisonment. *Furman,* 408 U.S. at 345–54. In *Gregg,* he critiques a study that purports to demonstrate that the death penalty is a greater deterrent than life imprisonment and concludes that the study is not convincing. *Gregg,* 428 U.S. at 233–36. The death penalty is therefore excessive because there is no rational reason to prefer it to life imprisonment as a deterrent to crime.

168. *Furman,* 408 U.S. at 332 (Marshall, J., concurring).

169. Selznick, *supra* note 155, at 53.

170. *Gregg,* 428 U.S. at 232 (Marshall, J., dissenting).

171. In Llewellyn, *Some Realism About Realism—Responding to Dean Pound,* 44 HARV. L. REV. 1222 (1931), Llewellyn attempts to characterize the work of legal realists. He insists that legal realism is a movement rather than a school. "A *group* philosophy or program, a *group* credo of social welfare, these realists have not. They are not a group." *Id.* at 1256.

172. *Id.* at 1237 (Legal realism is characterized by "[d]istrust of traditional legal rules and concepts insofar as they purport to *describe* what either courts or people are actually doing."); J. Frank, *Are Judges Human?,* 80 U. PA. L. REV. 17, 40 (1931) ("Rules, whether stated by judges or others, whether in statutes, opinions or textbooks by learned authors, are not the Law, but are only some among many of the sources to which judges go in making the law of the cases tried before them.").

173. Llewellyn stated that one of the "common points of departure" among realists is the "*temporary* divorce of Is and Ought for purposes of study." Llewellyn, *supra* note 171, at 1235–36. By this he meant that realists attempt to study the law objectively without being swayed by their views of what the law should be. "[T]he intrusion of Ought-spectacles *during the investigation of the facts* [makes] it very difficult to see what is being done." *Id.* at 1237. But Llewellyn recognized law as a means to social ends, not as an end in itself—"any part [of the law] needs constantly to be examined for its purpose, and for its effect, and to be judged in the light of both and of their relation to each other." *Id.* at 1236.

An example of an extreme realist point of view is presented in Nowak, *Realism,*

*Nihilism, and the Supreme Court: Do the Emperors Have Nothing but Robes?*, 22 WASH-BURN L.J. 246, 249 (1983). Professor Nowak divorces the realist approach entirely from any discussion of the "ought." "My premise . . . is that constitutional law is what Supreme Court justices do. It is no more, no less. There are no demonstrably right or wrong decisions." *Id.* (citation omitted). "The realist focus on power eliminated any basis for normative review of court rulings. Case decisions could be explained, but not proved right or wrong." *Id.* at 252.

174. Llewellyn and Frank are not necessarily the most representative figures of the movement. I discuss them here because they were the most adamant in seeing their views as a part of a movement, and because their positions received the most attention within the legal community. White, *From Sociological Jurisprudence to Realism: Jurisprudence and Social Change in Early Twentieth-Century America,* 58 VA. L. REV. 999 (1972), *reprinted in Patterns of American Legal Thought* 99, 121 (1978).

175. Llewellyn, *A Realistic Jurisprudence—The Next Step,* 30 COLUM. L. REV. 431, 464 (1930).

176. *Id.* at 449.

177. *Id.* at 447–48.

178. *Id.*

179. *Id.* at 464.

180. J. Frank, *Law and the Modern Mind,* 111 ("Law may vary with the personality of the judge who happens to pass upon any given case.").

181. Frank, *supra* note 172, at 28.

182. *Id.* Frank cited *United States v. Shipp,* 214 U.S. 386 (1908), where a pure question of fact was presented. The Court appointed a commissioner to take testimony and report it without comment. On the basis of the written testimony, the decision of the Court was split five to three on the question of fact. The two sides came to opposite conclusions, with each stating that theirs was the only conclusion to be drawn from the evidence.

183. *Id.* at 41.

184. They received support for this belief from Judge Hutcheson in *The Judgment Intuitive: The Function of the "Hunch" in Judicial Decision,* 14 CORNELL L.Q. 274, 278 (1928) ("I decide the case more or less offhand and by rule of thumb.") According to the judge, "the vital, motivating impulse for the decision is an intuitive sense of what is right or wrong for that cause, and . . . the astute judge, having so decided, enlists his every faculty and belabors his laggard mind, not only to justify that intuition to himself, but to make it pass muster with his critics." *Id.* at 285.

185. Llewellyn, *supra* note 171, at 1238–39.

186. Frank, *supra* note 172, at 37.

187. Llewellyn, *supra* note 171, at 1252–53.

188. *Id.* at 1253.

189. According to Llewellyn, "[T]he line of inquiry via rationalization has come close to demonstrating that in any case doubtful enough to make litigation respectable the available authoritative premises—*i.e.,* premises legitimate and impeccable

under the traditional legal techniques—are at least two, and that the two are mutually contradictory as applied to the case in hand. Which opens the question of what made the court select the one available premise rather than the other." *Id.* at 1239.

190. *Id.* at 1252–53.

191. *Id.* at 1253. Thus, a judge's blinding herself to policy considerations should have no more "sanctity" than any other way of working with precedent. She has chosen, for whatever reason, not to look at policy. *Id.*

192. J. FRANK, Courts on Trial: Myth and Reality in American Justice 275 (1949). Frank cites three devices that judges use to avoid applying a precedent they regard as undesirable: the "distinguishing" or "precise question" device, where the judge states that the rule in a prior case must be limited to the "precise question" involved in that earlier case; "verbal stability," or the act or pretending to preserve an old rule by keeping it verbally but stuffing the words of the rule with new meaning so that it becomes a new rule; and the "ratio decidendi" device, where the judge claims that the authoritative part of a decision is not the decision itself or the rule on which that decision was based, but the ratio decidendi, or right principle, which lies behind both. *Id.* at 275–80. Frank concludes that for precedential purposes a case means only what a judge in any later case says it means. It is authoritative only if the judge decides it is authoritative. Therefore, the doctrine or theory of *stare decisis* is very different than its actual application by judges. *Id.* at 279–80.

193. *Id.* at 265–71.

194. *Id.* at 271.

195. Frank, *supra* note 172, at 31; Llewellyn, *supra* note 175, at 431, 463 ("[A]s soon as one turns from the formulation of ideals to their realization, the [legal realist] approach here indicated is vital to his making headway. It is only in terms of a sound descriptive science of law . . . that ideals move beyond the stage of dreams.").

196. Llewellyn, *supra* note 171, at 1254–55 ("When the matter of *program in the normative aspect is raised,* the answer is: *there is none.*").

197. According to Professor White, the place of morals or ethics in the law was one of the two main issues on which Pound and Frank and Llewellyn sharply disagreed. The other was the worth of legal rules. WHITE, FROM SOCIOLOGICAL JURISPRUDENCE TO REALISM; JURISPRUDENCE AND SOCIAL CHANGE IN EARLY TWENTIETH-CENTURY AMERICA, *reprinted in* PATTERNS OF AMERICAN LEGAL THOUGHT 125 (1978).

198. Llewellyn, *supra* note 171, at 1254.

199. *Id.* at 1249.

200. *Id.*

201. Schmidhauser, *Stare Decisis, Dissent, and the Background of the Justices of the Supreme Court of the United States,* 14 TORONTO L.J. 194 (1962).

202. At least one commentator has stated that these writers "typify the neutral principles theorists." Nowak, *supra* note 173, at 253. Professor Nowak recognized that Professor Choper may not belong in the neutral-principles school, but grouped him with the others because of his work on the institutional role of the Supreme Court.

203. A. Bickel, The Least Dangerous Branch 16 (1962).

204. Wechsler, *Toward Neutral Principles of Constitutional Law*, 73 Harv. L. Rev. 1 (1959). For a discussion of Wechsler's neutral-principles theory as a part of what Henry Hart and Albert Sacks termed "reasoned elaboration," *see* White, The Evolution of Reasoned Elaboration: Jurisprudential Criticism and Social Change, *reprinted in* Patterns of American Legal Thought 136 (1978).

205. Wechsler, *supra* note 204, at 19.

206. *Id.* at 12.

207. *Id.* at 16.

208. *Id.* at 15.

209. *Id.* at 19.

210. *Id.* at 20–22.

211. *Id.* at 20–21.

212. *Id.* at 21.

213. *Id.*

214. Ely, *supra* note 26.

215. *Id.* at 87. Ely contends that there is no satisfactory method of finding "fundamental values" embedded in the open-ended clauses of the Constitution. *See generally id.* at 43–72.

216. *Id.*

217. *Id.* at 87.

218. *Id.* at 181.

219. *Id.* at 117.

220. *See id.* at 105–34.

221. *See id.* at 135–79.

222. *Id.* at 176.

223. 107 S. Ct. 1756, 1781 (1987) (Brennan, J., dissenting). Justice Brennan was joined in dissent by Justice Marshall, and by Justices Stevens and Blackmun in part.

224. J. Choper, Judicial Review and the National Political Process 64 (1980). This has been dubbed the "*Carolene Products* footnote 4 approach to constitutional law" by Professor Nowak. Nowak, *supra* note 173, at 253–54.

225. Choper, *supra* note 224, at 68.

226. *Id.* at 69.

227. *Id.* at 129–71.

228. *Id.* at 170.

229. *Id.* at 129–30.

230. *Id.* at 169, 175, 263.

231. *Id.* at 168.

232. *Id.*

233. *Id.*

234. *Id.*

235. Tushnet, *Critical Legal Studies: An Introduction to Its Origins and Underpinnings*, 36 J. Legal Educ. 505 (1986).

236. *Id.* at 510.

237. *Id.* at 506.

238. Fischl, *Some Realism About Critical Legal Studies,* 41 U. Miami L. Rev. 505, 525 (1987).

239. *Id.* at 525.

240. *Id.* at 524. Tushnet states that a second intellectual support for Critical Legal Studies is the progressive tradition in American historiography.

> The progressive historians, including Charles Beard and Vernon Parrington, argued that the best way to understand the course of American history was to pay attention to the play of interest groups in American society. Much of their work was devoted to debunking the claims of filiopietistic writers that the best way to understand the course of American history was as the working out of the idea of progress within a generally liberal political framework. The progressive historians looked at American policies and politics and saw much more of economic interest at work; for that they were, rather like CLS people today, called Marxists.—Tushnet, *supra* note 235, at 506 (citations omitted).

241. Of "liberalism," Kelman states: "While some CLS writers try to define what they mean by liberalism at considerable length . . . , more often 'liberalism' is little more than a very loose term for the dominant postfeudal beliefs held across all but the left and right fringes of the political spectrum." M. Kelman, A Guide to Critical Legal Studies 2 (1987).

242. *Id.* at 15–113.

243. *Id.* at 15.

244. *Id.*

245. *Id.* at 16.

246. *Id.* Additionally, Duncan Kennedy has posited that the ambivalence over choice of form is rooted in a greater ambivalence over substantive political issues. *Id.* at 16 (citing Kennedy, *Form and Substance in Private Law Adjudication,* 89 Harv. L. Rev. 1685 (1976)). Kennedy has claimed that rules express the substantive ideals of self-reliance and individualism, while standards correspond to the ideal of altruism. *Id.*

247. Kelman, *supra* note 241, at 27.

248. *Id.* at 64.

249. *Id.* at 3, 64–67. I confess that Kelman's discussion of this conflict baffles me. I understand the initial premise, but I could not apply it to save my life.

250. *Id.* at 86.

251. *Id.*

252. *Id.*

253. *Id.* at 87.

254. *Id.* at 89 (citation omitted).

255. *Id.* at 3–4.

256. *Id.* at 4.

257. *Id.* at 16.

258. *Id.* at 66. Kelman concludes that "the commitment to the subjectivity and arbitrariness of preferences implies a commitment to a merely 'facilitative' state, one that does not seek that particular good lives be led but simply allows persons to achieve their own vision of the good." *Id.*

259. *Id.* at 86–87.

260. *Id.* at 4. The dominant position of CLS is, however, *not* that the legal system is tilted in favor of capitalism. Tushnet, *supra* note 235, at 511. One argument in support of this is that rule skepticism makes it impossible to say that the system is tilted in any particular direction. Where judges can reach any conclusion they wish within the system, it is they who may be biased, not the system itself. *Id.*

261. *E.g.,* Tushnet, *Critical Legal Studies and Constitutional Law: An Essay in Deconstruction,* 36 STAN. L. REV. 623 (1984) [hereinafter Tushnet, *Critical Legal Studies and Constitutional Law*]; Tushnet, *Judicial Review,* 7 HARV. J.L. & PUB. POL'Y 77 (1984) [hereinafter Tushnet, *Judicial Review*]; Tushnet, *Darkness on the Edge of Town: The Contributions of John Hart Ely to Constitutional Theory,* 89 YALE L.J. 1037 (1980) [hereinafter Tushnet, *Darkness on the Edge of Town*].

262. Tushnet, *Judicial Review, supra* note 261, at 77.

263. *Id.*

264. *Id.*

265. *Id.*

266. *Id.*

267. *Id.*

268. *See generally* Tushnet, *The Dilemmas of Liberal Constitutionalism,* 42 OHIO ST. L.J. 411 (1981).

269. *Id.* at 412 (citing R. UNGER, KNOWLEDGE AND POLITICS (1975)).

270. *Id.* at 415.

271. *Id.*

272. *Id.*

273. *Id.* at 416 ("[T]hat particular form of check and balance, with Justices arriving and departing at irregular intervals, comes as close to guaranteeing long term incoherence as any institutional arrangement could.").

274. Tushnet, *Judicial Review, supra* note 261, at 79. Tushnet, however, suspects that we each have a threshold beyond which we would find some act to be majoritarian overreaching, thus requiring a quicker response than is available through the political process. *Id.*

275. Tushnet, *supra* note 268, at 424. He would, for example, look to which result would advance the cause of socialism. *Id.*

276. *Id.* at 425.

277. *Id.* at 425–26.

278. *Id.* at 415.

279. R. HALL, THE MORALITY OF CIVIL DISOBEDIENCE 15 (1971).

280. *Id.* at 20.

281. *Id.* at 30.

282. Campbell, *supra* note 5, at 44.

283. *Id.*

284. Schlegel, *Critical Legal Studies for the Intelligent Lawyer,* 60 N.Y. STATE BAR J. 13 (January 1988) (The realists "did not understand that, by arguing that the technique was not determinate and that the premises not authoritative, they were, in effect, undermining the entire structure of liberal political theory. They did not understand that all of a sudden they were opening the theory up to the claim that nothing constrains judicial decision.").

## Chapter 4

1. Garrett Epps, *Donning the Robe,* NATION, Sept. 26, 1994, at 314.

2. Memorandum from Law Clerk to Justice Thurgood Marshall, *Reed v. Florida,* 92–5222, Sept. 4, 1990, Container 397, Folder 12, in Papers of Justice Thurgood Marshall, Manuscripts Division, Library of Congress, Washington, D.C.

3. Memorandum from Law Clerk to Justice Thurgood Marshall, *Fields v. Illinois,* 90–5066, and *Hawkins v. Illinois,* 90–5328, September 11, 1990. Container 397, Folder 12, in Papers of Justice Thurgood Marshall, Manuscripts Division, Library of Congress, Washington, D.C.

4. Memorandum from Justice Thurgood Marshall to Justice John Paul Stevens, *Lankford v. Idaho,* 88–7247, October 11, 1991, Container 397, Folder 12, in Papers of Justice Thurgood Marshall, Manuscripts Division, Library of Congress, Washington, D.C.

5. Memorandum to Justice Thurgood Marshall from Law Clerk, *Lankford v. Idaho,* February 22, 1991, Container 397, Folder 12, in Papers of Justice Thurgood Marshall, Manuscripts Division, Library of Congress, Washington, D.C.

6. Memorandum to the Chief Justice from Thurgood Marshall, *Lankford v. Idaho,* 88–7247, March 5, 1991, Container 397, Folder 12, in Papers of Justice Thurgood Marshall, Manuscripts Division, Library of Congress, Washington, D.C.

7. *Id.*

8. Memorandum from Chief Justice William Rehnquist to Justice Thurgood Marshall, *Lankford v. Idaho,* 88–7247, March 6, 1991, Container 397, Folder 12, in Papers of Justice Thurgood Marshall, Manuscripts Division, Library of Congress, Washington, D.C.

9. Memorandum to Conference from Justice Thurgood Marshall, *Lankford v. Idaho,* 88–7247, March 7, 1991, Container 397, Folder 12, in Papers of Justice Thurgood Marshall, Manuscripts Division, Library of Congress, Washington, D.C.

10. Memorandum from Justice John Paul Stevens to Justice Harry Blackmun, *Lankford v. Idaho,* 88–7247, March 8, 1991, Container 397, Folder 12, in Papers of Justice Thurgood Marshall, Manuscripts Division, Library of Congress, Washington, D.C.

11. Neil A. Lewis, *In Marshall Papers, Rare Glimpse at Court,* N.Y. TIMES, May 25, 1993, at A1.

12. *Id.*

13. *Id.* at A16.

14. *Id.*

15. *Id.*

16. *See generally* R. O'Brien, Storm Center: The Supreme Court in American Politics (1986); B. Woodward and S. Armstrong, The Brethren (1979).

17. Kelman, *The Forked Path of Dissent,* 1985 Sup. Ct. Rev. 227, 263. Professor Kelman offers, as the paradigm of the "one-sided acceptance," the opinion pattern of Justice Black in the cases concerning an indigent criminal defendant's right to counsel decided between Betts v. Brady, 316 U.S. 455 (1942), and Gideon v. Wainwright, 372 U.S. 335 (1963). Black dissented in *Betts,* arguing for an absolute right to counsel in felony cases. The majority held that, absent "special circumstances," the trial court was under no obligation to appoint a lawyer for the defendant.

Given Black's reputation for tenacity in first amendment matters, Kelman was surprised by the results of his examination of the cases.

> Surely, I thought, in the many cases leading up to *Gideon,* Justice Black must have renewed his demand for an unrestricted right of counsel for indigent defendants. No. What Black actually did was to oscillate between his own anti-*Betts* views and an application (obviously a generous application) of the *Betts* exception. Sometimes he wrote separately to renew his call for an absolute right to an attorney; at other times he joined majority opinions that scraped together enough "special circumstances" to require the appointment of counsel (Justice Black even authored some of those opinions for the Court). Only rarely did Black write conjunctively, siding with the defendant on the basis of his own minority view as well as the *Betts* exception. There is even a case virtually on the eve of *Gideon* in which Justice Black elected to join the opinion of six Justices predicated on special circumstances rather than a separate concurring opinion by Justice Douglas, joined by Justice Brennan, directly attacking *Betts.*—Kelman, *supra* at 263–64 (footnotes omitted).

18. *See* Sumner v. Shuman, 107 S. Ct. 2716 (1987); Woodson v. North Carolina, 428 U.S. 280 (1976); Godfrey v. Georgia, 446 U.S. 420 (1980); Enmund v. Florida, 458 U.S. 782 (1982); Coker v. Georgia, 433 U.S. 584 (1977); Ford v. Wainwright, 106 S. Ct. 2595 (1986); Caldwell v. Mississippi, 105 S. Ct. 2633 (1985); Booth v. Maryland, 107 S. Ct. ___ (1987).

19. 458 U.S. 782, 801 (1982). ("For purposes of imposing the death penalty, Enmund's criminal culpability must be limited to his participation in the robbery, and his punishment must be tailored to his personal responsibility and moral guilt. Putting Enmund to death to avenge two killings he did not commit and had no intention of committing does not measurably contribute to the retributive end of ensuring that the criminal gets his just desserts. This is the judgment of most of the legislatures that have recently addressed the matter and we have no reason to disagree with that judgment for purposes of applying the Eighth Amendment."). *But see id.*

at 799 ("It would be very different if the likelihood of a killing in the course of a robbery were so substantial that one should share the blame for the killing if he somehow participated in the felony"); *see also* Tison v. Arizona, 107 S. Ct. 1676, 1688 (1987) ("[W]e hold that the reckless disregard for human life implicit in knowingly engaging in criminal activities known to carry a grave risk of death represents a highly culpable mental state that may be taken into account in making a capital sentencing judgment when that conduct causes its natural, though not inevitable, result.").

In *Enmund,* Justices Brennan and Marshall concurred. Justice O'Connor, joined by Chief Justice Burger and Justices Powell and Rehnquist, dissented.

In *Tison,* Justice O'Connor delivered the opinion of the Court, joined by Chief Justice Rehnquist and Justices White, Powell, and Scalia; Brennan dissented, joined fully by Marshall and in part by Justices Blackmun and Stevens.

20. Enmund v. Florida, 458 U.S. at 801 ("However, I adhere to my view that the death penalty is in all circumstances cruel and unusual punishment prohibited by the Eighth and Fourteenth Amendments. *See* Gregg v. Georgia, 428 U.S. 153, 227 (1976) (dissenting opinion).").

21. 433 U.S. 584 (1977).

22. *Id.* at 601–04. Powell would have held that on the facts of the case death was a disproportionate punishment for rape. But he would not have concluded that death was a disproportionate punishment for rape in all cases where a rape but not a murder had been committed.

23. *Id.* at 600.

24. 106 S. Ct. 2595 (1986).

25. As one commentator remarked:

> The unanimous decision and opinion in United States v. Nixon, 418 U.S. 683 (1974), was exceptional. The Justices have worked together to reach an institutional opinion in this way only two or three times in the last thirty years. The trend is now toward less consensus on the Court's rulings. The justices are increasingly divided over their decisions. Individual opinions have become more highly prized than institutional opinions. The Court now functions more like a legislative body relying simply on a tally of votes to decide cases than like a collegial body working toward collective decisions and opinions.—O'BRIEN, *supra* note 16, at 22.

> But conference discussions have less significance in the Burger Court's decision making. The cost of the practice of devoting less time to collective deliberation and consensus building is more divided decisions and less agreement on the court's rulings. Because the justices no longer have the time or inclination to agree on opinions for the Court, they file separate opinions. The reality of cases and less collective deliberation discourages the reaching of compromises necessary for institutional opin-

ions. Ideological and personal differences in the Burger Court are reinforced.—*Id.* at 231.

26. Ford v. Wainwright, 106 S. Ct. at 2598 (opinion of the Court) (holding that
the eighth amendment bars the execution of the insane); *id.* at 2602–06 (joined by
Brennan, Blackmun, and Stevens, JJ.); *id.* at 2606–11 (Powell, J., concurring in part
and concurring in the judgment). Justice Powell wrote separately to address the
meaning of insanity in the context of an imminent execution and to differ with
Marshall's views on the procedures for determining competency to be executed.

27. *Id.* at 2611–13 (while the eighth amendment does not create a substantive
right not to be executed while insane, Florida law does; in addition, Florida does not
provide the minimal procedural protections required by federal due process).

28. *Id.* at 2613–15 (finding it unnecessary to "constitutionalize" the already uni-
form view that the insane should not be executed; arguing that the most required by
the common law was that the executive make a determination of competency).

29. *Id.* at 2600 ("Now that the eighth amendment has been recognized to affect
significantly both the procedural and substantive aspects of the death penalty, the
question of executing the insane takes on a wholly different complexion. The adequacy of the procedures chosen by the State to determine sanity, therefore, will
depend on an issue that this Court has never addressed: whether the Constitution
places a substantive restriction on the State's power to take the life of an insane
prisoner.").

30. *Id.* ("There is now little room for doubt that the eighth amendment's ban
on cruel and unusual punishment embraces, at a minimum, those modes or acts of
punishment that had been considered cruel and unusual at the time that the Bill of
Rights was adopted.") (citations omitted).

Professor Kelman argues that, when a restrictive application of a precedent is
called for by the tallying of votes, the least credible choice as author of the Court's
opinion is one who originally dissented from the precedent-setting case. In his view,
"such an assignment carries an implication of hostility and of hidden agendas when
what is wanted is the appearance of objective analysis." Kelman, *supra* note 17, at
294. This criticism is not entirely apropos of *Ford,* as the facts and questions considered were thoroughly different from *Furman* or *Gregg,* although the criticism has
some merit. Kelman adds, in a footnote:

> I have a twofold objection to the recent employment of Justice Marshall
> to deliver the Court's reversal of the death sentence in Caldwell v. Mis-
> sissippi, 105 S. Ct. 2633 (1985). First, Justice Marshall's abiding belief
> in the unconstitutionality of capital punishment in any circumstances
> undermines his value as administrator of the Court's precedents in such
> cases. Second, in order to reach the Court's conclusion on the specific
> issue in *Caldwell,* concerning the propriety of prosecutorial argument to
> the jury, it was necessary to distinguish a two-year-old decision, Califor-
> nia v. Ramos, 463 U.S. 992 (1983), in which Justice Marshall was a
> dissenter. It should be pointed out, however, that the Chief Justice was

not responsible for the opinion assignment in *Caldwell*. That task fell to Justice Brennan (Marshall's alter ego on the subject of capital punishment) as senior member of the majority.—*Id.* at 294, n.268.

First, a comparison of Brennan's and Marshall's opinions in *Furman, supra,* and in *Gregg* reveals a wealth of subtle differences, so that it is superficial to call Brennan the alter ego of Marshall *simpliciter*. Second, Justice O'Connor, concurring in part and concurring in the judgment in *Caldwell,* was also able to distinguish *Ramos,* although on different grounds than those Marshall employed in Part IV-A of the opinion, the only part that was not also that of the Court. *Caldwell* at 2646–47 (O'Connor, J., concurring). In fact, the dissenting opinion in *Caldwell,* authored by Justice Rehnquist and joined by Chief Justice Burger and Justice White, made but a feeble attempt to refute the distinguishing of *Ramos. Caldwell* at 2651 (dissenting opinion) ("Although we noted in *Ramos* that the challenged information bore more than marginal relevance to the jury's sentencing determination, *Ramos* is not distinguishable from this case on that ground; there is no constitutional requirement that all information received by a sentencing jury be 'relevant' ").

As for Professor Kelman's larger contention, that the restrictive application of the precedent should not be entrusted to an original dissenter because to do so weakens the Court's institutional authority, there is, as I have said, some merit to the view, though in other contexts. But there again, as in so many other areas of the law, death is different. Because of the peculiar nature of the sustained dissent in death penalty cases, that of a running dialogue with the federalist notions of the "retentionists," and also because of the ethical overtones of the issue, I believe that the dissenters may safely be allowed to write opinions for the Court without questioning their motives or presuming a continued disrespect for the core holding of *Gregg*. What the Court has done since *Furman* and *Gregg* is to say when the state may execute and when it may not; without Brennan and Marshall there may have been a constitutional abdication of all influence on the question of when the state may not. The tension here is inevitable and necessary; I would suggest that it is even beneficial for the growth of the law. Of course the point is moot since the retirement of Brennan and Marshall from the bench.

31. Kelman, *supra* note 17, at 259.

32. *Id.* However, as Kelman noted, the

damage containment concern becomes operative only when there are four other votes on the Court for limiting the foundation decision and when an original dissenter can furnish the pivotal fifth vote. If a majority exists without him for a restriction of Case Alpha, it makes little difference whether the original dissenter adds a surplus signature to an already precedential opinion of the Court or keeps up a running opposition to the Case Alpha principle. And, on the other hand, if there is a current majority for an Alpha-extending decision, placing our justice again on the minority side, what is the advantage of arguing for a narrower reading of Alpha rather than repeating the justice's basic objections to Alpha itself?—*Id.* at 259–60 (footnote omitted).

33. *Id.* at 259.

34. *Id.* at 231. Kelman seems to have gleaned this term from an article by Justice Traynor, *Some Open Questions on the Work of State Appellate Courts,* 24 U. CHI. L. REV. 211 (1957):

> Paradoxically, the well-reasoned dissent, aimed at winning the day in the future, enhances the certainty of the majority opinion, now embedded in the concrete of resistance to the published arguments that beat against it. For that reason the thoughtful dissident does not find it easy to set forth his dissent.
>
> Once he has done so he has had his day. He should yield to the obligation that is upon him to live with the law as it has been stated. He may thereafter properly note that he is concurring under compulsion, abiding the time when he may win over the majority, but he should regard dearly enough the stability of the law that governs all the courts in the state not to renew the rataplan of his dissent. When the trial court properly follows the declared law and is duly affirmed by the intermediate court, he should not vote for a hearing on the basis of his dissent. Conversely, should the trial court be reversed on the basis of his dissent, he should vote for a hearing. When the court has granted a hearing in a case with multiple issues, including the ancient one, and there is a nucleus of dissenters on other issues, he should not cast his vote on the basis of his ancient dissent to achieve a reversal or affirmance that would not otherwise have materialized. To do so would work only mischief. The judge's responsibility to keep the law straight is no less when he is a dissenter.—*Id.* at 218–19. *Compare* Brennan, *In Defense of Dissents,* 37 HASTINGS L.J. 427, 437 (1986):

> This kind of dissent, in which a judge persists in articulating a minority view of the law in case after case presenting the same issue, seeks to do more simply than offer an alternative analysis—that could be done in a single dissent and does not require repetition. Rather, this type of dissent constitutes a statement by the judge as an individual: "Here I draw the line." Of course, as a member of the court, one's general duty is to acquiesce in the rulings of the court and to take up the battle behind the court's new barricades. But it would be a great mistake to confuse this unquestioned duty to obey and respect the law with an imagined obligation to subsume entirely one's views of constitutional imperatives to the views of the majority. None of us, lawyer or layman, teacher or student in our society must ever feel that to express a conviction, honestly and sincerely maintained, is to violate some unwritten law of manners or decorum. We are a free and vital people because we not only allow, we encourage debate, and because we do not shut down communication as

soon as a decision is reached. As law-abiders, we accept the conclusions of our decision-making bodies as binding, but we also know that our right to challenge the wisdom of that result must be accepted by those who disagree with us. So we debate and discuss and contend and always we argue. If we are right, we generally prevail. The process enriches all of us, and is available to, and employed by, individuals and groups representing all viewpoints and perspectives.—*Id.* at 437.

35. Kelman, *supra* note 17, at 269; Hudgens v. NLRB, 424 U.S. 507, 518 (1976) (*per* Stewart, J.); Burns v. Richardson, 384 U.S. 73, 99 (1966) (Stewart, J., concurring in the judgment) ("Time has not changed my views. I still believe the Court misconceived the Equal Protection Clause in Reynolds v. Sims [377 U.S. 533 (1964)] and its companion cases. But as long as those cases remain the law, I must bow to them."); Burns v. Richardson, 384 U.S. at 98 (Harlan, J., concurring in the judgment) ("Because judicial responsibility requires me, as I see things, to bow to the authority of Reynolds v. Sims, 377 U.S. 533, despite my original and continuing belief that the decision was constitutionally wrong (see my dissenting opinion, 377 U.S. at 589 *et seq.*), I felt compelled to concur with the Court's disposition of the case.").

36. *E.g.,* Furman v. Georgia, 408 U.S. at 384 (Burger, C.J., dissenting, joined by Blackmun, Powell, and Rehnquist, JJ.) ("[I]n a democracy the legislative judgment is presumed to embody the basic standards of decency prevailing in the society."); Gregg v. Georgia, 428 U.S. at 179–80 (opinion of the Court and of Stewart, Powell, and Stevens, JJ., *per* Stewart, J.) ("The most marked indication of society's endorsement of the death penalty is the legislative response to *Furman.* The legislatures of at least 35 states have enacted new statutes that provide for the death penalty for at least some crimes that result in the death of another person.").

37. Justice Powell's tightrope-walking style of adjudication may well be the stuff of which legends are made. *See, e.g.,* University of California Regents v. Bakke, 438 U.S. 265 (1978). In the context of the death penalty, *see* Booth v. Maryland, 107 S. Ct. 2529 (1987) (*per* Powell, J.) (reversing, by a 5–4 vote, a death sentence arrived at by a jury that considered "victim impact" evidence); McCleskey v. Kemp, 107 S. Ct. 1576 (1987) (*per* Powell, J.) (affirming, by a 5–4 vote, a death sentence in spite of statistical evidence indicating a strong probability that the sentencing decision was influenced by race). *Booth* was overruled in 1991. Payne v. Tennessee, 111 S. Ct. 2597 (1991).

38. An overall picture can be found in NAACP Legal Defense and Educational Fund, Inc., Death Row U.S.A. (April 24, 1991) (unpublished compilation). Although not simply a reflection of the maintenance of the sustained dissent by Brennan and Marshall, the raw numbers do reflect that position and the ad hoc alliances with other members of the Court, the influence of that alliance on the lower federal and state court system, and independent factors within the state court systems. The numbers also reflect, grimly, the influence of the retentionist justices. As of April 24, 1991 (in depositions since January 1, 1973):

Convictions reversed or sentences vacated: 1,091

Executions: 145

Suicides: 30

Commutations: 64 (including those by the governor of Texas resulting from favorable court decisions)

Died of natural causes or killed in fights while under death sentence: 58

39. Even in such a case, however, the position of Marshall and Brennan will not be without value for the development of the law. In the words of Llewellyn, who was not fond of dissenting opinions, "the dissent, by forcing or suggesting full publicity, rides herd on the majority." K. LLEWELLYN, THE COMMON LAW TRADITION: DECIDING APPEALS 26 (1960). Even Llewellyn could grudgingly concede that this was a useful function.

40. 408 U.S. 238, 257 (1972) (Brennan, J., concurring in the judgment); *id*. at 314 (Marshall, J., concurring in the judgment).

41. *Id*. at 240 (Douglas, J., concurring in the judgment); *id*. at 306 (Stewart, J., concurring in the judgment); *id*. at 310 (White, J., concurring in the judgment).

42. Kelman, *supra* note 17, at 268 ("Suppose that two justices support the Court's disposition of the case on the strength of legal analysis, X, and three others under a broader analysis, Y, with four justices dissenting (on anti-X and/or anti-Y grounds or for reasons unrelated to X or Y). Any future case which comes within the scope of anlaysis X should produce the same outcome in the Supreme Court, assuming no personnel changes on the Court and no shifting or original positions.") (footnote omitted); Gregg v. Georgia, 428 U.S. at 169 n.15 ("Since five justices wrote separately in support of the judgment in *Furman,* the holding of the Court may be viewed as that position taken by those members who concurred in the judgment on the narrowest grounds.").

43. An examination of the opinions of Justices Douglas, Stewart, and White in *Furman* reveals both subtle and substantive differences. Douglas relies primarily on the equal protection clause, *Furman* at 257. Stewart invokes the fourteenth amendment to apply the eighth amendment to the states and then remarks that "it is clear that these sentences are 'cruel' in the sense that they excessively go beyond, not in degree but in kind, the punishments that the states' legislatures have deemed to be necessary. Weems v. United States, 217 U.S. 349 (1910)." *Furman* at 309. Stewart's opinion then dovetails with White's by stating that "it is equally clear that these sentences are 'unusual' in the sense that the penalty of death is infrequently imposed for murder, and that its imposition for rape is extraordinarily rare." *Id*. (footnote omitted). Stewart does not rest here, however, but proceeds to conclude that the "Eighth and Fourteenth Amendments cannot tolerate the infliction of a sentence of death under legal systems that permit this unique penalty to be so wantonly and freakishly imposed." *Id*. at 310.

White's main concern seems to be that "as the statutes before us are now administered, the penalty is so infrequently imposed that the threat of execution is too attenuated to be of substantial service to criminal justice." *Id*. at 313. Because the death penalty produces "such negligible returns to the State," *id*. at 312, its imposition, under the legislative regimes before the Court, is violative of the eighth amendment.

It is no wonder, then, that state legislatures that wished to reenact the death penalty in the wake of *Furman* were so confused. The narrowest grounds for the holding is based on at least two separate rationales, with a third position seemingly a mixture of the first two. The constitutional results of this confusion can be found in *Gregg* and the companion cases: Proffitt v. Florida, 428 U.S. 242 (1976); Jurek v. Texas, 428 U.S. 262 (1976); Woodson v. North Carolina, 428 U.S. 280 (1976); and Roberts v. Louisiana, 428 U.S. 325 (1976).

The voting patterns in these first post-*Furman* cases are instructive; all the cases reaffirmed the core holding of *Furman,* that the death penalty is not per se unconstitutional. Stewart, Powell, and Stevens formed a bloc that announced the majority opinions in all five cases. In the cases that held the mandatory impositions of the death penalty unconstitutional (*Woodson* and *Roberts*), they were joined by Brennan and Marshall, who concurred in the judgment only on the basis of their opinions in *Furman* and *Gregg.* Burger, White, Blackmun, and Rehnquist dissented, separately or conjunctively. In the cases upholding the legislative schemes for channeled sentencing discretion (*Gregg, Proffitt,* and *Jurek*), Brennan and Marshall dissented, while the others concurred in the judgment.

44. For an analysis of the allocation of institutional responsibility by the Court as a whole, *see* Kamisar, *Taking Institutions Seriously: Introduction to a Strategy for Constitutional Analysis,* 51 U. CHI. L. REV. 366 (1984).

45. H.W. PERRY, JR., DECIDING TO DECIDE: AGENDA SETTING IN THE UNITED STATES SUPREME COURT 43 (1991).

46. *Id.* at 97.

47. *Id.* at 171.

48. *Id.* at 149.

49. *Id.* at 173.

50. Material for this section came from the recently released private papers of Justice Marshall. They are currently located in boxes arranged chronologically and by Term of the Court in the Manuscripts Division, Madison Building of the Library of Congress.

51. 498 U.S. 308 (1991).

52. 438 U.S. 586 (1978).

53. *Id.*

54. *Id.*

55. PERRY, *supra* note 45, at 172.

56. R. GOLDMAN AND D. GALLEN, THURGOOD MARSHALL: JUSTICE FOR ALL 21 (1992).

57. PERRY, *supra* note 45, at 176–77.

58. *Id.*

59. *Id.* at 174.

60. *Id.* at 97.

61. *Id.*

62. *Id.* at 41.

63. *See* L. YACKLE, POSTCONVICTION REMEDIES 1–2 (1981) (explaining that all states provide for direct review of state criminal judgments).

64. Gideon v. Wainwright, 372 U.S. 335 (1963).

65. Douglas v. California, 372 U.S. 353 (1963).

66. *See, e.g.,* McCrae v. State, 437 So. 2d 1388, 1390 (Fla. 1983) (finding that issues which were raised or could have been raised on direct appeal cannot be relitigated in state postconviction proceeding); Atkinson v. United States, 366 A.2d 450, 452–53 (D.C. 1976) (same).

67. 344 U.S. 443 (1953).

68. For a sampling of the academic debate surrounding the federal courts' redetermination of federal questions decided in state criminal proceedings, see generally Bator, *Finality in Criminal Law and Federal Habeas Corpus for State Prisoners,* 76 HARV. L. REV. 441 (1961); Brennan, *Federal Habeas Corpus and State Prisoners: An Exercise in Federalism,* 7 UTAH L. REV. 423 (1963); Friendly, *Is Innocence Irrelevant? Collateral Attack on Criminal Judgments,* 38 U. CHI. L. REV. 142 (1970); Neuborne, *The Myth of Parity,* 90 HARV. L. REV. 1105 (1977); Peller, *In Defense of Habeas Corpus Relitigation,* 16 HARV. C.R.-C.L. L. REV. 579 (1982); Robbins, *The Habeas Corpus Certificate of Probable Cause,* 44 OHIO ST. L.J. 307 (1983); Tague, *Federal Habeas Corpus and Ineffective Representation of Counsel: The Supreme Court Has Work to Do,* 31 STAN. L. REV. 1 (1978).

69. At some point between direct appeal and execution, the condemned inmate may seek executive clemency. On clemency generally, *see* EDMUND BROWN, PUBLIC JUSTICE, PRIVATE MERCY (1989); Hugo Bedau, *The Decline of Executive Clemency in Capital Cases,* 18 N.Y.U. REV. L. & SOC. CHANGE (1990–91); *Clemency and Pardons Symposium,* 27 U. RICHMOND L. REV. 177–371 (1993); DiSalle, *Comments on Capital Punishment and Clemency,* 25 OHIO ST. L.J. 71 (1964); Note, *Executive Clemency in Capital Cases,* 39 N.Y.U. L. REV. 136 (1964).

70. *See generally,* N.Y. TIMES, October 9, 1991, at A1: *Vote on Thomas Is Put off as Senate Backing Erodes over Harassment Charge; A One-Week Delay; Mitchell Says Integrity of Judge, Accuser and Senate Is at Stake; 7 House Women March to Senate in Attempt to Delay Thomas Vote; A Matter of Pragmatism: Delay of Thomas Vote Reflects Concerns of Declining Faith in Judge and Senate;* N.Y. TIMES, October 8, 1991, at A1: *Thomas' Accuser Assails Handling of Her Complaint; Judiciary Panel Attacked; Senate Vote Still Set for Today—Some Democrats Back Away from Nominee; The Senate and Sexism: Panels's Handling of Harassment Allegations Renews Questions About an All-Male Club;* N.Y. TIMES, October 12, 1991, at A1: *Thomas Accuser Tells Hearing of Obscene Talk and Advances; Judge Complains of "Lynching"; Drama in Senate; Court Nominee Rejects Charges Laid Out in Frank, Vivid Detail; On Thomas: More Questions, Not Fewer; In an Ugly Atmosphere, the Accusations Fly:* WASH. POST, October 12, 1991, at A1: *Hill Describes Details of Alleged Harassment; Thomas Categorically Denies All Her Charges;*

*Court Nominee Calls Ordeal Lynching for Uppity Blacks; A Distressing Turn: Activists Decry What Process Has Become; Grace, Grit and Gutter Fight; Never Has Country Seen a Hearing Like This;* WASH. POST., October 13, 1991, at A1: *Thomas, Allies Step Up Counterattack; Cry of "Lynching" Opens Wounds: Thomas' Words Evoke a Range of Emotions Among Blacks in Area; Decorum Is a Victim as Tempers Boil Over: Committee Members Scold One Another;* WASH. POST, October 11, 1991, at A1: *Second Woman Tells Committee of Incidents with Thomas; Hearings Strewn with Dangers for Senators, Too: Thomas' Judges Have Own Ethical and Image Problems;* N.Y. TIMES, October 13, 1991, at A1: *Thomas Backers Attack Hill; Judge, Vowing He Won't Quit, Says He Is Victim of Race Stigma; Fierce Questioning; Senators Level Additional Accusations That Law Professor Has Lied; Taboo Issues of Sex and Race Explode in Glare of Hearing; Spectacle of Degradation;* N.Y. TIMES, October 14, 1991, at A1: *Parade of Witnesses Support Hill's Story, Thomas' Integrity; A Calmer Session; Friends Say He Spoke Long Ago—Judge's Backers Laud Him; With Each Round of Testimony, the Mood at the Hearing Sways; White House Role in Thomas Defense: Initially Split, Bush Aides Opt to Attack Accuser;* N.Y. TIMES, October 16, 1991, at A1: *Senate Confirms Thomas, 54–48, Ending Week of Bitter Battle; "Time for Healing" Judge Says; Court's Second Black; Public Floods the Capitol with Calls During an All-Day Debate; Senate Futile Search for Safe Ground; Image More than Reality Became Issues, Losers Say.*

The Anita Hill–Clarence Thomas hearings are now history; Judge Thomas is Justice Thomas. Yet the memories linger on and on. Like witnesses to an accident, many who watched the three days of Senate hearings continue to replay the especially horrible moments. We compare our memories of cold accusation and heated denial; we weigh again the hours of testimony, vacuous and vindictive by turn. In them, even those of us who thought we were beyond surprise had underestimated the trauma.

Echoing Rosemary Bray, some of my women friends said that even before the hearings began the nomination of Clarence Thomas had taken on, for them, the quality of a nightmare. The particular dread they felt was one of betrayal—not a betrayal by President Bush, from whom they expected nothing—but by Thomas himself, who not only was no Thurgood Marshall but also gradually revealed himself to be a man who rejoined in burning the bridges that had brought him over. One described the kind of heartbreak that comes only to those still willing to call themselves race-women and race-men: people who feel, in the old and honorable sense, that African Americans should live and work and succeed not only for themselves but also for each other.

It is remarkable how much it still matters. I usually end my travels down this particular memory lane with an open letter to Anita Hill by Donella Meadows of Plainfield, New Hampshire, an adjunct professor of environmental studies at Dartmouth College. Whenever I read it—usually aloud—I keep it in the first person because Meadows's letter encapsulates so perfectly my own relationship with the Hill-Thomas issue:

I find that, like many Americans, I have been aroused by the events you crystallized in a way I can't forget. Whatever else you accomplished or meant to accomplish during that difficult week when you were the center of public attention, you were a great teacher. For that I want to express my deepest gratitude.

The first lesson you taught me was about my own anger. I didn't know it was there. I was one of the millions of dormant volcanoes on the issue of sexual harassment who erupted that week, letting up a molten core of hurt and fury that had been held down for years. I was astonished at the force of my own feelings.

My feelings, like those of others, came from direct experience, starting with my first job at age 16. Unlike you, I never told a soul. I thought that somehow what happened was my own fault. And I had no doubt, if I had complained, who would get fired. I went on working there. I went on working at every job where I encountered that problem. You explained the reason perfectly: To have quit would have meant letting one man's lewd behavior make my job decisions for me.

When the senators didn't understand that point, that was the moment my rage boiled over. Apparently they thought that the right and proper resolution of the issue would have been for you to end all association with Clarence Thomas. In the Senate debate, in media commentary, all over the nation, the fact that you didn't do that was labeled an "inconsistency" in your testimony.

Some people still don't get it. They still can't see the mote in their own eyes, their unquestioning acceptance of the idea that a man should have such power over a woman that if he humiliates her, she should leave—or shut up and take it. But believe me, Professor Hill, lots of us did get it. You showed us the extent to which we, the victims of that idea, had accepted it ourselves and had given away our own dignity and freedom.

Another thing you taught me was what to do with my anger. First, keep it specific—don't direct it at all men when only a few men deserve it. Second, don't stuff it down. Don't stay silent. However late, however long after the fact, bring it out. America has a lot of talking to do on this subject before men and women learn how to work together and to set each other straight, without rancor and without fear, on what their sexual relationships are to be.

Never again will I let sexual harassment go unchallenged if it happens to me, and especially if, to my knowledge, it happens to a young person just entering the workplace. You've given me a great line to use. I can look the offender in the eye and say, "You'd better hope you never get nominated to the Supreme Court!"

Your final lesson to me is the most precious of all. It is about means and ends. After I had spent a week in a rage on your behalf, on my behalf, on behalf of all women who had ever experienced the kind of undeserved, unsubstantiated character smears the Republican senators heaped on you, you went back to Oklahoma and held a last press conference.

By that time it was clear that the United States would have a Supreme Court justice who was perhaps a sexual harasser and perjurer, and who was for sure a willing tool of an ugly power play, a judge who had denied believing in nearly every opinion he had professed earlier. He had won. You had lost. And you weren't vengeful. You didn't say that you had gone through a week of hell for nothing. You were as calm as you had been throughout the process. You said only that you had told the truth and were grateful to have had the opportunity to be heard.

That was a stunning example of the central message of every religion, every spiritual tradition—the hardest message, always, for me to remember. Do your very best and let go of the result. Have the courage to change the things you can and the serenity to accept the things you cannot. Keep truth in the means, and let the ends take care of themselves. When you're up against others who will sacrifice anything to win, don't descend to their level. Hang on to your own integrity, and pray for them.

Thank you, Professor Hill. I needed to hear that. At a time when every American politician is being told to be dishonest in order to win, the nation needed to hear that, on Capitol Hill, under the spotlights, in prime time. It must have been very difficult for you. It must hurt you to see how many people didn't listen—to see, for example, how the Democrats are being chastised for not being as low and mean as the Republicans. I just want you to know that some of us did hear you, admired you, and will do our best to live up to your example.

During the Thomas confirmation hearings, when the judge said he had not discussed *Roe v. Wade* with anyone, most commentators were concerned that he was lying. I was worried that Thomas was telling the truth. Can you imagine having a Supreme Court Justice who will be making decisions affecting the reproductive rights of millions of American women who has not cared enough about receiving different views on the subject to discuss the issue with even one woman? After watching Thomas on the bench for five years, I now firmly believe he was not lying—not about Professor Hill, but about *Roe*.

I wondered if he even read things like the "Voices" Brief. A decade ago, starting with *Thornburgh v. American College of Obstetricians and Gynecologists*, 476 U.S. 747 (1986), the National Abortion Rights Action League began to submit an amicus brief in major abortion cases, now known as the "Voices" Brief. It consists principally of women's stories of their abortions. The accounts tell their reasons for having had abortions and their effects on the women's lives. Some of the stories illustrate the horrors of illegal abortions. The purpose of the brief is to show the justices of the Supreme Court—nine older people, seven of them men—what would happen if the guarantees of *Roe v. Wade* were stripped away. This is just one example of a powerful movement in legal theory of using narratives—stories—to give voices to those outside dominant groups.

How did we get from Anita Hill to neopuritanical fascists like Catharine MacKinnon and Andrea Dworkin, from making career advancement contingent upon the bestowing of sexual favors to the promulgation of campus speech codes?

71. BLACK'S LAW DICTIONARY (6th ed. 1990): "Policy of courts to stand by precedent and not to disturb a settled point."

72. BLACK'S LAW DICTIONARY (6th ed. 1990): "A thing or matter settled by judgment."

73. ALBERT CAMUS, NOTEBOOKS, 1942–1951, at 88 (1991; orig. 1942).

74. "First Draft," Opinion by Justice Thurgood Marshall, Dissenting from the Denial of Certiorari, *Ford v. Wainwright,* 85–5542, November 22, 1985, Container 397, Folder 12, in Papers of Justice Thurgood Marshall, Manuscripts Division, Library of Congress, Washington, D.C.

75. Memorandum from Justice William Brennan to Justice Thurgood Marshall, *Ford v. Wainwright,* 85–5542, Container 397, Folder 12, Papers of Justice Thurgood Marshall, Manuscripts Division, Library of Congress, Washington, D.C.

76. "Second Draft," Opinion by Justice Thurgood Marshall, with whom Justice Brennan joins dissenting from denial of certiorari, *Ford v. Wainwright,* 85–5542, December 2, 1985, Container 397, Folder 12, Papers of Justice Thurgood Marshall, Manuscripts Division, Library of Congress, Washington, D.C.

78. Memorandum from Justice William Rehnquist to Justice Thurgood Marshall, *Ford v. Wainwright,* 85-5542, Container 397, Folder 12, Papers of Thurgood Marshall, Manuscripts Division, Library of Congress, Washington, D.C.

79. Memorandum from Justice Byron White to Justice Thurgood Marshall, *Ford v. Wainwright,* 85–5542, Container 397, Folder 12, Papers of Thurgood Marshall, Manuscripts Division, Library of Congress, Washington, D.C.

80. Memorandum from Justice William Brennan to Justice Thurgood Marshall, *Ford v. Wainwright,* 85–5542, Container 397, Folder 12, Papers of Thurgood Marshall, Manuscripts Division, Library of Congress, Washington, D.C.

81. Memorandum from Justice Lewis Powell to Justice Thurgood Marshall, *Ford v. Wainwright,* 85–5542, June 5, 1986, Container 397, Folder 12, Papers of Thurgood Marshall, Manuscripts Division, Library of Congress, Washington, D.C.

82. Memorandum from Justice Harry Blackmun to Justice Thurgood Marshall, *Ford v. Wainwright,* 85–5542, June 9, 1986, Container 397, Folder 12, Papers of Thurgood Marshall, Manuscripts Division, Library of Congress, Washington, D.C.

83. Memorandum from Justice Thurgood Marshall to Justice Lewis Powell, *Ford v. Wainwright,* June 16, 1986, Container 397, Folder 12, Papers of Thurgood Marshall, Manuscripts Division, Library of Congress, Washington, D.C.

84. Memorandum from Justice John Paul Stevens to Justice Thurgood Marshall,

*Ford v. Wainwright,* 85–5542, June 17, 1986, Container 397, Folder 12, Papers of Thurgood Marshall, Manuscripts Division, Library of Congress, Washington, D.C.

85. Memorandum from Justice Lewis Powell to Justice Thurgood Marshall, *Ford v. Wainwright,* 85–5542, June 17, 1986, Container 397, Folder 12, Papers of Thurgood Marshall, Manuscripts Division, Library of Congress, Washington, D.C.

86. Memorandum from Justice Byron White to Justice Sandra Day O'Connor, *Ford v. Wainwright,* 85–5542, June 17, 1987, Container 397, Folder 12, Papers of Thurgood Marshall, Manuscripts Division, Library of Congress, Washington, D.C.

87. Memorandum from Chief Justice Warren Burger to Justice William Rehnquist, *Ford v. Wainwright,* 85–5542, June 19, 1986, Container 397, Folder 12, Papers of Thurgood Marshall, Manuscripts Division, Library of Congress, Washington, D.C.

88. Defense counsel stated: "It's going to be your decision. . . . You are the judges and you will have to decide his fate. It is an awesome responsibility, I know—an awesome responsibility." 472 U.S. 320, 324 (1985).

89. *Id.* at 325.

90. *Id.*

91. Papers of Thurgood Marshall, Library of Congress, Manuscripts Division, Container 374, Folder 4.

92. *Id.*

93. *Id.*

94. *Id.*

95. *Id.*

96. *Id.*

97. *Id.*

98. *Id.*

99. *Id.*

100. *Caldwell,* 472 U.S. at 330 (quoting Woodson v. North Carolina, 428 U.S. 280, 305 (1976)); *see also, e.g.,* Mills v. Maryland, 108 S. Ct. 1860, 1870 (1988) ("The decision to exercise the power of the State to execute a defendant is unlike any other decision citizens and public officials are called upon to make. Evolving standards of societal decency have imposed a correspondingly high requirement of reliability on the determination that death is the appropriate penalty in a particular case.").

101. *Caldwell,* 472 U.S. at 329.

102. *Id.* (quoting California v. Ramos, 463 U.S. 992, 998–99 (1983)).

103. *Id.* at 341.

104. *Id.* at 330.

105. *Id.* (quoting *Woodson,* 428 U.S. at 304). He stated further: "[W]hen we held that a defendant has a constitutional right to the consideration of such factors . . . we clearly envisioned that that consideration would occur among sentencers who were present to hear the evidence and arguments and see the witnesses." *Id.* at 330–31.

106. *Id.*

107. *Id.* at 331.

108. *Id.* at 332.

109. *Id.* at 333.

110. *Id.*

111. *Id.*

112. *Id.*

113. *Id.* at 333–34.

114. *Id.* at 336–37.

115. 416 U.S. 637 (1974). The *Donnelly* Court examined the prejudicial effect of a prosecutor's remark to the jury, in reference to defendant and his counsel: "They said that they hope that you find him not guilty. I quite frankly think that they hope that you find him guilty of something a little less than first-degree murder." *Id.* at 640. The Court held that this remark, though ambiguous, stood corrected by the trial court's specific disapproving instructions. *Id.* at 644–45. The Court emphasized the distinction between "ordinary trial error of a prosecutor" and "that sort of egregious misconduct" that would amount to a denial of constitutional due process. *Id.* at 647–48.

116. *Caldwell,* 472 U.S. at 337–40.

117. 463 U.S. 992 (1983). In *Ramos,* the Court upheld the constitutionality of California's statutory requirement that capital-sentencing juries be instructed about the governor's power to commute a sentence of life imprisonment without parole to a lesser sentence with the possibility of parole. *Id.* at 997. The Court determined that the provision served a legitimate state interest of accurately informing jurors of the significance of their sentencing decision. *Id.* at 1009.

118. *Caldwell,* 472 U.S. at 336.

119. *Id.*

120. *Id.*

121. *Id.* at 342 (O'Connor, J., concurring).

122. *Id.*

123. Justice O'Connor stated:
> Should a state conclude that the reliability of its sentencing procedure is enhanced by accurately instructing the jurors on the sentencing procedure, including the existence and limited nature of appellate review, I see nothing in *Ramos* to foreclose a policy choice in favor of jury education. . . . Laypersons cannot be expected to appreciate without explanation the limited nature of appellate review, especially in light of the reassuring picture of "automatic" review evoked by the sentencing court and prosecutor in this case.—472 U.S. at 342, 343 (O'Connor, J., concurring).

124. *Id.* at 342 (O'Connor, J., concurring). Justice O'Connor, who wrote the majority opinion in *Ramos,* misinterpreted and exaggerated Marshall's treatment of *Ramos.* He wrote that a death sentence should never be imposed merely on the basis

of the availability of the appellate review. In that context, Marshall viewed appellate review as a factor "wholly irrelevant to the determination of the appropriate sentence." *Id.* at 336. Although O'Connor argued that informing a jury of the limited scope of appellate review may be important to enhance its sense of responsibility, there is nothing in Marshall's opinion to show that the plurality would not favor such jury instructions if used to increase the reliability of capital sentencing.

O'Connor may have been reacting to a misperception that the Court was abandoning *Ramos*. Indeed, Marshall referred favorably to that part of O'Connor's language in *Ramos* that emphasized the "indispensability of sentencers who appreciat[e] . . . the gravity of their choice and . . . the moral responsibility reposed in them as sentencers." *Caldwell,* 472 U.S. at 336 (quoting *Ramos,* 463 U.S. at 1011).

125. *Id.* at 343 (O'Connor, J., concurring) (citation omitted).

126. *Id.* at 349 (Rehnquist, J., dissenting).

127. *Id.* at 349–50 (Rehnquist, J., dissenting).

128. 472 U.S. at 351 (Rehnquist, J., dissenting).

129. 114 S. Ct. __ (1994).

130. Because Justice O'Connor wrote a separate concurrence, the *Caldwell* opinion is, technically, a plurality opinion. This in no way diminishes the precedential power of the case for purposes of this chapter, because Justice O'Connor's brief concurrence expresses only her disagreement with the plurality's treatment of California v. Ramos, 463 U.S. 992 (1983), and its suggestion that an accurate and nonmisleading instruction about appellate review might be invalid because it would serve no valid state penological interest. Prefacing her discussion, the justice clearly stated that she joined "the judgment *and* the opinion of the Court, with the exception of Part IV-A. I write separately to express my views about the Court's discussion of *California v. Ramos.*" 472 U.S. at 341 (O'Connor, J., concurring) (emphasis added). O'Connor fully joined in the fundamental thrust of Marshall's analysis, the conclusion that "it is constitutionally impermissible to rest a death sentence on a determination made by a sentencer who has been led to believe that the responsibility for determining the appropriateness of the defendant's death rests elsewhere." *Id.* at 328–29. Thus, the essential teachings of the *Caldwell* opinion represent the majority view of the Court, not merely a plurality opinion.

The Court resolved any ambiguity on this score in Romano v. Oklahoma, 114 S. Ct. __ (1994). Even before *Romano,* however, when other justices writing in subsequent opinions have cited *Caldwell,* they have referred to it as the view of "this Court." *E.g.,* Steffen v. Ohio, 108 S. Ct. 1089, 1090 (1988) (Brennan, J., joined by Marshall, J., and Blackmun, J., dissenting from denial of certiorari); Darden v. Wainwright, 106 S. Ct. 2464, 2473 n.15, 2476 (1986) (Blackmun, J., dissenting). In *Steffen,* Justice Brennan explained that "this Court laid down a general prohibition against trial comments that minimize a jury's sense of responsibility for a death sentence." 108 S. Ct. at 1090. Brennan went on to describe the portion of the opinion that was the product of "a four-justice plurality," one not joined by Justice O'Connor. *Id.* at 1091. With the exception of that part of *Caldwell,* the body of the opinion is a majority view. Indeed, Justice Rehnquist, dissenting in *Caldwell* itself, made frequent references to "the Court's" faulty anlaysis, rather than to the opinion of a mere plurality. *E.g., Caldwell,* 472 U.S. at 350 (Rehnquist, J., dissenting) ("I therefore find unconvincing the Court's scramble to identify an independent Eighth Amendment norm that was violated by the statements here").

Even before *Romano, Caldwell* had been perceived, effectively, as a majority opinion by the supreme courts of the several states that have addressed *Caldwell* claims. The Supreme Court of Virginia stated that in *Caldwell* "Justice Marshall, writing for a majority of five, found that unreliability ad bias inhere in death sentences following state-induced suggestions that the sentencing jury may shift its stint of responsibility to an appellate court." Frye v. Commonwealth, 231 Va. 370, 396, 345 S.E.2d 267, 285 (1986). The *Fyre* court noted that "[o]ne section of Justice Marshall's opinion speaks for only a plurality of the Court, as Justice O'Connor wrote separately to express her view of the application of *California v. Ramos.*" *Id.* at 396 n.5, 345 S.E.2d at 287 n.5. Similarly, the Supreme Court of Colorado, in *People v. Drake,* referred to *Caldwell* as the decision of "the United States Supreme Court" and held it to be fully controlling. 748 P.2d 1237, 1258–59 (Colo. 1988) (finding reversible error where prosecutor told sentencing jury that "you have a shared responsibility" because the job of passing on the death penalty is, ultimately, on the trial court). The New Jersey Supreme Court, in *State v. Ramseur,* finding error in the trial court's instructions that the jury's sentencing role was "merely to apply the law," held that "as the United States Supreme Court has recently made clear" jury instructions must never lead capital sentencers to believe that their responsibility is diminished. 106 N.J. 123, 316, 524 A.2d 188, 286 (1987). In fact, in virtually every state supreme court opinion that has addressed similar *Caldwell* claims, the *Caldwell* opinion is referred to as that of "the Court." *See, e.g.,* Hooks v. State, 502 So. 2d 401, 401 (Ala. Crim. App. 1987); People v. Milner, 45 Cal. 3d 227, 753 P.2d 669, 246 Cal Rptr. 713 (1988); Combs v. State, 525 So. 2d 853, 856 (Fla. 1988); People v. Lego, 116 Ill. 2d 323, 350, 507 N.E.2d 800, 810 (1987); Matthews v. Commonwealth, 709 S.W.2d 414, 421 (Ky. 1985); State v. Clark, 492 So. 2d 862, 871 (La. 1986); Booker v. State, 511 So. 2d 1329, 1332 (Miss. 1987); Mazzan v. State, 733 P.2d 850, 851 (nev. 1987); State v. Buell, 22 Ohio St. 3d 124, 489 N.E.2d 795 (1988); Commonwealth v. Baker, 511 Pa. 1, 21, 511 A.2d 777, 791 (1986); Modden v. State, 721 S.W. 2d 859, 862 (Tex. Ct. App. 1986); Petition of Jeffries, 110 Wash. 2d 326, 752 P.2d 1338 (1988).

131. *Romano,* 114 S. Ct., at ___.

132. *Id.* at ___.

133. 114 S. Ct. ___ (1994).

134. *E.g.,* Kordenbrock v. Commonwealth, 700 S.W.2d 384, 391 (Ky. 1985) ("The importance of *Caldwell v. Mississippi* is that it makes clear that what is critical is telling the jury that its sentence is only a recommendation, without regard to the argument over whether the word 'recommendation' is technically correct.").

135. On Private Eddie Slovik's case generally, *see* W. HUIE, THE EXECUTION OF PRIVATE SLOVIK (1954). On the "Slovik syndrome" generally, *see* Paduano & Smith,

*Deadly Errors: Juror Misperceptions Concerning Parole in the Imposition of the Death Penalty*, 18 COLUM. HUM. RTS. L. REV. 211, 213 n.3 (1987) ("perhaps a majority of jurors" refuse to believe that the death sentence they impose will be carried out); *Special Project: Parole Release Decisionmaking and the Sentencing Process*, 84 YALE L.J. 810, 812 (1975) (describing the "Slovik syndrome" as a juror's expectation that the sentence will not be fully carried out).

136. HUIE, *supra* note 135, at 169; *see also id.* at 173, 188.

137. *Caldwell*, 472 U.S. at 333–35.

138. Fleming v. State, 240 Ga. 142, 146, 240 S.E.2d 37, 40 (1977) (reversible error where prosecutor told jury that death sentence would be reviewed by trial judge and by appellate court); Ward v. Commonwealth, 695 S.W.2d 404, 408 (Ky. 1985) (prosecutor impermissibly sought to divert jury from responsibility by telling jury that judge has ultimate sentencing role); State v. Tyner, 273 S.C. 646, 659, 258 S.E.2d 559, 565–66 (1979) (death sentence invalid where prosecutor argued that trial court would review any recommendation of death); Lyons v. Commonwealth, 204 Va. 375, 379, 131 S.E.2d 407, 409–10 (1963) (improper for prosecutor to tell jury that, if it errs, trial court can correct mistake).

139. *Caldwell*, 472 U.S. at 328–29 (emphasis added).

140. *Id.* at 333.

141. *Id.*

142. S. WISHMAN, ANATOMY OF A JURY (1986); *see also* A. OSBORN, THE MIND OF THE JUROR 55, 207 (1937).

143. *See generally* 1 ABA STANDARDS FOR CRIMINAL JUSTICE § 6-1.3 (1986).

144. Starr v. United States, 153 U.S. 614, 626 (1894).

145. *Caldwell*, 472 U.S. at 333.

146. *Id.* at 330–33.

147. Tedder v. State, 322 So. 2d 908, 910 (Fla. 1975).

148. CAL. PENAL CODE § 190.1 through § 190.5 (West 1988); KY. REV. STAT. ANN. § 532.025(1)(b) (Baldwin Supp. 1988); OHIO REV. CODE ANN. § 2929.03 (Baldwin 1986); VA. CODE ANN. § 19.2-264.2 through § 19.2-264.5 (1983 & Supp. 1988).

149. *E.g.*, VA. CODE § 19.264.5 (The court must either impose sentence in accordance with the verdict fixing punishment at death or "set aside the sentence of death and impose a sentence of imprisonment for life." The court may only set aside a death sentence after consideration of a probation officer's report and "upon good cause shown.").

150. Rogers v. Ohio, 474 U.S. 1002 (1985) (order summarily granting certiorari and reversing and remanding for reconsideration in light of *Caldwell* in *Rogers v. State*) (comments to jury that its sentencing determination was "only a recommendation," although technically an accurate statement of applicable law, may be misleading); Tucker v. Kemp, 474 U.S. 1001 (1985) (order summarily reversing and remanding for reconsideration in light of *Caldwell*; prosecutor's comments that jury

was only "last link" in a process that included police officers, district attorney, and trial judge).

151. Wheat v. Thigpen, 793 F.2d 621, 628–29 (5th Cir. 1986) (prosecutor's comments that jury's sentencing decision was not final and would be reviewed by the trial judge and appeals courts were impermissible under *Caldwell*); Mann v. Dugger, 844 F.2d 1446, 1458 (11th Cir. 1988) (en banc) (prosecutor's and trial court's references to jury's advisory sentencing as mere recommendation a violation of eighth amendment); Wainwright, 804 F.2d 1526, 1528–33 (11th Cir. 1986), *modified sub nom. on other grounds,* Adams v. Dugger, 816 F.2d 1493 (11th Cir. 1987) *rev'd on other grounds sub nom.* Dugger v. Adams, __, U.S. __ (1989). But *see* Haarich v. Dugger, 844 F.2d 1464, 1472–75 (11th Cir. 1988) (en banc) (trial court's instructions that it would make the final sentencing determination did not diminish weight of jury's advisory sentencing role); Julius v. Johnson, 840 F.2d 1533, 1544 (11th Cir. 1988) (prosecutor did not diminish jury's sentencing responsibility by accurately informing it that its advisory sentencing verdict was subject to review by trial court); Davis v. Kemp, 829 F.2d 1522, 1530 (11th Cir. 1987) (no reversible error when prosecutor emphasized jury's role as final link in long judicial process); Celestine v. Butler, 823 F.2d 74, 79 (5th Cir. 1987) (use of word "recommendation," in view of entire jury instructions, did not diminish jury's sentencing authority); Mulligan v. Kemp, 818 F.2d 746, 748 (11th Cir. 1987) (trial court's use of word "recommend" did not diminish jury's sense of responsibility where jury was also informed that court would be bound by jury's recommendation); Tucker v. Kemp, 802 F.2d 1293, 1297 (11th Cir. 1986) (en banc) (prosecutor's comments that jury was "last link" in process that included police, district attorney, and trial judge did not render sentencing proceedings fundamentally unfair); Thomas v. Wainwright, 788 F.2d 684, 689 (11th Cir. 1986) (trial court's instructions that jury had only an advisory sentencing role not improper); Brooks v. Kemp, 762 F.2d 1383, 1410–11 (11th Cir. 1985) (en banc) (prosecutor's reference to roles of all participants in judicial process, although ambiguous, did not undermine jury's responsibility for its sentencing decision).

152. Parks v. Brown, 840 F.2d 1496, 1503–04 (10th Cir. 1987) (prosecutor's comments regarding jury's sentencing role as part of larger criminal justice system did not minimize importance of jury's determination), *rev'd on other grounds,* __ U.S. __ (1990); Dutton v. Brown, 812 F.2d 593, 593–96, 596–97 (10th Cir. 1987) (no error where prosecutor emphasized that jury was part of whole criminal justice system).

153. Frye v. Commonwealth, 231 Va. 370, 397–98, 345 S.E.2d 267, 284–87 (1986) (prosecutor's statements that the responsibility for sentencing is not jury's, and that "the judge will be the person that fixes sentence," constituted reversible error).

154. *Id.* at 397, 345 S.E.2d at 285.

155. People v. Drake, 748 P.2d 1237, 1258–60 (Colo. 1988).

156. Matthews v. Commonwealth, 709 S.W.2d 414, 421–22 (Ky. 1985) (although brief reference to jury's decision as a "recommendation" did not require reversal, "court and prosecutor must be extremely careful to avoid leaving the jury with any

impression that would diminish its 'awesome responsibility' in imposing the death sentence"); Holland v. Commonwealth, 703 S.W.2d 876, 880 (Ky. 1985) (trial court erred when it advised jury that the judge "can change" the penalty imposed by the jury); State v. Buell, 22 Ohio St. 3d 124, 142–44, 489 N.E.2d 795, 811–13 (1986) (instruction to jury that its determination regarding death penalty was nonbinding on trial court did not diminish jury's sense of responsibility); People v. Lego, 116 Ill. 2d 323, 348, 507 N.E.2d 800, 810 (1987) (state attorney's brief suggestion that jury decision was only a recommendation, in light of further amonishments regarding seriousness of task, did not shift jury's sense of responsibility); State v. Roberts, 709 S.W.2d 857, 869 (Mo. 1986) (prosecutor's statement that jury would make a sentencing recommendation, although not reversible error, should be avoided hereafter); State v. Hance, 254 Ga. 575, 578, 332 S.E.2d 287, 291 (1985) (comments that jury would not be any more responsible for death sentence than police officers, grand jury, district attorney, or trial judge did not tend to diminish jury's sense of responsibility); People v. Milner, 45 Cal. 3d 227, 753 P.2d 669, 246 Cal. Rptr. 713 (1988) (prosecutor's assurances that jury need not "shoulder the responsibility" because "the law protects" them in their capital sentencing determination impermissibly misled jury as to its responsibility in imposing death sentence); Johnson v. State, No. 83-241-III, 1988 WL 3632 (Tenn. Crim. App. Jan. 20, 1988) (prosecutor's statements that sentencing jury was "just a part of the process" for determining punishment impermissibly lessened the jury's sense of its decision-making role); Hooks v. State, 502 So. 2d 401, 401 (Ala. Crim. App. 1988) (prosecutor's statements regarding jury's advisory role were accurate and nonmisleading); State v. Ramseur, 106 N.J. 123, 316, 524 A.2d 188, 186–87 (1987) (trial court's instructions that jury's task was "merely to apply the law" were prejudicial error); Combs v. State, 525 So. 2d 853, 858 (Fla. 1988) (trial court's instructions that jury would issue an advisory sentence was accurate statement of Florida law and did not violate dictates of *Caldwell*).

157. Combs v. State, 525 So. 2d 853, 858 (Fla. 1988). But *cf.* Garcia v. State, 492 So. 2d 360, 367 (Fla. 1986) (failure to stress importance of jury role would violate *Caldwell*).

158. *E.g.,* Tedder v. State, 322 So. 2d 908, 910 (Fla. 1975).

159. *E.g.,* ALA. CODE § 13A-5-47(e) (1982).

160. *E.g.,* State v. White, 286 N.C. 395, 404, 211 S.E.2d 445, 450 (1975) (prosecutor's argument to jury regarding availability of judicial review of death sentence "was clearly intended to overcome the jurors' natural reluctance to render a verdict of guilty to murder in the first degree by diluting their responsibility for its consequences").

161. *E.g.,* Radelet, *supra* at 1413 ("The first observation that can be made from these data is that jurors are less likely to favor the imposition of a death sentence than are judges."); KALVEN & ZEISEL, THE AMERICAN JURY 434–49 (1971).

162. Lockhart v. McCree, 106 S. Ct. 1758, 1764–70 (1986) (process of "death-qualifying" jurors—identifying and excluding from service venire members with conscientious scruples against the death penalty—held constitutional).

163. *E.g.,* Caldwell v. Mississippi, 472 U.S. 320, 330 (1985); California v. Ramos, 463 U.S. 992, 998–99 (1983); Beck v. Alabama, 447 U.S. 625, 637–38 (1980); Lockett v. Ohio, 438 U.S. 586, 604 (1978); Gardner v. Florida, 430 U.S. 349, 357–58 (1977); Woodson v. North Carolina, 428 U.S. 280, 305 (1976).

164. As Justice Marshall wrote in *Caldwell,* the capital sentencer must consider "those compassionate or mitigating factors stemming from the diverse frailties of humankind." *Caldwell,* 472 U.S. at 330 (quoting Woodson v. North Carolina, 428 U.S. at 304). Although Marshall noted that appellate courts were not suited to evaluate the appropriateness of the death penalty in the first instance, *id.,* data describing the history of jury overrides in Florida strongly demonstrate that trial judges are far more likely to impose a death sentence than are jurors. As discussed in Chapter III, in some 120 cases a jury was not willing to recommend that the defendant be put to death, whereas the trial judge chose to disregard the jury's sentiment and impose the death penalty.

165. Interview with Florida circuit judge John Rudd, conducted for Geimer & Amsterdam, *Why Jurors Vote Life or Death: Operative Factors in Ten Florida Death Penalty Cases,* 15 AM. J. CRIM. L. 1, 1 (1988).

166. *See Caldwell,* 472 U.S. at 333–34.

167. *Id.* at 328–29.

168. The Court noted that states have long recognized the importance of maintaining a jury's sense of responsibility in noncapital cases as well, albeit not as a matter of eighth amendment doctrine. *Id.* at 334. Although the ramifications of diluting a jury's role in these contexts is arguably less profound than in the capital setting, the body of state law condemning such a result is no less abundant. Regardless of the punishment at stake, the general prohibition is well established: actions that have the effect of minimizing the jury's task are intolerable as a matter of law and are grounds for reversal. *E.g.,* United States v. Fiorito, 300 F.2d 424, 427 (7th Cir. 1962) (trial court's instruction, during narcotics trial, that court of appeals would review outcome was prejudicial and required reversal); Blount v. State, 509 S.W.2d 615, 616 (Tex. Crim. App. 1974) (state law violated by prosecutor's statements during sentencing phase of robbery trial that jury need not concern itself with granting probation); People v. Smith, 206 Cal. 235, 239, 273 P. 789, 790 (1929) (instructions during embezzlement trial were reversible error under state law where jury was told that trial court could reduce punishment); Hodges v. State, 15 Ga. 117, 122 (1854) (stabbing conviction reversed where trial court instructed jury that defendant could seek appeal to state supreme court: "Again we must condemn, as we have had occasion to do heretofore, this remark. If defendants have the advantage, as intimated by the Court, it is one which they are entitled to under the law; and it does not relieve either the Court or the Jury from the obligation to mete out to them, not only the full measure of their legal rights, but in cases of doubt, to give to prisoners the benefit of these doubts. To administer justice in mercy, less than this cannot be done.").

169. Sawyer v. Butler, __ U.S. __ (1990).

170. State v. Biggerstaff, 17 Mont. 510, 514, 43 P. 709, 711 (1896) ("The lan-

guage complained of was highly improper and reprehensible, and we think the court should, of its own motion, have prevented its use, or directed the jury to wholly disregard it."); Monroe v. State, 5 Ga. 85, 139 (1848) ("We think, too, that the remark which fell from the Court, reminding the jury of the existence of an appellate tribunal, . . . however well intentioned, was calculated, nevertheless, to lessen their sense of their own responsibility.").

171. Wiley v. State, 449 So. 2d 756, 762 (Miss. 1984) (finding reversible error in prosecutor's remarks).

172. *Id.* (emphasis added).

173. *E.g.,* Williams v. State, 445 So. 2d 798, 810–12 (Miss. 1984) (state law required that death sentence be reversed and remanded for new sentencing hearing where state argued that defendant had "eight stages of appeal" ahead of him); Hill v. State, 432 So. 2d 427, 439 (Miss. 1983) (although procedural bar precluded reversal, "[A]ny argument by the state which distorts or minimizes this solemn obligation and responsibility of the jury is serious error. . . . [I]n a death penalty case a jury should never be given false comfort that any decision they make will, or can be, corrected").

174. Caldwell v. State, 443 So. 2d 806, 816 (Miss. 1983) (Lee, J., dissenting, joined by Patterson, C.J., Prather, J., and Robertson, J.).

175. *E.g.,* Pait v. State, 112 So. 2d 380, 383–86 (Fla, 1959) (prosecutor's comments to jury that defendant's death sentence would be subject to appeal by state supreme court violated state law and required reversal); Fleming v. State, 240 Ga. 142, 146, 240 S.E.2d 37, 40 (1977) (death sentence reversed where prosecutor, contrary to state law, told jury that penalty would be reviewed by trial judge and state supreme court); Prevatte v. State, 233 Ga. 929, 931, 214 S.E.2d 365, 367 (1975) (prosecutor's remarks to judge, in jury's presence, that trial court could reduce death sentence had "inevitable effect" of encouraging jury to "attach diminished consequences to their verdict, and take less than full responsibility for their awesome task. . . ."); State v. Henderson, 226 Kan. 726, 737, 603 P.2d 613, 622 (1979) (district attorney's remarks that homicide conviction could be reversed upon appeal amounted to reversible error under state law); Ward v. Commonwealth, 695 S.W.2d 404, 408 (Ky. 1985) (Kentucky law forbids prosecutor's attempt to diminish jury's sense of responsibility by describing jury's death sentence as "only a recommendation"); Ice v. Commonwealth, 667 S.W.2d 671, 676 (Ky. 1984) (prosecutor's references to jury's sentencing decision as recommendation impermissible under law of commonwealth); State v. Willie, 410 So. 2d 1019, 1034 (La. 1982) (prosecutor's argument that jury's decision was not final lessened its "awesome responsibility" and required reversal under state law); State v. Berry, 391 So. 2d 406, 420 (La. 1980) (Calogero, J., dissenting) ("[T]he overwhelming consensus of cases from other jurisdictions is to the effect that 'comments by the prosecuting attorney . . . to the jury on the power of the court to suspend sentence . . . are calculated to induce the jury to disregard their responsibility, and are improper") (quoting 75 Am. Jur. 2d *Trial* § 230, 309); State v. Jones, 296 N.C. 495, 251 S.E.2d 425 (1979) (prosecutor's impermissible references to possibility of appellate review and commutation required re-

versal under state law); State v. White, 286 N.C. 395, 211 S.E.2d 445 (1975) (prosecutor's argument regarding judicial review of death sentence was "clearly intended to overcome the jurors' natural reluctance" by diluting their sense of responsibility); State v. Tyner, 273 S.C. 646, 658, 258 S.E.2d 559, 565–66 (1979) (death sentence reversed where prosecutor, disregarding state law, commented that jury's decision would be reviewed by trial judge and appellate court); State v. Gilbert, 273 S.C. 690, 698, 258 S.E.2d 890, 894 (1979) (jury's sense of responsibility was diminished by prosecutor's argument that trial judge would review death sentence). *But see* State v. Monroe, 397 So. 2d 1258, 1270 (La. 1981) (reference by prosecutor to appellate review, in light of entire argument, did not amount to reversible error under Louisiana law); State v. Berry, 391 So. 2d 406, at 418 (prosecutor's brief reference to appellate review did not render proceedings fundamentally unfair).

176. *E.g.,* Ward v. Commonwealth, 695 S.W.2d 404, 407–08 (Ky. 1985) (prosecutor's comment that jury would make "only a recommendation" of sentence, although technically accurate, violated commonwealth's law by impermissibly reducing jury's sense of responsibility).

177. People v. Morse, 60 Cal. 2d 631, 649, 388 P.2d 33, 44–47, 36 Cal. Rptr. 201, 215 (1964) (prosecutor's argument that trial judge could reduce death sentence tends to reduce jury's sense of responsibility in imposing the death penalty); People v. Johnson, 284 N.Y. 182, 188, 30 N.E.2d 465, 467 (1940) (arguments emphasizing defendant's right to appeal constituted reversible error); State v. Mount, 30 N.J. 195, 212, 152 A.2d 343, 351 (1959) (reversible error in trial court's instructions to venireperson that appellate review would follow death sentence).

178. People v. Johnson, 284 N.Y. at 188, 30 N.E.2d at 467 (emphasis added).

179. California v. Ramos, 463 U.S. 992, 998–99 (1983); *see also* Mills v. Maryland, 108 S. Ct. 1860, 1866–67 (1988); Eddings v. Oklahoma, 455 U.S. 104, 110–12 (1982); Lockett v. Ohio, 438 U.S. 586, 602–05 (1978); Gardner v. Florida, 430 U.S. 349, 357–58 (1977); Woodson v. North Carolina, 428 U.S. 280, 305 (1976).

180. *Caldwell,* 472 U.S. at 329.

181. *E.g.,* Combs v. State, 525 So. 2d 853, 858 (Fla. 1988) (trial court's instructions that jury could issue an advisory sentence was accurate statement of Florida law and did not violate dictates of *Caldwell*); Pope v. Wainwright, 496 So. 2d 798, 805 (Fla. 1986) (trial judge may explain to the jury its advisory role "as long as the significance of [the jury's] recommendation is adequately stressed"); Hooks v. State, 502 So. 2d 401, 401 (Ala. Crim. App. 1988) (statements regarding jury's advisory role were accurate and nonmisleading).

182. *E.g.,* ALA. CODE § 13A-5-47(e) ("In deciding upon the sentence, the trial court shall determine whether the aggravating circumstances it finds to exist outweigh the mitigating circumstances it finds to exist. . . ."); FLA. STAT. 921.141(3) ("Notwithstanding the recommendation of a majority of the jury, the court, after weighing the aggravating and mitigating circumstances, shall enter a sentence of life imprisonment or death. . . ."); IND. CODE § 35-50-2-9(e) ("The court shall make the final determination of the sentence, after considering the jury's recommendation,

and the sentence shall be based upon the same standards that the jury was required to consider. The court is not bound by the jury's recommendation.").

183. Fla. Stat. § 921.141(3).

184. Although *Tedder* requires a judge to give great deference to a jury's recommendation of a *life* sentence, the Florida Supreme Court subsequently held that the same standard extends to a jury's recommendation of *death* as well. *E.g.,* Smith v. State, 515 So. 2d 182 (Fla. 1987); LeDuc v. State, 365 So. 2d 149, 151 (Fla. 1978) (jury's sentence of death "should not be disturbed if all relevant data was [sic] considered, unless there appears strong reasons [sic] to believe that reasonable persons could not agree with the recommendation").

185. Tedder v. State, 322 So. 2d 908, 910 (Fla. 1975).

186. *E.g.,* DuBoise v. State, 520 So. 2d 260, 266 (Fla. 1988); Wasko v. State, 505 So. 2d 1314, 1318 (Fla. 1987); Garcia v. State, 492 So. 2d 360, 367 (Fla. 1986); Huddleston v. State, 475 So. 2d 204, 206 (Fla. 1985); Lusk v. State, 446 So. 2d 1038, 1043 (Fla. 1984); Richardson v. State, 437 So. 2d 1091, 1095 (Fla. 1983); McCampbell v. State, 421 So. 2d 1072, 1075 (Fla. 1982); Jacobs v. State, 396 So. 2d 713, 717–18 (Fla. 1981); Ross v. State, 386 So. 2d 1191, 1197 (Fla. 1980); Stone v. State, 378 So. 2d 765, 772 (Fla. 1979); Shue v. State, 366 So. 2d 387, 390 (Fla. 1978); Burch v. State, 343 So. 2d 831, 834 (Fla. 1977); Provence v. State, 337 So. 2d 783, 787 (Fla. 1976).

187. Indeed, the Florida Supreme Court has rejected this notion, holding: "If the jury's recommendation, upon which the judge must rely, results from an unconstitutional procedure, then the entire sentencing process necessarily is tainted by that procedure." Riley v. Wainwright, 517 So. 2d 656, 659 (Fla. 1987); *accord* Thompson v. Dugger, 515 So. 2d 173 (Fla. 1987). The best description of how the Florida courts treat jury error is in Mann v. Dugger, 844 F.2d 1446 (11th Cir. 1988) (en banc).

188. Espinosa v. Florida, 112 S. Ct. 2926 (1992); Parker v. Dugger, 498 U.S. 308 (1991); Spaziano v. Florida, 468 U.S. 447, 461–62, 465 (1984) (although Constitution does not require capital sentencing by jury, jury input serves as "community voice" in the sentencing process); Dobbert v. Florida, 432 U.S. 282, 295 (1977) (*Tedder* standard affords defendant "significant" safeguards).

189. Mann v. Dugger, 844 F.2d 1446, 1454–55 (11th Cir. 1988) (en banc) ("Because the jury's recommendation is significant in these ways, the concerns voiced in *Caldwell* are triggered when a Florida sentencing jury is misled into believing that its role is unimportant. Under such circumstances, a real danger exists that a resulting death sentence will be based at least in part on the determination of a decisionmaker that has been misled as to the nature of its responsibility."); Adams v. Wainwright, 804 F.2d 1526, 1530 (11th Cir. 1986) ("Clearly, then, the jury's role in the Florida sentencing process is so crucial that dilution of its sense of responsibility for its recommended sentence constitutes a violation of *Caldwell*."), *modified sub nom. on other grounds,* Adams v. Dugger, 816 F.2d 1493 (11th Cir. 1987), *rev'd on other grounds,* ___ U.S. ___ (1989).

190. *Mann,* 844 F.2d at 1454.

191. The Eleventh Circuit acknowledged the effect that political considerations might have upon a capital-sentencing judge. "It would indeed be surprising were the trial judge, who in Florida is also an electorally accountable official, not powerfully affected by the result of that [jury recommendation] process." *Id.; see also* State v. Roberts, 709 S.W.2d 857, 872 (Mo. 1986) (Blackman, J., concurring) ("Under the climate presently prevailing a circuit judge would risk his career if he were to set aside a death verdict rendered by a jury."); Radelet, *supra* note 16, at 1414. The saga of Chief Justice Rose Bird and her two colleagues on the California Supreme Court illustrates this point. The three were targeted by conservative lobbyists critical of their record on death penalty reversals. Spurred on by the ensuing multi-million-dollar campaign to unseat the justices, California voters denied them reconfirmation in the 1986 elections. L.A. DAILY J., Nov. 6, 1986, at 1; *id.*, Aug. 26, 1986, at 1.

As Radelet explains, there is no central data source for tracing cases where a trial judge sentenced a defendant to life after a jury recommendation of death. Nevertheless, Radelet's research indicated that no more than a dozen such overrides occurred, as compared at the time to nearly ninety death sentences following a jury recommendation of life. Radelet, *supra* note 16, at 1454.

192. Delaware, which only recently required both jury and judge to participate in capital sentencing, appears also to be adopting the *Tedder* standard for governing disagreements between decision makers. *See* Pennell v. State, 604 A.2d 1368, 1377–78 (Del. 1992). There have to date been no death sentences imposed under Delaware's new statute after jury life recommendations.

193. Combs v. Cook, 238 Ind. 392, 397, 151 N.E.2d 144, 147 (1958) (a statute is to be examined and interpreted as a whole, giving common and ordinary meaning to its words); *Ex parte* Jones, 456 So. 2d 380, 382–83 (Ala. 1984); *Ex parte* Madison County, Ala., 406 So. 2d 398, 400 (Ala. 1981).

194. As the Indiana Supreme Court held: "[I]t seems unlikely . . . that the legislature would specifically require the court to consider the jury's recommendation if that consideration amounted only to a book entry noting the recommendation. This court regards the practical effect of the jury's recommendation as significant." Williams v. State, No. 985-S-372, slip op. at 8 (Ind. July 8, 1988).

195. *E.g.,* Hooks v. State, 3 Div. 460, slip op. at 62 (Ala. Crim. App. Mar. 10, 1987) ("The trial judge's and prosecutor's remarks clearly defined the jury's role in the sentencing scheme. Thus, the jury could not have been confused as to its responsibility in the sentencing process. The remarks here were a correct statement of the law and did not tend to mislead or misinform the jury, [and] thus we conclude the remarks were not improper under *Caldwell*."). But compare *Hooks* to cases where errors were made at the penalty phase, before an "advisory" jury, and were held not harmless and grounds for reversal of sentence. *E.g., Ex parte* Whisenhant, 482 So. 2d 1247, 1248 (Ala. 1984) (state's improper references to other crimes allegedly committed by defendant rendered penalty phase unfair and required new sentencing hearing). Alabama's mixed message, then, is one of both minimizing and maintaining the significance of the jury's sentencing role.

196. ALA. CODE § 13A-5-46.

197. Although the Eleventh Circuit's *Mann* decision focused on the jury override provisions of the Florida system, its analysis of the powerful psychological impact that a jury's advisory sentence has upon a trial judge also applies to the systems of Alabama, Indiana, and Delaware:

> In analyzing the role of the sentencing jury, the Supreme Court of Florida has apparently been influenced by a normative judgment that a jury recommendation of death carries great force in the mind of the trial judge. . . . We do not find it surprising that the supreme court would make this kind of normative judgment. A jury recommendation of death is, after all, the final stage in an elaborate process whereby the community expresses its judgment regarding the appropriateness of the death sentence.—Mann v. Dugger, 844 F.2d 1446, 1453–54 (11th Cir. 1988) (en banc).

198. Beck v. Alabama, 447 U.S. 625, 645 (1980); *cf.* Baldwin v. Alabama, 472 U.S. 372 (1985). Under Alabama's 1975 sentencing scheme (since repealed), a jury was required, upon finding a defendant guilty of first-degree murder, to issue a "recommendation" sentence of death. The *Baldwin* Court held that this provision was not unconstitutional, because judges were aware that juries had no opportunity to consider mitigating circumstances and that the advisory sentence conveyed "nothing more than a verdict of guilty." *Baldwin,* 472 U.S. at 388. The 1975 statute, unlike its current successor, did not contain language requiring the judge to "consider" the jury's recommendation.

199. Alabama has in essence a trifurcated system for sentencing defendants to death. A jury first determines whether an accused is eligible for the death penalty by reaching a decision regarding guilt or innocence. ALA. CODE § 13A-5-43 (1982). If a defendant is found guilty of a capital offense, the case then moves to a sentencing hearing before the same jury. ALA. CODE §§ 13A-5-45, -46 (1982). After hearing evidence and argument, the jury provides a penalty recommendation to the trial court, which imposes sentence. ALA. CODE §§ 13A-5-46(d), (g), -47 (1982).

200. 396 So. 2d 645 (Ala. 1981).

201. 447 U.S. 625 (1980).

202. *See Beck v. State,* 396 So. 2d at 660 (solution to problem "cannot be effected by the elimination of the jury's participation in the sentencing process").

203. *Id.* at 659. *See also* Prothro v. State, 370 So. 2d 740, 743 (Ala. Crim. App. 1979) (jury function in capital cases has been "assiduously . . . guarded" throughout the years). *Beck* examined the jury role as established by state penal codes dating back to the early 1800s. In the early nineteenth century death sentences were mandatory following a jury determination of guilt for certain offenses. *Id.* at 648–49. Each of the ten statutes considered by the *Beck* court from the 1840s until the law was revised in 1975 required the jury to make the capital-sentencing decision under a grant of discretion. *Id.* at 649–652. *See, e.g.,* ALA. CODE § 15-15-24(a) (1982) ("The court

shall not in any event, however, impose capital punishment without the intervention of a jury.").

204. Alabama's current capital statute was amended in 1981 to address *Beck*. One pertinent difference between the present law and the statute *Beck* addressed is that a trial court's ability to reject a jury verdict of life without parole is now permitted by statute, ALA. CODE § 13A-5-47 (1982), whereas that power under the earlier law was made express by judicial ruling. *See Ex parte* Hays, 518 So. 2d 768, 775–76 (Ala. 1986).

205. Alabama's unbroken adherence to the involvement of a jury in any capital-sentencing procedure has led to the unusual requirement that a judge cannot accept a plea of guilty to a capital offense and impose a life-without-parole punishment without jury participation. ALA. CODE § 13A-5-42 (1982); *see also* Youngblood v. State, 372 So. 2d 34 (Ala. Crim. App. 1979) (trial court in capital case could neither determine guilt nor fix punishment of defendant without intervention of jury, even though defendant sought to plead guilty); Prothro v. State, 370 So. 2d at 746 (Alabama law does not permit trial court, without jury, to fix punishment in capital case). *See also* Johnson v. State, 502 So. 2d 877, 879 (Ala. Crim. App. 1987) (jury plays "key role" in sentencing phase of capital case, as is clear in *Beck*); Edwards v. State, 452 So. 2d 487, 493 (Ala. Crim. App. 1982), *rev'd on other grounds,* 452 So. 2d 503 (Ala. 1983) (*Beck* makes clear that jury participates in sentencing scheme).

206. The statute requires a full hearing that must comport with due process and that provides the jury with every element traditionally associated with a penalty phase proceeding. Richardson v. State, 376 So. 2d 205 (Ala. Crim. App. 1978), *aff'd* 376 So. 2d 228 (Ala. 1979). After hearing evidence, argument, and instruction, ALA. CODE § 13A-5-46(d) (1982), the panel must have sufficient votes to reach a capital-sentencing determination (ten votes for death or seven for life), or a mistrial is declared and a new jury is empaneled. ALA. CODE §§ 13A-5-46(f), (g) (1982). (The jurors must, of course, be death-qualified, *see* Edwards v. State, 452 So. 2d at 493, and must be "life-qualified" upon request by the defense. Bracewell v. State, 506 So. 2d 354, 358 (Ala. Crim. App. 1986). The jury's participation can be waived only if both parties and the judge concur. ALA. CODE § 13A-5-46(c) (1982).

207. 556 So. 2d 744 (Ala. 1987).

208. ALA. CODE § 13A-5-49(1) (1982).

209. *Ex parte* Williams, 556 So. 2d at 745.

210. *Id.*

211. *E.g., Ex parte* Stewart, No. 1920509 (Ala. Sept. 3, 1993); Jefferson v. State, 473 So. 2d 1100 (Ala. Crim. App. 1984), *cert. denied,* 479 U.S. 922 (1986); *see also* Hallford v. State, 548 So. 2d 536 (Ala. Crim. App. 1988) (jury must be given limiting instruction on heinous, atrocious, or cruel aggravating factor). New jury hearings have also been ordered where improper argument might have influenced deliberations. *See, e.g.,* Guthrie v. State, 616 So. 2d 914, 932 (Ala. Crim. App. 1993) ("We see this as a clear infringement upon the jury's important and critical discretion in determining whether to recommend a sentence of death or of life imprisonment

without parole.''); *Ex parte* Rutledge, 482 So. 2d 1262, 1263–65 (Ala. 1984); *Ex parte* Whisenhant, 482 So. 2d 1247, 1249 (Ala. 1984), *cert. denied,* 496 U.S. 943 (1990), or where improper evidence was presented to the jury at the penalty phase. *See, e.g.,* McGahee v. State, 554 So. 2d 454, 471 (Ala. Crim. App. 1989), *aff'd,* 554 So. 2d 473 (Ala. 1989); *see also* Coulter v. State, 438 So. 2d 336, 349 (Ala. Crim. App. 1982).

212. ALA. CODE § 13A-5-47(e) (1982).

213. *E.g.,* Stockwell v. State, CR 89-225 (Ala. Crim. App. Dec. 30, 1993), slip op. at 50 (no Alabama law specifies weight trial court is to accord jury's advisory sentence); State v. Taylor, No. CR-92-1313 (Ala. Crim. App. July 8, 1994), slip op. at 28 n.3 (same); Hadley v. State, 575 So. 2d 145, 158 (Ala. Crim. App. 1990) (''Alabama Supreme Court has yet to formulate a distinct standard'') (quoting Martinez-Chavez v. State, 534 N.E.2d 731, 734 n.2 (Ind. 1989)). *See* Colquitt, *The Death Penalty Laws of Alabama,* 33 ALA. L. REV. 13, 328 (1981) (trial judge's seminal analysis of Alabama's capital statute, in which it is noted that ''Alabama appellate courts can reasonably be expected to develop and apply restrictions to a trial judge's power to reject a sentence recommended by a jury'').

214. Circuit court judges, who face partisan elections every six years, adjudicate Alabama capital cases. ALA. CODE § 17-2-7 (1982).

215. *E.g.,* State v. Bush, No. CC-81-1335 (Montgomery County 1991); State v. Duncan, No. CC-87-271 (Dallas County 1988); State v. Musgrove, No. CC-83-1476FL (Madison County 1985); *see also* State v. Myers. No. CC-91-988 (Morgan County 1994) (jury life verdict ''single strongest mitigating factor'').

216. The Alabama statute directs trial courts only as to the weighing of aggravation and mitigation. ALA. CODE § 13A-5-47(e) (1982). *E.g.,* Murry v. State, No. CC-82-211G (Montgomery County 1982) (stating belief that jury verdict can only be considered as mitigator).

217. *E.g.,* State v. Crowe, No. CC-83-2727 (Jefferson County 1984); State v. Harrell, No. 82-1147 (Jefferson County 1983); State v. Jones, No. CC-81-610 (Baldwin County 1982).

218. Still other courts strive to resolve their dilemma by viewing the advisory verdict not as a full mitigating circumstance under the law but as an ''aspect'' of mitigation that still must somehow be made part of the weighing process. *E.g.,* State v. Johnson, No. CC-84-0331 (Morgan County 1985) (jury verdict an ''aspect of mitigation separate and apart and in addition to'' statutory and nonstatutory factors); State v. McMillian, No. CC-87-137 (Monroe County 1988) (jury verdict weighed independently as aspect of mitigation separate and apart from other factors); *see also* State v. Owens, No. CC-84-455 (Russell County 1985) (''The Court finds that the aggravating circumstances outweigh the mitigating circumstances when the jury recommendation of life without parole is also taken into consideration.'')

219. Godfrey v. Georgia, 446 U.S. at 429 (sentencer's interpretation of factor matter of ''sheer speculation''). *E.g.,* State v. Neelley, No. CC-82-276 (DeKalb County 1983) (court has ''weighed the aggravating and mitigating circumstances . . .

and has given consideration to the recommendation of the jury"); *see also* State v. Flowers, No. CC-89-65 (Baldwin County 1990); State v. McNair, No. 90-086 (Henry/Montgomery Counties 1993).

220. *E.g.*, State v. Turner, No. CC-83-340-SW (Etowah County 1983).

221. *E.g.*, State v. Lindsey, No. CC-82-212 (Mobile County 1982) (court "judicially aware" of advisory verdict).

222. *E.g.*, State v. McGahee, No. CC-85-251 (Dallas County 1992); State v. Sockwell, No. CC-88-1244-HRT (Montgomery 1991); State v. Starks, No. CC-88-23 (Pike County 1989).

223. *E.g.*, State v. Knotts, No. CC-91-2537-PR (Montgomery County 1993); State v. Wesley, No. 83-2501-FDM (Mobile County 1988); State v. Williams, No. CC-88-2742 (Mobile 1990); State v. Gentry, No. CC-89-1345 (Jefferson County 1992); State v. Neelley, No. CC-82-276 (DeKalb County 1983).

224. *E.g.*, Frazier v. State, CC-85-3291 (Mobile County 1986) ("if this were not a proper case for the death penalty to be imposed, a proper case could scarcely be imagined"); *see also Ex parte* Hays, 518 So. 2d 768, 777 (Ala. 1986) (agreeing that jury life recommendation was "unquestionably a bizarre result"), *cert. denied*, 485 U.S. 929 (198). This approach resembles Florida's standard. *See* Tedder v. State, 332 So. 2d 908, 910 (Fla. 1975) (facts for death must be "so clear and convincing that virtually no reasonable person could differ" before a jury life recommendation can be rejected).

225. State v. Murry, No. CC-82-211G (Montgomery County 1982).

226. State v. Murry, No. CC-82-211G (Montgomery County 1989).

227. The courts have sustained challenges to the override in two ways. First, they have noted that it is allowed by statute: *e.g.*, Harrell v. State, 470 So. 2d 1303, 1309 (Ala. Crim. App. 1984), *cert. denied*, 474 U.S. 935 (1985); Jones v. State, 456 So. 2d 366, 373 (Ala. Crim. App. 1983), *cert. denied*, 470 U.S. 1062 (1985); and *Ex parte* Lindsey, 456 So. 2d 393, 394 (Ala. 1984), *cert. denied*, 470 U.S. 1023 (1985). Second, they have cited to the decisions in Proffitt v. Florida, 428 U.S. 242 (1976), or Spaziano v. Florida, 468 U.S. 447 (1984), approving the placing of sentencing authority in two decision makers: *e.g.*, Crowe v. State, 485 So. 2d 351, 364–65 (1984), *rev'd on other grounds*, 485 So. 2d 373 (1986); Frazier v. State, 562 So. 2d 543, 550 (Ala. Crim. App. 1989), *rev'd on other grounds*, 562 So. 2d 560 (Ala. 1989); and Williams v. State, 627 So. 2d 985, 992 (Ala. Crim. App. 1991), *cert. denied*, 114 S. Ct. 1387 (1994). The Alabama courts have disregarded the Florida system's *Tedder* standard as an "extra" protection that is not constitutionally required. Owens v. State, 531 So. 2d 2, 16 (Ala. Crim. App. 1986), *rev'd on other grounds*, 531 So. 2d 21 (Ala. 1987); Jones v. State, 456 So. 2d at 382–83.

228. *E.g.*, State v. Stephens, 580 So. 2d 11, 25–26 (Ala. Crim. App. 1990), *cert. denied*, 112 S. Ct. 176 (1991).

229. *E.g.*, State v. Neelley, 494 So. 2d 669, 680 (Ala. Crim. App. 1985) (court states that "[t]he jury imposed a sentence of life without parole" in assessing *Witherspoon* challenge; no further mention is made of sentence), *cert. denied*, 480 U.S. 926

(1987); Turner v. State, 521 So. 2d 93, 94 (Ala. Crim. App. 1987) ("He was found guilty of the capital offense, and, after a sentencing hearing, the jury recommended that he be punished by life imprisonment without parole. . . . [T]hereafter, the trial court sentenced appellant to death by electrocution.").

230. *E.g.,* Freeman v. State, 555 So. 2d 196, 213–14 (Ala. Crim. App. 1988) ("The trial judge's findings clearly showed that he considered the jury's advisory verdict."), *cert. denied,* 496 U.S. 912 (1990); Harrell v. State, 470 So. 2d at 1309 ("The trial judge considered the jury's recommendation . . . in his written finding."); Carr v. State, No. CR-92-362 (Ala. Crim. App. Mar. 4, 1994), slip op. at 22 ("The trial court's sentencing order reflects the fact that the court gave 'consideration to the recommendation of the jury in its advisory verdict that the defendant be sentenced to life without parole.' "). Even in cases of override, the supreme court's examination of a death sentence is generally limited to the basic concern with passion and prejudice and proportionality accorded all sentences of death and found in most death penalty statutes. ALA. CODE § 13A-5-53(b), (c) (1982). *See* Clemons v. Mississippi, 494 U.S. at 744 (Mississippi Supreme Court's performance of proportionality review and finding that death was appropriate when aggravation was compared to mitigation did not salvage death sentence where potentially arbitrary element not specifically addressed).

231. *E.g.,* Coral v. State, 628 So. 2d 988 (Ala. Crim. App. 1992); Musgrove v. State, 519 So. 2d 565 (Ala. Crim. App. 1986); Jackson v. State No. 4 Div. 388 (Ala. Crim. App. Aug. 21, 1992), slip op. at 46–47.

232. *E.g.,* Rieber v. State, No. 91-1500 (Ala. Crim. App. June 17, 1994); White v. State, 587 So. 2d 1218, 1231–32 (Ala. Crim. App. 1990), *cert. denied,* 112 S. Ct. 979 (1992).

233. *E.g.,* McMillian v. State, 594 So. 2d 1253 (Ala. Crim. App. 1991), *remanded,* 594 So. 2d 1288 (Ala. 1992).

234. Gentry v. State, 595 So. 2d 578 (Ala. Crim. App. 1991).

235. Tarver v. State, 500 So. 2d 1232 (Ala. Crim. App. 1986); McNair v. State, No. CR 90-1556 (Ala. Crim. App. Jan. 21, 1994).

236. *E.g.,* Boyd v. State, 542 So. 2d 1247, 1259–60, 1269–70 (Ala. Crim. App. 1988), *cert. denied,* 493 U.S. 883 (1989); Crowe v. State, 485 So. 2d 351 at 364–65. In affirming a small number of overrides, the courts have provided an analysis that could approximate a standard of review. *E.g., Ex parte* Hays, 518 So. 2d at 777 (approving trial court's override because jury life recommendation for man convicted in lynching was "unquestionably a bizarre result"); Jackson v. State, No. 4 Div. 388 (Ala. Crim. App. Aug. 21, 1992), slip op. at 44–45 (upholding override where seasoned trial judge determined this was most heinous crime he had ever encountered). Yet while one Alabama Supreme Court justice has averred that the court "is especially sensitive" in evaluating overrides, *Ex parte* Tarver, 553 So. 2d 633, 634 (Ala. 1989) (Maddox, J., concurring), *cert. denied,* 494 U.S. 1090 (1990), this declaration is not borne out by any reasonable review of the cases.

237. 632 So. 2d 501 (Ala. Sup. Ct. 1994).

238. 534 N.E.2d 731, 734 (Ind. 1989).

239. Schiro v. State, 451 N.E.2d 1047 (Ind. 1983), *cert. denied,* 464 U.S. 1003 (1987).

240. *Martinez Chavez,* 534 N.E.2d at 733.

241. *Id.* at 735. Other Indiana cases defer to the *Martinez Chavez–Tedder* standard. In Minnick v. State, 544 N.E.2d 471, 482 (Ind. 1989), the state supreme court upheld a judge override of a life recommendation on the *Martinez Chavez* rule that "no reasonable person would find a death sentence inappropriate here." In *Minnick,* the Indiana Supreme Court concluded that in *Martinez Chavez* there were two men, one of whom could be viewed by reasonable people as less culpable in the murder. *Id.* The court then reasoned that because Minnick was acting alone, there was no basis for comparison. *Id.* This distinction was weak and may indicate a dissatisfaction with the *Martinez Chavez* test. The sweeping assertion that no reasonable person could find death to be inappropriate in Minnick's case indicates a willingness to allow the overriding of jury recommendations. Further, despite the apparent high standard for override, the Indiana court did not find it improper for a judge to tell a capital jury that their sentence was "a recommendation to the trial judge who would make the final determination." Evans v. State, 563 N.E.2d 1251, 1256 (Ind. 1990).

In another case, the same standard was used to order resentencing in an inappropriate override. Kennedy v. State, 578 N.E. 2d 633, 637 (Ind. 1991), *cert. denied,* 112 S. Ct. 1299 (1992). In *Kennedy,* the court remanded a case in which the judge overrode a jury's recommendation of life imprisonment, directing the trial court to reconsider the sentence in light of the *Martinez Chavez* standard. *Id.*

242. *Kennedy v. State,* 578 N.E.2d 633 (Ind. 1991), *cert. denied,* 112 S. Ct. 1299 (1992).

243. *Id.* at 637 (emphasis added).

244. *Daniels v. State,* 561 N.E.2d 487 (Ind. 1990).

245. Williams v. State, __ N.W.2d __, __ (Ind. 1988) (quoting Brewer v. State, 417 N.E.2d 889, 909 (Ind.), *cert. denied,* 458 U.S. 1122 (1981)); *see also* Chavez v. State, 534 N.E.2d 731, 735 (Ind. 1989).

246. Mann v. Dugger, 844 F.2d at 1454.

247. *Jacobs v. State,* 361 So. 2d 640, 650–51 (Ala. 1978) (Jones, J., dissenting) (footnote omitted).

248. For example, there were eight capital convictions in Montgomery County, Alabama, between January 1, 1986, and August 8, 1988. In seven cases, the judge and jury agreed on the sentence. In one case, the judge sentenced the defendant to life without parole after the jury recommended death. *See* Letter from Wendy Parker to Eva Ansley, Aug. 15, 1988. In author's possession.

249. Ward v. Commonwealth, 695 S.W. 2d 404, 408, 409 (Ky. 1985) (Leibson, J., concurring).

250. *Caldwell's* "no effect" test has been subsequently applied by the Court in one other capital sentence case. Hitchcock v. Dugger, 107 S. Ct. 1821 (1987) (Court rejected state's harmlessness argument because it could not "confidently conclude"

that excluded evidence "would have had *no effect* upon the jury's deliberations") (emphasis added).

251. David Bruck, Does the Death Penalty Matter?, Address Given at Austin Hall, Harvard Law School (Oct. 22, 1990).

252. PERRY, *supra* note 45, at 176–79.

253. Recall that there is an informal rule that it takes six votes to dispose of a case summarily.

254. Perry goes on to observe:

> Prior to this response there was a good lesson for me on interviewing. By the time I interviewed this justice, I had heard the term "defensive denial" many times and assumed that the term was used universally. Other justices knew exactly what I meant when I used the term. However, when I asked this justice about defensive denials, he looked very puzzled and asked me to repeat the question. Then I was puzzled, because I could not understand why he was confused. After I posed the question again, he launched on a long exposition of why it was rare and unnecessary to write in defense of denial. Obviously, he is aware of the strategy of defensively denying, but evidently he does not use the terminology.—Perry, *supra* note 45, at 201–2.

## Epilogue

1. 466 U.S. 668 (1984) (Brennan, J., concurring in part and dissenting in part) (Marshall, J., dissenting).

2. *Furman,* 408 U.S. 238 (1972) (Brennan, J., concurring) (Marshall, J., concurring).

3. *Furman,* 408 U.S. 238 (1972); *Strickland,* 466 U.S. 668 (1984).

4. Professor Kelman refers to repeated dissent on the same issue as "sustained dissent." Kelman, *The Forked Path of Dissent,* 1985 SUP. CT. REV. 227, at 248–58.

5. Linda Greenhouse, *Court Discourages Late Claims of Innocence from Death Row: 6–3 Ruling Allows Only "Truly Persuasive" Cases,* N.Y. TIMES, Jan. 26, 1993, at A1.

# INDEX

▼   ▼   ▼

judicial decisionmaking (*cont.*)
Hart's secondary rules of, 276n. 106, 278n. 132, 278n. 136; inverse seniority, 86–87; Marshall's influence on, 37–38, 79–80, 165–67; number of written opinions, 171; "one-sided acceptance," 267n. 10, 288n. 17; "one-sided" dissents, 262n. 317; retentionist bloc, 165; sentencing responsibility, 193–204; seriatim opinions, 85, 86–90, 90–94, 97, 242n. 15, 243n. 27, 243n. 31; strategic legitimacy of dissents, 157–207; unanimity v. dissents, 85–86, 90–94, 125–26, 242n. 9, 289n. 25; Warren's influence on, 68–69
judicial Fabianism, 165–66
judicial restraint, 25, 26–27, 28, 122, 149–51, 154, 250n. 97
jurisprudence: autonomous law, 271n. 62; Black's philosophy of, 115–16, Brennan's philosophy of, 25–28, 29–32, 36, 274n. 90, 275n. 100; Critical Legal Studies, 151–55, 156, 285n. 240, 286n. 260; Douglas' philosophy of, 166; feminist, 151; Frankfurter's philosophy of, 25, 26–27, 28; Harlan's philosophy of, 122, 125; Holmes' philosophy of, 65, 112, 129; instrumentalist, 133–34, 141; judicial conservatives, 25, 26–27, 28; judicial restraint, 25, 26–27, 28, 122, 149–51, 153, 154, 250n. 97; legal realism, 144–47, 154, 156, 246n. 53, 281nn. 171–73; legitimate use of judicial power, 127–56; Marshall's philosophy of, 81, 82–83; and morality, 129–30, 268n. 21; natural-law theory, 72, 133, 134–37, 156, 271n. 62, 272n. 66, 273n. 78, 274n. 90; neutral-principles theory, 125, 147–48, 283n. 202; original intent doctrine, 23, 30, 31, 67, 81; positivism, 97–98, 133, 137–41, 156, 274n. 89, 276n. 112; procedural fairness in, 148–49;

repeated dissents and ultimate justice, 127–56; responsive law, 272n. 67; result oriented, 133–34; sociological, 65–68, 107, 109, 133–34, 137, 141–44, 146, 274n. 89, 279n. 154; and stare decisis, 131–34; strict constructionists, 115–16
jury: misinformation given to, 180, 183–84, 189; racist jurors, 58; selection of 190–91, 307n. 162; sense of responsibility of, 180, 182–204, 308n. 168
jury trial, right to, 101, 118, 120, 123, 262n. 327, 264n. 342; waiver of, 103
justifications for imposing death penalty, 75–76, 77, 281n. 167
juvenile offenders, 209–10

Kansas: sentencing responsibility in, 192
*Katz v. United States,* 120
Kelman, Mark, 151–53, 164, 165–66, 278n. 137, 288n. 17, 290n. 30, 291n. 32
Kennedy, Duncan, 285n. 246
Kennedy, John F., 28, 70
Kennedy, Robert, 70
Kentucky: sentencing responsibility in, 189–90, 192, 202
Kluger, Richard: *Simple Justice,* 38–39
*Knickerbocker Ice Co. v. Stewart,* 110
Ku Klux Klan, 61

*Lankford v. Idaho,* 158–61
*Lathrop v. Donahue,* 118
*Leach v. Carlile,* 113
Lee, Justice, 192
legal realism, 144–47, 154, 156, 246n. 53, 281nn. 171–73
legislative supremacy, 97–98, 102–3, 109–10, 111, 122, 131, 132–33, 139, 149, 165
Leman, Nicholas, 80
Lewis, Anthony, 37; *Make No Law,* 24
libel and slander, 24–25, 264n. 342
Library of Congress, justices' papers do-

discrimination test, 32–35; proof of, 32–35; sentencing discretion and, 10
racist jurors, 58
Randolph, Edmund, 87–88
Ransom, Leon, 48
Raz, Joseph, 139, 140–41, 156, 276nn. 115–29
Reed, Stanley, 59, 64, 68
Rehnquist, William, 161, 163; dissent in *Caldwell,* 181, 184; dissent in *Ford,* 165, 177, 180; *Herrera* opinion, 81–82; on Marshall, 210; on papers given Library of Congress, 9; on *Plessy,* 38–39; on review of sentencing, 215n. 35; on sentencing standards, 12
Rehnquist Court, 5, 126, 171, 204
restrictive housing covenants, 64–65
retirement: of Brennan, 4, 8, 35–36; of Frankfurter, 28; of Marshall, 4, 13; of White, 8
retroactive application of rulings, 120–21
Richman, Daniel B., 163
Roane, Spencer, 91
*Roe v. Wade,* 29, 299, 300n. 70
Rogers murders, 58
*Romano v. Oklahoma,* 184, 303n. 130
Roosevelt, Franklin D., 114
Roosevelt, Theodore, 106
*Roth v. United States,* 23, 25, 116
Rowland, Gail, 218n. 39
Rutledge, Wiley B., 261n. 311

Safire, William: *The First Dissident,* 84–85
sanity determinations. *See* insane accused
Savage, David, 157
Scalia, Antonin, 34, 171, 214n. 35, 215n. 35, 221n. 79
*Schenck v. United States,* 256n. 241
searches and seizures, 31, 119, 262n. 323
segregation, 37, 38–39, 40, 41–44, 45, 46, 51–57, 60, 104, 263n. 334. *See*

*also* Jim Crow; separate but equal doctrine
self-incrimination, privilege against, 29, 103, 119, 262n. 323, 264n. 342
Selznick, Phillip, 133, 142, 144, 271n. 62, 272n. 66, 272n. 67, 272n. 70, 280n. 154
sentencing standards, 5; aggravating circumstances in, 11, 193, 197,198, 199, 200; arbitrary and capricious, 76–77; in Critical Legal Studies, 152; cruel and unusual punishment standards and, 10–11, 76–77, 79; and due process, 10–13, 149; guided discretion, 11–13, 77, 182, 184, 186, 198, 199, 200, 201–2; intrinsic unfairness of, 6–7; judge's role in, 184–90, 193–204; jury's responsibility in, 182–204, 308n. 168; mandatory death penalty, 77, 269n. 33; mitigating circumstances in, 11, 77, 182, 193, 198, 199, 200, 221n. 77, 313n. 198; need for reliability and, 181–83, 191, 193; in noncapital cases, 306n. 168
separate but equal doctrine, 38, 52–55, 57, 65, 67–68, 69, 104
sexual harassment, 297–300
*Shapiro v. Thompson,* 122
*Shelley v. Kraemer,* 64–65
Sherman Anti-Trust Act of 1890, 102–3, 111–12
Sipuel, Ada Lois, 65
sixth amendment, 119, 264n. 342
*Skipper v. South Carolina,* 178
Slovik phenomenon, 185, 305n. 135
Smith, Ed, 64
*Smith v. Allwright,* 64
social legislation, 106, 107, 108, 109, 110
sociological jurisprudence, 65–68, 107, 109, 133–34, 137, 141–44, 146, 274n. 89, 279n. 154
solicitor general, office of, 71–72, 172–73

South Carolina: sentencing responsibility in, 192
*South Carolina v. Gathers,* 78
*Southern Pacific Co. v. Jensen,* 110
Spenkelink, John, 9
*Spiuel v. University of Oklahoma,* 65–66
*Standard Oil Co. v. United States,* 103
stare decisis doctrine, 100–101, 108, 115, 116, 121, 123, 125–28, 130–34, 165; and Critical Legal Studies, 153, 155; departure from precedent, 130–31, 130–34; in jurisprudence, 131–34; and legal realism, 144, 145–47; and moral values, 127–34; in natural-law theory, 135; and positivism, 137–38, 139, 140; repeated dissents and, 127–56; and sociological jurisprudence, 142–43
state sovereignty, 27, 96, 98–100, 102, 109–10, 111, 113, 121, 122, 123, 124, 165
*State v. Murry,* 199
statistical studies of sentencing patterns, 32–35, 78, 149
*Steel Mill Case,* 199
Stephenson, Gladys, 60–61
Stephenson, James, 61
*Stettler v. O'Hara,* 108
Stevens, John Paul, 161, 163, 164, 165, 169, 180, 181
Stevenson, Adlai, 21
Stewart, Potter, 10–11, 28, 119, 164, 294n. 43
Stone, Geoffrey, 22–23
Stone, Harlan Fiske, 65, 108, 109
Story, Joseph, 92, 94, 248n. 68
strategic legitimacy of dissents, 157–207
Steiker, Jordan, 79
*Strickland v. Washington,* 5, 209
Sullivan, Kathleen, 39
Sullivan, L. B., 24
Sunday closing laws, 261n. 307
Swayne, Justice Noah, 261n. 311
Sweatt, Herman Marion, 66

*Talbot v. Seeman,* 90
*Tedder v. State,* 194, 200
Tennessee: racism in, 60–63; sentencing responsibility in, 189–90
Texas: death penalty in, 6, 7, 209–10; segregation in, 66; voting rights in, 64
*Texas v. Johnson,* 24
thirteenth amendment, 104
Thomas, Clarence, 81, 171–72, 297–300
Thompkins, Philip D., 162
Thompson, Justice Smith, 92
*Thornburgh v. American College of Obstetricians and Gynecologists,* 299–300
*Tison v. Arizona,* 5–6, 289n. 19
Traynor, Justice Robert, 292n. 34
trespass cases, 120–21, 125
Trimble, Justice Robert, 92
Truman, Harry, 63, 117
Tune, John Henry, 20
Tushnet, Mark, 153–54
*Tyson & Brother v. Banton,* 109

United Nations: congress on prevention of crime, 75–76; study on capital punishment, 178
*United States v. American Tobacco Co.,* 103
*United States v. Bland,* 113, 114
*United States v. Kras,* 74–75
*United States v. MacIntosh,* 113, 114
*United States v. Nixon,* 289n. 25
*United States v. Schwimmer,* 113

Vanderbilt, Arthur, 18–19, 20–21, 22
victim impact statements, 78
Vietnam War protests, 121
Villard, Oswald Garrison, 42
Vinson, Fred, 67–68
Virginia: executions in, xi, 37; sentencing responsibility in, 189
"Voices" Brief, 299–300
voir dire process, 190–91
von Drehle, David, 214n. 35
voting districts, 124, 265n. 366

voting rights, 42–43, 43, 64, 72, 104, 124
Voting Rights Act of 1965, 72

Walling, William English, 42
Warren, Earl, 26, 27, 38, 68–69
Warren Court, 171
Washington, Booker T., 40
Washington, Bushrod, 92
Wechsler, Herbert, 125, 147–48
*West Coast Hotel v. Parrish,* 258n. 261
*West River Bridge v. Dix,* 248n. 71
*West Virginia State Board of Education v. Barnette,* 129
*Wheeling Steel Corp. v. Glander,* 115
White, Byron: *Bowers* case, 163; *Caldwell* case, 181; dissents of, 120, 125, 165; *Enmund* case, 164; *Ford* case, 177,

180; *Furman* case, 294n. 43; papers of, 8; on random nature of death penalty, 11
White, Walter, 49, 56
Wilder, Douglas, xi
Wilkison, J. Harvie, III, 231n. 200
Will, George, 214n. 35
Williams, Juan, 8–9
Wilmer Cutler & Pickering, xi
Wilson, Justice James, 87, 89
Wilson, Woodrow, 106
*Wiscart v. D'Auchy,* 89
Wise, Professor, 137–38
Wishman, Seymour, 186
*Wolf v. Colorado,* 119, 264n. 342
Woodbury, Justice Levi, 101, 248n. 71
Wright, Robert, 79

Zimring, Frank, 203–4